THE REIGN OF RICHARD LIONHEART

THE MEDIEVAL WORLD

Editor: David Bates

John Moorhead	Ambrose
John Moorhead	Justinian
Janet Nelson	Charles the Bald
Paul Fouracre	The Age of Charles Martel
Richard Abels	Alfred the Great
M.K. Lawson	Cnut
H.R. Loyn	The English Church, 940–1154
Malcolm Barber	The Cathars
James A. Brundage	Medieval Canon Law
John Hudson	The Formation of the English Common Law
Lindy Grant	Abbot Suger of St-Denis
David Crouch	William Marshal
Ralph V. Turner	The Reign of Richard Lionheart
Ralph V. Turner	King John
Jim Bradbury	Philip Augustus
Jane Sayers	Innocent III
C.H. Lawrence	The Friars
David Abulafia	The Western Mediterranean Kingdoms 1200–1500
Jean Dunbabin	Charles I of Anjou
Jennifer C. Ward	English Noblewomen in the Later Middle Ages
Michael Hicks	Bastard Feudalism

THE REIGN OF RICHARD LIONHEART

Ruler of the Angevin Empire, 1189–99

RALPH V. TURNER
and
RICHARD R. HEISER

Longman

An imprint of **Pearson Education**

Harlow, England · London · New York · Reading, Massachusetts · San Francisco
Toronto · Don Mills, Ontario · Sydney · Tokyo · Singapore · Hong Kong · Seoul
Taipei · Cape Town · Madrid · Mexico City · Amsterdam · Munich · Paris · Milan

Pearson Education Limited
Edinburgh Gate
Harlow
Essex CM20 2JE
England

and Associated Companies throughout the world

Visit us on the World Wide Web at:
http://www.pearsoneduc.com

Transferred to digital print on demand, 2005

ISBN 0 582 25659 3 (PPR)
ISBN 0 582 25660 7 (CSD)

British Library Cataloguing-in-Publication Data
A catalogue record for this book is available from the British Library

Library of Congress Cataloging-in-Publication Data
Turner, Ralph V.
    The reign of Richard Lionheart : ruler of the Angevin empire, 1189–1199 / Ralph
V. Turner and Richard R. Heiser.
        p. cm. — (The medieval world)
    Includes bibliographical references (p.   ) and index.
    ISBN 0-582-25660-7 (alk. paper) — ISBN 0-582-25659-3 (pbk. : alk. paper)
    1. Great Britain—History—Richard I, 1189–1199.   2. Richard I, King of England,
1157–1199.   3. Great Britain—Kings and rulers—Biography.   4. Crusades—Participation,
British.   5. Crusades—Third, 1189–1192.   I. Heiser, Richard R.   II. Title.   III. Series.
DA207. T87   2000
942.03'2'092—dc21   00–022160
    [B]

Typeset by 35 in 11/13pt Baskerville MT
Produced by Pearson Education Asia Pte Ltd.
Printed and bound by Antony Rowe Ltd, Eastbourne

CONTENTS

CONTENTS

EDITOR'S PREFACE

Richard Lionheart is one of the most interesting, and also one of the most controversial of medieval kings. Generally admired by his contemporaries, the rationalism of the Enlightenment, followed by the Whig history and the administrative history of the later nineteenth and twentieth centuries, denigrated the reputation of a ruler whose main interests lay in crusading and warfare, and of a king of England who spent only a few months of his ten-year reign in his kingdom. Over the last twenty or so years, a further revision has occurred and the consensus of opinion has, to a considerable degree, swung back in Richard's favour. Although this reassessment has largely been based on the view that his life and rule should be interpreted according to the values that his contemporaries recognised as those of a good king, some historians have gone as far as to argue that Richard was also a skilled administrator and a capable politician, qualities that even the most supportive of previous commentators had denied him.

This new book by Ralph Turner and Richard Heiser tackles the issue that is central to all the modern controversies, namely, the character of Richard's rule of the immense territories that are normally described as the Angevin Empire. In order to do this, the events and conduct of the Third Crusade are largely left to one side, except in so far as they illuminate the book's main themes. Relying principally on the extraordinarily plentiful government records from England and, to a lesser extent, Normandy, the authors construct a compelling and entirely new portrait of Richard as a ruler who emerges as a great soldier, but also as cruel, wilful and greedy. The narrative ranges across all Richard's lands, devoting sections to Anjou and Aquitaine, as well as to accounts of such topics as the failed chief justiciarship of William Longchamp, the devious manoeuvring of Richard's brother John, the successful regimes of Walter of Coutances and Hubert Walter and the ever growing demands made on the duchy of Normandy. While Richard's abilities were obviously exceptional ones, he appears as insensitive to the scale and scope of the financial demands he was making of his subjects. It is also pointed out that his military achievements, though very great, were not decisive; he had contained his opponent, the wily Philip Augustus, rather than defeated him.

Ralph Turner is a distinguished historian of twelfth- and thirteenth-century English law and government, who has already contributed *King John* to the Medieval World series. Richard Heiser is a young scholar who has worked extensively on the records of the English government during Richard's reign. Their combined expertise has produced a volume that is a particularly welcome addition to the series, not just because of its new approach to an important subject, but because, taken together with *King John*, it supplies a meaningful account of the end of the Angevin Empire and the tensions that led to Magna Carta in 1215. Instead of laying the blame mostly or exclusively with Richard or John, as historians have on occasion been prone to do, we have instead a coherent analysis of the two reigns together which demonstrates how problems accumulated over time.

David Bates

AUTHORS' PREFACE

Just as twelfth-century scholars admitted that they were standing on the shoulders of giants, so we must acknowledge that if our study of Richard Lionheart's reign advances knowledge of the subject it is because it builds on the earlier work of many students of the Angevin 'empire'. Not least of these is John Gillingham, with whom we have not always agreed, but who always has encouraged us and generously sent across the Atlantic to us copies of his papers and books. We regret that his latest book, *Richard I* (Yale University Press 1999) appeared too late for us to take into account in this work. We also regret that our friend Thomas K. Keefe, a longtime colleague in Angevin studies who stimulated us with his enthusiasm and his insights, did not live to see this book. Other members of the Charles Homer Haskins Society have listened to our papers on Richard and his Angevin kin for many years, and their patience as well as their comments and encouragement are greatly appreciated. A number of associates who sent us offprints of their papers, who allowed us access to their theses, and who answered our queries must be recognised by name: David Balfour, David Bates, Nick Barratt, George Beech, David Carpenter, Kathy Carter, David Crouch, Claude Fagnen, Marie Hivergneaux, Brock Holden, Sir James Holt, Marie Lovatt, Olivier Jeanne-Rose, Jane Martindale, Stephen Morillo, Vincent Moss, Daniel Power, David Spear, Ilicia Sprey, Robert Stacey, Kathleen Thompson, and Nicholas Vincent.

Along with the publishers, we are grateful to the following presses for permission to reproduce copyright material: Map I from Edmund King, *Medieval England 1066–1485*, Phaidon Press, Oxford (1988); Map II from Clayton and David Roberts, *A History of England*, vol. 1, *Prehistory to 1714*, Prentice Hall, Inc., Englewood Cliffs NJ, USA (1995); Map III from R. Allen Brown, *The Normans and the Norman Conquest*, Thomas R. Crowell Inc., New York, USA (1968); Map VI from Kate Norgate, *England under the Angevin Kings*, vol. 2, Macmillan and Co., London (1987). We have been unable to trace the copyright holder of Maps IV and V from Elizabeth Hallam, *The Plantagenet Chronicles*, originally published by Phoebe Phillips Editions, London (1986), and would be grateful for any information that would enable us to do so.

Ralph V. Turner would like to thank first Rick Heiser, for participating in this undertaking as co-author and for bringing to it his knowledge of the personnel of English government under the Lionheart and for his share in its completion, despite other powerful demands on his time. Thanks are due to the History Department of the Florida State University for travel funds and research semesters that it granted. I also thank the Bibliothèque nationale, Paris, for providing a microfilm copy of the collection of Richard I's charters made by Achille Deville. Additionally, my gratitude to William P. Lawrence, travel companion and driver on a trip to France to visit various sites associated with Richard Lionheart's life, must be acknowledged.

Richard R. Heiser would like to thank the two colleges where he has served while working on this project, namely Nyack College in New York and Presbyterian College in South Carolina. These institutions have contributed funds for travel, conferences, and other professional activities that have advanced the completion of the task. Also I would like to thank the staffs at the two colleges' libraries who cheerfully and eagerly ordered books and other resources needed when these materials could not be acquired in person. Finally, I would be grossly remiss not to express my appreciation and respect for my mentor, Ralph Turner. I was profoundly honoured to have been asked to join this project, for I knew that Ralph could have completed it most admirably without my contribution. It is my privilege, then, to add my name to the title page with a scholar who is one of the giants of the profession and from whose shoulders I have been better able to see.

Finally, we both wish to express the heartiest gratitude to David Bates, the capable general editor of the Medieval World series. His professional and personal encouragement has undergirded this effort from its inception.

ABBREVIATIONS

AHR	*American Historical Review*
ANS	*Anglo-Norman Studies*
Baldwin	*The Government of Philip Augustus*
BEC	*Bibliothèque de l'Ecole des Chartes*
BIHR	*Bulletin of the Institute of Historical Research*
BN	Bibliothèque Nationale, Paris
Boussard	*Le Gouvernement d'Henri II Plantegenêt*
BSAO	*Bulletin de la Société des antiquaires de l'Ouest*
Cal. Docs. Fr.	*Documents Preserved in France*, I, *918–1206*
CCM	*Cahiers de civilisation médiévale*
ChanR . . . RI	*Chancellor's Roll . . . Richard I*
Coggeshall	*Radulphi de Coggeshall Chronicon Anglicanum*
Delisle/Berger	*Recueil d'actes de Henri II*
Devizes	*The Chronicle of Richard of Devizes*
Diceto	*Radulphi de Diceto, Opera Historica*
EHR	*English Historical Review*
Gerald of Wales	*Gerald Cambrensis Opera*
Gervase	*Gervase of Canterbury, Historical Works*
Gesta Regis	*Gesta Regis Henrici Secundi Benedicti Abbatis*
Gillingham, *Coeur de Lion*	*Richard Coeur de Lion: Kingship, Chivalry, and War in the Twelfth Century*
Gillingham, *Richard*	*Richard the Lionheart*
Howden	*Chronica Rogeri de Hovedene*
HSJ	*Haskins Society Journal*
JBS	*Journal of British Studies*
JMH	*Journal of Medieval History*
Landon	*Itinerary of King Richard I*
MSAO	*Mémoires de la Société des antiquaires de l'Ouest*
Newburgh	*Historia Rerum Anglicarum of William of Newburgh*
Pat. Lat.	*Patrologiae Latinae*
Powicke, *Loss*	*The Loss of Normandy*
PRS	Pipe Roll Society
PR . . . HII	*Great Roll of the Pipe . . . Henry the Second*

PR . . . J	*Great Roll of the Pipe . . . John*
PR . . . RI	*Great Roll of the Pipe . . . Richard I*
RS	Rolls Series
Rot. Chart.	*Rotuli Chartarum 1199–1216*
Rot. Norm.	*Rotuli Normanniae 1200–1205*
Sanders	*English Baronies*
Stapleton	*Magni Rotuli scaccarii normanniae*
TRHS	*Transactions of the Royal Historical Society*
Vigeois	*Geoffroi de Vigeois Chronique*

CHAPTER ONE

The historians' balance-sheet

King Richard I (1189–99), son of Henry II and Eleanor of Aquitaine, is the best known of all the medieval kings of England. Still a leading character in novels, films and television series, he is presented in the media today much as he has been for centuries: a model of kingly virtues because of his military exploits, chivalric courtesy and crusading ardour. Indeed, the periodisation of his reign reflects the dominance of war: first, his preparations for the Third Crusade, from the spring of 1189 to summer 1190; then the crusading expedition, 1190–92; followed by his capture on the return journey and imprisonment in Germany throughout 1193; and finally, following his release early in 1194 until his death in April 1199, five years of warfare protecting his French possessions from Philip Augustus, king of France.

Although popular histories have consistently admired Richard Lionheart, the same is not true of serious historians. Richard's historiographical ups and downs are a useful example of how historians' judgments of leaders are periodically revised according to different ages' priorities. Any examination of the reign of Richard Lionheart presents the dilemma of the sharply differing standards applied by medieval chroniclers, later historians and today's scholars in assessing leaders' achievements. The definition of a model ruler today is hardly the same one that Richard's contemporaries, living in an era of religious fervor and warrior ethos, applied to their monarch. Because medieval and modern writers have such dramatic differences of methodology, purpose and perspective regarding Richard I and because of contributions to historical understanding made by specialists in recent years, it is important to look again at the reign of this remarkable medieval English king.

A sketch of historical opinion on Richard Lionheart demonstrates the shifting values and priorities that biased authors. First to express opinions about Richard I were his contemporaries in their chronicles. The late twelfth

1

century was 'a golden age of historiography in England',[1] and it would be unwise to reject the chroniclers' findings simply because their aims and procedures differed from modern historical method. Although all chroniclers writing during Richard's reign were in clerical orders, only four were monks; three others – Roger of Howden, Ralph of Diss and Gerald of Wales – were secular clerks with close ties to the royal court. Indeed, the chronicle composed by Roger of Howden, a royal clerk, is considered a 'quasi-official record of the central government'.[2] He did not, nor did Ralph of Diss, dean of St Paul's, share the anti-government bias of most monastic writers, notorious among the thirteenth-century St Albans chroniclers.

As churchmen, the historians who were Richard Lionheart's contemporaries held liberation of the Christian holy places from the Muslims as the highest priority, indeed the highest goal of the chivalric lord.[3] Thus, medieval chroniclers saw the Third Crusade as the central event in Richard's life, and they painted their portraits of him accordingly. Richard of Devizes' account of the Lionheart's crusade, for example, sketches 'a heroic portrait consciously drawn to inspire unreserved admiration and to justify military failures'; other writers also depicted the crusading monarch as a hero akin to the heroes of chivalric romances, hailing him as a perfect knight and model king because of his courtesy and military prowess.[4] Admiration of the Lionheart led some ecclesiastics to tolerate behaviour for which they would not have forgiven his father or his brother. Gerald of Wales and Roger of Howden both saw Henry II's rejection of the 1185 plea for military assistance by the patriarch of Jerusalem as the turning point in the king's life. Peter of Blois, another courtier, joined them in interpreting Henry's tragic end in 1189 as God's judgment on his indifference to the fate of the holy places.[5]

Not all writers in Richard's day were clerics learned in Latin; vernacular poetry composed for aristocratic audiences reflects the violent warrior ethos embedded in the cult of chivalry. With its definition of the perfect knight's qualities of prowess, loyalty, largess and courtesy, chivalry profoundly influenced thinking about kingship by the late twelfth century. For noble

---

1   B. Smalley, *Historians in the Middle Ages* (New York, 1974), 113; A. Gransden, *Historical Writing in England c. 550–1307* (Ithaca, NY, 1974), 219.
2   Gransden, *Historical Writing in England*, 222, 225–8, 332, 368–9.
3   M. Keen, 'War, Peace, and Chivalry', in *Nobles, Knights and Men-at-Arms in the Middle Ages* (London, 1996), 2.
4   N. Partner, *Serious Entertainments: The Writing of History in Twelfth-Century England* (Chicago, 1977), 175. Other works include one in French verse, *L'Estoire de la Guerre Sainte* and one in Latin prose, *Itinerarium Peregrinorum et Gesta Regis Ricardi*.
5   R. Bartlett, *Gerald of Wales* (Oxford, 1982), 76; R.W. Southern, 'Peter of Blois and the Third Crusade', in H. Mayr-Harting and R.I. Moore (eds), *Studies in Medieval History Presented to R.H.C. Davis* (London, 1985), 208; Gillingham, 'Roger of Howden on Crusade', in *Coeur de Lion*, 141–53.

listeners to troubadours or *trouvères*, a successful king was a mighty warrior, exhibiting qualities of the chivalrous knight. Richard's martial skills and generous spirit won him the admiration of his contemporaries, who found embodied in him all the chivalric virtues.[6] A verse history of the Third Crusade described Richard: 'His deeds of chivalry so great / And such fair prowess as to stun / and to bewilder everyone'; and an Aquitanian lament composed on Richard's death said similarly, 'Never was there a king so faithful, so valiant, so fearless, so generous.'[7]

Not even in the Middle Ages did all writers evaluate monarchs solely according to their success as generals. An old principle of kingship that professed the ruler's responsibility for his people's well-being, equating the ruler–subject relationship with a father's care for his minor children, was familiar to the learned in the twelfth century. The *Dialogus de Scaccario*, *c*. 1177–79, explained that God had entrusted the monarch with 'the special care of his subjects'. A letter written for Richard's justiciar by Peter of Blois about 1195 employs such terms as 'the welfare of all' and 'the public business of the king'.[8] Some writers who lived under Richard's rule found him guilty of neglecting the general responsibility for his subjects' care that constituted good kingship. For example, William of Newburgh condemned as irresponsible a number of the new king's actions on taking power in 1189; and Ralph of Coggeshall, who praised Richard extravagantly at the beginning of his reign, later saw the unworthy manner of his death as divine punishment for the financial extortions of his last years.[9]

Historians since the seventeenth century have measured Richard by yardsticks adapted to their own ages' preconceptions about kingly duties. By the end of the nineteenth century, scholars, having become preoccupied with 'nation-building' and 'administrative kingship', had demoted Richard Lionheart to the category of bad rulers. Bishop William Stubbs, writing in late nineteenth-century Oxford, was not impressed with Richard, and his comments represent a Victorian verdict on rulers which was 'essentially a moral judgment upon an individual sinner'.[10] Stubbs set the pattern for

---

6   See A. Bridge, *Richard the Lionheart* (New York, 1989), 241–2, for comments on Richard as *preux chevalier par excellence*.

7   S. Painter, *French Chivalry* (Baltimore, 1940), 28–64; for the Limousin troubadour's poem, A. Richard, *Histoire des comtes de Poitou* (Paris, 1903), 2: 327, note.

8   Charles Johnson (ed. and trans.), *Dialogus de Scaccario* (London, 1950), 1, 101; *Pat. Lat.*, 207: cols. 403–04, epist. 135; translation, C.R. Cheney, *Hubert Walter* (London, 1967), 158.

9   D. Carpenter, 'Richard by his Contemporaries. Was he a "Model King"? England in 1189', unpublished paper, Colloque aux Archives du Calvados (Caen April 1999); also Carpenter, 'Abbot Ralph of Coggeshall's Account of the Last Years of Richard and the First Years of John', *EHR* 3 (1998), 1210–30.

10   V.H. Galbraith, 'Good Kings and Bad Kings in English History', *History*, 30 (1945), 120, 128; reprinted in his *Kings and Chronicles* (London, 1982).

accounts of the Lionheart with his denunciation of him as 'an unscrupulous and impetuous soldier', whose cardinal trait was 'the love of warfare'. He judged him a failure as a statesman, with an 'utter want of political common sense' and with 'none of the tact of a wise prince'.[11] Stubbs has continued to exercise powerful influence upon our views of medieval England, for generations of British students were brought up on his *Constitutional History*, and scholars still depend on his editions of medieval chronicles.

Scholars since Stubbs have continued to disparage the Lionheart's pre-occupation with war. Absorbed with law and administration, they neither know nor care about medieval warfare, which they dismiss as a series of aimless raids punctuated by pointless sieges of castles, led by undisciplined knights fighting for personal glory – in short, a mêlée little different from urban gang activity. They refuse to accept that such warriors were capable of any larger plan worthy of the term 'strategy'. Typical is the contemptuous comment by H.G. Richardson and G.O. Sayles, two iconoclastic British scholars, that medieval warfare 'called for little strategy, for little military science'.[12] Such writers with their secular outlook and historical hindsight dismiss Richard's crusade as a futile venture, and they are no more capable of grasping its significance than medieval chroniclers would understand America's 1960s quest to land a man on the moon.

The early twentieth century saw the beginnings of the welfare state, and historians no longer feared 'big government', but favoured bureaucrats as those who actually made government work for the public good. As a result, they shifted their studies from individual statesmen to institutions and administrative agencies. In addition, Marxist doctrines emphasising imper-sonal socio-economic forces discredited the 'great man' theory of history. The disasters of the twentieth century – deficient military leadership in the First World War and politicians' failures in solving post-war problems or preventing the Second World War – caused many British scholars to disavow heroes in history.[13] Any notion that a leader could merit glory and admira-tion as a result of military exploits was also numbered among the casualties. Negative assessments of Richard became common, and they gained currency

---

11 W. Stubbs, *Historical Introductions to the Rolls Series*, ed. Arthur Hassall (London, 1902), 317–23; see also Bridge, *Richard the Lionheart*, 244–9, on Stubbs' influence on modern interpretations. A.L. Poole followed Stubbs in his volume in the *Oxford History of England, From Domesday Book to Magna Carta, 1087–1216*, 2nd edn (Oxford, 1954), 351. H.G. Richardson and G.O. Sayles, while protesting Stubbs' version of English history, agreed that in political and administrative matters, '[Richard's] acumen was deficient' (*The Governance of Mediaeval England* (Edinburgh, 1963), 366, 329).

12 For example, Richardson and Sayles, *Governance*, 366.

13 H. Summerson, 'Problems of Biography: Revising the DNB', *Medieval Prosopography*, 17 (1996), 210–11.

through repetition in popular texts on the Middle Ages, as seen in one current textbook's dismissal: 'Richard was an attractive man and a thoroughly bad monarch. . . . War was his one delight, and his only interest in England was as a source of funds for his crusade and his bitter war with Philip Augustus.'[14]

In recent years scholars employing different criteria have undertaken a re-evaluation of Richard by seeking to place him in his proper late twelfth-century context and to judge him by the standards of his own age. Among the battlefields on which they have waged war for Richard's reputation are his preoccupation with war, his apparent disregard for the governing enterprise and his financial demands. Taking the lead are John Gillingham, J.C. Holt and J.O. Prestwich. Signposts of the revision are three collections of papers: *Riccardo Cuor di Leone nella Storia e nella Leggenda*, a colloquium at Rome in 1981 sponsored by the Accademia dei Lincei; *Richard Coeur de Lion in History and Myth*, a colloquium sponsored by King's College London to mark the 800th anniversary of Richard's coronation in 1989; and John Gillingham's 1994 volume of his collected writings, *Richard Coeur de Lion: Kingship, Chivalry, and War in the Twelfth Century*.[15]

After Richard's return from the Third Crusade by 1194, his priority was a defence of his continental patrimony against King Philip (II) Augustus of France who was bent on depriving him of all his French lands.[16] As a result, traditional depictions of Richard as ruler showed him as, above all, a warrior – *rex ille bellicosus* – in Ralph of Coggeshall's words.[17] All recent biographies of Richard Lionheart – James A. Brundage's 1974 book, John Gillingham's 1978 work and Antony Bridge's 1989 publication – follow tradition in depicting Richard as primarily a military man.[18]

---

14   S. Painter and B. Tierney, *Western Europe in the Middle Ages 300–1475*, 3rd edn (New York, 1978), 310. Similar is B. Lyon's entry on Richard in *Dictionary of the Middle Ages*, ed. J.R. Strayer (New York, 1982–89), 10: 383–4.

15   *Riccardo Cuor di Leone nella Storia e nella Leggenda*, Accademia dei Lincei (Rome, 1981); *Problemi attuali di scienza e di cultura*, no. 253, prints three papers: J.O. Prestwich, 'Richard Coeur de Lion: Rex Bellicosus', 3–15; J.C. Holt, 'Ricardus Rex Anglorum et Dux Normannorum', 17–33; J. Gillingham, 'Some Legends of Richard the Lionheart: Their Development and Their Influence', 35–50. *Richard Coeur de Lion in History and Myth*, ed. J. Nelson, King's College London Medieval Studies, 7 (London, 1992), reprints Prestwich's piece, 1–16, and Gillingham's piece, 51–69, from *Riccardo Cuor di Leone*. Holt's piece was reprinted in his *Magna Carta and Medieval Government* (London, 1985), 67–83. Gillingham's collected papers, *Richard Coeur de Lion*, also reprints his piece from the Italian colloquium.

16   K. Norgate, *England under the Angevin Kings*, 2 vols (London, 1887; rprt New York, 1969), 2: 363; Baldwin, 87.

17   Coggeshall, 49.

18   J.A. Brundage, *Richard Lion Heart* (New York, 1974); J. Gillingham, *Richard the Lionheart* (London, 1978); and Bridge, *Richard the Lionheart*.

John Gillingham's biography of Richard is recognised as the standard work on this king today. Like the Lionheart's knightly contemporaries, he sees fighting as the most fitting activity for medieval rulers, the fullest evidence of their ability; and he argues that, therefore, Richard should be judged as a warrior.[19] Gillingham assigns a high value to contemporary writers, admitting that his research materials are more likely to be chroniclers' narratives than chancery or exchequer records; and he adopts the traditional definition of monarchs' chief function as making war. Like Antony Bridge, he admires the warrior-king's courage, his plunging into the thick of battle alongside his men.[20] According to Gillingham, Richard's subjects recognised his wars as 'reasonable and honorable', just struggles in defence of his rights.[21] He complains that modern historians' misconceptions about medieval warfare lead them to conclude that Richard did not need much intellect, planning capacity or organisational ability to be a successful warrior, but he finds in Richard's military strategies evidence of competent and effective administration. He writes, 'Whether we like it or not, leadership in war was a vital aspect of kingship, and successful leadership required many qualities besides those of brute courage and physical strength.'[22]

Gillingham judges Richard as 'one of the outstanding rulers of European history', successful in fulfilling his kingly responsibility to defend the Plantagenet patrimony. He constantly contrasts Richard Lionheart, 'a model of medieval generalship', with his younger brother John Lackland, whom he paints as a hopeless incompetent, evidenced by his military failures.[23] Gillingham is convinced that the loss of most Angevin lands north of Gascony was entirely King John's responsibility. The dates for his chapter 'The Crisis of the Angevin Empire' in his book on the Angevin Empire are 1199–1206, dates that place the loss of Normandy squarely on John's shoulders. He insists that Normandy and Anjou fell to the Capetian king because 'John did not know how to rule'.[24]

---

19   Gillingham, *Coeur de Lion*, Introduction, xiii, xvi–xvii. In *Richard*, 4, he chides other historians who 'prefer to study man as a socio-political animal rather than as a fighting animal'.

20   Bridge, *Richard the Lionheart*, 245.

21   J. Gillingham, 'Conquering Kings: Some Twelfth-century Reflections on Henry II and Richard I', in *Warriors and Churchmen in the High Middle Ages: Essays Presented to Karl Leyser* (London, 1992), 174, 177–8.

22   J. Gillingham, 'Richard I and the Science of War in the Middle Ages', *Coeur de Lion*, 211–26. See also Partner, *Serious Entertainments*, 101, commenting on William of Newburgh's attitude, 'War is what kings do.'

23   Gillingham, *Richard*, 285 and 2. For a brief, forthright statement of Gillingham's view of King John, see 'The Fall of the Angevin Empire' in *Coeur de Lion*, 193–200.

24   Gillingham sees John's loss of Normandy and Anjou as less due to structural factors than to 'the contingencies of war and politics', *Richard*, 304; J. Gillingham, *The Angevin Empire* (New York, 1984), 46; and recently, J. Gillingham, 'The Fall of the Angevin Empire', in N. Saul, ed., *England in Europe 1066–1453* (New York, 1994).

J.O. Prestwich also argues for the priority of warfare in assessing the monarch's achievement and ability. He, like Gillingham, justifies Richard's wars as necessary defence of his patrimony and Angevin dynastic interests; he states, 'Richard fought his campaigns not to win territory but to defend or to recover the rights of the house of Anjou.'[25] In his view, the Lionheart's campaign to rescue the Holy Land was not solely a religious mission, but also served a dynastic purpose, for a junior branch of the house of Anjou ruled the kingdom of Jerusalem, descended from Richard's great-grandfather, Count Fulk V.[26] Prestwich's scrutiny of the Third Crusade reveals to him Richard's sound grasp of strategy, not only in combat on land but also his appreciation for the significance of sea power. Richard I's qualities of 'valour and versatility in war' sustained the morale of his fighting men.[27]

Since the First World War, a number of historians have moved toward the study of bureaucracy, sensing that administrative records give a truer picture than mere reliance on medieval chroniclers' presuppositions and prejudices, enabling them to write more objective history. Concentration on administration has led them to demote Richard and to elevate John on the list of favoured English monarchs; the preoccupation of the Lionheart's successor with England's administration appears to them as a positive quality.[28] Overlooking Richard's reign as a mere hiccup of chivalric combat between the reigns of his father and younger brother that brought major administrative, legal and constitutional changes to England, such writers neglect the sweeping governmental changes implemented under his justiciar, Hubert Walter. They denounce what they view as Richard's neglect of England; he made only two visits to his island kingdom, spending less than six months there. They see his almost constant warfare on the continent as a diversion from his proper task of constructing a strong English government, and they compare him unfavourably with his predecessor and his successor. Bryce Lyon sums up the opinions of this generation of historians by writing, 'Richard failed to appreciate the responsibilities of rule, and . . . left that boresome task to clerks and humdrum men.'[29] Although Gillingham has recently challenged these perceptions, declaring that Richard's administrative record 'at least matches his father's' and may even surpass it, they have clung doggedly to the Lionheart.[30]

For several years, the increasing sway of administrative or bureaucratic history has led to attempts to place Richard Lionheart within the context

---

25 Prestwich, 'Rex Bellicosus', 7.
26 Prestwich, 'Rex Bellicosus', 6–7.
27 Prestwich, 'Rex Bellicosus', 14.
28 See R.V. Turner, *King John* (London, 1994), ch. 1, 'King John in his Context: A Comparison with his Contemporaries', 1–19.
29 B. Lyon, *A Constitutional and Legal History of Medieval England* (New York, 1960), 234.
30 Gillingham, 'Conquering Kings', 173.

of 'administrative kingship'. The phrase, coined by John W. Baldwin and C. Warren Hollister, does not mean a king actually heading the administration, but a monarchy powered by administrative and financial machinery that can operate according to fixed routine without constant royal supervision. It means, in sum, a monarchy that has moved beyond governing through simple *ad hoc* arrangements within the royal household and toward specialised agencies that assumed wider responsibilities for the king's subjects' well-being than he could oversee personally.[31] Twelfth-century England is an early example of 'administrative kingship' with its two centres of royal government. One centre was the itinerant royal household, chiefly occupied with war and diplomacy and with corralling the great nobles through patronage and penalties; the second centre, operating according to established procedures under the justiciar's supervision, took responsibility for enforcement of internal order and for raising revenues to achieve the monarch's diplomatic and military goals.

Richard's reign is now recognised as a crucial period for England's creation of administrative and financial structures; a soundly constructed machine of central government reaped seemingly inexhaustible wealth for him, easily harvested even during his long absences. M.T. Clanchy sees it as paradoxical that Richard I, 'who seems to have taken no interest in England except as a source of revenue', helped create a formidable administrative machine for his kingdom because of his need to finance his wars on the continent.[32] Yet it is not such a paradox. While modern historians, like Clanchy, have been reluctant to acknowledge it, Richard I fits the description of an administrative monarch. A medieval king, more like an American president than a constitutional monarch, was a shaper of policy and a decision-maker. He needed to avoid over-entanglement in administrative detail, to escape turning into a bureaucrat himself, and to free himself for coping with larger issues: in Richard's case, confronting the Capetian military threat and finding money for his armies. To argue that he cared little for England fails to apply properly the definition of administrative kingship. England was placed under the supervision of the Lionheart's bureaucratic servants so that he could pursue pressing matters of war and diplomacy on the continent.

The strength of administrative kingship in current historiography is demonstrated by the tendency of some historians to defend Richard as an administrator, perhaps because of the praise heaped on his father Henry II and brother John in this century. One of the first scholars to seek to situate Richard within the context of administrative kingship is J.C. Holt. As a

---

31 Hollister and Baldwin, 'The Rise of Administrative Kingship: Henry I and Philip Augustus', *AHR* 83 (1976).

32 M.T. Clanchy, *England and its Rulers 1066–1272* (London, 1983), 138.

result of his study of Angevin charters, Holt argues that Richard was aware of important issues relating to England because of the numerous charters bearing the attestation *teste me ipso*, and also his attention to those seeking justice at his court.[33] Although fewer royal records survive from Richard's reign than from his brother's, Holt's study shows the king intervening 'frequently and persistently' in English affairs, as actively involved as he could be, given his absence from the kingdom. Holt finds, however, that his involvement centred on raising men and *matériel* for his wars; other royal interventions came at the initiative of petitioners willing to seek him out on the continent.[34]

Looking at Richard's military record, J.O. Prestwich maintains that his command of the crusading forces is proof of his administrative skill; he notes, 'Few commanders understood better than Richard the importance of mobilizing money and spending it to the best effect.'[35] John Gillingham argues, in an indirect swipe at King John, that over-involvement by a monarch in the daily work of administration was 'unnecessary and counter-productive'.[36] He either finds John devoting too much time to administration or else finds modern historians unduly influenced by the quantity of administrative records showing him busy at his work of governing. John's embrace of administration, which earns him admiration from scholars centuries later, won him his own subjects' condemnation as an oppressor. Yet Gillingham himself tries sometimes to place Richard in the context of 'administrative kingship', pointing out that success in warfare required effective administration. He writes further: 'Not only did [Richard] live up to contemporary ideals of kingship, but even by such modern criteria as the management of patronage, administrative competence, and the politician's ability to project an image, he was a master of the art.' Gillingham depicts Henry II as 'a more bellicose and aggressive ruler' than historians have acknowledged in order to argue that the Lionheart was no less concerned with the art of government than his father.[37]

A successful head of any large institution must choose able assistants, and Richard gave close attention to appointments in both the English Church and secular government. Even Bishop Stubbs grudgingly admitted that he 'did his best to choose good ministers'.[38] Scholars can discern the wisdom of

---

33 J.C. Holt, 'Ricardus Rex Anglorum et Dux Normannorum', in *Magna Carta and Medieval Government* (London, 1985), 70–82.

34 Holt, 'Ricardus Rex', 71; Gillingham, 'The Art of Kingship,' 97. Also Gillingham, 'Conquering Kings', in *Coeur de Lion*, 105–18.

35 Prestwich, 'Rex Bellicosus', 11–13.

36 Gillingham, 'The Art of Kingship', 99.

37 First quotation in Gillingham, *Coeur de Lion*, Preface, x; second quotation in Gillingham, 'Conquering Kings', 164. See also Gillingham, 'Richard I and the Science of War', 90.

38 Stubbs, *Historical Introductions*, 321.

9

Richard's selections, ensuring continued governmental efficiency in England. They have long recognised that his naming of Hubert Walter, his choice as archbishop of Canterbury, to be also justiciar at the end of 1193 was a brilliant one. Indeed, Richardson and Sayles state that the Lionheart's 'best service to England was to leave the government of the country to Hubert Walter and [his successor] Geoffrey fitz Peter'.[39] Hubert Walter made innovations that mark the culmination of twelfth-century 'administrative kingship' in England at the same time that Philip Augustus was introducing similar reforms in France. One of Hubert's biographers, Charles R. Young, depicts his twenty-year career – Ranulf de Glanvill's assistant in the 1180s, Richard's justiciar from 1193 to 1198, and John's chancellor until 1205 – as the link between Henry II's innovations and the fully developed machinery of King John, and he acknowledges Hubert's 'singular inventiveness' in governmental experiments.[40] Using his enormous energy and organising skill in all spheres of royal government, Hubert Walter raised it to a peak of effectiveness, despite his master's absence. But he did not act unilaterally, for as Gillingham argues, Hubert's implementation of major administrative changes had to await Richard's personal approval.[41]

Much attention has been paid to Hubert Walter, and rightly so, but recent study has resulted in similar praise for other of Richard's justiciars, William Longchamp and Walter of Coutances. A full-length study of William Longchamp finds the chancellor to have been a competent enough supervisor of royal business early in the reign when the king's absence was keenly felt, though certainly not without character flaws that eventually undermined his power as chief justiciar.[42] Peter A. Poggioli's work on Walter of Coutances, archbishop of Rouen, describes his justiciarship as skilful and tactful though undramatic. He concludes his study of Walter's career as justiciar with the succinct statement that 'his political acumen had quietly saved Richard's throne'.[43] Geoffrey fitz Peter, the only other man to serve as justiciar during Richard I's reign, did not serve long before the king was killed, but Geoffrey's ability and many years in service to the Angevins place him within the tradition of Hubert Walter and the others. Richard's record in selecting capable regents to preside over the administration while he was out of the kingdom is striking and worthy of historians' accolades. Yet not all scholars agree with this assessment of Richard's track record in appointing chief

---

39 Richardson and Sayles, *Governance*, 329.
40 C.R. Young, *Hubert Walter, Lord of Canterbury and Lord of England* (Durham, NC, 1968), 160–9.
41 Gillingham, 'Conquering Kings', 165–6.
42 D. Balfour, 'William Longchamp: Upward Mobility and Character Assassination in Twelfth-century England', PhD dissertation (University of Connecticut, 1996), 263–9.
43 P. Poggioli, 'From Politician to Prelate: The Career of Walter of Coutances, Archbishop of Rouen, 1184–1207', PhD dissertation (Johns Hopkins University, 1984), 101–2.

justiciars. Some argue that his appointment of William Longchamp was disastrous and reflects adversely on the king's political judgment.[44]

Below the level of justiciar, more work on the personnel of Richard's government remains to done, and recent scholarship must be incorporated into any judgment of his reign. The co-authors of this work have made contributions with their prosopographical studies of royal servants. Richard Heiser's study of witness-lists of royal charters identifies the members of the Lionheart's household and indicates his intimates, those who appeared at court most frequently.[45] Also important for a proper assessment of Richard's administration is an accurate account of second-rank royal servants, those who carried out the daily work of government away from the court. Another of Heiser's studies analyses appointments of sheriffs; it shows the king on his two visits to the kingdom playing 'a substantial role' in selecting those key local agents.[46] Ralph Turner's work on royal justices has shown that by 1194 a core of justices who can be called professionals or at least proto-professionals began to sit regularly at Westminster.[47] They were not *familiares regis*, but most owed their appointments to the justiciar.

So far no scholar has tackled the tedious task of sifting administrative and judicial records that would permit completion of a rounded portrait of Richard as ruler of England. Gillingham admits that his biography 'made no effort to use the voluminous English records as the basis for a detailed study'.[48] This is a noteworthy omission, for Richard's reign holds great significance, marking the time that English central administration first functioned effectively under the justiciar during a king's prolonged and, at times, distant, absence. The only modern book-length study, John T. Appleby's 1965 work, *England Without Richard*, grew out of his work of editing the *Chronicle of Richard of Devizes*. Limited to Richard's English holdings, it relies almost entirely on chronicle sources, borrowing a similar annalistic approach. As the title of Appleby's book indicates, he finds Richard Lionheart to have been 'king in name only', interested in England solely as 'an inexhaustible source of money'. He scathingly condemns Richard 'for [having] done almost everything possible to break up the firm and orderly government that his father had imposed on the country'. Such a sweeping conclusion is

---

44 For example, D. Carpenter, 'Richard by his Contemporaries'.

45 R. Heiser, 'The Royal *Familiares* of Richard I', *Medieval Prosopography* 10 (1989), 25–50. See also D. Bates, 'The Prosopographical Study of Anglo-Norman Royal Charters', in K.S.B. Keats-Rohan, *Family Trees and the Roots of Family Politics: The Prosopography of Britain and France from the Tenth to the Twelfth Century* (Woodbridge, 1997), 89–102, for caveats about this methodology.

46 R. Heiser, 'Richard I and His Appointments to English Shrievalties', *EHR* 112 (1997), 1–19.

47 R. Turner, *The English Judiciary in the Age of Glanvill and Bracton c. 1176–1239* (Cambridge, 1985).

48 Gillingham, *Coeur de Lion*, Preface, x.

not entirely justified, yet recent research shows that in at least one sphere Richard undid Henry II's work, for his land grants dissipated 'virtually overnight' his father's restoration of the royal demesne.[49]

Much of England's strong government was geared to Richard's need to raise enormous sums of money, a third problem in assessing his reputation. His demands earned him, along with his father and brother, a reputation for greed, a vice for which chroniclers often condemned medieval monarchs. Richard of Devizes records how Richard at the beginning of his reign 'most obligingly' lightened the load of those weighed down with money and observes that his readers should have been forewarned of coming hardship by the king's joke that he would have sold London but for a buyer.[50] A long-time clerk of the Angevins who became their harsh critic, Gerald of Wales, expressed a widely held view when he wrote, 'The King is like a robber permanently on the prowl, always probing, always searching for the weak spot where there is something for him to steal.'[51] Today medievalists accept Gerald's point in depicting early medieval government as predatory, stressing the exploitative character of administrative kingship for the benefit of the royal family, the aristocracy and the courtiers. Historians tend to view government as less benign than historians earlier in the twentieth century had depicted it, and they find royal officials more concerned with their own and their relatives' advancement than with performance of public services.[52]

Study of the Angevin monarchs' financial demands is rewarding for twentieth-century historians because of the elaborate set of financial records surviving from twelfth-century England, the earliest of any European state. Recent studies on Richard's and John's finances afford an opportunity for more accurate comparisons of financial exploitation of the English by the Lionheart, his father and his brother. Both Richard and John needed more money than Henry II had required because the strain of costly warfare was worsened by inflation which raged in England c. 1180–1220. Hubert Walter explained to assembled magnates in 1198, 'With smaller resources and forces [Richard] was struggling against a very powerful king, who was straining every nerve to disinherit and ruin him.'[53]

---

49 J.T. Appleby, *England Without Richard, 1189–1199* (Ithaca, NY, 1965), 36, 233–4; N. Barratt, 'The English Revenue of Richard I', unpublished paper presented at the Colloque aux Archives du Calvados (Caen, April 1999).

50 Devizes, 9.

51 Gerald of Wales, 8: 316; translation of Gillingham, *Richard*, 133. On Gerald's outlook, see Gransden, *Historical Writing*, 242–3; Bartlett, *Gerald of Wales*, 58–61.

52 P. Freedman and G. Spiegel, 'Medievalisms Old and New: The Rediscovery of Alterity in North American Medieval Studies', *AHR* 103 (1998), 689–90.

53 D.L. Douie and H. Farmer (eds), *The Life of St. Hugh of Lincoln*, 2 vols, Medieval Texts (London, 1961–62), 2: 98.

Several studies show the Lionheart in a desperate search for funds, expanding his father's exploitation of lordship over the English barons in ways that foreshadow his younger brother's financial exactions.[54] As the king's quest for money became steadily more desperate, contemporaries recognised Richard's reign as marking a turning point for the Angevin 'empire'. Competition with Philip Augustus was forcing Richard and John to organise England as a 'war economy', and their rule over the kingdom took on a 'strong military colour'.[55] Because only a flow of funds from England could supply resources needed for this struggle against the Capetian king, their agents had to be inventive in finding the necessary moneys.

Clearly, the Plantagenets' financial exploitation of England and their conflicts on the continent are inextricably linked, yet most histories have treated Richard Lionheart solely as king of England. Typical is an American authority's reproachful comment, 'He is an exclusively French prince caring not for England but for its money.'[56] The history of the Angevin 'empire' has not attracted historians' attention, largely for nationalistic reasons; since the early nineteenth century, histories have tended to concentrate on the evolution of the nation-states. Scholars in France show little interest in the Angevins' lands until they passed into Capetian hands, to be absorbed into the French kingdom. Most histories by English-speaking authors share the anglocentric view of Bishop Stubbs and his fellow Victorians, failing to appreciate that England was only one of Richard's domains and not necessarily closest to his heart. Few British historians saw significance in such a short-lived collection of territories; Normandy was lost by 1204, and all the English kings' French possessions – except Gascony – were lost by the 1230s. It is clear, however, that one of Richard's primary concerns was the protection and preservation of his continental domains; and his reign cannot be understood without grasping the character of the Angevin 'empire'.

Widening study of Richard's reign to include his rule over the Angevin territories in France poses logistical problems. Because masses of administrative records survive from medieval England, an evaluation of the Lionheart's personal role in English government is easier than for elsewhere. Yet questions related to Richard's lordship over his French domains must be

---

54 See articles cited in Chapter 8, 'The government of England under Hubert Walter and Geoffrey fitz Peter'.

55 J.O. Prestwich, 'War and Finance in the Anglo-Norman Realm', *TRHS*, 4th ser., 4 (1954), 20; J.E.A. Jolliffe, 'The Chamber and Castle Treasuries under King John', in R.W. Hunt, W.A. Pantin and R.W. Southern (eds), *Studies in Medieval History Presented to F.M. Powicke* (Oxford, 1948), 118. See also F.M. Powicke, 'England: Richard I and John', in *Cambridge Medieval History*, 6 (Cambridge, 1929), 216–17; J.C. Holt, 'The End of the Anglo-Norman Realm', in *Magna Carta and Medieval England* (London, 1985), 36.

56 B. Lyon, *A Constitutional and Legal History of Medieval England*, 234.

addressed to set alongside new evaluations of his governance of England. While earlier historians condemned the king for his absences from England, scholars in the age of the European Union should recognise that Richard remained within his larger realm when perambulating his French territories. Any study of Richard's reign needs to abandon a nineteenth-century perspective that visualised the Middle Ages as moving inexorably toward the modern nation-states of France and Britain, and instead, to depict Richard's reign in its medieval, pre-national setting. Too many scholars dismiss Richard's continental lands as poorly governed, afflicted by 'feudal anarchy', draining resources from England, and distracting him from his duties as England's king. For example, the traditional textbook version of the king's death at Chalus-Chabrol Castle in the Limousin presents the siege as resulting from a quixotic quest for buried Roman treasure. As John Gillingham has shown, however, Richard went south to crush a dangerous revolt by two powerful vassals in the Angoumois and Limousin who controlled vital routes connecting Poitou and Anjou to Gascony.[57]

While new work on the Norman exchequer can answer questions concerning Normandy's contribution to its defence,[58] a dearth of documents from Anjou, Maine, Touraine and Aquitaine discourages scholarly evaluations of governance of the Lionheart's remaining French territories. Even after John Lackland's chancellor began keeping charter rolls, patent and close rolls for England around 1200, it was not considered necessary to keep separate rolls for official documents of the continental domains beyond Normandy. One surviving Norman roll of writs for John's early reign is labelled 'Normandy, Poitou and Anjou', lumping together the three regions.[59] No financial records earlier than the Capetian takeover survive, if any ever existed at all. Annals and chronicles from Richard's southern possessions are largely limited to local concerns, chiefly those surrounding the great abbeys that produced them, for example, Saint-Martial at Limoges. Chroniclers in northern France and England were usually ill-informed about events in Aquitaine. Three English chronicles, those of Roger of Howden, 'Benedict of Peterborough' and Ralph of Diss, are an exception, however; and Ralph's work especially shows interest in Aquitaine.[60] Charters remain the fundamental

---

57 Gillingham, *Richard*, ch. 2, 'At the Castle of Chalus-Chabrol,' 9–23. See also
   J. Gillingham, 'Unromantic Death of Richard I,' *Coeur de Lion*, 155–80.
58 Prestwich, 'War and Finance in the Anglo-Norman Realm', 20; Jolliffe, 'The Chamber and Castle Treasuries under King John', 118. See also Powicke, 'England: Richard I and John', 216–17; Holt, 'The End of the Anglo-Norman Realm', 36.
59 *Rot. Norm.*
60 Smalley, *Historians of the Middle Ages*, 113. Major chroniclers for the South under the Angevins are Geoffroi de Vigeois (d. 1185) and Bernard Itier (d. 1225). For English chroniclers, Gransden, *Historical Writing*, 235. For Roger of Howden as author of 'Benedict

source for reconstructing Richard's and his father's governance of their French domains, an indication that nothing close to administrative kingship existed there. J.C. Holt has devoted years to collecting all the *acta* of Henry II and Richard I, and although his work is not yet complete, his collection of Richard's *acta* shows a heavy preponderance of documents from England and Normandy rather than the southern regions.[61]

No recent study of Richard Lionheart confronts the problem of the economies, societies and governments of his French territories. The principal book in English treating the continental lands is Sir Maurice Powicke's magisterial work, *The Loss of Normandy, 1189–1204*, first published in 1913 and revised in 1961. The dates that Powicke assigned to his book lend support to a view that Richard's reign marks the beginning of the Angevin 'empire's' collapse. While John Gillingham's 1984 work, *The Angevin Empire*, treats territories on both sides of the Channel, it is a work of less than 100 pages that cannot treat adequately its large subject.[62] Apparently feeling that he had covered Richard I's reign in his earlier biography, he largely skips over the last decade of the twelfth century in this work.

Jacques Boussard's monumental 1956 study, *Le gouvernement d'Henri II Plantegenêt*, never translated into English, is the most complete study of the Angevin kings' government of their French lands: Normandy and Brittany, Anjou, Maine, Touraine and Aquitaine. As the title shows, it does not claim to consider the fate of the Angevin lands after Henry's death in 1189. Also it suffers from an attempt to fit Plantagenet government into an outdated 'feudal' framework, failing to take into account striking structural differences between the constituent parts of the Angevin 'empire' that made it imposs-ible to impose a single pattern of government. Recent revisionist work on feudalism raises questions about the amount of public authority surviving and the extent of 'feudalisation' within its component parts. Contrasts between the societies in England and Normandy and the other Plantagenet lands are greater than the similarities, for nobles' lands elsewhere had not yet become fully dependent tenures, held in return for specified feudal services. Richard had to govern with whatever materials he had available in his various provinces, and he was unlikely to have succeeded in transplant-ing to his French lands south of Normandy the Anglo-Norman pattern of

---

of Peterborough', see D.M. Stenton, 'Roger of Howden and Benedict', *EHR* 58 (1953), 574–82.

61   J.C. Holt, 'The Acta of Henry II and Richard I of England 1154–1199: The Archive and its Historical Implications', in P. Rück (ed.), *Fotografische Sammlungen mittelalterlicher Urkunden in Europa* (Sigmaringen, 1989); page 139 gives 433 English, 117 Norman and 40 for other domains.

62   Gillingham, *Angevin Empire*; reprinted in Gillingham, *Coeur de Lion*, 1–91.

'fiscal feudalism' that efficient exchequers enabled him to impose on the nobility of England and Normandy.

In her 1887 book, *England under the Angevin Kings*, Kate Norgate concluded: 'Richard had spent the first half of his reign in fighting for a lost cause in Palestine; he spent the other half in fighting for a losing cause in Gaul.'[63] John W. Baldwin, author of *The Government of Philip Augustus*, characterises the 1190s as 'the crucial decade' for the Capetian monarchy, years when Philip set his sights on destruction of his Plantagenet rival. Yet John Gillingham rejects any notion that the Angevin 'empire' was in grave danger before Philip Augustus's campaigns in Normandy against King John, 1202–03, absolving Richard from any responsibility for loss of lands. These conflicting views raise questions of the viability of the Plantagenet block of territories, particularly its resources compared to those of Richard's antagonist, Philip Augustus of France. Key questions involve the public powers that Richard could exercise over his subjects in Anjou and Aquitaine, particularly his ability to levy taxes, and his privileges of feudal lordship over the aristocracy of those regions compared to his near-sovereign power over his English and Norman subjects. Although Anjou and Aquitaine contained flourishing ports, productive fields and fruitful vineyards, doubts remain about the adequacy of the king/duke's machinery for tapping their riches. Answering these questions is essential for any assessment of Richard as an 'administrative monarch'. The effectiveness of officials in the French parts of his 'empire' must be evaluated, yet his administrators outside England have not received equal scholarly attention. Closely linked to the problem of tying his possessions together with an able and loyal civil service is another – the challenge of cultivating a sense of shared identity among his diverse subjects that could counter the growing ideology of French unity under the Capetian royal line.

Such questions can only be answered by examining the patterns of government in both England and Richard's continental possessions. The time is right for an assessment of Richard Lionheart that goes beyond traditional narrative sources to incorporate record materials, not only extensive English exchequer rolls, but also the meagre number of charters surviving from the French domains. A balanced study of the Lionheart's reign must not neglect either his role as military commander or his position as prince and feudal lord imposing obligations, law and order on his assorted subjects, English and French. Such an approach, unlike previous studies, centres more on the character of governance during his decade-long reign than on his personal character.

---

63   Norgate, *England under the Angevin Kings*, 2: 357, 361.

CHAPTER TWO

The character of the Angevin 'empire'

Richard Lionheart was not simply king of England but lord of wide domains in western France. His father, Henry II Plantagenet, had assembled a block of lands that included his Angevin patrimony of the three counties of Anjou, Maine and Touraine (called for convenience Greater Anjou), his mother's Anglo-Norman kingdom and duchy, and the possessions of his queen, Eleanor, countess of Poitou and duchess of Aquitaine. [see Map I] These Angevin dominions formed 'an elegant geographical bloc stretching from Northumberland to the Pyrenees'.[1] Yet describing the nature of this assemblage of territories is not an easy task. Henry's 'empire' proved to be short lived, threatened by Philip Augustus throughout Richard's reign, and much of it conquered by 1204 when the French monarch wrested Normandy and Greater Anjou from John Lackland. Because of the failure of the Angevin 'empire' to endure, historians have debated its essential character, its potential for achieving political stability, and even Henry's and his sons' intentions for its permanence.

Most scholars conclude that neither Henry, Richard nor John sought to mould their possessions into a permanent political entity, that they saw them only as a means of providing for their offspring, who would take their lands and go their own ways. They perceive little evidence for a concept of imperial doctrine or permanent union. For example, J.C. Holt wrote that Plantagenet government did not rest on any political theory, but only on 'an amalgam of feudal practices and family rights'. He asked, 'In the absence of theory, can we speak of an "empire"?' Indeed, French scholars today eschew the word 'empire', preferring the expression *espace plantagenêt*. The

---

1   E. Hallam, *Capetian France, 987–1328* (London, 1980), 180.

historian of the Capetians, Robert-Henri Bautier, observes that there was never an Angevin 'empire', only 'an odd conglomeration of diverse powers over territories of widely differing status'. Another French scholar, Robert Fawtier, writes of 'the artificial union brought about by Henry II, just strong enough to hold together in his own lifetime', while the American authority C. Warren Hollister stated that the concept of an 'Angevin Empire' is 'nothing more than a convenient invention of modern historians'.[2]

Nineteenth-century preoccupation with 'nation-building' as a theme for medieval history long made it inconceivable that parts of both modern Britain and France might have been moulded into a single, stable political unit.[3] Yet state boundaries are, after all, human creations, not results of geography. Although the Plantagenets' continental lands incorporated the two strikingly different cultures of northern Europe and the Langue d'oc, potential existed for their integration with the sea, the Seine, the Loire and the Garonne providing easy access to such commercial centres as Rouen, Tours, La Rochelle, Bordeaux and Bayonne, while old Roman roads running south from Normandy afforded land links. Some scholars have noted possibilities for a 'sea-borne empire' with commerce serving as the network.[4] As John Le Patourel pointed out, 'The effective political units from 1066 until sometime in the fourteenth century were not England and France . . . , but a Norman empire and an Angevin Empire and a kingdom of France . . . overlapping and interpenetrating.'[5]

The Angevin block of lands lacked an attribute associated with a successful pre-modern 'hegemonic' empire, to use the language of modern military historians.[6] The object of hegemonic rulers was not installing direct rule over their conquests, but indirect exploitation. The Angevin 'empire', however, had no central zone in a geographical, economic or administrative sense

---

2 J.C. Holt, 'Aliénor d'Aquitaine, Jean sans Terre et la succession de 1199', *CCM* 29 (1986), 100; R.-H. Bautier, 'Conclusion. "Empire Plantagenêt" ou "Espace Plantagenêt". Y eut-il une civilisation du monde Plantagenêt?', *CCM* 29 (1986), 139–47; quotation, Bautier, 'Le traité d'Azay et la mort de Henri II Plantagenêt: un tournant dans la première guerre de Cent ans entre Capétiens et Plantagenêts (juillet 1189)', article 5 in his *Etudes sur la France Capétienne* (London, 1992), 33; R. Fawtier, *The Capetian Kings of France*, trans. L. Butler and R.J. Adam (London, 1960), 145; C.W. Hollister, 'Normandy, France and the Anglo-Norman *Regnum*', in *Monarchy, Magnates and Institutions in the Anglo-Norman World* (London, 1986), 56.

3 For example, Powicke, *Loss*; for a study of a French sense of 'manifest destiny', see G. Duby, *La dimanche de Bouvines* (Paris, 1973).

4 Y. Renouard, 'Essai sur le rôle de l'empire angevin dans la formation de la France et de la civilisation française aux XIIe et XIIIe siècles', in *Etudes d'histoire médiévale*, 2 vols (Paris, 1968), 2: 851–4; reprint from *Revue historique*. 195 (1945), 289–304.

5 J. Le Patourel, *Feudal Empires, Norman and Plantagenet* (London, 1984), 308.

6 See R. Hassig, *Aztec Warfare: Imperialism, Expansion and Political Control* (Norman, OK, 1988); E. Luttwak, *The Grand Strategy of the Roman Empire from the First Century A.D. to the Third* (Baltimore, 1976). These references are owed to Prof. Stephen Morillo.

from which to overawe outlying subject states. Its geographical centre, linking the Anglo-Norman realm to the north with Aquitaine to the south, was the patrimony of the counts of Anjou lying in the Loire River valley. Yet this central region does not meet the historians' criterion as an effective power-base, for England and Normandy generated the bulk of the Angevin rulers' wealth. Treasuries at Chinon and Loches castles, centres for paying and supplying armies, attest to Greater Anjou's strategic significance, but the coin stored in those fortresses was collected in England and Normandy.

The Plantagenets' northernmost possessions, the kingdom of England and the duchy of Normandy, constituted their economic powerhouse. In this so-called 'Anglo-Norman realm', the king/duke held powers approaching sovereignty, which made for efficient raising of funds for mercenary forces in Anjou-Maine and farther south. Scholars today no longer assume that William the Conqueror and his sons welded their ancestral duchy and their new kingdom into a single Anglo-Norman *regnum*.[7] None the less, both territories combined ancient traditions of public authority with effective administrative structures that set them apart from other western European countries before the thirteenth century. England's unity, assured by geography and history long before the Angevin kings' accession, enabled them to rule in an authoritarian, if not absolutist manner even when absent for long periods. County and hundred courts surviving from the Anglo-Saxons settled free subjects' disputes, and the central political authority possessed the coercive power needed to enforce the public tribunals' judgments. Henry II's legal reforms created new ties between the monarch and the knightly class, strengthening a direct ruler–subject relationship. Wider access to the *curia regis* afforded by his innovations threatened the barons' traditional control over the countryside.

Much of the Angevin monarchs' might came from exploitation of their tenurial relationship with the English baronage, imposing ever heavier financial burdens as 'feudal' obligations. The Angevins exercised control over inheritance of baronies, and they loaded down the barons with feudal payments, often assessed arbitrarily, that left them heavily in debt to the king. Other English nobles became crown debtors through purchase of custodies or other favours by which they hoped to swell their fortunes. Such gamblers

---

7   On a single Anglo-Norman realm, see Hollister, 'Normandy, France and the Anglo-Norman *Regnum*', in *Monarchy, Magnates and Institutions*, 17–58, reprinted from *Speculum*, 51 (1976); and J. Le Patourel, *The Norman Empire* (Oxford, 1976). Questioning the concept are D. Bates, 'Normandy and England after 1066', *EHR* 104 (1989), 851–76; J. Green, 'Unity and Disunity in the Anglo-Norman State', *Historical Research* 63 (1989), 115–34; and D. Crouch, 'Normans and Anglo-Normans: A Divided Aristocracy?', in D. Bates and A. Curry (eds), *England and Normandy in the Middle Ages* (London, 1994), 51–67.

became dependent on the king for future favours and for remission of debts owed for past favours. Under Henry II and his sons, commands for extra-judicial seizures of lands for default of payments or services became routine, and as a result, English barons lived in fear of the royal *ira et malevolentia*.[8] Paradoxically, it was the authority of Richard and his predecessors as sovereigns in the Anglo-Saxon or Frankish mould, executed by professional administrators armed with written records, that garnered the resources required to enforce 'feudal' obligations on their baronage. In short, English 'feudalism' is characterised by early 'territorialisation' of obligations imposed by the Anglo-Norman monarchs on the fiefs that their baronage held of them and, in turn, imposed by the barons on tenants of knights' fees. Despite the importance of England as a source of funds, neither Henry nor his two immediate successors, Richard and John, viewed themselves as English. All valued England chiefly for the wealth its strong government enabled them to tap.

While traditions and institutions of a strong state survived in England, a basic question about the nature of the Angevins' rule over their continental lands is the extent to which such 'public power' survived from the Carolingians under Henry II and Richard Lionheart. As Léopold Génicot wrote when reviewing several studies of medieval French principalities, 'The fundamental problem is always the same: public authority and its exercise.'[9] Historians of western Europe generally have seen a complete collapse or 'feudal transformation' of Frankish comital authority by the early to mid-eleventh century. The received view is that 'public power' disappeared from much of France during the eleventh-century 'feudal revolution', and intensely localised societies emerged, centred on castellans who dominated the surrounding countryside. These renegade castellans appropriated the powers of counts and dukes who had succeeded to the Carolingian monarchs' authority. They stripped peasant farmers of their freedom, and usurped comital and ducal rights by exercising police powers, presiding over justice, even *haute justice*, collecting tolls and taxes, and monopolising village resources, leaving counts and dukes with full military, judicial and financial powers only within their direct domains.[10] Scholars today are questioning the extent of this eleventh-century transformation; Dominique Barthélemy reminds readers that it is 'only a system for interpreting very scattered facts', and he advocates

---

8 J.E.A. Jolliffe, *Angevin Kingship*, 2nd edn (London, 1963); also R.V. Turner, 'King John's Concept of Royal Authority', *History of Political Thought* 17 (1996), 157–78.

9 L. Génicot, 'Provinces de France au coeur du moyen âge', *Revue d'histoire ecclésiastique*, 72 (1977), 614–15; reprinted in his *La noblesse dans l'Occident médiéval* (London, 1982).

10 A standard account is J.-P. Poly and E. Bournazel, *The Feudal Transformation 900–1200* (New York and London, 1991).

a gradualist view of 'successive adjustments' in the tenth and eleventh centuries.[11] The loss of public power was far from complete, and comital or ducal control over castellans varied from region to region according to their lords' resources. For example, in Anjou the counts continued to exercise considerable authority inherited from the Carolingians; and England and Normandy experienced expansion of royal/ducal power because William the Conqueror had inherited his Anglo-Saxon and Frankish predecessors' public powers. Public authority grew weaker in eleventh- and twelfth-century Aquitaine – a 'classic' feudal territory in the traditional sense – where castellans ruled as sovereigns over 'a network of tiny independent states'.[12]

Key aspects of Carolingian public power or sovereignty are a monopoly over the minting of coins, control over fortifications, continuance of public courts and supervision of the Church. This last is a good test for the survival of the Carolingians' authority among their successors in French counties and duchies. Richard Lionheart had to accept differing degrees of authority over ecclesiastical matters in his different domains. In Normandy, as in England, he succeeded in preserving tight royal/ducal supervision. In the province of Tours, rivalry with the French monarchs denied the Angevins command over the archbishop; yet in the Loire valley and in Brittany, some episcopal elections remained subject to pressures from Henry II and Richard. In the churches farther south, Richard had no more success in imposing his nominees on episcopal electors than his father or his maternal ancestors, reflecting the frailty of ducal control over Aquitaine and Gascony. The contrast between Richard's active role in naming bishops to Anglo-Norman sees and his feebleness in Aquitaine is striking.[13]

Just as the Angevins' loss of control over the Church in their diverse territories varied in degree, so too did erosion of other aspects of their public power differ from one region to another. While something close to a 'classic' feudal regime prevailed in much of western France, with the counts' public functions challenged by local lords, such a breakdown of public order seems to have been less complete in Greater Anjou. Richard's great-grandfather,

---

11 D. Barthélemy, *La Mutation de l'an mil, a-t-elle eu lieu?* (Paris, 1997), 17, 28.

12 G. Beech, *A Rural Society in Medieval France, the Gâtine of Poitou in the 11th and 12th Centuries* (Baltimore, 1964), 43–4; also S. Painter, 'Castellans of the Plain of Poitou in the Eleventh and Twelfth Centuries', rpt. *Speculum* 31 (1956) in F. Cazel Jr. (ed.), *Feudalism and Liberty* (Baltimore, 1961), 23–4, and M. Garaud, *MSAO*, 4th ser. 8 'Les Châtelains de Poitou et l'avènement du régime féodal, xie et xiie siècles' (1964), 22. For recent views, see T. Bisson, 'The "Feudal Revolution"', *Past and Present* 142 (Feb. 1994), 6–42; and the resulting 'Debate', 152 (Aug. 1996), 196–223; 155 (May 1997), 177–225.

13 R.V. Turner, 'Richard Lionheart and English Episcopal Elections', *Albion* 29 (1997), 1–13; and R.V. Turner, 'Richard Lionheart and the Episcopate in his French Domains', *French Historical Studies* 21 (1998), 517–42.

Count Fulk V, and his grandfather, Geoffrey le Bel, had succeeded in preserving or restoring comital control over their castellans in the early twelfth century, and Henry II 'prudently and patiently' continued their work of asserting comital authority.[14] Limited evidence for Greater Anjou hints, for example, that public justice had not disappeared entirely in the eleventh century and that Henry expanded it in ways similar to his expansion of royal and ducal justice in England and Normandy.

Aquitaine, in contrast with Anjou, afforded little opportunity for Richard to enforce ducal authority over a nobility traditionally characterised by historians as 'turbulent and undisciplined vassals'.[15] His ducal ancestors had not succeeded either in preserving public authority or forcing 'feudal' obligations on their nobility. By the beginning of the eleventh century, public tribunals were no longer functioning effectively in Aquitaine, and ducal attempts to reassert their jurisdiction by seizing control of the Church's peace movement had failed.[16] The dukes' situation actually worsened during the twelfth century, as some nobles in Aquitaine absorbed neighbouring castellans' territories to create substantial regional lordships of their own.

Despite these differences within his domains, Richard's possessions are usually lumped together under the convenient term Angevin or Plantagenet 'empire'. How he conceptualised these disparate lands, however, is difficult to discover. Neither he, his father nor his brother had a name for the block of lands that they ruled. Their seals bore the inscription *Rex Anglorum, Dux Normannorum et Aquitanorum et comes Andegavorum*, and they never imposed a common coinage bearing their portraits. In the Middle Ages, a single ruler's domination of several different peoples was not uncommon, and such rulers frequently dreamed of reviving the prerogatives and prestige of Roman emperors. Yet neither Henry II, Richard nor John ever dared call their body of possessions an 'empire'.[17] None of the three made much attempt to

---

14 F.M. Powicke, 'The Angevin Administration of Normandy II', *EHR* 22 (1907), 36.

15 André Debord, *La Société laïque dans les pays de la Charente XIe–XIIe siècles* (Paris, 1984), 397. Earlier is Kate Norgate, *England under the Angevin Kings* (London, 1887; rpt New York, 1969), 2: 203, on the Aquitanian nobility's 'love of strife for its own sake'. Guillaume le Breton spoke of Poitou as 'terre belliqueuse, et de foi instable', cited by E.-R. Labande, 'La civilisation d'Aquitaine à la fin de la période ducale', *Bulletin du Centre International d'Études Romanes* 1–2 (1964), 19. See Jane Martindale on historiography of the region, 'Eleanor of Aquitaine', in *Richard Coeur de Lion in History and Myth*, reprinted in *Status, Authority and Regional Power* (Aldershot, 1997), 24–33, for doubts about Aquitaine's 'anarchy'.

16 A. Debord, 'The Castellan Revolution and the Peace of God in Aquitaine', in T. Head and R. Landes (eds), *The Peace of God: Social Violence and Religious Response in France around the Year 1000* (Ithaca, NY, 1992), 156–9.

17 R. Folz, *The Concept of Empire in Western Europe from the Fifth to the Fourteenth Century*, trans. S. Ogilvie (London, 1985); R.R. Davies, 'Presidential Address: The Peoples of Britain and Ireland, 1100–1400, Identities', *TRHS* 4, 6th ser. (1994), 11–12.

impose uniformity on their possessions, and Henry rarely imposed identical laws on his diverse territories, issuing only four 'imperial acts' binding throughout his lands. The administrative pattern that he authorised soon after his sons' 1173–74 rebellion recognised the constituent parts of his 'empire' as separate regional units. From 1175, he gave each of his domains its own seneschal or viceroy, comparable to the English justiciar. In two of his provinces – Aquitaine and Brittany – his agents were his second and third sons, Richard and Geoffrey. After Geoffrey's premature death in 1186, his widow nominally ruled Brittany under the supervision of Henry and his seneschal.

The little evidence for the Angevins' own view of their domains must be teased out of their changing plans for the succession. Henry II unwisely assumed that advance arrangements would forestall quarrels among his sons over their inheritances. Like most aristocratic fathers, he wished his assemblage of lands to continue as a family unit, conserving the Plantagenet patrimony and England's crown for his eldest son and namesake, Young Henry; yet he was torn by a conflicting desire to provide some land for his three younger sons, Richard, Geoffrey and John. He assumed that some cohesion for his congeries of territories would continue through a common family interest despite partition among his sons, for he expected natural family affection, strengthened by ties of homage, to bind his younger sons to their eldest brother.

Long before and long after Henry II, great families sought to preserve their landed wealth as a unit in order to protect their standing and to preserve a prominent role in public life. Tradition reaching back to the Carolingians painted a picture of royal government as 'a family firm', in which sons were expected to take their places in the family business at an early age, serving in various posts until capable of governing sub-kingdoms as their father's viceroys.[18] In the eleventh-century county of Anjou and duchy of Normandy, fathers, sons and siblings had often cooperated for family advantage. In thirteenth-century France, younger sons of the Capetian royal family would rule apanages, accepting their royal elder brother's priority within the kingdom without rancour.[19]

Models for the disposition of Henry's 'empire' came not so much from public law as from a body of customary law prevailing across northwestern

---

18   J. Nelson, *Charles the Bald* (London, 1992), 43.
19   B. Bachrach, 'Henry II and the Angevin Tradition of Family Hostility', *Albion* 16 (1984), 112–30; E. Searle, *Predatory Kinship and the Creation of Norman Power, 840–1066* (Berkeley, CA, 1988); C. Wood, *The French Apanages and the Capetian Monarchy, 1224–1328* (Cambridge, MA, 1966); A. Lewis, *Royal Succession in Capetian France: Studies on Familial Order and the State* (Cambridge, MA, 1981).

France.[20] In the eleventh century, princely families had abandoned old Frankish traditions of division of possessions among heirs; and instead, they adopted a patrilinear model to safeguard the patrimony, rejecting equal partition among sons in favour of male primogeniture. A strictly linear pattern never became universal, however; and many territorial princes made some provision for younger sons, while passing the bulk of their lands to their eldest son. In some regions, custom decreed that any landed inheritance that the mother brought to her husband's family should pass to the second son. Aristocrats often limited land grants to only one or two younger sons. If more survived, either marriages to heiresses or ecclesiastical posts provided for the youngest ones, or else they were left to seek their own fortunes.

In parts of France, particularly in Normandy, the custom of *parage* arose. While giving preference to the eldest son, it required that younger sons be given some holdings out of their father's possessions. A deceased tenant's sons made private agreements providing shares of the fief for younger sons, yet family unity was preserved by the homage of the eldest son alone for the *caput* or chief castle, with his brothers holding some land of him and assisting him in performing feudal services. A recent study of early Normandy's ducal family describes *parage* as 'a kind of partible inheritance under the chairmanship of one son'.[21] A variation on *parage*, passing the patrimony intact to the eldest son but allowing the father to apportion his own acquisitions among younger sons, spread to England after 1066. This custom seems to have governed succession to the Anglo-Norman lands following William the Conqueror's death. His eldest son, Robert Curthose, already held the ducal title in Normandy. William felt free, however, to bequeath his conquest, England, to his second son, William Rufus, leaving only a large treasure to Henry, his third son. Apparently a custom of making acquisitions more freely disposable than the patrimony was already 'thoroughly familiar' to late eleventh-century Normans.[22]

When the counts of Anjou rose to power in the tenth century, they accumulated additional lands in the Loire region by marriage, conquest or other means; and the Angevin dynasty sought to keep its possessions intact, preserving the largest part of inherited land and acquisitions for the eldest son, although providing other sons with small portions. For example, after Count Fulk V of Anjou gained Maine through his marriage to its heiress,

20. For Angevin succession plans, R.V. Turner, 'The Problem of Survival for the Angevin "Empire": Henry II's and His Sons' Vision versus Late Twelfth-Century Realities', *AHR* 100 (1995), 82–91.

21 Searle, *Predatory Kinship*, 143.

22 E. Tabuteau, 'The Role of Law in the Succession to Normandy and England 1087', *HSJ* 3 (1991), 144–69.

that county was not made an apanage, but passed with Anjou to Geoffrey le Bel, his eldest son. Geoffrey's own succession plans are a subject for scholarly dispute, but Henry II took control of both Greater Anjou and his mother's Anglo-Norman lands, leaving his two younger brothers with only minor holdings.[23]

When the time came for devising succession plans for his own 'empire', Henry II drew on the traditions of both his Anglo-Norman and Angevin ancestors. Like them, he sought a 'broadly based and flexible' network of family ties that would preserve the unity of the family's domains and at the same time would provide for each son in a manner suiting his status.[24] Henry refused to accept strict primogeniture, which would have left his younger sons landless, but his failure to solve issues of inheritance proved his undoing. A plan for the succession set forth at Montmirail, Maine, in 1169 aimed at allaying fears of Louis VII by appearing to sanction partition. It specified that the eldest son, Young Henry, was to have the core principalities in the Loire region, together with the Anglo-Norman realm; and he was crowned king of England the next year. Younger sons would take outlying appendages in a secondary zone outside the central territory. The second son, Richard, was promised his mother's duchy of Aquitaine and installed formally as count of Poitou in 1172, in accord with a not uncommon custom of awarding the mother's inheritance to the second son. Ties to the Capetian king would be strengthened through Richard's betrothal to Alix, a daughter of Louis VII, and sister of Margaret, already married to Young Henry. The third boy, Geoffrey, would become count of Brittany, to whose heiress he had been betrothed in 1166. John 'Lackland', born only in 1167, had no place in this tripartite partition. Henry II named his last-born son lord of Ireland in 1177, but later attempts at providing a larger legacy for John increased tensions with his elder sons that ignited into open warfare.

Henry's proposals for his younger sons call to mind the later Capetian apanages, a practical means of providing for cadets while protecting dynastic interests. Yet the French royal apanage did not take shape until the thirteenth century, too late to serve Henry as a model. Under such a grant descending only to direct male heirs, chances of mortality meant that holdings given to cadets under its restricted conditions would often revert to the senior line. The Angevins had not yet devised such strategies as the Capetian apanages or late medieval English barons' entailed estates that similarly encouraged reversions to the head of the senior line.

---

23 J. Le Patourel, 'Angevin Successions and the Angevin Empire', in *Feudal Empires, Norman and Plantagenet.*
24 Bachrach, 'Henry II and the Angevin Tradition of Family Hostility', 126, 129–30.

Henry's ancestors' experience with *parage* led him to expect that his sons could maintain an alliance despite partitions, with shared ties of vassalage to the eldest providing cohesion and consultation on common measures. He expected his sons to share with him the task of governing his far-flung domains; as Henry's modern biographer observes, 'He conceived the future of the Angevin dominions not as an *empire* but as a *federation*.'[25] Henry II was to be deeply disappointed, however, for his arrangements demanded strong fraternal affection, younger brothers' acceptance of their limited portions and willingness to cooperate with their senior brother, all of which his sons lacked. His periodic proposals for changes in the succession fuelled their resentment of him and their jealousy of each other. His failure to share power with his namesake in the Angevin heartland especially aroused Young Henry's bitterness. The Young King saw his father thwarting him from reaching full manhood, forcing him to seek riches and fame alongside other landless youths in actual warfare or in mock combat at tournaments.

In 1173–74, Young Henry's frustration and his mother's fury against her unfaithful husband exploded into a large-scale rebellion, the most serious threat to confront Henry II. Eleanor of Aquitaine, for all practical purposes estranged from Henry by 1169, had returned to Poitiers and sought revenge against him by means of their sons. The Young King's brothers Richard and Geoffrey, urged on by their mother and by King Louis VII of France, soon joined the revolt that was suppressed with difficulty. As Henry continued to tinker with the succession to his territories in the years after the rebellion, new schemes sowed dissension among his three elder boys, arousing jealousy among them and against their youngest brother, John Lackland, the old king's favourite. Louis VII and his son Philip Augustus took advantage of the hostility between Henry and his sons and among siblings; later Philip exploited the rivalry between Richard and John and that between John and his nephew, Arthur, son of Geoffrey of Brittany. These costly struggles threatened to exhaust Plantagenet resources, even if they did not succeed militarily in splitting apart their lands.

The king sought a feudal means of guaranteeing the unity of his domains in January 1183 by proposing that his second son Richard do homage as count of Poitou to his elder brother, Henry the Young King; but Richard refused to acknowledge his brother as his superior, 'since they had been born of the same father and the same mother'.[26] As Richard protested, their previous homage to the French monarch made the two equals; and because both held directly of Philip Augustus, he could not be made subject to his

---

25 W.L. Warren, *Henry II* (Berkeley and Los Angeles, CA, 1987), 561–2, 627.
26 Diceto, 2: 18–19.

elder brother by doing homage to him. Because Aquitaine, the maternal inheritance, had never been subject either to the Anglo-Norman kings or to the counts of Anjou, Richard also feared that homage to his brother would make it a dependency of the Plantagenet territories. Richard's refusal pushed the Young King into another rebellion, seeking to oust his brother from Aquitaine, which ended with Young Henry's death in June 1183 as his revolt was collapsing.

New schemes, aimed at providing for John after the death of Young Henry and after Geoffrey of Brittany's death in 1186, rankled Richard. The soft spot in Henry's heart for John Lackland moved him to seek a larger legacy for him than the last-born son in any aristocratic family could expect, and the old king paid a price in Richard's disaffection and rebellion. It is unlikely that Henry II actually proposed replacing Richard with John as heir to his royal title and to his Angevin patrimony; more likely, he was simply unwilling to acknowledge this publicly. According to Gerald of Wales, however, the king contemplated in 1187–88 leaving to Richard only the English crown and the Norman duchy, consigning all his other French fiefs to John.[27] Philip Augustus inflamed Richard's animosity toward his father, cultivating Richard's friendship and endeavouring to strengthen their ties by urging that the Lionheart finally marry his long-time fiancée, Alix, the French king's sister. The French king's friendship for Richard Lionheart would not last long after Henry II's death, however.

Henry II's hope of permanence for his domains was doomed by mutual mistrust among father, mother and sons, exacerbated by the meddling of two Capetian monarchs, Louis VII and Philip Augustus. For Henry's off-spring, the bond of vassalage to their Capetian lord proved stronger than the force of filial affection. Despite mistrust within the family, accidents of mortality kept the Plantagenet domains intact until John's reign. Richard Lionheart succeeded unchallenged to all his father's domains in 1189, thanks in part to his mother's efforts in England. Eleanor had accumulated treasures of energy during her 1174–89 imprisonment that she would expend without counting the cost during her two sons' reigns.[28] Despite her failed marriage, she seems never to have doubted that her ancestral lands belonged within the larger Angevin 'empire' that her husband Henry II had assembled, and she fought to hold together for Richard Lionheart and later for John Lackland the far-flung Plantagenet possessions.

Despite tendencies toward uniformity in the governments of England and Normandy, the Plantagenets never conceived of shaping their various

27   Gerald of Wales, 8: 232.
28   R. Pernoud, *Aliénor d'Aquitaine* (Paris, 1965), 257.

possessions into a centralised state. Jacques Boussard, in his study of twelfth-century Anjou and in his larger book, *Le Gouvernement d'Henri II Plantegenêt*, found an organising principle for the Angevin 'empire' in 'feudalism'. In his view, Greater Anjou had emerged as a fully feudal society by the mid-twelfth century, and he saw the post-1175 pattern for Henry's possessions as a strongly organised 'feudal state'. He found this pattern continuing to function effectively under Richard I, despite his long absences on crusade and in captivity. Henry II and Richard Lionheart are described by Boussard and other historians as attempting to rescue Anjou and Aquitaine from the anarchy of 'classic' feudalism by 'territorialising' feudal relationships. Supposedly, Henry and Richard redefined their nobles' earlier vague obligations of vassalage to advance the notion that they held their patrimonies as fiefs; and a tenurial relationship of vassals and fief-holders to a feudal lord was replacing loyalty and public services of subjects to the Carolingian rulers and their successors, that is, a private relationship supplanting political allegiance.[29] In Boussard's version, they were extending elsewhere obligations of homage and services already owed by their English and Norman vassals, cementing personal ties to bind together the dynasty and the nobles of their different territories in a chain of 'feudal' relationships.[30]

A chronological problem appears, however, when seeking an effective 'feudal' basis for Plantagenet rule in the late twelfth century. The 'territorialisation' associated with the rise of strong 'feudal' principalities proceeded at far different rates in the various domains of Henry II and Richard I. Their powers ranged from 'the intensive and authoritative' in their English kingdom and their duchy of Normandy to 'the diffused and occasional' in the domains brought to Henry by his marriage to Eleanor of Aquitaine.[31] In fact, the law of fiefs and vassals had barely reached any degree of definition outside the Anglo-Norman realm before the end of the twelfth century. For a number of years, studies by French regional historians have challenged textbook versions of 'feudalism', and now Susan Reynolds' book, *Fiefs and Vassals*, demands that students confront the new evidence and revise received views. Reynolds writes, '[I]n so far as anything like feudo-vassalic institutions existed, they were the products not of weak and unbureaucratic government in the

---

29 G. Duby, *La Société aux XIe et XIIe siècles dans la région mâconnaise* (Paris, 1971), 159–8.

30 Also in J. Boussard, 'La diversité et les traits particuliers du régime féodal dans l'Empire Plantagenêt', *Annali della Fondazione italiana per la storia amministrativa* 1 (1964), 158, Henry's administration described as 'fondée justement sur les principes essentiels et immuables du régime féodal'. See also Debord, *Charente*, 380–1, for a more recent presentation of application of 'feudal' principles in Aquitaine.

31 R.R. Davies, *Domination and Conquest: The Experience of Ireland, Scotland and Wales, 1100–1300* (Cambridge, 1990), 46.

early middle ages but of the increasingly bureaucratic government and expert law that began to develop from about the twelfth century.'[32]

Before the marriage of Henry and Eleanor, the power of the duke of Aquitaine came chiefly from the prestige of his office and the force of his personality or from his ties of clientage and *convenientia* with the aristocracy, in the absence of 'feudal' ties of vassalage and fief holding.[33] While the nobles of Aquitaine and Gascony vaguely acknowledged ducal lordship, doing homage as an act of reconciliation after rebellion, their 'feudal' obligations remained ill-defined, subject to frequent renegotiation. Indeed, in the extreme Mediterranean south, vassalage and homage often denoted a degree of servility or subjection that the aristocracy viewed as demeaning.[34] Furthermore, much land continued to be classed as alods, not as fiefs subject to 'feudal' obligations, but as property theoretically subject to performance of 'public' services. French regional studies show substantial alodial estates persisting throughout the twelfth century, and terms such as *feodum* or *allodium* lacked the precise meaning that modern scholars prefer.[35]

Henry II and his son are incorrectly described as rescuing Aquitaine and Gascony from 'feudal anarchy', converting their nobles' patrimonies into fiefs, and dictating to them explicit obligations of homage, fealty and services.[36] That portrayal of Angevin lordship seems more the creation of historians' minds than an accurate depiction of reality in the southwest. In the Loire valley, definition of obligations had gone little further. There nobles' homage and fealty symbolised bonds of friendship or political subjection; it did not transform their patrimonies into comital or ducal fiefs, even if their Plantagenet lords granted them some estates as fiefs. Not until the thirteenth century was a process of 'territorialisation' under way with lords enforcing

---

32 S. Reynolds, *Fiefs and Vassals* (Oxford, 1995), 320, also 479–80. For references to the French literature, see T. Bisson, 'The "Feudal Revolution"'; and the 'Debate' that followed, *Past and Present* no. 152 (Aug. 1996); no. 155 (May 1997).

33 Debord, *Charente*, 269, 370.

34 L. Paterson, *The World of the Troubadours: Medieval Occitan Society c. 1100–1300* (Cambridge, 1993), 16–17, 31, 35.

35 T. Evergates, 'Nobles and Knights in Twelfth-century France', in T.N. Bisson (ed.), *Cultures of Power: Lordship, Status, and Process in Twelfth-century Europe* (Philadelphia, 1995), 27 and n. 82. Also Duby, *Société dans la mâconnais*, 481–2, depicting alods in the Mâconnais gradually reduced to fiefs, 1160–1240. In a 1208 charter's account of a land dispute between the great abbey of La Sauve-Majeure near Bordeaux and a knight, the claimant acknowledged that the properties in question did not pertain to his *feodum*, but were *allodiales*, and that they ought to belong to the abbey *feodaliter*; C. Higounet and A. Higounet-Nadal (eds), *Grande Cartulaire de la Sauve Majeure*, Etudes et documents d'Aquitaine, 8 (Bordeaux, 1996), 2: 618–19, no. 1116.

36 For example, K. Norgate, *England under the Angevin Kings*, 2: 203; Powicke, *Loss*, 22–3; C. Petit-Dutaillis, *La Monarchie féodale en France et en Angleterre* (Paris, 1933; rpt 1971), 164; and Debord, *Charente*, 380–1.

military and financial services as obligations owed from fiefs, enforceable by juridical and fiscal means, rather than as consequences of personal ties with their castellans or 'vassals'. In thirteenth-century Anjou and Poitou, as in much of France, this was largely the work of royalist lawyers once Capetian annexation had brought them into the French royal demesne.

Henry II and Richard Lionheart as counts of Anjou and dukes of Aquitaine could not introduce the 'fiscal feudalism' that their control over tenants in England and Normandy enabled them to enforce there. Beyond their Anglo-Norman realm, supervisory tools were missing for extending the control of the *curia regis* to the baronage in the outlying countryside. Sources from Greater Anjou and Aquitaine give no evidence for demands for relief, the 'feudal aids' or the 'feudal incidents' that textbooks define as standard financial obligations owed by nobles to their lords from their fiefs. In fact, such payments did not become common on the continent before the very end of the twelfth century; the Capetian monarchs, for example, did not levy reliefs on their great lordships until the time of Philip Augustus. Such 'feudal' resources, unacknowledged by the aristocracy of Anjou or Aquitaine, could have raised little money for Henry II and Richard Lionheart outside their Anglo-Norman realm.

Military service is a test of the feudal character of the Angevin 'empire'. Outside Normandy, French landlords' military service does not appear to have been a condition by which they held their property.[37] The first surveys of knight-service from twelfth-century France that are comparable to the 1166 English Inquest come from Normandy and Champagne in 1172. Except in Angevin-ruled Brittany, whatever quotas were assessed elsewhere in the twelfth century were mainly for castle-guard. When Henry II summoned the great men of his continental lands to join his host, only the Norman barons brought fixed numbers of knights, the rest only whatever number their status warranted. Angevin and Aquitanian aristocrats answered his call to arms because warfare was their profession and on account of lingering notions of military service as a public duty. Even in England and Normandy, the feudal levy of knights was less useful than textbooks portray it, important chiefly in offensive warfare. Collection of scutage in lieu of personal military service raised the necessary funds from England and Normandy to pay mercenaries.

As Georges Duby wrote of knights in the Mâconnais, 'The old Frankish public service of *defensio patriae* was not forgotten in the twelfth century.' Military service of *ost et chevauchée* surviving the eleventh-century 'feudal transformation' in much of France was as much an ancient responsibility of

---

37 Reynolds, *Fiefs and Vassals*, 131. Also Boussard, 419, 428, 565; and Norgate, *England under the Angevin Kings*, 1: 461–2, where she stresses the magnates' desire for military glory.

freemen as a feudal obligation of fiefholders.[38] Henry II endeavoured to reactivate his subjects' old public obligation of military service, issuing a decree in 1180 for his continental lands comparable to the English Assize of Arms. All freemen possessing moveable goods worth at least £100 *angevin* had to equip themselves with a horse, shield and armour, sword and lance, while his less wealthy subjects were to bear less costly weaponry. Despite attempts to require military service from their subjects, however, Henry II, Richard Lionheart and John depended much more upon mercenaries in their military forces fighting in France, infantry companies of *Brabançons* from the Low Countries and from Wales, than on their nobles' 'feudal' contributions. They relied upon paid infantry, mobile tactical forces readily shifted about their far-flung possessions as needed, and siege engineers to construct and operate complex siege machines to reduce rebel strongholds. Though efficient, such military forces cost the Angevins both in money and in their subjects' esteem.

Richard's mode of governing Aquitaine and Gascony, both in his father's lifetime and afterwards, consisted largely of a series of punitive expeditions of foreign mercenaries against rebel barons. He spent a quarter century in almost unrelieved war against the magnates of his duchy, razing their fortifications only to see them swiftly rebuilt in time to resist another siege. These wars consumed vast sums of money, and discussion of revenues portends differences between the Plantagenet territories rather than unity. No financial records comparable to the English or Norman pipe rolls survive for the southern lands, and no other surviving sources point toward adequate tax-collecting or accounting machinery for exploitation of the south's wealth. Outside the Anglo-Norman territories, Richard's revenues consisted chiefly of domanial dues from his estates and easily collected tolls or duties from his growing towns in the Loire valley and to the south along the Atlantic coast of Aquitaine, where commerce plainly was prospering.

In the absence of surviving financial records, no conjecture can be made of the amount of 'public' revenues that comital or ducal agents could collect outside their own demesne. None the less, some scholars insist that the flourishing commerce of the Loire, Charente and Garonne regions would have produced income that more than offset Richard's costs in suppressing incessant rebellions.[39] Perhaps due to a dearth of evidence from the continent, 'feudal' revenues extorted from English and Norman barons – the enormous reliefs, scutages and fines for favours inscribed upon the pipe

---

38 Duby, *Société dans la mâconnais*, 328–9; T. Evergates, *Feudal Society in the Bailliage of Troyes under the Counts of Champagne, 1152–1284* (Baltimore, 1975), 49, 58.
39 Gillingham, *Richard*, 46–7; J. Dunbabin, *France in the Making 842–1180* (Oxford, 1985), 344, follows Gillingham, as does Hallam, *Capetian France*, 165–8.

rolls – have most impressed English-speaking historians.[40] Evidence points toward taxation of England's wealth to fund warfare in defence of the southern domains as early as Henry II's 1159 campaign against the Count of Toulouse.[41] Both father and son continued to deplete England's treasure in endless conflicts on the Continent against rebellious vassals and against the Capetian monarch. Only Normandy generated substantial sums for its own defence, and its resources were seriously stretched by 1198–99. It seems apparent that Richard's wealth harvested in England and Normandy bought him skilled professional soldiers whose prowess could crush rebellious nobles, who lacked resources to reinforce their castles with walls thick enough to resist his siege engines. His unending quest for funds and his demands for service in far-away lands also provoked loud protests from the English.

Since the Angevin 'empire' does not conform comfortably to the 'feudal' model, the terminology of recent writers on warfare suggests an alternate model, defining it as hegemonic rather than territorial. The aim of Henry II, Richard I and John was the same as that of most pre-modern imperial rulers: indirect exploitation of acquired lands without displacing entirely local or regional lords. In such a system, the imperial power maintained its homeland as a central zone of direct control – the 'royal demesne' in feudal terminology – from which armed forces could be dispatched to a surrounding zone consisting of vassals' lordships to demand obedience and collect tribute. The three Loire valley counties of Anjou, Maine and Touraine (Greater Anjou) formed such a geographical centre, linking Normandy and Aquitaine, and crucial to the Plantagenets for repelling the Capetians.

Aquitaine and Gascony fell into a second zone, where the Plantagenet dukes appeared as little more than first among equals in a loose 'confederation' of nobles. In the absence of administrative structures, effective government proved possible only when mutual friendship and respect prevailed between the duke and his nobility. When amicable relations were lacking – as in Angoulême or the Limousin on Poitou's southern fringes or near the Pyrenees – then periodic punitive expeditions to cow these second-zone nobles followed. Beyond the zone of indirect control lay a third zone, where control was dubious because a rival power centre – in the Plantagenets' case, the Capetian monarchy – could lure local leaders into its orbit, for example, the counts of Toulouse.

Henry II's marriage to Eleanor had made him a party to the age-old rivalry between the counts of Toulouse and the dukes of Aquitaine. Eleanor's

---

40   For example, J.O. Prestwich, 'War and Finance in the Anglo-Norman Realm', *TRHS* 5 ser. 4 (1954), 82.

41   E. Amt, *The Accession of Henry II in England: Royal Government Restored 1149–1159* (Woodbridge, 1993), 182–7.

ducal predecessors had laid claim to lordship over Toulouse by right of Duke William IX's marriage to its heiress; but because of seizure of the county by the girl's uncle, Raymond of St Gilles, the dukes struggled to realise their rights.[42] The legal aspects of the story no doubt gave the dukes of Aquitaine reasons for their actions, but the economy of this region must have motivated them as well, for control of Toulouse would have given the dukes dominion over a wealthy trading zone stretching from the Atlantic coast and their Garonne valley lands to the Mediterranean Sea.[43] Henry II had been vigorous in asserting his wife's rights in Toulouse, eventually succeeding in forcing the count to do homage to him in 1173; and not surprisingly, Richard followed a parallel policy. A frequent focus for this conflict was the county of Quercy with its chief town of Cahors, lost by Toulouse in 1159 and temporarily regained during Young King Henry's final rebellion of 1183, then continuously in Plantagenet hands after 1186. Devastating war between Duke Richard and Count Raymond V broke out on several occasions, the most damaging to Raymond in 1186 and 1188 when he lost Quercy, and loss of more land threatened had not Philip Augustus intervened.

Yet the Angevin 'empire' imperfectly fits this hegemonic 'model' for pre-modern states because England and Normandy – second-zone territories geographically – were central in resources, providing the bulk of Henry II's and Richard Lionheart's wealth. A great failing of the Plantagenets was their inability to create out of these various power zones a political entity with some cohesion whose inhabitants – or elites, at least – would share loyalty to the Plantagenet dynasty. Reliance upon military force to control Aquitaine proved counter-productive. The more ruthless the Plantagenets' punitive expeditions and the more rapacious their mercenaries' plundering in that zone, the more hostility they aroused. The *Brabançons* contributed to the region's confusion, often continuing to fight and plunder on their own behalf after formal hostilities had ended. Their looting of the countryside caused suffering among the peasantry and aroused the clergy's loud laments; more than once, Aquitanian bishops had to raise their own troops to protect their flocks from marauding soldiers.

Emblematic of the hegemonic character of the Angevins' block of lands is the failure of Henry II and Richard to create a cosmopolitan ruling class, drawn from all their possessions, united in loyalty to the dynasty and committed to preservation of the 'empire'. In their northern kingdom and duchy,

---

42   R. Benjamin, 'A Forty Years War: Toulouse and the Plantagenets, 1156–1196', *Historical Research* 61 (1988), 270–83.

43   Martindale, 'Eleanor of Aquitaine', 26–7; J. Gillingham, *The Angevin Empire* (New York, 1984), 26.

royal or ducal servants saw exercise of their master's power as a pathway to their own enrichment through enforcing his feudal prerogatives, winning for themselves custodies of minors or marriages to rich widows or heiresses. Numerous English and Norman servants of the Plantagenets had a stake in continued growth of royal power. The absence of a similar corps of Angevin- or Aquitanian-born *familiares* reaping rewards through service to the Lionheart is noticeable, however, for his English and Norman subjects are disproportionately represented.

Even within the Anglo-Norman domains, fewer Normans were finding administrative posts in England than earlier, although some Normans still joined the royal household as clerks and earned English bishoprics as reward. Some of the Normans who did secure secular office across the Channel aroused the bitter resentment of the English, for example, William Long- champ. A Norman layman who served as an administrator on both sides of the Channel was Robert de Tresgoz, a knight of the Cotentin, where he served as *bailli*. William Longchamp named him sheriff of Wiltshire and constable of Salisbury Castle in 1190–91; and he lost those posts on Long- champ's disgrace, but later regained custody of Salisbury and gained cus- tody of Bristol. In 1198, Robert managed to marry the heir to the barony of Ewyas Harold, Herefordshire. The flow of personnel was more often in only one direction, however, with English royal servants transferring to Normandy; pointed examples are the two highest officials in the duchy under Richard: Archbishop Walter of Rouen and William fitz Ralph, the English-born seneschal of the duchy.

Among the handful of members of the Lionheart's household who were with him continuously – both in England and across the Channel – hardly any Angevin or Poitevin names occur, mainly English ones, for most of the Lionheart's royal *familiares* had belonged to his father's household. The only prominent Norman official was Archbishop Walter of Rouen, actually a native of Cornwall; the rest held posts in England.[44] Joining Richard on his 1194 visit to England as the fifth-ranked witness to royal charters was a Poitevin knight captured with him on the return from Palestine, William de l'Etang; and a Norman, Robert de Tresgoz, was the tenth-ranked witness.[45] During the Lionheart's extended stay on the Continent, 1194–99, following

---

44   The others were Hugh du Puiset, bishop of Durham; Hugh de Nonant, bishop of
      Coventry, Norman by birth; Godfrey de Lucy, bishop of Winchester; John Marshal and
      his brother, William. R.R. Heiser, 'The *Familiares* of the Court of King Richard I', MA
      thesis (Florida State University, 1988), 75.

45   Tresgoz continued to witness fairly frequently in 1197 and 1199; R.R. Heiser, 'The Royal
      Familiares of Richard I', *Medieval Prosopography* 10 (1989), Tables, 44, 49. For De l'Etang,
      Debord, *Charente*, 384.

his second visit to his island kingdom, 'a military nucleus' headed by William Marshal and William de l'Etang dominated his witness lists. Also a Norman baron and a Norman administrator ranked high among the attestors. Fourth in frequency was Robert de Harcourt, scion of an old Norman family, who held lands of the honour of Beaumont-le-Roger and also seven manors spread over six shires in England; and seventh was the English-born William fitz Ralph, the Norman seneschal.[46]

The paucity of southerners among Richard's intimates as king is remarkable, since he must have known well many Aquitanian notables since youth; of the sixty-seven most frequent witnesses to Richard I's royal charters, only seven came from Aquitaine. It is not surprising, given the military nature of the Lionheart's rule in Aquitaine, that the few Poitevins who did move from ducal service with him were knights in his military household. Besides William de l'Etang, they included knights who had accompanied him on his journey across France for embarkation for the voyage to Palestine, notably William de Forz, Andrew de Chauvigny and Geoffrey de la Celle, whom Richard later appointed seneschal of Poitou.[47] Conspicuous by the almost total absence among the names of companions of Richard – either as count of Poitou or as king – are the great men of Anjou, Aquitaine and Gascony. Richard rarely held great councils on the Continent that would have gathered together his English and French magnates, lay and clerical, to reinforce their shared ties of *fidelitas* to the Plantagenet dynasty.

Viewed from the perspective of the Angevins, Poitevins and Gascons, Normandy and England were 'peripheral colonies', acquisitions of the ruling family that concerned them little.[48] Yet they may well have felt themselves 'colonised' by the Anglo-Normans, for Richard's southern subjects profited little from his rule of a vast empire. Few ties of tenure or marriage bound the Plantagenets' nobles in Greater Anjou to the nobility north of the Loire valley, and ties between the Poitevin or Gascon nobility and Anglo-Norman barons were even looser. Anglo-Norman nobles neither acquired land-holdings in Aquitaine nor married southerners in any significant numbers. Only a handful of marriages united the nobilities of the two regions. Richard married Denise de Déols to one of his Poitevin knights, Andrew de Chauvigny; and he married Hawise, countess of Aumâle, Normandy, and lady of Skipton, Yorkshire, to another of his knights, William de Forz, member of a family that had long served the counts as *prévôts* in Poitou.

---

46 Heiser, MA thesis, 125; Tables, 45, 49; Powicke, *Loss*, 342–3.
47 Heiser, 'Royal *Familiares*', 29, 32, 34, and Table, 46–50.
48 J.C. Holt, 'The Loss of Normandy and Royal Finances', in *War and Government in the Middle Ages* (Woodbridge, 1984), 105; Dunbabin, *France in the Making*, 339.

Antagonism between the culture of northern France (which dominated among the English aristocracy) and the Mediterranean society of Aquitaine and Gascony actually reached back into the Dark Ages. With the partition of the Carolingian Empire into different *regna*, Aquitaine and Gascony had been separated from *Francia*. The southerners had long thought of themselves as a separate *gens* or *natio*, a group sharing a common descent, yet somehow still belonging to the larger kingdom of France.[49] Aquitanian and Gascon barons developed a distinct culture unlike that of lands to the north; indeed, John of Salisbury in 1166 took note of 'the peculiar customs and strange laws of the folk of Aquitaine', unfamiliar to outsiders.[50] The particularist attitude of Henry II's Poitevin and Gascon subjects had limited his appointment of Anglo-Normans to posts there, although he had occasionally assigned them to military commands in the south.[51] Prejudice ran in both directions, however. After John's loss of Normandy along with much of Poitou in 1204, rancour against alien soldiers appointed to posts in England made 'Poitevin' into a party political label, even though most of those bitterly resented aliens actually came from Touraine.

Even the long-time links between England and Normandy were beginning to weaken by the end of the twelfth century. Lucien Musset finds that 'the old equilibrium between England and Normandy had reversed itself completely, in favor of England'.[52] Regardless of expansionist Capetian policies, native Normans were finding that their union with the English under Plantagenet rule no longer benefited them, for patronage was flowing chiefly to the English. Within Normandy, lords in such frontier zones as the Vexin had no ties to England; they held estates beyond the Norman frontiers, often located in Capetian territory, and can be labelled more 'Franco-Norman' than 'Anglo-Norman'.[53] Few Normans would regret their separation from England in 1204.

At the same time, the descendants of Norman settlers in England had become thoroughly assimilated, and the fate of Normandy concerned them less and less. Family and tenurial ties no longer bound together the two

---

49 K. Werner, 'Les nations et le sentiment national dans l'Europe médiévale', *Revue Historique* 244 (1970), 292–5; Renouard, 'Essai sur le rôle de l'empire angevin', vol. 2: 850–4; also S. Reynolds, *Kingdoms and Communities* in Western Europe, 900–1300 (Oxford, 1984), 254–5, 280.

50 *Letters of John of Salisbury* 2: 179, letter 176.

51 For the paucity of English or Norman officials in Poitou, see Pierre Boissonade, 'Administrateurs laïques et ecclésiastiques Anglo-Normands en Poitou à l'époque d'Henri II Plantagenêt (1152–1189)', *BSAO* 3rd ser. 5 (1919), 156–90; for Richard's avoidance of Poitevins as officials in England, see Heiser, 'Royal *Familiares*'.

52 L. Musset, 'Quelques problèmes posés par l'annexion de la Normandie au domaine royal français', in R.-H. Bautier (ed.), *La France de Philippe Auguste* (Paris, 1982), 294.

53 D. Crouch, 'Normans and Anglo-Normans: A Divided Aristocracy?', 51–67.

branches of Anglo-Norman families as they had in the Anglo-Norman period. Even those barons in England who still held large estates across the Channel were growing steadily more English and less Norman in outlook, and most would choose the island kingdom over the duchy after John's loss of it in 1204. The majority, without significant Norman holdings, had less and less interest in supporting warfare for Normandy's defence with their taxes, much less with their own military service. Below the baronial level, most English knights had lost any sense of Norman identity, and only a small number still had landholdings in their ancestral land. The increasingly narrow English concerns of these landholders diverged sharply from their monarch's broader continental outlook. Late in Richard's reign, some English ecclesiastical tenants-in-chief, soon to be followed by their lay fellows, were questioning their obligation to supply knights for fighting across the sea in Normandy.

A major factor compromising the Angevins' creation of a successful hegemonic regime was their status as vassals of the Capetian monarch for their continental possessions. Philip Augustus's suzerainty gave him opportunities for fomenting conflict, not only between Henry II and his sons or between Richard Lionheart and his brothers, but also between the head of the Plantagenet house and the nobility of his French lands. Before the accession of Philip Augustus in 1180, vassalage and fief still had not become linked; and homage by the counts of Anjou and dukes of Normandy to the Capetian monarch had signified no more than 'a tenuous non-aggression pact'.[54] Only the surviving prestige that still attached to the name of king, despite the Capetians' weakness, caused their counts and dukes to acknowledge any obligations to them.[55] *Hommage de paix* or *hommage en marche* might mark a meeting on neutral ground between the Capetian king and one of the French territorial princes, sealing a pact of friendship, 'a sign of alliance rather than a mark of subordination'.[56]

The eleventh-century count of Anjou, Fulk Nerra, exemplifies this, for he accepted his status as the French king's vassal and *fidelis*, but interpreted it as only an expression of alliance and friendship. Fulk did not consider his county of Anjou a fief held of the French crown. He acknowledged only that he held some scattered lands and privileges of the king, but no sources before 1106–09 assert that the count held his comital *honour* as a French fief. None the less, the counts of Anjou had closer ties to the French monarchs than the dukes of Normandy or the dukes of Aquitaine. The counts insisted

---

54 J. Strayer, 'Fief', in *Dictionary of the Middle Ages* (New York, 1982–89), 5: 59.
55 O. Guillot, *Le Comte d'Anjou et son entourage*, 2 vols (Paris, 1973), 16–17; see also Reynolds, *Fiefs and Vassals*, 35–40.
56 Hallam, *Capetian France*, 94–7.

on a 'more dignified dependence' than ordinary vassals, symbolised by their claim to the honorific title 'seneschal of France'.[57]

The homage that the Anglo-Norman kings did to the Capetian monarch for their duchy of Normandy meant no more to them than personal allegiance without any admission that Normandy was a French fief. Indeed, William of Poitiers, writing near the end of the eleventh century, wrote that William the Conqueror was 'neither the friend nor the vassal of the Capetians', and no evidence survives for any 'formal links of fidelity' with the French king.[58] Certainly the homage that some Anglo-Norman kings did to the French monarch for their duchy of Normandy on its frontiers meant little in terms of concrete obligations; they never sent their knights to join the Capetians' feudal host.

The question of the relationship of the dukes of Aquitaine to the French monarchs is even more confusing than that of the dukes of Normandy or counts of Anjou. Its status had remained murky for much of the post-Carolingian period. The duke, who was also count of Poitou, was one of the great lords of France, and he preserved some of the prestige of the Carolingian sub-kings. Apparently, Eleanor's ducal predecessors in Aquitaine had acknowledged the French monarch's supremacy by the eleventh century; but if they sometimes joined the Capetian royal host, they fought as allies, not as vassals of the French monarch. The dukes of Gascony had freed themselves from any subjection to the French kings some time before the union of the two duchies in 1058, and by the twelfth century, Gascony still appeared to be an alod free of any attachment to the French monarchy. Richard Lionheart felt safe in endowing his bride Berengaria with Gascony as her dower-right in 1191 without securing Philip Augustus's permission, but he had done homage to the Capetian kings for the county of Poitou in 1169 and again in 1188.[59]

Henry II several times admitted that he was the 'man' of the French monarch, doubtless still thinking of his homage as purely personal. As duke of Normandy, he travelled to Paris in 1151 to render homage to Louis VII, although earlier dukes had insisted on doing their homage only on the Norman frontier. At that time, Henry needed the French king's recognition to buttress his claim to the duchy against a rival, Eustace of Boulogne, son

---

57   Powicke, *Loss*, 13–14.
58   Cited by D. Bates, *Normandy before 1066* (London and New York, 1982), 59–60 and n. 33, where he translates *militem* as 'vassal'.
59   P. Chaplais, 'Le Traité de Paris de 1259 et l'inféodation de la Gascogne allodiale', *Le Moyen Age* 61 (1955), 127–8, 133; reprinted in his *Essays in Medieval Diplomacy and Administration* (London, 1981). See Martindale, 'Eleanor of Aquitaine', 28–31, who finds Aquitaine under Louis VII 'an autonomous political entity which could not be conceptually absorbed into a pre-existing scheme of political or juridical views on the character of royal power'.

of King Stephen. In February 1156, Henry again did homage to Louis for Normandy, and also for Anjou and Aquitaine, thereby becoming the first crowned king of England to do homage to the French ruler. The ceremony took place once more on the Norman frontier. Again he needed his suzerain's guarantee of his authority over his 'empire', this time in the face of claims by his younger brother, Geoffrey.[60] An English chronicler wrote that in 1183, Henry II did homage and fealty 'for all his holdings across the sea to King Philip of the French, for which he never before this [occasion had] wished to do homage'.[61] The superior prestige that the Capetian king enjoyed as Henry's lord was displayed during Henry's expedition against Toulouse in 1159, when he raised the siege of the town because of Louis's presence there. He dared not threaten the life of his lord, the anointed *rex Francorum*.

Henry allowed his heirs to do homage to Louis VII and Philip Augustus for continental territories nominally in their hands, giving the French monarch a means of fostering hostility between father and sons. Young Henry did homage for Anjou in 1169, acknowledging that he held it as a fief of the French king and receiving recognition of his title of French royal seneschal, belonging hereditarily to the counts of Anjou.[62] It is unclear whether Richard Lionheart's promise to pay Philip Augustus 24,000 silver marks in 1189 on his succession to his father's continental lands constituted a recognition of them as French fiefs. It was merely an increase of 4,000 marks over an indemnity that the desperate and defeated Henry II had agreed to pay days before his death. At Messina in 1191, the Lionheart on his way to the Holy Land acknowledged that he was Philip Augustus's *ligius homo* for all the fiefs that his predecessors had held of the French kings, and he conceded to Philip, as lord of those lands, a part to play in their succession.

Only in the later twelfth century, as hierarchical thought patterns among Paris philosophers and theologians won acceptance for notions of a hierarchy of property, did writers interpret earlier forms of homage as *hommage vassalique*, which created a vassal's dependent relationship with his lord and bound him to performance of definite services. None the less, all rituals of homage required a 'posture of dependence', symbolising submission to a superior. Although the ceremony may have signified for the participants little more than an exalted subject's expression of respect for his monarch, or in 'feudal'

---

60 For 1151, G. White, 'The End of Stephen's Reign', *History* 75 (1990), 4; for 1156, Hollister, 'Normandy, France and the Anglo-Norman *Regnum*', in *Monarchy, Magnates and Institutions*, 50; Warren, *Henry II*, 65.

61 *Gesta Regis*, 1: 306; see also Warren, *Henry II*, 227; Boussard, 544; Hallam, *Capetian France*, 94–7, 168–72.

62 Warren, *Henry II*, 227; *Chronicle of Robert of Torigny*, in R. Howlett (ed.), *Chronicles, Stephen, Henry II and Richard I*, RS (London, 1884), 4: 240.

terms, a man's respect for his lord, it still suggested subordinate status and an obligation of service that gave the Capetians leverage.

Henry II, his sons and their courtiers seemed less aware of the implications of these newer doctrines of a feudal pyramid for their relations with the French crown than did the Capetians and their counsellors, swayed by intellectual currents at the Paris schools. Louis VII and even more his son, Philip, pressed the view that ties of homage and fealty meant that the dukes and counts of France held their territories by fealty to the French crown as fiefs, subject to judgments of the royal court, while they themselves owed fealty to no one.[63] Indeed, the term 'fief' only gained a precise definition in Philip's time, meaning reduced property rights based on military obligations to one's lord. In the twelfth century, chroniclers, in telling of English kings' homage to the Capetians, called the Plantagenets' possessions 'fiefs' far less often than do modern scholars.[64] Philip Augustus used new feudal definitions to intervene freely in the territories of France's dukes and counts, seeking to interpose his suzerainty between them and their own vassals. He also turned the more precise definitions to financial advantage, collecting previously neglected feudal dues to fill his war chest for campaigns against Henry's sons.[65] Ironically, both Richard I and John contributed to Philip's treasury through large sums paid him on their accessions.

The Capetians reinterpreted the bonds of fealty in order to construct through them a political and territorial hierarchy that students are accustomed to visualise as a 'feudal pyramid'. With Capetian claims to lordship over all France, the royal court at Paris constituted an alternative power centre, encouraging appeals for assistance from discontented Angevin vassals, including Henry's own sons. The Angevins' French subjects did not consider the Capetians their enemy; Aquitanians often dated their charters by the regnal years of both their Angevin lord and their Capetian overlord. As long ago as 1887 Kate Norgate wrote: 'Paris and its king, even when his practical authority was at its lowest ebb, had always been in theory the accepted rallying-point of the whole kingdom, the acknowledged head of the body politic.'[66] The attraction of Paris – cultural as well as political – was too strong for the Plantagenets to counteract.

---

63 K. Werner, 'Kingdom and Principality in Twelfth-century France', in T. Reuter (ed.), *The Medieval Nobility* (Amsterdam, 1978), 264, 273–4.

64 Reynolds, *Fiefs and Vassals*, 273, although Abbot Suger used the term *feodum* for French principalities; Poly and Bournazel, *Feudal Transformation*, 204.

65 Baldwin, ch. 11, 'The King as Seigneur'; Jacques Boussard, 'Philippe Auguste et les Plantagenêts', in R.-H. Bautier (ed.), *La France de Philippe Auguste* (Paris, 1982), 263–87.

66 Norgate, *England under the Angevin Kings*, 2: 361.

CHAPTER THREE

The problem of Philip Augustus and growing French royal power

Once Philip Augustus returned from the Third Crusade in mid-1191, his goal was no longer simply enforcing lordship over Richard Lionheart but expelling his over-mighty vassal from the continent.[1] During Richard's German captivity, 1192–93, Philip made inroads along the Norman frontiers that proved permanent; Richard could not recover the castles of the Eure and Avre valleys.[2] The character of the centuries-long conflict between the two dynasties changed, and it was no longer Angevin wars of aggression, but now defensive campaigns by Richard Lionheart against his French lord. Kate Norgate commented that Richard faced within his domains 'a process of disintegration which his father had been unable to check, and against which he himself was well-nigh helpless'.[3] As she recognised, the warfare between the French king and Richard Lionheart following their crusade marked a shift in the balance of power away from the Angevins and toward the Capetians.

Other scholars view the scattered domains assembled by Henry II as impossible to govern and conclude that, had Richard lived longer, he would have confronted a crisis similar to his brother John's and found it equally insurmountable. Pinpointing the genesis of the Angevins' crisis is not easy, but it precedes John's accession. The period when England and the Angevins' continental possessions first began to split apart, abetted by a newly strengthened

---

1 K. Norgate, *England under the Angevin Kings*, 2 vols (London, 1887), 2: 363; Baldwin, 87.
2 D. Power, 'The Norman frontier in the twelfth and early thirteenth centuries', PhD thesis (Cambridge, 1994), 344.
3 Quotation, Norgate, *England under the Angevin Kings*, 2: 361; also R.V. Turner, 'The Problem of Survival for the Angevin "Empire": Henry II's and His Sons' Vision versus Late Twelfth-century Realities', *AHR* 100 (1995), 78–96.

Capetian monarchy, can be viewed as starting with Philip Augustus's accession in 1180; or perhaps its crucial years are the decade of Richard's reign, certainly the period following Philip's return from the crusade in the summer of 1191, if not the time of Richard's German captivity.

Philip Augustus left Palestine prematurely, at the end of July 1191 following the fall of Acre to the crusaders. While using illness as a pretext, his departure was due in large part to frustrations over his rivalry with Richard Lionheart which dated to their encampment at Messina in the winter of 1190–91. Richard on his arrival at Acre had overshadowed Philip in the siege operations, and he continued to upstage the French king, taking the spotlight in both crusading chronicles and subsequent histories.[4] The death of Philip of Flanders on crusade was likely a more significant factor in the Capetian ruler's return to France, however; for it presented him with an opportunity to continue his northeastward expansion, which had begun with his annexation of the county of Amiens. Now he obtained Artois and parts of Vermandois.[5] Naturally, this Capetian expansion had serious implications for Normandy, threatening communications with Flanders.

The Capetian ruler's trials on crusade had sharpened his hostility toward Richard Lionheart, and he began to threaten the duchy of Normandy almost as soon as he returned to the West. Although he had sworn to protect Richard's lands while he was away on crusade, he was determined not only to seize large chunks of Normandy, but to enforce his lordship over all the Plantagenets' continental possessions. Indeed, in the view of some scholars, Philip's 'supreme task upon his return from the crusade was to dislodge the Angevins from their continental possessions', and his arrival from Palestine initiated more than a decade of conflict, broken briefly by sporadic unstable truces.[6] Warfare would centre on two theatres where the Capetian ruler pressured Richard – the Vexin of Normandy and the border between Poitou and Berry – while he also encouraged surrogate attacks on Richard by his nobles on Poitou's southern borders in the Angoumois and Limousin. Clearly, the Plantagenet prince now was on the defensive against his French lord.

Major changes were under way within the French royal domain that strengthened Philip Augustus, enabling him to engage in a long series of struggles that slowly wore down his Plantagenet rivals, culminating in John's defeats in 1204 and 1214. As Philip's most recent biographer has noted, the Capetian king's earlier successes against Henry II and Richard 'had worked like a dripping tap wearing away their hold on the continental lands'.[7]

---

4 Baldwin, 77–8.
5 J. Bradbury, *Philip Augustus: King of France 1180–1223* (London, 1998), 92–5; Baldwin, 99.
6 Baldwin, 87; and earlier, Norgate, *England under the Angevin Kings*, 2: 363.
7 Bradbury, *Philip Augustus*, 159.

Indeed, recent scholarship makes clear that Philip Augustus's entire reign, 1180–1223, marks a turning point for the Capetians' power. Examples of scholarly recognition of the importance of Philip's reign are papers given at a 1980 Paris symposium, *La France de Philippe Auguste: le temps de mutations*, and John W. Baldwin's 1986 work, *The Government of Philip Augustus*. Basic changes in the structure of French royal government made during the 1190s, years of Philip's rule coinciding with Richard's, 'constituted a great divide between the government bequeathed by the early Capetians and that crafted for the future by Philip Augustus'.[8] The years on either side of the Third Crusade also can stand as a turning point in the history of the Angevin 'empire' with implications for its survival.

Recent calculations estimate Capetian revenues in 1180, the date of Philip Augustus's accession, at about 47 per cent of Henry II's income, or £7,365 compared to £15,467 (both sterling).[9] These studies point to stunning increases in royal revenues under Philip, whose innovations apparently ended the Angevins' superiority in resources, tipping the balance in the Capetians' favour by the first years of the thirteenth century. Since the earliest surviving French royal accounts date only from 1202–03, any comparisons of Plantagenet and Capetian revenues before John's loss of Normandy are largely surmises. None the less, Baldwin in his book on Philip Augustus can point to his reign as the period when Capetian resources first surpassed those of the Angevins. Indeed, French studies of Capetian finances published as long ago as 1932 first raised questions about the comparative resources of the two monarchies at the opening of the thirteenth century.[10] Yet scholars – impressed by the earlier elaborate English and Norman financial accounts – long assumed that the Capetians could not have matched the Angevins in revenue raising.

Now Baldwin's study shows confidently that Capetian revenues had expanded by 22 per cent in his first decade, that they had outstripped Angevin funds by 1202–03, increasing by 72 per cent, and increasing by 69 per cent in the years after 1203.[11] Calculations from the earliest surviving records, the registers of 1202–03, do not necessarily reflect total Capetian revenues, for they only record income received under certain headings. Extraordinary revenues that might have increased royal resources were not recorded on

---

8   R.-H. Bautier (ed.), *La France de Philippe Auguste: le temps de mutations* (Paris, 1982); Baldwin, Part Two, 'The Decisive Decade, 1190–1203', 101.

9   N. Barratt, 'The English Revenue of Richard I', unpublished paper presented at the Colloque aux Archives du Calvados (Caen, April 1999), 9, summarising work by Baldwin and Moss.

10 F. Lot and R. Fawtier, *Le premier budget de la monarchie française, le compte générale de 1202–03* (Paris, 1932); J.W. Baldwin and M. Nortier, 'Contributions à l'étude des finances de Philippe Auguste', *BEC* 138 (1980).

11 Baldwin, 99–100, 152–75, 247.

the registers. An example of such an unrecorded resource is the *prisée des sergents*, a wartime obligation on towns of the royal domain and royal abbeys to provide foot soldiers and wagons or a cash equivalent; this obligation, dating from the 1190s, produced £26,453 *parisis* (almost £10,000 sterling) in 1202–03.[12]

Study of Richard Lionheart's revenues shows him in a quest for money that points toward his younger brother John's extortionate policies. His captivity in Germany necessitated the raising of an enormous ransom, adding to the desperation. Richard, while making his way westward from the Holy Land, fell captive to the Austrian duke, who delivered his prisoner to the German emperor, Henry VI, in January 1193. Richard remained a prisoner until February 1194, when terms for payment of a ransom of 150,000 silver marks were finally settled. It was agreed that the English king would be released on delivery of 100,000 marks and the sending of hostages to guarantee payment of the remainder.[13]

Recent work on Angevin royal finances shows that the fiscal crisis in Richard's reign caused a dramatic divergence between Henry II's relatively modest demands for money and his sons' heavy demands.[14] Raising Richard's ransom required the imposition of staggering levies on his subjects and on the churches of his domains. After the ransom was raised, endless warfare against Philip Augustus waged with mercenaries required that more and more resources be squeezed out of England and Normandy. A comparison of English royal revenues – omitting sums gathered for England's share of the ransom – before and after Richard's return from captivity confirms his raging thirst for more money. Before 1194, annual royal revenues were modest, averaging slightly less than £12,000; the 1190 income totalling over £30,000 was exceptional, explained by unprecedented efforts at fundraising for the crusade. For the final five years of the reign, revenues rose to an average of around £25,000, figures that exceed those from John's early years.[15] Evidently, Hubert Walter's hyperbolic assertion to Richard that he had raised over a million marks for him contains a kernel of truth, for the government was plainly trying to extract all the resources that it possibly could from the kingdom.

Even wealthy Normandy was becoming dependent on sums shipped across the Channel from England for its defence. As revealed by recent financial studies that an earlier generation of scholars would never have undertaken, the destruction of warfare and heavy financial demands were rapidly exhaust-

---

12 Baldwin, 171–2.
13 Landon, 71–83.
14 See Turner, *King John*, ch. 4, 'Crises of John's Reign: Continuing Financial Problems', 87–114.
15 Barratt, 'English Revenue of Richard I', 3–5.

ing Normandy's resources. As F.M. Powicke's magisterial work, *The Loss of Normandy*, suggested early in this century, late twelfth-century Normandy's defence rested on massive infusions of money shipped across the Channel from England. Evidence for a flow of funds from England surfaces on the 1184 English pipe roll, and the pipe rolls throughout Richard's reign continue to give testimony to treasure shipments from his island realm. Vincent Moss's recent paper on the Norman pipe rolls concludes that by 1195 English contributions of money 'had become systematic'.[16] That year it proved necessary to send clerks from the English treasury to the Norman treasury to deal with the influx of funds.[17] By then, Richard had already burdened the duchy with debt for his ransom, and Norman financiers turned over to German envoys £16,000 *angevin*.[18] Richard was also spending heavily on castle construction and renovation. None the less, Moss's recent attempt to calculate Richard's finances in the Norman duchy downplays the significance of treasure transferred from England, concluding that the figures have been generally overestimated.[19]

J.C. Holt and John Gillingham attempted to calculate Richard's Norman revenues, and now Vincent Moss in his doctoral thesis and Nick Barratt as part of his studies of King John's finances have recalculated revenues for comparison with Gillingham's and Holt's earlier findings. Their task is complicated by the survival of Norman pipe rolls for only two years of Richard's reign, 1195 and 1198. Holt calculated Normandy's revenues at £13,991½ sterling (£55,966 *angevin*) in 1195, while Gillingham suggested a sum of £20,000 sterling or £60,000 *angevin*; Moss's more detailed analysis results in an estimate of between £51,000 and £76,000 *angevin*; and Barratt calculates net Norman receipts in 1195 as £42,122 *angevin*. All these scholars arrive at figures for the Lionheart's ducal revenues in 1198 that present a picture of a duchy squeezed to the limit, pushing revenues to unprecedented heights since 1195 despite reduced income from some areas on account of the devastation of warfare. Holt computes a rise in revenue to £38,282 sterling (£153,131 *angevin*) by 1198; and Gillingham's estimate results in a total slightly smaller than Holt's: £34,000 sterling (or £136,000 *angevin*). Moss places Richard's 1198 revenue at a more modest amount, somewhere

---

16 *PR30HII*, xxiii; *PR5RI*, 37, 44, payments for the clothing of mercenaries in Normandy; *PR6RI*, 176, 177, 213; *PR7RI*, 204; *ChanR 8RI*, 60, 69, 290; *PR9RI*, 17, 24; *PR10RI*, 23, payments for ships, etc., for transfer of unspecified amounts of treasure. Quotation from V. Moss, 'Normandy and England in 1180: Pipe Roll Evidence', in D. Bates and A. Curry (eds), *England and Normandy in the Middle Ages* (London, 1994), 188.

17 Hugh of Winchester, clerk of the treasury, and his assistant, *PR7RI*, 205.

18 Powicke, *Loss*, 233, citing Stapleton, 1: 136.

19 V. Moss, 'Normandy and the Angevin Empire: A Study of the Norman Exchequer Rolls 1180–1204', PhD thesis (University of Wales College Cardiff, 1996), 14.

between £97,100 and £100,400 *angevin* (about £25,000 sterling), which he none the less notes to have been 'untypically high'.[20] Barratt's figure for 1198 is £52,151 *angevin*, excluding £47,531 in extraordinary taxes. The 1198 roll does include extraordinary income, such as an *auxilium exercitus* or *tallagium servientium*, similar to the French *prisée des sergents*, to which all towns contributed.[21] The significance of these figures is that they show Normandy in 1198 producing as much or more income for the Lionheart than England, which averaged annually £24,975 sterling after 1194.[22]

Gillingham refuses to acknowledge that Richard's financial exploitation was attaining levels that approached John's, or that Richard, had he lived, might have equalled John in extorting money from his Anglo-Norman subjects. Although he writes of Richard's 'insatiable demands for money and soldiers', he refuses to draw the logical conclusion, writing that, to contemporaries, 'It seemed right and proper that a king should strain every nerve to recover the lands of which he had been treacherously deprived.'[23] This seems slightly disingenuous, for he knows of chroniclers' loud outcries against the Lionheart's greed. Ralph of Coggeshall wrote not long after Richard's death: 'No age can remember or history tell of any king, even one who ruled for a long time, who demanded and took so much money from his kingdom as this king extorted and amassed within five years after his return from captivity.' With this quotation in mind, David Carpenter argues convincingly that Richard's popularity was seriously blemished by the brutal tax measures.[24]

Gillingham argues both in his biography of Richard and in his *Angevin Empire* that Angevin resources surpassed the Capetians' because of great riches drawn from Aquitaine, but this is difficult to document. Although both Greater Anjou and Aquitaine contained flourishing ports, productive fields and fruitful vineyards, questions remain about the adequacy of the king/ duke's machinery for tapping their riches. Richard's rule over Aquitaine, both in his father's lifetime and afterwards, consisted largely of a series of punitive expeditions of foreign mercenaries against rebel barons in the

---

20 J.C. Holt, 'The Loss of Normandy and Royal Finance', in *War and Government in the Middle Ages* (Woodbridge, 1984), 95–6; Gillingham, *Coeur de Lion*, 72; Moss, 'Normandy and the Angevin Empire', 36–53. Moss points out that the 1198 pipe roll is incomplete, lacking returns from three bailliages. Poggioli sees reduced ducal revenues after 1194, pointing out that receipts from the bailliage of Verneuil suffered a 35 per cent reduction in 1195, from £700 to £450, citing Stapleton, 1: 237.

21 C. Stephenson, 'The Aids of the French Towns in the Twelfth and Thirteenth Centuries', in B. Lyon (ed.), *Medieval Institutions: Selected Essays* (Ithaca, NY, 1954), 16.

22 Barratt, 'English Revenue of Richard I', 5.

23 Gillingham, *Richard*, 271.

24 Coggeshall, 92–3; Gillingham's translation, *Richard*, 303. D. Carpenter, 'Abbot Ralph of Coggeshall's Account of the Last Years of Richard and the First Years of John', *EHR* 11 (1998), 1210.

Angoumois and Limousin. This is evidence in itself of an absence of effective administrative structures in his southernmost territories. While Greater Anjou had stronger comital administrative machinery, nothing suggests that surpluses generated there were sufficient for exporting sums to Normandy for expenditure on mercenary forces. Further evidence is the paucity of charters issued by Richard I for his southern subjects; apparently, they found less value in his confirmations of his privileges or letters of protection than did his English and Norman subjects. Most surviving comital/ducal charters from the southern provinces record grants to religious houses of what scholars would classify as 'seignorial' dues or 'public' obligations, for example, grants of tolls or cash allowances from *prévôtés*, that is, surrender of ducal resources.[25]

Richard could neither practise the 'fiscal feudalism' in Anjou, Aquitaine and Gascony that efficient exchequers enabled him to impose on the nobility of England and Normandy nor demand the fixed quotas of knights that his Anglo-Norman magnates owed him. Consequently, J.C. Holt found no evidence for funds flowing northward from Anjou or Aquitaine for Normandy's defence; in his opinion, money more likely flowed southward from England and Normandy.[26] It was chiefly cash collected in England and Normandy that bought the professional soldiers and siege equipment needed to demolish southern castles.

Holt attempted to calculate figures for comparing overall Angevin and Capetian revenues in 1195 and 1198. Admitting that his effort 'involves a structure of guesswork of Byzantine complexity', he none the less estimates Richard Lionheart's total revenues at no more than 45 per cent of Philip Augustus's revenues in 1195 and 74 per cent in 1198.[27] Moss's recent study confirms Holt's conclusion that Angevin resources under Richard were inferior. He calculates that 'Capetian France had the greater disposable collected revenue', although he judges the Norman exchequer as more efficient under Richard than previous scholars had reckoned. Moss concludes that any Plantagenet ruler, however able, would have failed to defend the

---

25 For example, *Cal. Docs. Fr.*, 382, no. 1081: Richard, count of Poitou, grants £100 to Fontevraud, half from the wine levy of Benon; 426, no. 1188: Richard's grant of his share of tolls at Angers to Marmoutier Abbey, a sum of £150 *angevin*; A.W. Lewis, 'Six Charters of Henry II and his Family for the Monastery of Dalon', *EHR* 110 (1995), 662–3: confirmation of Dalon's immunity from all tolls and customs, including the ban on selling salt.

26 Holt, 'The Loss of Normandy and Royal Finances', 105; also Stapleton, 2: 303, xvi: 6,859 marks in sterling sent for soldiers' wages in 1198. Extant records from John's reign show funds transferred from England to Gascony, e.g. 6,000 marks in 1200, *Rot. Norm.*, 36; 2,200 marks in 1208, T.D. Hardy (ed.), *Rotuli litterarum patentium*, Record Commission (London, 1835), 83.

27 Holt, 'The Loss of Normandy and Royal Finances', 96, 99–100; and J.C. Holt, 'Ricardus Rex Anglorum et Dux Normannorum', in *Magna Carta and Medieval Government* (London, 1985), 78–9. See also Bates, 'The Rise and Fall of Normandy', 34.

Angevin 'empire' in the first decade of the thirteenth century because of the impossibility of matching the Capetians' growing revenues.[28]

Since only the sketchiest of French financial information is available before 1202–03, comparisons of revenues before then are problematic. Comparisons between John's and Philip's revenues can be more solidly based, although scholars arrive at conflicting figures because they calculate by different methods and apply different terminologies. An examination recently undertaken by Nick Barratt finds that Capetian total net revenues had surpassed the Angevins' in 1202–03; he places the Angevin figure at either 71 per cent or 74 per cent of the Capetian total. According to Barratt's calculations, however, King John possessed for use in the war zone 78 per cent of Philip Augustus's revenues, placing John at a disadvantage, though not a disastrous one. Jim Bradbury, Philip's biographer, concludes that the French king had an even greater financial advantage over King John, pointing out that John's most extortionate increases in his English income came only after 1204. Bradbury accepts Baldwin's figure of £115,000 *parisis* (over £42,200 sterling) for French ordinary income, excluding such extraordinary sums as the *prisée des sergents* or John's relief of 20,000 marks. Gillingham is the odd man out. Confident of substantial though undocumented revenues flowing from Greater Anjou and Aquitaine, he insists that the Angevins' wealth continued to surpass that of Philip Augustus. He states: 'All in all there is not much doubt that the overall resources of the Angevin Empire were a good deal greater than those at the disposal of Philip Augustus.'[29]

Disparity in the Angevins' success in drawing money out of their lands reflects the diversity and dispersed resources of Richard's and John's dynastic heritage. Few historians today see much likelihood for their shaping their legacy into a lasting political entity. While it had some advantages that gave it potential for unity, steady pressure from the Capetians broke apart Henry II's collection of principalities before the Plantagenets had time to implant any sense of unity or dynastic loyalty among their diverse subjects. A fundamental distinction separated the British Isles from their continental possessions: in England, they were sovereign lords bearing a royal title, while on the Continent they acknowledged a superior, the French monarch.[30]

---

28 Moss, 'Normandy and the Angevin Empire', 6–7; Conclusion, 237.
29 N. Barratt, 'The Revenues of John and Philip Augustus Revisited', in S.D. Church (ed.), *King John: New Interpretations* (Woodbridge, 1999), Tables 1–3, comparisons of Capetian and Angevin revenue 1202–03 based on Holt's and Baldwin's calculations for Capetian totals; Table 7, 'Analysis of Utilised Revenue in the War Zone', Capetian revenues of £122,225 *angevin* and Angevin £93,954. Baldwin, 154; Bradbury, *Philip Augustus*, 159–60, 263–9; Gillingham, *Coeur de Lion*, 72–4.
30 J. Dunbabin, *France in the Making, 842–1180* (Oxford, 1985), 346; Norgate, *England under the Angevin Kings*, 2: 186.

Once Philip Augustus returned from the Third Crusade, he was determined to enforce his lordship over the princes of France, especially the Plantagenets whose position as 'super-princes' within France was so threatening to the Capetians.[31] With Philip's power on the rise, neighbouring lords, such as the counts of Blois-Chartres and Champagne, who had once feared Plantagenet expansion, had to come to an accommodation with him to gain his protection. New feudal doctrines had justified his father and him in their exploitation of the hostility between Henry II and his sons; and after Henry's death, the French monarch was prepared for aggressive use of his lordship to play John against Richard, and later John against his nephew, Arthur of Brittany. Theories of homage, fiefs and feudal hierarchy became instruments for converting Philip's 'nominal authority into something like effective jurisdiction'.[32] For Philip Augustus, as for his father Louis VII, French suzerainty was not simply a theory. Both aimed to apply it as a powerful weapon for subverting their English rivals' authority, affording them a pretext for intervention in the Angevin provinces of western France.

Yet their Angevin rivals stubbornly refused to recognise the dangers in their fealty to the French monarch at the same time that they were busy subjecting their English barons to their own *curia regis*, treating their baronies as dependent tenures. They devised no doctrine to counter the Capetians' cloaking of themselves in memories of Carolingian royal authority, which gave them near-sacred status and enhanced their claim to supremacy over all territories lying within the historic kingdom of France. Capetian suzerainty, coupled with the Plantagenet propensity for rivalry between father and son and also between brothers, spelled disaster for the Angevin 'empire'.

The Angevin rulers, apparently awed by the French monarchy's prestige, accepted Capetian assertions of feudal suzerainty over their continental possessions. Henry II's sons submitted to requirements that conceded their dependent status. After Count Geoffrey of Brittany's death at the Capetian ruler's court from a tournament wound in 1186, Philip Augustus demanded wardship of his posthumous son, Arthur. Later Philip exacted relief payments from both Richard and John on their succession to the Plantagenets' French possessions, and in the 1191 treaty of Messina Richard acknowledged that he was Philip Augustus's *ligius homo*, holding his French territories of him as fiefs, opening up the possibility of Philip's intervention within those lands.[33] Later John, with the treaty of Le Goulet in 1200, formally

---

31 K.F. Werner, 'Kingdom and Principality in Twelfth-century France', in T. Reuter (ed.), *The Medieval Nobility* (Amsterdam, 1978), 263–4.
32 S. Reynolds, *Fiefs and Vassals* (Oxford, 1995), 270–6.
33 Landon, app. H, 229–31.

acknowledged that his vassalage to the Capetian monarch meant subjection to the French *curia regis*.[34] Soon Philip Augustus's right to summon
the Plantagenets to his court and to judge them gained acceptance among
their subjects, and his royal court at Paris became an alternative power to
which their subjects could appeal. Such a plea initiated by John Lackland's
Lusignan vassal in 1201 set in motion a series of disasters that ended in his
loss of Normandy, his Loire valley patrimony and much of Poitou. Few of
John's magnates doubted Philip's right to condemn him as a contumacious
vassal for his defiance of the authority of his *curia regis*.[35]

One aspect of Philip Augustus's suzerainty over the Plantagenet lands in
France was his assertion of a role in their succession. Richard appears to
have given little thought to dynastic continuity or preservation of the unity
of the Plantagenet holdings. He showed few worries about the succession,
confident that he would survive the dangers of an expedition to the Levant
or fighting in France and would live long enough to sire heirs.[36] The
Lionheart's first attempt to deal with the problem of the succession came
during his Sicilian stopover en route to the Third Crusade in October
1190; as part of a marriage alliance with Tancred of Lecce, he named his
nephew, Arthur of Brittany, his heir.[37] No doubt, the Lionheart's chief consideration was to name an heir who would not try to usurp his royal crown
or his French lordships during his long absence in the East. Arthur, a young
child, was less likely to provide a focus for conspiracies to seize power than
his brother John, count of Mortain, who had been given a power-base in
England and who had already displayed his dubious fidelity. Furthermore,
Richard expected that he would take Arthur into his custody and place him
in the care of trusted servants.

In England, where it was commonly believed that the king would not
survive the crusade, his recognition of his nephew as heir undermined his
regency government's position, prompting Count John to stir up trouble.
Prior to Richard's designation of an heir at Messina, John had been quiet;
but after the announcement, he began scheming to strengthen his position,
should disaster overtake Richard and leave the English throne vacant.
Certainly Richard perceived some potential danger, for, according to one
chronicler, he urged his viceroy in England, William Longchamp, to seek the

---

34 P. Chaplais (ed.), *Diplomatic Documents Preserved in the Public Record Office* (London, 1964), I,
    no. 5; for Le Goulet, no. 9. John made a similar agreement in 1194; J.C. Holt, 'The End
    of the Anglo-Norman Realm', in *Magna Carta and Medieval Government* (London, 1985), 41, n. 3.
35 Dunbabin, *France in the Making*, 346.
36 For example, the March 1191 treaty with Philip of France made provision for anticipated
    sons; Landon, 230.
37 Settlement with Tancred of Lecce; Landon, 43.

Scottish king's promise of help in assuring Arthur's succession to England's crown.[38] The Lionheart's patronage to Count John in his strongly governed kingdom and his wealthiest French province had established the count in so powerful a position that some of the king's subjects suspected that he did not expect to return to England, and they feared that if he did, 'His brother, already no less powerful than he and eager to rule, would defeat him and drive him out of the kingdom.'[39] Richard's grants to John seemed an implicit declaration of his intent, should he die overseas; an explicit statement would have encouraged the count's bad behaviour much sooner, as Henry II's unhappy experience with Young King Henry showed.

Subsequent succession schemes accepted Capetian suzerainty over the Plantagenets' French lands. Part of an agreement made between the French and English kings at Messina in March 1191 before setting sail for the Holy Land dealt with the succession. It was assumed that a yet unborn son of Richard would succeed to the English crown and would hold the bulk of the Plantagenets' continental lands in-chief of the French monarch, while an anticipated second son would hold a county or duchy, either Normandy, Greater Anjou or Aquitaine. Such a scheme, while following family traditions of providing portions for younger sons, threatened the unity of his inheritance from Henry II and Eleanor of Aquitaine. Philip Augustus succeeded in asserting the French crown's suzerainty and forcing Richard to agree that any younger son would hold his domain also in-chief of the Capetian king, not as an apanage of his elder brother.[40] A similar agreement between Philip and Richard's brother John, made in January 1194 before the crusader king's release from captivity, also provided that if John had two or more sons, each would hold fiefs directly of the French king.[41] Such arrangements would have precluded continued unity for the Plantagenet domains, preventing Richard's or John's eldest son and heir from binding his younger brothers to him by a bond of vassalage. In effect, political circumstances – a need to come to terms with the French king, lord of their continental possessions – forced Henry II's two sons into sanctioning a future partitioning of the Angevin patrimony among their sons.

Richard and Berengaria's marriage remained childless, and uncertainty lingered about the Plantagenet succession. The nomination of Arthur is noteworthy for its acceptance of the 'representative principle' – the young duke of Brittany as representative of his late father, Geoffrey, who was Richard's younger brother – and its rejection of Count John, Richard's sole surviving

---

38   Landon, app. E, 197–8.
39   Devizes, 6.
40   Treaty of Messina, Chaplais, *Diplomatic Documents*, I, no. 5.
41   A. Teulet (ed.), *Layettes du trésor des Chartes*, 5 vols (Paris, 1863–1909), 1: no. 412.

brother; this had not yet become a fixed rule in the law of inheritance. Arthur of Brittany, poisoned by the anti-Plantagenet sentiments of his mother, Constance, and his protector, Philip Augustus, was unacceptable as Richard Lionheart's heir. His very name was 'a badge of Breton independence and hostility toward the Plantagenets'.[42] Philip had claimed custody over little Arthur, born after his father's death in 1186, perhaps on grounds that Geoffrey of Brittany had done homage to him after his flight to Paris. Henry II also claimed custody, since Brittany was a vassal-state of the duchy of Normandy; but Constance was determined to keep her son from falling into Angevin hands, either Henry's or later Richard's. She and the Breton aristocracy harboured powerful antagonism against the Plantagenets after her husband Geoffrey's death in 1186; and her hatred for her in-laws aroused a desire by Eleanor of Aquitaine to block little Arthur from becoming head of the Plantagenet house.[43] Constance's fury against the Angevins blinded her to the advantage that an upbringing at his Angevin uncle's court would have given her son, an opportunity to strengthen ties with Richard that might have won him formal nomination as the childless king's heir. In 1196, when the Lionheart demanded custody of young Arthur, the boy was hidden away until he could be spirited out of the duchy to Philip Augustus's court.[44]

By 1197, the childless Richard seems to have rejected his nephew, Arthur of Brittany, as his heir and tacitly acknowledged his brother, Count John, and certainly Eleanor of Aquitaine preferred him to her grandson, young Arthur, as successor. The Lionheart is thought to have confirmed his choice on his deathbed in April 1199.[45] Yet the Breton duke remained 'a trump card' for his Capetian protector. On Richard's death without an heir of his body, uncertainty arose over the succession, with the English and Norman magnates opting for John Lackland and the nobles of Anjou, Maine and Touraine proclaiming Arthur of Brittany as their lord. The disputed succession enabled the Capetian monarch to revive his family's great political game of pitting one member of the Plantagenet family against another, and he supported the claims of young Arthur.[46]

Perhaps, as C. Warren Hollister maintained, the Angevin princes saw that the French monarch was 'the ultimate source of [their] authority on the continent', the 'foundation' of their command over their French

42 M. Meade, *Eleanor of Aquitaine* (New York, 1977), 332.
43 K. Carter, 'Arthur I, Duke of Brittany, in History and Literature', PhD dissertation (Florida State University, 1996), 200–3; E.-R. Labande, 'Pour une image véridique d'Aliénor d'Aquitaine', *BSAO* 4th ser., 2 (1952), 225–6.
44 Gillingham, *Richard*, 260–1.
45 Y. Hillion, 'La Bretagne et la rivalité Capétiens–Plantagenêts. Un exemple: la duchesse Constance (1186–1202)', *Annales de Bretagne* 92 (1985), 118–19; Landon, app. E, 207–8.
46 Powicke, *Loss*, 133.

lands.[47] If so, such a theoretical weapon was a double-edged sword, affording Richard and John slender safety. In fact, Capetian suzerainty was an insurmountable barrier, preventing the Angevins from moulding their possessions into a coherent whole; and coupled with the Plantagenet propensity for family rivalries, it spelled disaster for their 'empire'. As J.C. Holt has pointed out, it is no coincidence that the only two territories remaining under Plantagenet rule after 1214 were England and Gascony, lands that were not subject to the French crown.[48]

Richard spent his last years, 1196–99, in Normandy defending his duchy from the Capetian king, and the devastation and brutality of those military campaigns alienated the Normans. Responsibility for the duchy's defence passed from the Normans themselves to mercenaries and foreigners, English knights, Welsh recruits and the dreaded *Brabançons*. The English pipe rolls reveal numbers of Welsh serjeants – both mounted and foot – and knights enlisted for Norman service, beginning in Henry II's last years. At least 2,100 foot soldiers were sent in 1196, and that same year, Richard desperately demanded 300 knights from his English tenants for a year's service in Normandy.[49]

This predominance of foreign fighters meant that the conflict became more threatening to the lives of non-combatants and to their property. Repeated invasions by Philip Augustus undermined the Norman clergy's traditional allegiance to their duke in Richard's last years. It appeared to them that Richard's rule was growing more oppressive, yet less successful in protecting ecclesiastical property from plunder either by his mercenaries or by Capetian invaders. The Lionheart granted Archbishop Walter of Rouen 300 *modia* of wine annually in 1195–96 as compensation for damages that Philip Augustus's forces had inflicted upon his properties.[50] The prelate quarrelled fiercely with the duke over Les Andelys, site for the construction of Château-Gaillard. He placed Normandy under an interdict and fled to Rome in November 1196; settlement of the dispute under papal pressure 'marked the end of Walter's services to the Angevins'. Convinced that Richard could not protect the Norman Church, he began to pursue a policy of neutrality, seeking peace between the warring rulers to safeguard the Church's possessions.[51] The endemic warfare led the archbishop and

---

47 Hollister, 'Normandy, France and the Anglo-Norman *Regnum*', 53–4.
48 J.C. Holt, 'The End of the Anglo-Norman Realm', in *Magna Carta and Medieval Government*, 54.
49 *PR33HII*, 63, 131; *ChanR 8RI*, xvii–xviii, 41, 42, 60, 88. Powicke, *Loss*, 213.
50 *Cal. Docs. Fr.*, no. 67; BN ms. lat. nouv. acq. 1244, f405. One *modium* equalled eight gallons of wine; R.E. Latham, *Revised Medieval Latin Word-list* (Oxford, 1965), 302.
51 P. Poggioli, 'From Politician to Prelate: The Career of Walter of Coutances, Archbishop of Rouen, 1184–1207', PhD dissertation (Johns Hopkins University, 1984), 116, 125–8; Powicke, *Loss*, 103–4, 113–16.

the rest of the Norman clergy to sever their longstanding ties to a ducal government that no longer seemed to guarantee peace and stability.

The Norman clergy began to look favourably upon the prospect of peaceful rule under Philip Augustus, who was presenting himself as a protector of ecclesiastical liberties, less exploitative of Church property and less likely to impose his will on episcopal electors. Ecclesiastics in Normandy found it easy to embrace the concept of loyalty to a larger France; writers of the period sometimes reflected on the contrast between their own troubled times and the age of Charlemagne, when all the Franks had been united.[52] Culture was drawing the Norman clergy toward the schools of Paris, and when rebuilding their churches, they found inspiration in the pointed arches and spires of the new Gothic-style churches springing up throughout the Ile de France.[53] Yet it was not only the Norman clergy who were feeling a pull toward Paris; the knights felt it as well. The Capetian court was becoming the centre of a chivalric culture, expressed in the French vernacular, that attracted the nobility of all France, including the Plantagenet-ruled territories. By the end of the twelfth century, many Normans – both lay and clerical – were longing for peace, even at the price of annexation by the French king.[54]

The Angevins suffered a severe handicap because of their inability to propagate a dynastic 'myth' or ideology that would unite their assorted subjects and counteract that of the Capetians. Richard's authority over his assorted territories was recent, lacking an ancient origin that could compete with the superior prestige of the Capetian house. Philip Augustus's royal title evoked the sacral monarchy of its Carolingian predecessors and placed him above all the other noble houses of his realm, no one's vassal. He promoted his familial ties to Charles the Great, and he achieved some success; the pope once stated, 'It is common knowledge that the king of France is descended from the lineage of Charlemagne.' As a result, the Angevin monarchs remained 'ideologically inferior to the [Capetian] king even when they were materially superior'.[55] This gave the Capetian monarch an advantage over his Angevin rival in the sense of community, however

---

52 Powicke, *Loss*, 17, 127.

53 L. Grant, 'Gothic Architecture in Southern England and the French Connection in the Early Thirteenth Century', in P. Coss and S. Lloyd (eds), *Thirteenth Century England*, 4 (Woodbridge, 1991).

54 Powicke, *Loss*, 301–3; Roger Jouet, *Et la Normandie devint française* (Paris, 1983), 61; and R.W. Southern, *Medieval Humanism and Other Studies* (New York, 1970), 135–57, who follows Gerald of Wales.

55 Papal statement, Bradbury, *Philip Augustus*, 220–1, quoting Georges Duby, *France in the Middle Ages*, trans. J. Vale (Oxford, 1991), 226; quotation, Werner, 'Kingdom and Principality', 275; also Bates, 'The Rise and Fall of Normandy', 34–5.

vague, that survived in all regions formerly part of the old Frankish kingdom. The inhabitants even saw themselves as sharing a common descent. Philip Augustus and his successors combined such old myths of collective ancestry and traditions of kingship's sacred character together with stronger governmental institutions in a way that the Angevins could not. The French kings fostered a 'regnal solidarity' that the Angevins, ruling over diverse peoples with widely differing governmental structures, could not achieve.[56]

Considerable literature circulating at the Angevin comital court had recorded their ancestors' exploits and asserted their claims to rule as *principes*, that is, as legitimate rulers wielding authority according to the law. Lacking the divine sanction of the Carolingians' lawful successors, Henry II's Angevin predecessors had turned instead to chivalry to enhance their stature. Writers at their courts stressed their ancestors' conduct as perfect knights earning their position through services to the people, and contrasting them with the old nobility whose standing had derived solely from inherited lands and titles.[57] Jean of Marmoutier's *Historia Gaufredi Ducis*, written *c.* 1180, depicts Geoffrey le Bel as 'an ideal count and an ideal knight'.[58] Richard, his father, and his brother proved unable to foster myths that would elevate their status higher, approaching the Capetians' dignity and challenging their mantle of longstanding legitimacy.

The Plantagenets had formal ceremonies to mark their installation as dukes of Aquitaine and Normandy, yet they never took a title that symbolised their superior status as suzerains over diverse lands and peoples; and they never devised rituals of sacral authority to contest the Capetians' supremacy. Their English royal crown enhanced their prestige, but bestowed no authority beyond the British Isles; only an imperial title would have sufficed, but that was too bold an ideological step. Poets under Angevin patronage made some attempts to popularise Arthurian legends, perhaps linking the Plantagenets with the legendary king of the ancient Britons as a counter to propaganda linking the Capetians to the Carolingians. Yet such an ideological campaign seems puny in comparison with the efforts of the monks at Saint-Denis. They had begun late in the twelfth century composing a pro-Capetian version

56 Susan Reynolds, 'Medieval *Origines gentium* and the Community of the Realm', *History* 68 (1983), 380–7.
57 Geoffrey Koziol, 'England, France, and the Problem of Sacrality in Twelfth-century Ritual', in T.K. Bisson (ed.), *Cultures of Power: Lordship, Status, and Process in Twelfth-century Europe* (Philadelphia, 1995), 132–3; also Michael Schaffer, 'Rhetorics of Authority: Feudal Ideologies in Twelfth-century Anjou', unpublished paper presented at the International Congress of Medieval Studies (Kalamazoo, MI, May 1992).
58 J. Bradbury, 'Geoffrey V of Anjou, Count and Knight', in C. Harper-Bill and R. Harvey (eds), *The Ideals and Practices of Medieval Knighthood*, vol. 3, *Papers from the Fourth Strawberry Hill Conference, 1988* (Woodbridge, 1989), 38.

of history that focused French national unity on the person of the king and stressed his connections with Charlemagne.[59]

Although the Angevins outstripped the Capetians in constructing administrative agencies in England and Normandy for subduing their magnates and for revenue raising, governing by such mechanisms tended to desacralise their political authority. Their power in England and Normandy encouraged arbitrary acts that undercut archaic notions of tutelary kingship and called into question any sacred source for their political authority. Furthermore, Louis VII and Philip Augustus worked to promote a reputation for Christian morality and good lordship that contrasted with the Angevins' alleged despotism. In the eyes of clerical critics, Plantagenet governance suffered by comparison with Capetians' good lordship; and incorporation into the French kingdom appeared to many of their subjects as an attractive alternative to continued Angevin rule.[60] Outside the Anglo-Norman lands, the Plantagenets neither constructed strong governments nor devised an ideology that would inspire their subjects' devotion; the constant pressure exerted by Philip Augustus would not allow Richard or John the leisure to perform such tasks.

With all these threats to his possessions from his Capetian suzerain, it is hardly surprising that Richard proved unable to shape his inheritance into a coherent political entity or to foster any sense of dynastic loyalty among his polyglot subjects. Yet he never seems to have lost confidence in the continued existence of his Angevin 'empire'. After his return in 1194 from crusade and captivity, he dedicated his energies to warfare for its protection and preservation, despite his own childlessness and his doubts about his brother's capability.

---

59 Georges Duby suggested that Henry II 'deliberately scoured the culture of the British isles for material out of which he might build an ideological edifice to rival the ideology of the Frankish monarchy'; *The Three Orders: Feudal Society Imagined*, trans. A. Goldhammer (Chicago, 1980), 287; also E. Mason, 'The Hero's Invincible Weapon: An Aspect of Angevin Propaganda', in C. Harper-Bill and R. Harvey (eds), *The Ideals and Practices of Medieval Knighthood*, vol. 3, 136. On St-Denis, G. Duby, *The Legend of Bouvines: War, Religion and Culture in the Middle Ages*, trans. C. Tihanyi (Cambridge, 1990), 7–9.

60 See Turner, 'The Problem of Survival for the Angevin "Empire": Henry II's and His Sons' Vision Versus Late Twelfth-century Realities', 93–4; also Koziol, 'England, France and the Problem of Sacrality', 144–5.

CHAPTER FOUR

Richard's apprenticeship: count of Poitou 1172–89

Though born in England, Richard Lionheart grew up in Poitou under the tutelage of his mother, and it was the place where he felt most at home. Henry II's 1169 plan for the succession designated him as heir to Eleanor of Aquitaine's possessions, likely in accord with noble custom that acknowledged the second son as inheritor of his mother's patrimony. In 1172, splendid ceremonies in the church of Saint-Hilaire at Poitiers and the cathedral of Limoges marked his installation as count of Poitou. Perhaps this recognition at age 12 bolstered the special bond between Richard and his mother that historians acknowledge.[1] They traditionally have turned to Richard's youth spent in Eleanor's ancestral lands and the singular affection that grew up between his mother and him as the explanation for his character. He seems to have shared with Eleanor 'an undeniable sense of regional attachment and shared experience' that both bound them together and bound them both to Aquitaine.[2]

Richard served a long apprenticeship in war and government in his mother's territories. The young count did not take charge immediately after his designation as heir to Poitou and Aquitaine in 1169, however, for both his mother and father continued to claim some authority over those territories. Between 1167 and 1173, Eleanor issued all major administrative *acta* under her own seal and in either her own or Richard's name; but Henry II reserved for himself control over finances and command of the military host.[3]

---

1   For example, J.A. Brundage, *Richard Lion Heart* (New York, 1974), 247.
2   J. Martindale, 'Eleanor of Aquitaine', rpt in *Status, Authority and Regional Power* (Aldershot, 1997), 22.
3   M. Hivergneaux, 'Aliénor d'Aquitaine: le pouvoir d'une femme à la lumière de ses chartes', Colloque de Thouars (29 April–1 May 1999).

Richard's frustration with these limitations and handicaps may have paved the way for his attachment to his elder brother, Young Henry, in the great rebellion of 1173–74. He joined the Young King in the spring of 1173 at Paris, where Louis VII knighted him. Without maturity, reputation or respect, the 16-year-old count of Poitou can hardly have played a pivotal role in the uprising against his father. None the less, his first exercise of independent authority over Poitou came in the autumn of 1173 after his mother was banished to England, although his leadership was far from successful. When the citizens of the port town of La Rochelle slammed shut their gates in his face, the young prince moved on to the Charente valley city of Saintes, a commercial rival of La Rochelle, only to be driven out by his father in the spring of 1174. Henry then took control of Poitou for the duration of the uprising, and Young Richard found refuge in the near-impregnable fortress of Taillebourg. By late summer 1174, young Richard, contemptuous of his lacklustre brothers, stood alone until the end of September, when all three sons came to terms with their father. As part of Henry II's settlement with his repentant sons ending the great rebellion of 1173–74, Richard received only half the revenues of Poitou and two 'fitting dwelling-places'.[4]

By the spring of 1175, Henry had given young Richard command over the army of Poitou, sending him to reduce castles whose walls had been reinforced during the recent rebellion.[5] Little is known of these campaigns save that Richard in August, after a two-month siege, captured the rebel castle of Castillon-sur-Agen, known for its natural and architectural advantages. Shortly afterward, Richard began serving as his father's veritable viceroy in Aquitaine and Gascony, once Henry II's reorganisation of his territories had assigned each constituent part its own regional governor. Richard continued to be Henry's agent in Aquitaine and Gascony for much of the rest of his reign, securing practice on the battlefield and earning a reputation as a soldier. Since he lacked weapons other than the threat of force in restraining the aristocracy of Aquitaine, the years that he spent in Aquitaine did not give him equal experience in supervising advanced administrative structures comparable to those of England or Normandy.

If the duchy of Aquitaine was in Henry's view merely an outlying appendage of the hegemonic Angevin 'empire', in Richard's eyes it was his maternal legacy properly descending to him as second-born son. Yet Henry II reserved for himself the title 'duke of Aquitaine' throughout his reign, and Richard usually bore the lesser title 'count of Poitou'. In Henry's charter confirming the liberties of La Rochelle, dating from the 1170s, Richard is

---

4   Delisle/Berger, 2: 19, no. 468, dated Oct. 1174.
5   Howden, 2: 72; *Gesta Regis*, 1: 81.

referred to as *dominus Pictavie, heredus meus.*[6] Yet Henry's periodic tinkering with the succession fed Richard's uncertainty and resentment of his father, and it inflamed his brothers' jealousy of each other. The young count felt strongly the longstanding traditions of Aquitanian autonomy, refusing his father's demand in 1183 that he do homage to his elder brother, Young Henry. He feared that such homage might imply that his maternal inheritance was a dependency of the Plantagenet territories. In 1187–88, Richard again showed his attachment to his mother's domains by rejecting his father's proposal to surrender Aquitaine in exchange for assurances of his succession to England and Normandy. Henry's sons continued their rebellions after the great 1173–74 one, and they spilled over into Poitou, for some Aquitanian nobles knew how to take advantage of Plantagenet family strife to thwart Richard's ambition of strengthening ducal authority.

The Lionheart had gained experience in Aquitaine as a military commander and had earned acclaim for heroism well before he succeeded Henry II in 1189 as head of the Angevin 'empire'. Constant warfare had characterised the reigns of his eleventh- and early twelfth-century predecessors. His grandfather, William IX, the 'troubadour duke', had spent much of his time in hard-fought struggles with powerful enemies, far different from the ritualised battles depicted in chivalric romances.[7] Henry II had tried direct rule over Eleanor's possessions in the years shortly after their marriage, seeking to impose his will by military might, but he aroused powerful resistance from the great nobles.[8] A rebellion in 1168 led by the lords of Lusignan resulted in an ambush that took the life of Henry's lieutenant, Earl Patrick of Salisbury; but problems elsewhere forced the Angevin prince to abandon attempts to take revenge. By 1169, he had given up any idea of imposing direct rule and placed his queen, Eleanor of Aquitaine, in charge of her possessions along with their second son, Richard.

Few institutions existed to enforce ducal authority over a bellicose aristocracy who showed an independent spirit, even a tendency toward anarchy.

---

6 Delisle/Berger, 2: 83, no. 519, dated 1172–73, 1178; also J.C. Holt, 'Aliénor d'Aquitaine, Jean sans Terre et la succession de 1199', *CCM* 29 (1986), 98. A charter of the viscount of Thouars was dated 'In the year of the incarnation of our Lord 1188, in the time of Philip king of the French, of Henry king of the English, of Richard *consule Pictavorum* . . .'; cited by H. Beauchet-Filleau, 'Recherches sur Airvaux, son château et son abbaye', *MSAO* 24 (1857), 291.

7 For pre-Plantagenet Aquitaine's endemic warfare, J. Martindale, 'Aimeri of Thouars and the Poitevin Connection', *ANS* 7 (1985), 224–45; and J. Martindale, '"Cavalaria et orgueill": Duke William IX of Aquitaine and the Historian', in C. Harper-Bill and R. Harvey (eds), *The Ideals and Practice of Knighthood* (Woodbridge, 1988), 2: 87–116; both reprinted in her *Status, Authority and Regional Power*.

8 C. Higounet, *Histoire de l'Aquitaine* (Toulouse, 1971), 180; A. Debord, *Société laïque dans les pays de la Charente X^c–XII^c siècles* (Paris, 1984), 380.

Monastic charters often record these nobles' repentance for the harm done to churches and the evil customs imposed on their lands and men in the absence of strong government.[9] Eleanor's ancestors had lost most powers outside their ducal or comital demesne lands during the eleventh-century 'feudal transformation', when castellans had thrown off the count/duke's control to dominate the surrounding countryside. Lacking administrative agencies to extend his control to his nobles' lands lying beyond the ducal domain, Richard could only control them by cementing ties of friendship and counting on their personal loyalty. Yet the slight evidence supplied by attestations of Richard's comital charters suggests that he did little to encourage his great men's presence at court, where bonds of allegiance could have been bolstered. The most frequent witnesses were local notables in the lands where the ducal domain lay holding office as seneschals or *prévôts*, not viscounts, castellans or prelates.[10]

Because personal bonds proved insufficient to secure obedience, Richard had to rely on intimidation or actual military force to assert his authority. During the Lionheart's twenty-five years as duke of Aquitaine and as king of England, war against the magnates of his duchy was almost ceaseless. After Henry II and Eleanor's marriage brought the region under Angevin rule, nine different rebellions challenged the Plantagenets: in 1168, 1173–74, 1176, 1178–79, 1182–83, 1188, 1192, 1193–94 and 1199. When war broke out, the impossibility of raising an effective army from the Aquitanian aristocracy forced Richard and his father to rely upon foreign mercenary forces or, occasionally, on allies from across the Pyrenees. An additional complication was the meddling of the Capetian monarchs, constantly seeking to add to Henry's and Richard's difficulties.

Richard learned quickly from his struggles against Aquitanian rebels that the victor was unlikely to be the impetuous hero impatient to meet a hostile army head-on. Like other capable military leaders in the Middle Ages, he sought to avoid pitched battle, and he pursued success through plundering his enemy's resources and besieging his castles. As John Gillingham has

---

9 For example, D.P. de Monsabert, ed., *Chartes et documents pour servir à l'histoire de l'abbaye de Charroux*, Archives Historiques du Poitou, 39 (Poitiers, 1910), no. 45, charter of Adelbert V, count of La Marche, *c.* 1177; A. Leroux and A. Boisvieux (eds), *Chartes de chroniques et mémoriaux pour servir à l'histoire de la Marche et du Limousin* (Tulle and Limoges, 1886), no. 68, grant by Boso de Mamuriac, knight, to St-Martial, Limoges, 'in expiation for wrongs caused by his late father'; P. Marchegay (ed.), *Cartulaires du Bas-Poitou* (Les Roches-Baritaud, 1877), no. 27, a 1209 charter of William de Mauléon to the priory of La Chaise-le-Vicomte, in recompense for 'damages that [the prior and monks] said were done by me and my men . . . when there was war between me and Aimery, viscount of Thouars'.
10 R.V. Turner, 'The Households of the Sons of Henry II', Colloque de Thouars; also Debord, *Charente*, 384, table of witnesses to 18 of Richard's *acta*, 1174–89.

observed from the *Chanson de Guillaume le Maréchal*, 'pillage and robbery' were fundamental aspects of chivalric warfare.[11] Richard's force roved rebels' territory, not seeking battle, but laying waste and plundering their lands, applying pressure by impoverishing their peasants and securing dominance over the countryside by taking castles.

Richard, like his father, came to depend upon companies of mercenary infantrymen, the so-called *Brabançons*, and hired siege engineers, skilled at operating machinery capable of smashing rebel strongholds. The barbarity of these mercenaries, not bound by the chivalric code, became infamous; perhaps this made them more useful to the Angevins, since they terrorised rebel territories. Most famous of Richard's mercenary captains is Mercadier, who served him almost continually from 1183 until the king's death in 1199. Toward the end of his life he described his relations with Richard Lionheart, referring to himself as the king's *famulus*: 'I fought for him with loyalty and strenuously, never opposed his will, prompt in obedience to his commands; and in consequence of this service I gained his esteem and was placed in command of his army.'[12]

Richard Lionheart served his military apprenticeship combating Aquitanian lords based in the counties along the southern frontier of Poitou, where their predecessors had carved out regional lordships. Although the relationship between Richard and these lords was phrased in the language of feudal dependence, their vassalage proved to be largely conjectural, and these nobles were practically independent. In their turbulent lands in the lower Charente and upper Vienne valleys lay 'the soft underbelly of the Angevin Empire', potentially splitting the Plantagenet's southern domains.[13] In enemies' hands, they could block the old Roman roads that linked Poitou and Gascony, connecting Richard's three chief administrative centres in the south: Poitiers, Saintes and Bordeaux. [See Map V]

Just below Poitou proper lay the lands of such regional lords as the Taillefer counts of Angoulême, the counts of Périgord and the viscounts of Limoges, who habitually flouted ducal authority. The Taillefers – Vulgrin III and his brothers, William and Adémar – participated prominently in all revolts against the Angevins, despite periodic defeats and demolition of their castles. Other nobles with less exalted titles such as the lords of Lusignan or the lords of Rancon shared the hostility to the Plantagenet count/duke. The Lusignan brothers coveted the county of La Marche, whose count had

---

11 J. Gillingham, 'War and Chivalry in the History of William the Marshal', rpt. in
     Anglo-Norman Warfare, (ed.) Matthew Strickland (Woodbridge, Suff., 1992), 263.
12 H. Géraud, 'Mercadier: Les routiers au treizième siècle', *BEC* 3 (1841–42), 427–43;
     translation, Powicke, *Loss*, 232.
13 J. Gillingham, 'The Unromantic Death of Richard I', 41.

sold it to Henry II in 1177. Geoffrey II de Rancon dominated the Aunis and Saintonge, with his commanding fortress of Taillebourg and the castle of Marcillac, both on the Charente River, plus the castle at Pons, and he also held fortresses in Poitou proper. Off and on for most of his life, Richard would be engaged in suppressing rebellions radiating out from southern Poitou inspired by these bothersome nobles and their castellans. They succeeded in taking advantage of the hostility of Richard's brothers, Henry the Young King and Geoffrey of Brittany, to merge their rebellions into the succession struggles periodically threatening the stability of Henry II's 'empire'.

Farther south in Gascony, Richard could not hope to impose his author-ity over the entire duchy; and he largely limited his efforts to exercising direct control over its richest portions, the Garonne valley and the routes that led to the Pyrenean passes and Spain.[14] None the less, he had to deal occasionally with Gascon nobles who were often drawn into the rivalries of neighbouring princes of the Spanish kingdoms and of the South of France. Richard had to be on guard there against aggressive tendencies by Alfonso II, king/count of Aragon and Barcelona, or Raymond V, count of Toulouse. Although Richard repeatedly disciplined his fractious nobles, defeating them and demolishing their strongholds, he could never permanently subdue them. Rebel castles such as Taillebourg, razed in the course of one revolt, promptly rose again with higher walls ready to resist the count in the next rebellion.

On appointment as his father's viceroy in Aquitaine in 1175, young Richard was assigned the task of reducing the castles that had been rebel centres during the great rebellion of 1173–74. He began to build his military reputation by moving against the castle of Le Puy de Castillon in the county of Agen, which he took and demolished after a two-month siege.[15] Then in 1176, Richard had to face a rebellion led by the sons of the count of Angoulême with their allies, the viscounts of Limoges, Ventadour and Chabannes, centred on the crucial southern frontier of Poitou. Apparently the threat of this coalition caused Richard to go to England to consult with his father early in 1176. Surprisingly, this rebellion may have had a connec-tion to events in England, specifically to the succession to the earldom of Cornwall; for Aimar V, viscount of Limoges, was married to Earl Richard's eldest daughter. When the earl died with only three daughters as heirs, Henry II refused to follow the normal English practice of partition among co-heiresses and seized into his own hand the bulk of the earldom's estates, leaving only a small portion to the daughters. Aimar saw the prospect of his

---

14   Boussard, 149–50.
15   *Gesta Regis*, 1: 101; A. Richard, *Histoire des comtes de Poitou* (Paris, 1903), 2: 183.

succession to important English estates or even to the title of earl slip away, and his disappointment may have pushed him into rebellion.[16]

The fighting broke out in the spring of 1176 with an invasion of Poitou proper by Vulgrin Taillefer, son of the count of Angoulême, while Richard was in England with his father. It was left to Richard's constable in Poitou, Theobald Chabot, and the bishop of Poitiers to organise resistance to Vulgrin. Young Richard returned to Poitou to take charge of the campaign, and, armed with money from his father, he gathered a large force of *Brabançons* and knights from neighbouring territories won by the wages that he paid them. With this army, he defeated the rival force of *Brabançons* hired by the count of Angoulême in a pitched battle near the western frontier of the Angoumois. Then Richard moved into the territory of the viscount of Limoges, taking Viscount Aimar's castle of Aixe, and next taking the city of Limoges after a few days' siege. Now accompanied by his elder brother, Henry the Young King, the two youths marched to Vulgrin's fortress of Châteauneuf on the Charente River, which fell after a two-week siege. As had occurred in the great rebellion, Young Henry soon abandoned his brother, and Richard was left to battle alone. Undeterred, he set out for the city of Angoulême, where his enemies Vulgrin and his father the count, their ally Aimar of Limoges, and other rebel chiefs had taken refuge. Richard quickly forced them to surrender, and he sent the defeated rebel leaders off to his father in England, where they begged him for mercy. Later, in the autumn of 1177, both Henry II and Richard campaigned for a month in the Limousin, punishing the rebels; they forced them to hand over their chief fortresses to Plantagenet officials. None of these victories proved permanent, and the defeated nobles promptly regained their possessions. Yet the young Count was doubtlessly earning their admiration or their fear.

During the years 1176–77, Richard also had to deal with the nobility of Gascony, a region that needed to be kept safe for the pilgrims en route to Santiago de Compostella.[17] He occupied in January 1177 the city of Dax, which Pierre III, viscount of Dax, and Centule, count of Bigorre, had fortified against him. Richard confiscated the lands of Pierre III, took control of the tower dominating the town of Dax, and placed Dax under his own rule. He then marched on Bayonne, defended by its viscount, Ernald Bertram, and he took it in ten days. Young Richard moved on to the Spanish border, captured the castle of Saint-Pierre at the base of the Pyrenees, which he then razed, and required the Basques and the Navarrese to observe peace. Once he had pacified the region, ensuring pilgrims' safe passage, he returned

---

16   Gillingham, *Richard*, 72–3.
17   P. Courteault, *Histoire de la Gascogne et de Béarn* (Paris, 1938), 78–9; Boussard, 153, 154.

to Poitou. Unrest on his southern frontier was ever lurking, however, and he had to return to Gascony in the autumn of 1178. His recent adversary, the count of Bigorre, had fallen foul of the citizens of Dax, who managed to imprison him. Alfonso II, king/count of Aragon and Barcelona (1162–96), interceded on the count's behalf; and Richard set him free in return for Alfonso's surety for his good behaviour and his surrender of two castles. In fact, the 1178 expedition may have been meant as a warning to Alfonso against any ideas of his expansion beyond the Pyrenees.[18] By 1187, Richard had brought the young viscount of Béarn, Gaston VI, under his control. Earlier Béarn had fallen into the Spanish kingdom's sphere of influence, with the viscount declaring himself the vassal of both the king of Aragon and the duke of Gascony.

Yet another rebellion confronted Richard in 1178–79 with the most powerful lord of Aunis and Saintonge, Geoffrey de Rancon, as his chief foe. Richard's campaign took the form of sieges of the Rancon castles lying in the Charente valley; he besieged Geoffrey's castle of Pons in December, but for months was unable to take it. By Easter 1179, part of his army was still surrounding Pons, unable to force its surrender; so he moved on to take and demolish the castle of Richemond and several other rebel fortresses in the region. Richard distinguished himself by besieging the supposedly im-pregnable fortress of Taillebourg situated on cliffs high above the Charente, seat of Geoffrey de Rancon, a challenge that one chronicler described as 'a most desperate task that none of his ancestors had dared attempt'. Here Richard's strategies and battle plans were devised. He ordered his forces into the surrounding countryside to destroy everything of value, from peas-ants' huts to villages, from fields to vineyards, from barnyards to forests. Daringly pitching his army's tents under this fortress's awesome walls, the Lionheart personally led the assault that broke into the surrounding town. He succeeded in forcing the castle's surrender on Ascension Day in May 1179, establishing his reputation 'as an acknowledged expert in the vital art of siege warfare'.[19] After that, Geoffrey de Rancon sought terms with Richard, and he surrendered all his castles, including Pons. The Lionheart's brilliant victory led to a pacification of Angoulême as well. Within a month, Vulgrin of Angoulême opened his gates to Richard and turned over to him his chief castles, Montignac and the citadel at Angoulême, which the young count of Poitou ordered demolished.

Aquitaine enjoyed an interval of peace from these noble rebellions, chiefly because a number of the nobility was absent on pilgrimage to Jerusalem.

---

18 Gillingham, *Richard*, 79–80; K. Norgate, *Richard the Lion Heart* (London, 1924), 29.
19 Diceto, 1: 431–2; Gillingham, *Richard*, 81.

An added element in the pacification of Poitou was Henry II's purchase of the county of La Marche in December 1177 from its childless count, who was anxious to join the pilgrims. Richard took advantage of the calm to leave Poitou and visit England in the summer of 1179. His next military activity took place in the summer of 1181 with another expedition to Gascony. There Richard asserted his control over the viscounty of Lomagne near the Toulousan frontier, accepting the submission of the young viscount, Vézian, whom he knighted. In the autumn, Richard felt free to leave Gascony for the upper Loire valley to join his brother, the Young King Henry, in a campaign against the count of Sancerre.[20]

In 1182 Richard had to face still another rebellion by his subjects on the southern fringes of Poitou, one that soon merged into the rivalry between Henry II's sons. Allegedly, the rebellion arose because Richard was 'oppressing with violence and harrying unjustly' the Poitevins. The 'soul' of the conspiracy, however, was Aimar, viscount of Limoges; and the rebels, centred again in the Limousin, the Angoumois and Périgord, included Aimar's fellow viscounts of the Limousin, his Taillefer half-brothers William and Adémar of Angoulême, Elie, count of Périgord, Geoffrey, lord of Lusignan, and other magnates in the region.[21] Adding to the general chaos was the troubadour Bertrand de Born, whose conflict with his brother for their ancestral castle of Hautefort in southwestern Périgord inspired him to plot against Richard. This half-Limousin and half-Périgordin petty noble loved war for its own sake, and also for the plunder that it earned him and similar minor nobles; as Bertrand wrote in one of his *sirventes*, 'I would fain have the great barons ever wroth with one another.'[22]

The rebels leveled heavy charges against Richard, accusing him of raping the wives and daughters of his free subjects; and then, 'After the ardor of his lust had died, he handed them over to his knights as common prostitutes.' A more likely explanation is alarm at the young count's 'iron rule',[23] notably his vigorous effort to enforce 'feudal' privileges over the nobility of Aquitaine. On the death of Count Vulgrin in 1179, Richard claimed custody of the county of Angoulême on behalf of the count's daughter, a claim successfully disputed by Vulgrin's two surviving brothers, William and Adémar.[24] Henry II's purchase of the county of La Marche from its childless count

---

20   Norgate, *Richard the Lion Heart*, 38–9.

21   Norgate, *Richard the Lion Heart*, 41–3.

22   L. Clédat, *Du rôle historique de Bertrand de Born 1175–1200* (Paris, 1879), 38–9; translation, K. Norgate, *England under the Angevin Kings* (London, 1887; rpt New York, 1969), 2: 212.

23   Norgate, *Richard the Lion Heart*, 40.

24   Quotation, Diceto, 2: 19; trans. E. Hallam, *The Plantagenet Chronicles* (New York, 1986), 172; Gillingham, *Richard*, 85–6, expresses the view that the Angoulême inheritance was at the root of the rebellion.

had already disturbed the balance of power in the region. Addition of La Marche to the ducal demesne alarmed the Taillefers of Angoulême, and it angered the Lusignan family, distant relatives of the count of La Marche with a claim to the county for themselves.

Richard heard rumours of the planned uprising, and he took pre-emptive action, seizing the citadel of Périgueux in April 1182. A temporary peace settlement failed to hold, and soon Henry II realised that Richard was in danger of losing Poitou unless he came to his aid. By mid-May 1182, he had arrived in the south, and he summoned his eldest son, Henry the Young King, to join them. By midsummer, the combined forces of the father and his two sons had convinced the viscounts of Limoges and Périgord to seek peace terms; but war in the region continued, for the lords of Angoulême remained in rebellion. An ominous change in the conflict's character occurred when Young King Henry was goaded into challenging his brother, supposedly by Bertrand de Born's songs. A nineteenth-century French historian characterises this struggle as 'a war of succession, with this especially odious circumstance, that the father whose heritage the sons were disputing was not yet dead and [he] took part in the conflict'.[25] Because of this turn of events, the viscount of Limoges renounced the peace settlement and rejoined the conflict. The rebels turned to the Young King, charmed like many others by his chivalry; and they expressed their desire to have him rule over them instead of Richard, doubtless preferring his fecklessness to Richard's persistence. Young Henry's chronic discontent transformed the rebellion into a contest between two brothers.

Young Henry found an excuse for initiating conflict with his brother in Richard's construction of the castle of Clairvaux just below the Loire River on the ill-defined Poitevin–Angevin frontier, apparently lying within the county of Anjou and under the Young King's jurisdiction. It is likely that Richard meant his new castle to be more of a provocation to the viscount of Châtellerault, an important Poitevin baron, than to his elder brother. Nonetheless, it goaded Young Henry into rash action; and at the 1182 Christmas court at Caen, he admitted that his anger over construction of Clairvaux had impelled him to ally with the rebel Aquitanian nobles.

To settle his sons' quarrel, Henry II took the new castle into his own hand, but this incident forced him to acknowledge the potential for war between his sons following his death and to seek a stable succession plan. He tried to impose a permanent settlement between his sons at Le Mans in early January 1183, but the arrangement knitted together there soon unravelled. As part of the proposed succession settlement, Richard was asked

---

25 Clédat, *Bertrand de Born*, 52.

to do what must have seemed to him an outrageous request, namely to do homage to his elder brother, the Young King, for his mother's lands. Richard's angry refusal to make proud Aquitaine into a dependency of his landless brother led to war between the Plantagenet siblings. Another of the brothers, Geoffrey of Brittany, entered the conflict when his father, seeking peace, sent him south to negotiate with the rebels; but in fact, he went to plot with them against Richard. In February 1183, the forces of Geoffrey and Young Henry joined the mercenaries of Viscount Aimar of Limoges in his chief city, and marauders began making forays into Richard's lands. Soon Henry II, fearing the count's defeat at the hands of his brothers, marched to Limoges to come to his aid; and they gathered a large army to besiege the town's citadel of Saint-Martial, but proved unable to take it. While Henry Senior pressed the siege of Limoges, Richard worked to deliver the Angoumois and Saintonge of rebels and plunderers.

The struggle in the south quickly developed into a major crisis with princes from outside the region seeking to take advantage of the Angevins' family strife to weaken Henry II. Philip Augustus, always eager to complicate the problems of his Plantagenet rivals, sent his brother-in-law, Young Henry, aid in the form of mercenaries. The duke of Burgundy and Raymond V, count of Toulouse, came in person to fight alongside the Young King.[26] Raymond's entry into the 1183 conflict enabled Richard Lionheart to recruit to his side Toulouse's chief rival in the region, Alfonso II of Aragon, whose ambition of expanding his power along France's Mediterranean coast conflicted with that of Raymond of Toulouse.

For a time, it appeared that Richard's rule over Aquitaine would fail, but Young Henry's charm and courtesy were inadequate substitutes for material resources. He quickly ran through his always insufficient resources and was forced to finance his war by plundering the people he supposedly had come to protect from his brother's greed. He plundered the abbey of Saint-Martial at Limoges and died on 11 June 1183, not long after having looted Rocamadour, one of the most famous shrines in western Christendom. Young Henry's death caused the collapse of the rebel coalition, but Henry II continued the siege of Limoges; and once the city surrendered on 24 June, he destroyed the walls of its citadel, 'not leaving one stone upon another'. Henry and Richard, with their ally Alfonso II of Aragon, proceeded to take other castles, among them Hautefort, seat of Bertrand de Born, the troubadour warrior who had sought by his lyrics to inflame the Young King's resentments. Once having pacified Poitou and Gascony by taking and razing

---

26   Richard, *Comtes*, 2: 211; Gillingham, 'Unromantic Death', 39; R. Benjamin, 'A Forty Years War: Toulouse and the Plantagenets, 1156–1196', *Historical Research* 61 (1988), 276.

castles, the Plantagenet monarch kept in his hand the castles that he had earlier given to Richard to hold, giving them to his own custodians.[27]

Henry's action left Richard uncertain about his position in Aquitaine, for the deaths of Young Henry in 1183 and Geoffrey of Brittany in 1186 would upset Henry's succession plans; and he had to rethink his proposals, apparently aiming in 1187–88 to transfer Richard to Normandy and to replace him in Aquitaine with John Lackland. He demanded that Richard surrender Aquitaine to his mother, and he named his own deputies to administer the region. After Henry gave up this scheme, he kept a closer rein on Richard's administration, placing ducal castles and their custodians under his direct control.[28] More and more, Richard began to fear that Henry's inordinate love for his youngest son, John Lackland, would result in cheating him – the eldest surviving son – of the province that he saw as 'his own especial possession'.[29] He voiced sharp refusals to suggestions aired by his father that he fill the Young King's position as heir to the principal Plantagenet holdings and surrender Aquitaine to John.

Richard, in the period following his brother Henry's death, was soon in the saddle, engaged in fighting. In 1184, he endured an invasion by John Lackland and Geoffrey of Brittany, who were trying to take by force his lands that he had refused to surrender. Two years later, Richard decided to punish Raymond V of Toulouse for his part in the 1183 campaign. This conflict centred on Quercy or the county of Cahors, a region that Henry II had conquered in 1159, but that had somehow fallen again into the count's hand. On 14 April 1185 or 1186, the Lionheart made a treaty with Alfonso II of Aragon, promising mutual aid in a campaign against Raymond V of Toulouse. In 1186, Henry II gave Richard a huge sum of money to hire *Brabançons* for a large-scale campaign against Toulouse, apparently in alliance with the Aragonese ruler.[30] Richard's force advanced into Toulouse, meeting little opposition, until Philip Augustus, exasperated by unsuccessful negotiations with Henry II, went to war.

The demise of Young Henry in 1183 followed by the death in 1186 of Geoffrey of Brittany, Henry's third son, threatened conflict between Henry II and Philip Augustus of France. The Norman Vexin, dowry of the Young King's widow Margaret, Philip's sister, presented a threat to Normandy's safety. Negotiations between the two monarchs resolved that problem with Margaret's acceptance of an annuity in exchange for her dowry and the transfer of the Norman Vexin to another of Philip's sisters, Alix, who had

---

27 *Gesta Regis*, 1: 293, 302–3; Richard, *Comtes*, 2: 222; Norgate, *Richard the Lion Heart*, 55–6.
28 Diceto, 2: 40; Richard, *Comtes*, 2: 232.
29 Quotation, Norgate, *Richard the Lion Heart*, 59.
30 *Gesta Regis*, 1: 345; Norgate, *Richard the Lion Heart*, 65.

been in Henry's custody since her betrothal to Richard in 1169, along with Henry's promise that their much-delayed marriage would finally take place. Geoffrey's death led to rivalry between Philip and Henry for custody of his heir, Arthur of Brittany. Also these two deaths forced the Capetian ruler to rethink his policy toward the Plantagenets. Earlier he had assumed that the bulk of their possessions would pass to his friends, the Young King and Geoffrey of Brittany. He had counted them as allies and also calculated that they lacked their father's political sagacity.[31] Now Philip set out to win Richard's friendship, endeavouring to strengthen their ties by insisting that the Lionheart finally marry his fiancée, Alix. Richard continued to balk at the marriage, however.

In the spring of 1187, Philip dispatched a force to threaten Poitou and the Loire Valley by invading Berry, having secured in advance the support of two important nobles, the lords of Issoudun and Fréteval. Both the Capetians and the Plantagenets held parts of Berry, and they continually tried to expand their spheres of influence there. Berry's strategic location linking Touraine with the troubled territories of southern Poitou made it one of the Capetians' chief pressure points against the Plantagenets. This Capetian threat aided Count Raymond V in his struggle against the Lionheart, forcing Richard to turn aside from Toulouse in order to deal with the Capetian menace to eastern Poitou. His father sent a large Angevin army to relieve him at Châteauroux, but the Angevin and Capetian monarchs made a truce at the last minute, and a pitched battle between their forces was barely avoided.

The war with Toulouse merged with still another rising that occurred in 1188, led by some of the usual provocateurs on Poitou's southern fringes, Count Adémar of Angoulême, Geoffrey of Rancon, and Geoffrey, lord of Lusignan. Apparently, Geoffrey de Lusignan's killing of one of Richard's *familiares* in an ambush triggered the conflict; and it was rumoured that the rebels received encouragement from Henry II, who allegedly sent Geoffrey de Lusignan men and money. In any case, the Lusignan clan was still upset by Plantagenet acquisition of the county of La Marche. Richard responded with great harshness, waging 'war without pity', besieging and demolishing castles, burning cities, seizing plunder, even uprooting fruit-trees.[32] He took for a second time the Rancon stronghold of Taillebourg, rebuilt after he had razed it in his first great victory. When the rebels sought peace, the Lionheart granted it only on condition that they take the cross; and at least one of them, Geoffrey de Lusignan, quickly departed for Palestine.

---

31   W.L. Warren, *Henry II* (Berkeley and Los Angeles, CA, 1987), 610–11.
32   Richard, *Comtes*, 2: 241.

In the course of this conflict, Richard's quarrel with the count of Toulouse revived. Raymond V had been harassing merchants who were Richard's subjects, and the Lionheart in retaliation again invaded the county, taking prisoner one of Raymond's important officials. In the spring of 1188, Richard threw his mercenaries into a massive assault, occupying a number of castles, ravaging the countryside, and approaching the town of Toulouse. This prompted Philip Augustus to come to the aid of Richard's opponent by undertaking another invasion of Berry. The fall of Châteauroux in mid-June 1188 diverted Richard from Toulouse in order to attend to his eastern frontier of Poitou. Henry II, alarmed at Philip's progress and at the threat posed to the Loire valley, raised an army in England to cross the Channel and apply pressure on Normandy's borders with Capetian territory. Once the French monarch learned of the landing of this large force on 11 July, he had to withdraw from Berry to safeguard his Norman frontier. This war continued until Henry II's death the next summer. Richard's discovery that his father had supported his enemy, Geoffrey de Lusignan, and had sent him subsidies led to the final break between father and son, turning the Lionheart into an ally of Philip Augustus. In any case, the interests of Henry II and Richard diverged, with Henry primarily concerned about the Capetian threat to Normandy and willing to make concessions in the south that were objectionable to Richard.

After a confrontation between father and son at Bonmoulins in November 1188, inflamed by Richard's fears that Henry II was planning to deprive him of his inheritance, he defied his father by doing homage to his arch-enemy, Philip Augustus of France. The conflict in the south thus expanded into a campaign by Richard against his father, in alliance with the Capetian king. Negotiations in the weeks after Easter 1189 failed to defuse the crisis, for Henry appeared to be seeking to disinherit Richard in favour of John Lackland. In the summer of 1189, Richard Lionheart and Philip Augustus invaded Anjou to harry the ailing Henry II.

In this final struggle against Henry II, Philip Augustus and his new ally sought to drive a wedge into the Angevin heartland in the Loire valley, prying Normandy apart from Aquitaine. They attacked the castle of La Ferté-Bernard in northwest Touraine, where the English king and the Capetian ruler had just met for a parley; and once it fell, they moved on to attack Le Mans on 12 June, forcing Henry to flee toward Chinon. Meanwhile, Richard and his Capetian ally overran Maine, prompting several of the county's leading nobles to transfer their loyalty to Richard, doubtless aware that he would soon succeed his father as their lord. The two allies moved on to besiege Tours, taking it only days before the old king's death. On the fall of Tours, the defeated Henry met his adversaries two days before his death and meekly submitted to all their demands. He promised to do homage to

Philip Augustus for all his French possessions, and he acknowledged Capetian supremacy over the county of Auvergne and over two lordships in Berry, Graçay and Issoudun. Furthermore, he recognised Richard as lawful heir to all his lands, he promised to pay the French king a 20,000 mark indemnity, and he agreed to French occupation of three castles in either the Vexin or in Anjou as a pledge for fulfilment of the agreements. Weakened from his final illness and depressed by the desertion of his favorite son, John Lackland, Henry no longer had the will to continue the struggle, and he headed for Chinon Castle where he died on 6 July.

Richard succeeded to rule over his father's domains, experienced in warfare and already known as 'Lionheart'. Years spent opposing the tumultuous and treacherous nobility of southern Poitou and protecting his position from both those foes and his family had sharpened his judgment of his associates' capabilities and character, a useful talent for an absentee ruler over widely dispersed lands who must depend on efficient and faithful officials. His own duchy of Aquitaine had lagged behind the territories personally ruled by Henry II in administrative innovations, however, denying him experience in presiding over complex machinery of finance or justice. No doubt, he delighted at the prospect of raising immense sums of money from his father's lands and calling his new vassals to account for their misdeeds before his *curia regis*, powers that he had not wielded in Aquitaine, but potentially attainable with his augmented assets. As he travelled north for his coronation in the summer of 1189, his feelings must have been much like those of James VI of Scotland as he journeyed southward to claim his new English kingdom in 1603.

CHAPTER FIVE

Richard's accession and preparations for the Third Crusade

By taking Henry II to his grave on 6 July 1189, disease and death had removed the obstacle threatening Richard's sure succession to the Angevin realm and smoothed the way for his crusade. Richard's emotionless presence at the abbey of Fontevraud where his father's body lay awaiting ceremony and burial suggests that little had been lost to the new king. Indeed much had been gained, for an undisputed succession to the Plantagenet domains had occurred for the first time in many years. Richard's leisurely pace from Anjou to England to be crowned indicates an awareness of security, and just as well, for it gave him time to think about how best to preserve his dynastic interests and to draw from his various territories the resources necessary for his adventure *ultra mare*.

Richard moved quickly to impress upon his subjects in Anjou his intention to rule them firmly. Besides his imprisonment of Henry II's seneschal, Stephen of Tours, he occupied the lands of three important nobles who had deserted his father in his last days: Guy de Laval, Ralph of Fougères and Juhel de Mayenne.[1] Richard remained in Anjou for several days, visiting Fontevraud to pay respect to his deceased father. No ceremony of installation as count of Anjou was celebrated, however, since the Angevins had never devised a formal service for bestowing the comital dignity.

Having already been elevated to the titles of count of Poitou and duke of Aquitaine, Richard had no need to return there for any ceremonial invest-iture, so immediately upon leaving the church at Fontevraud, he travelled north toward the Anglo-Norman provinces. Although Richard showed little regard for his father, he owed much to the old king for his peaceful, even

---

1   *Gesta Regis*, 2: 71–2.

uneventful, accession to power over all the Angevin lands. Richard's own tireless and ruthless efforts earlier in Aquitaine had gone far in subduing that region's unruly nobility. Had Richard needed to make good his claim to authority over the southern lands, it would have postponed his crusading for an indefinite period.

The well-governed and orderly areas north of the Loire valley did not pose the same threat, for Normandy and England had within them loyal royal servants who sought an orderly and sure transition of power. Richard's mother, Eleanor of Aquitaine, released from long imprisonment in England for her role in her sons' 1173–74 revolt, worked to smooth the succession. Escorted by Walter of Coutances, archbishop of Rouen, and Archbishop Baldwin of Canterbury, Richard arrived in Rouen to be belted with the sword of the duchy of Normandy and receive the allegiance of his Norman subjects. Presided over by the archbishop of Rouen, these events occurred on 20 July 1189, a fortnight after the death of Henry II. After a conference on the Norman border with his overlord Philip Augustus of France, Richard set his course for England where he landed on 13 August at Portsmouth.

Chroniclers record that Richard's English subjects greeted him with great joy as they lined the streets to catch a glimpse of the hero of Taillebourg, crusader and their new sovereign. Richard's progress toward London and his coronation was leisurely; he took time to witness the marriages of his own and his father's men and to give them gifts. He even gave consideration to leading a force against the Welsh who had begun raiding the borders soon after his arrival in England, but his mother counselled against that until he had been duly crowned – advice he chose to follow. Richard worshipped in St Paul's Cathedral, London, on 1 September, marking the beginning of the festivities that would surround the new king's coronation.[2]

The vivid and precise details of Richard's coronation ceremony left by chroniclers resulted in its becoming a model for English coronations for generations.[3] It was a splendid affair. Prelates and magnates escorted the new sovereign into Westminster Abbey where he swore on the Gospels and other holy relics the threefold pledge that he would preserve the Church in peace and honour, ferret out wicked laws and evil customs, and promote justice and goodness to the benefit of those subjected by God to his rule. Richard was then clothed in his regalia and anointed, but before proceeding to the oath, Archbishop Baldwin of Canterbury cautioned the anointed

---

2 Gervase, 1: 457.
3 W. Stubbs (ed.) *Itinerarium Peregrinorum*, in *Chronicles and Memorials of the Reign of Richard I*, RS (London, 1864), 1: 142; Gervase, 1: 457; Diceto, 2: 68–9; *Gesta Regis*, 2: 78–83; Howden, 3: 9–11.

against accepting these responsibilities and binding them with oaths if he lacked intention of carrying them out. Upon receiving the new monarch's assurances, Baldwin took the crown from Richard who had lifted it from the high altar and crowned him King Richard. From his throne and surrounded by the great men of the realm, the king watched as the archbishop said mass, afterwards laying aside his ceremonial vestments and presiding over the festivities and celebrations that accompanied this grand occasion.

By early September 1189, therefore, Duke Richard of Aquitaine had been installed by formal ceremonies as duke of Normandy and king of England, but what of other lands, notably Brittany and Ireland? Richard had Plantagenet relatives with prior claims to these two territories. Richard's brother, Geoffrey Plantagenet, count of Brittany, who had died in 1186, left a son, Arthur; still a toddler at the time of Richard's accession, the boy posed no threat. Ireland had been given by Henry II to his youngest son, John Lackland, in 1177, and though the land was not entirely under his authority, he held the title *dominus Hiberniae*. Richard, nevertheless, regarded himself as suzerain over Ireland. He requested that William Longchamp's papal legateship extend to all England and Wales, and to those parts of Ireland where John exercised jurisdiction, and he unilaterally made land grants there to the Lacy and Marshal families.[4]

Richard celebrated his succession to the Plantagenet legacy by a profound generosity toward his family and friends. Whether this was consistent with Poitevin custom, chivalric convention, political good sense or his personal style, it became part of the lore associated with this king. The first to receive from the king's bounty was his beloved mother, Eleanor of Aquitaine, who had been imprisoned for years in varying degrees of severity. Richard ordered her released and empowered her to hold England until his arrival. He met her at Winchester soon after his landing, and she remained a prominent force in England, enforcing royal directives, granting lands, prohibiting the movement of papal legates, attesting royal charters and attending gatherings of the king's *magna curia regis*.[5] Though rich and powerful in her own right as duchess of Aquitaine, Eleanor was also honoured by her son with additional lands and moneys. He confirmed her dower lands that she had received from her late husband and added the lands that Kings Henry I and Stephen had bestowed upon their queens.[6] Later, Richard would settle on his bride,

4   Diceto, 2: 83; Landon, 87; W.L. Warren, 'King John and Ireland', in J. Lydon (ed.) *England and Ireland in the Later Middle Ages* (Dublin, 1981), 31–2; M. Flanagan, *Irish Society, Anglo-Norman Settlers, Angevin Kingship: Interactions in Ireland in the Late Twelfth Century* (Oxford, 1989), 281–4.
5   F. West, *The Justiciarship in England, 1066–1232* (Cambridge, 1966), 65; Landon, 2, 13, 16, 18, 26.
6   Howden, 3: 27.

Queen Berengaria, lands in Gascony and the rights to the English queens' dower, but the latter were to come to her only after the death of his mother.[7]

Richard poured even more lavish gifts upon John Lackland, his sole surviving legitimate brother. Besides rumoured plans of Henry II for replacing Richard in Aquitaine with John, the old king had reiterated late in his life his desire to see his youngest son married to an English heiress and invested with English and Norman territories along with his Irish title. These wishes were carried out by Richard in 1189. Before crossing from Normandy to be crowned king, Duke Richard belted John with the sword of the Norman county of Mortain. Within days of landing in England, Richard gave his brother the hand of Isabelle of Gloucester along with her father's earldom, disregarding the archbishop of Canterbury's protests that the marriage was within the prohibited degrees. Shortly thereafter, John received an unprecedented block of territories in the Southwest and Midlands that included entire counties (Somerset, Dorset, Devon, Cornwall, Nottinghamshire and Derbyshire) and great honours (Lancaster and Wallingford), although the king retained certain crucial castles in his hand. [See Map II] These latter lands alone, according to Bishop Stubbs' calculations, were valued at £4,000 per year.[8] By Richard's departure in December, therefore, Count John had been invested with great wealth, and his power had no English parallel, for he held these lands as liberties not subject to the exchequer. Richard had satisfied his father's wishes in a way that one historian describes as being 'beyond the limits of worldly wisdom and sound policy'.[9]

Since John was an Angevin prince, John Gillingham asks, 'Why was he not ruling Anjou? Or Aquitaine, or Brittany, or Normandy, or England?'[10] Richard would never have considered this in light of twelfth-century Angevin succession custom which made some provision for younger sons but left the bulk of the family lands with the eldest living son. What he supplied appears consistent with accepted practice. He was certainly not obliged to do more, and furthermore, it would have been dangerous. As Richard well knew, grants in the central or southern lands would have been far more dangerous, for the institutions of control there were much weaker than the English and Norman administrative machines or non-existent. Furthermore, had John

---

7   M. Mitchell, *Berengaria: Enigmatic Queen of England* (Burwash, 1986), 49–51, 62. Mitchell argues that Eleanor was an obstacle to Berengaria's assuming her proper role as Richard's wife, and that 'Eleanor's death can only have freed Berengaria from the frustration she suffered as a result of Richard's mother-fixation'; 97.

8   *Gesta Regis*, 2: 72–3, 78, 99; Howden, 3: 6, 27. Some of the castles withheld included Wallingford, Tickhill and Nottingham; W. Stubbs, *Historical Introductions to the Rolls Series*, ed. A. Hassall (London, 1902), 205–6.

9   K. Norgate, *Richard the Lion Heart* (London, 1924), 105.

10 Gillingham, *Richard*, 136.

become a duke on the continent, he would have been Richard's feudal equal, holding of the French crown directly and thus a greater danger diplomatically. Richard understood first-hand the benefits of tenancy-in-chief, having refused to do homage to his older brother, Henry the Young King, for Aquitaine in 1183. The holdings settled on Count John by his older brother actually blunted rather than unleashed his ambitions. It is possible that one of the causes for John's later rebellion is the difference between what his father had once sought for him and the lands and powers, though substantial, that he actually received.

Magnanimity toward family members, no matter how sincere, does not remove the charge of foolhardiness. The lands and powers given to John in England and Normandy were enormous, and the grant has earned Richard the criticism of scholars, who have described his decision to provide for his brother so richly as 'most imprudent and dangerous', 'liberal to the extent of folly', and 'lavish improvidence'.[11] H.G. Richardson and G.O. Sayles stated: 'No administrator would have displayed his princely generosity . . . by making over to his brother the revenues and administration of six English counties.'[12] What could have motivated a king to do something as seemingly unwise as this? To say he was devoid of the knowledge of governance is simplistic and disregards Richard's years of rule over a turbulent duchy that had revealed him as active and effective; and it also overlooks actions that the king took to box in the count. Neither is the conclusion credible that Richard rewarded John richly because he had joined him in rebellion against his father.[13] Consistent with Richard's views on political infidelity, John deserved rough treatment but did not receive it, for various accounts make clear that Richard had little appreciation for those who had abandoned their lord in his moment of crisis. The converse also occurred, for those who had stood with Henry II received generosity from their new lord, as the example of William Marshal testifies.

It has been suggested that the Lionheart might have spared himself much trouble if he had scattered John's huge holdings rather than handing him blocks of English territory or if he had retained control of the administrative apparatus in those shires.[14] While true enough, John's holdings were scattered in the broader context of the Angevin 'empire'; and import-

---

11 Norgate, *Richard*, 104; A.L. Poole, *From Domesday Book to Magna Carta*, 2nd edn (Oxford, 1955), 348; Stubbs, *Historical Introductions*, 447.

12 H.G. Richardson and G.O. Sayles, *The Governance of Mediaeval England* (Edinburgh, 1963), 328.

13 Richardson and Sayles, *Governance*, 328.

14 Norgate, *Richard*, 105; D. Carpenter, 'Richard by his Contemporaries: Was he a "Model King"? England in 1189', unpublished paper, Colloque aux Archives du Calvados (Caen, April 1999).

antly, they were located in its best governed parts, lying entirely within the Anglo-Norman provinces. John's handful of counties in England, one in Normandy, and lordship over unruly Ireland meant that his power when compared to his brother's can be considered inconsequential, safeguarded by the advanced governmental system of the Anglo-Norman realm. In the context of the whole of the Plantagenet possessions, it is possible to see Richard's grants in a different light. In 1189 Richard may have reasoned that John needed an income befitting a prince, but he hardly elevated the count to a position that threatened him.

Richard's grants to Count John can be explained in part as following from family tradition. As witnessed in Henry's various succession plans, it was part of the Angevin mentality to provide something for everybody in the family; and the Angevins had historically treated rebellious family members leniently, as noted in Henry II's handling of his sons following their revolt in the 1170s. Throughout his reign, Richard was amply generous to his brother; yet he could not safely have left John landless in the way that his father had left Young King Henry. For Richard to give John the grants that he did in order to keep him pacified, therefore, was not unwise; he may well have been attempting to avoid the disastrous results following from his father's stinginess toward his eldest son.

In fact, John may well have realised his advantage, for his trouble-making in England did not begin until after Richard had formally announced Arthur of Brittany as his heir late in 1190. Even when John made a bid for the throne during Richard's 1193 German captivity, the relationship between the two brothers would not be ruptured for long. Gestures of generosity quickly followed on the Lionheart's return from Germany in 1194. John lost most of his lands, and he gave up his household to join his brother's entourage, but was granted an allowance from the exchequer of £2,000 per year. Soon he received a commission to lead troops into battle against his former French ally.

Richard treated Geoffrey Plantagenet, one of Henry II's illegitimate sons and his father's chancellor, in much the same way that he did John. Geoffrey had too much ambition for Richard I to rest easily; because of his ambition, one historian calls him a 'formidable bastard'.[15] The royal blood in Geoffrey's veins, though tainted by illegitimacy, may have encouraged in him visions of someday wearing the crown of England himself.

Possibly more worrisome for Richard was Geoffrey's military reputation. His actions in the great rebellion of 1173–74 had won him Henry II's high accolades, and Geoffrey's role in preparing the castles of Anjou and

---

15   D.L. Douie, *Archbishop Geoffrey Plantagenet and the Chapter at York* (York, 1960), 3.

Normandy in the final war of Henry's life could only be fresh memories for Richard.[16] Henry had persistently pushed Geoffrey toward high ecclesiastical office, but the youth showed no enthusiasm for the religious life, even resigning the bishopric of Lincoln in response to the pope's ultimatum to undergo ordination as a priest or step down. None of Henry's inheritance schemes had made provision for Geoffrey, but on his deathbed, the old king sought either the rich see of Winchester or York for his lone faithful son. Richard put this wish into effect in 1189, the same time that John was vested with Mortain, by giving instructions to the chapter at York to elect Geoffrey as the new prelate.

The new king's placement of Geoffrey in York not only corresponded to Henry II's wish, provided Geoffrey with the prestige and wealth of a great ecclesiastic and squashed any hope of his for a monarchical future; it also moved his centre of activity from his continental holdings in Anjou and Touraine to England, that much-governed kingdom. Geoffrey held the castle of Baugé in Anjou and the castle of Langeais in Touraine, both located near Tours and of strategic and administrative significance.[17] Richard seized Geoffrey's castles early in the reign, however, and sold them back to him at great cost.[18] A recent doctoral thesis has shown that Geoffrey also had custody of the huge Giffard estates in Normandy and England, given him by Henry II; but Richard granted those lands to William Marshal and Richard de Clare in 1189, each magnate receiving half. The Norman half of this great estate, Longueville, went to Marshal, a person of known loyalty and dependence, demonstrating royal efforts at moving Geoffrey's interests away from the continent.[19]

Only one other man could claim descent from Henry II: William Longsword, the other of Henry's known bastards, probably born *c*. 1170. In 1189 Richard did not enrich him; he does not even appear in the records until 1191 when Richard gave him the manor of Kirton-in-Lindsey. Later in the reign, upon the death in 1196 of William fitz Patrick, earl of Salisbury, Longsword married the heir of the deceased and succeeded to the earldom. Salisbury was a lesser earldom with no castle attached to it. Longsword served with the king on the continent, often attesting charters when the king was at Les Andelys, but little else is known of his activities during Richard's lifetime.[20]

---

16 M. Lovatt, 'The Career and Administration of Geoffrey Plantagenet, Archbishop of York, ?1151–1212', PhD thesis (Cambridge University, 1975), 12, 21, 24–5; W.L. Warren, *Henry II* (Berkeley and Los Angeles, CA, 1987), 625.

17 *PR2RI*, 74; Lovatt, 'Geoffrey Plantagenet', 17–19; Stubbs, *Historical Introductions*, 268.

18 *PR2RI*, 74; Howden, 3: 17.

19 Lovatt, 'Geoffrey Plantagenet', 17–19.

20 B. Holden, 'The Rise of a Royal Bastard: William Longespée, Earl of Salisbury, 1198–1226', MA thesis (Florida State University, 1996).

In the first months of his reign, Richard's generosity extended beyond the family circle to include many who had served his father with the promise of rewards in return. William Marshal, the knight errant who had become indispensable to the Angevin house and who had fought for Henry II against Richard, was reconciled to his new lord and given the heiress, Isabelle of Striguil. This young woman brought to the marriage vast wealth in lands in the Welsh marches, Wales proper and Ireland. In addition, William received the Norman half of the rich Giffard estate, was appointed sheriff of Gloucester with its castle, farmed the forest of Dean, and was named one of the *appares* or associate justiciars who were to govern England during the king's absence on crusade. William's brothers also gained from the king's largess toward the Marshal clan, John becoming a royal escheator and sheriff of Yorkshire, and Henry, dean of York Minster.[21] Baldwin de Béthune, a man of the calibre of William Marshal but who never attained his level of fame and wealth, had also been promised an heiress, Denise, lady of Déols and Châteauroux, crucial lordships in Berry on the Poitevin border facing French royal territory. Richard decided against fulfilling Henry II's intention, for he had promised this prize to Andrew de Chauvigny, a favourite Poitevin knight who had been captured during Richard's 1188–89 rebellion. Baldwin was consoled with promises of compensation, eventually realised in his marriage to the countess of Aumâle, widow of another of Richard's military associates in Poitou, William de Forz, who had won her marriage from Richard in the early days of the reign.[22] William Longchamp, the ducal chancellor, became royal chancellor, justiciar, bishop of Ely and papal legate. Finally, many of Henry II's curial servants were elevated to episcopal office, a common Angevin means of rewarding loyal service.

Richard's patronage reveals a premeditation of plan that appears to have been missed by other historians, who credit Richard's open-handedness as nothing more than Poitevin chivalry. Patronage played a substantial role in bolstering royal power by buying the political loyalty of barons and *curiales*, what has been called 'an essential part of the art of kingship'.[23] The men-at-arms who knew Richard's favour received rewards that placed them in

---

21 D. Crouch, *William Marshal: Court, Career, and Chivalry in the Angevin Empire, 1147–1219* (London, 1990), 58–72.

22 Gillingham, *Richard*, 125–6; R.V. Turner, 'William de Forz, Count of Aumale', *Proceedings of the American Philosophical Society* 115 (1973), 222–3.

23 Gillingham, *Richard*, 125. Also J.E. Lally, 'Secular Patronage at the Court of King Henry II', *BIHR* 49 (1976): 159–84; R.W. Southern, 'The Place of Henry I in English History', in *Medieval Humanism and Other Studies* (New York, 1970), 208–28; T.K. Keefe, *Feudal Assessments and the Political Community under Henry II and His Sons* (Berkeley and Los Angeles, CA, 1983); R.V. Turner, *Men Raised from the Dust: Administrative Service and Upward Mobility in Angevin England* (Philadelphia, 1988), 1–19.

potential trouble spots. Andrew de Chauvigny's castles in Berry covered a key invasion route into Angevin territory, as did the county of Aumale into northeastern Normandy, given in succession to William de Forz and Baldwin de Béthune. William Marshal, though of unquestioned loyalty, needed lands and patronage of his own. Without these, he was 'but a small creature', unimpressive as one of England's associate justiciars.[24] Another of the associate justiciars, Geoffrey fitz Peter, acquired similar resources when he won the earldom of Essex through his wife's disputed claim.[25] The same held true for those capable clerics who had worked tirelessly and competently for Henry II. By elevating them to the episcopate, Richard established them as members of the king's great council and, therefore, among the social and political elite. His reliance on these individuals is attested by their continued presence at court and at Westminster.

Some of these men were destined to play leading roles in safeguarding Richard's interests while the king was away on crusade. Richard had committed himself to the Third Crusade in 1187 while duke of Aquitaine, an enterprise that he was determined to prosecute, unlike his father. Consequently, he had several goals that had to be achieved: establish law and order in his domains, ensure peace and security from hostile neighbours, and devise a regency plan to perpetuate Plantagenet authority during his absence. Helping him construct these ideas and plans was a combination of great men, his father's *curiales* and his own *familiares*. For instance, William Marshal, Maurice de Craon, the most powerful magnate of Anjou, and Gilbert Pipard, an administrator who had served on both sides of the Channel, were immediately brought into the new king's council at Fontevraud, and the archbishops of Canterbury and Rouen soon joined Richard's entourage.[26] Count John, Archbishop-elect Geoffrey Plantagenet, Earl Robert of Leicester and Gerard de Camville were men of note found with the king early. Camville received the king's first charter which gives a list of names of other men who had joined the court, such as William Longchamp; William du Hommet, constable of Normandy; two Norman nobles, Hugh de Gournay and Robert de Harcourt; Walkelin de Ferrers, a Norman chamberlain; William de Saint John; and Hugh Bardolf. The bishops of Rochester, Lincoln, Coventry, Durham, Worcester and Evreux were found at Richard's court soon after his arrival in England, as were his mother Eleanor and Ranulf de Glanvill, Henry II's chief justiciar.[27]

---

24   Crouch, *William Marshal*, 54.
25   *PR2RI*, 111; Turner, *Men Raised from Dust*, 55–8.
26   Paul Meyer (ed.), *L'Histoire de Guillaume le Maréchal*, Société de l'Histoire de France (Paris, 1891–1901), ll. 9304–51; Diceto, 2: 67.
27   Landon, 1–3.

Many came for no other reason than to fulfil protocol for the coronation, but once the king had begun to issue charters, the list of leading members of court, determined by attestations, demonstrates that his closest companions in 1189 would be given important roles during his absence, 1190–94. Of the ten chief attestors of charters issued while the king was in England, seven were men who held crucial posts in England's regency, such as justiciars, *appares* or sheriffs. Similarly, when Richard crossed the Channel, his two leading attestors were the highest-ranking men in Normandy's regency, William fitz Ralph, seneschal, and William du Hommet, constable.[28] Richard's plans, therefore, were formulated with the advice and counsel of those entrusted with discharging them. Since many of these men were experienced with the administration of the Anglo-Norman provinces, they brought wisdom to the council chamber. His counsel was balanced through the inclusion, through meetings of the *magna curia regis*, of the English magnates. Charters witnessed while the king held a council at Pipewell Abbey, where major decisions regarding the form of the English regency were determined, show that the earls of Gloucester, Leicester, Essex, Warenne, Warwick, Clare, Arundel, Salisbury, Roger Bigod, claimant to the earldom of Norfolk, David, brother of the Scottish king, and Ranulf de Glanvill were present. Also among the witnesses were Roger de Préaux and Stephen Longchamp, stewards, Ralph fitz Godfrey and Geoffrey de Chauvigny, chamberlains, and Guy de Dive, marshal, all members of Richard's comital household, who were most likely as trusted by the new monarch as the baronage of England.[29]

Similar patterns are observed when the Lionheart held councils on the continent. At La Réole in the South in February 1190, Aquitanian ecclesiastics, the seneschal of Gascony, and counts and viscounts were in attendance on the king-duke; and the next month at Nonancourt in Normandy, many of those at Pipewell were present along with leading Normans such as William fitz Ralph and Robert de Harcourt.[30] Clearly, Richard at the beginning of his reign was receiving advice and counsel from a broad spectrum of his subjects. What and whose advice he chose to heed opens a huge area of historical speculation, but it should be noted that though the decisions of 1189 needed to be made quickly, Richard's decision-making process was carried out in much the same context as that of his father's.

The defence of the Plantagenet lands from hostile attack clearly occupied Richard's mind as he prepared for his departure. Several actions were to alleviate this concern as much as possible, given the circumstances and the

---

28   R.R. Heiser, 'The Royal *Familiares* of Richard I', *Medieval Prosopography* 10 (1989), 39–40.
29   Landon, 6–8.
30   Landon, 25–7.

untrustworthiness of those whose lands bordered the Angevin possessions. On the frontiers of Normandy and Maine lay an uncomfortably vulnerable area adjacent to the lands of the counts of Perche, who held estates of both the Angevin and Capetian monarchs and also of the counts of Blois. Through their territory Richard and Philip Augustus had crashed to rout Henry II in the Angevin heartland weeks earlier, and Richard hoped to pull Perche firmly into the Angevin orbit by marrying his niece, Matilda of Saxony, to Count Geoffrey.[31] An invasion route into Aquitaine that caused alarm passed through the sensitive border region of Berry, and in order to shore up defences there, Richard relied on a Poitevin, Andrew de Chauvigny, to whom was given the heiress of the castles of Déols and Châteauroux. Along Normandy's northeastern frontier, Philip Augustus's acquisition of the county of Amiens in 1185 had expanded Capetian power, and the Lionheart sought to secure this region through marriages: first by marrying his co-justiciar, William de Mandeville, to the countess of Aumâle; and later by marrying her to the king's military associate, William de Forz. By these marriage arrangements, Richard safeguarded his continental frontiers as best he could.

Tours, captured by Richard in his last war with his father, and the surrounding area were also strategic for the preservation of the empire, for through this province passed major communications lines linking North to South, East to West.[32] Animosity existed between the counts of Anjou and the city's two principal ecclesiastical institutions, the archbishopric of Tours and the powerful abbey of Saint Martin. Seizing upon this, the Capetians used their position as protectors of the French Church to make them espionage centres for tracking movements and plans of the English kings. An agreement between the archbishop and Richard concerning their respective rights in the city in March 1190 helped resolve problems that had kept the prelates of Tours closely aligned with the French monarchy. The abbey of Saint Martin was also neutralised by an agreement between Richard and Philip Augustus after they met at Corbigny near Vézelay, July 1190. Richard's attempts to patch up these problems were fairly short lived, however, and they never translated into any major coups over the Capetians.

While Richard had been recently allied with Philip Augustus against Henry II, his accession to the lordship of the Angevin 'empire' moved the new

---

31 *Gesta Regis*, 2: 73; Gillingham, *Richard*, 126, 231. The counts of Perche worked to maintain a balance between their Angevin and Capetian lords as seen in the career of Geoffrey's father, Rotroud; he led a delegation from Philip Augustus to Richard relaying the French king's crusade plans; he stood with Philip at Messina and sailed with him to the Holy Land. He also witnessed Richard's gifts to his bride on Cyprus (*Gesta Regis*, 2: 92, 128–9; Howden, 3: 19; Landon, 49).

32 Powicke, *Loss*, 9–12.

monarch from Capetian friend to foe. The mutual distrust between Richard and Philip, about which the poet Bertrand de Born complains, was no doubt mollified by the fact that both were going on crusade.[33] None the less, Richard and Philip met on the Norman frontier and worked out a treaty designed to tie up loose ends in July 1189 two days after the Lionheart's investiture as duke of Normandy. Still unresolved was Richard's proposed marriage to Philip's half-sister, Alix, an issue involving Plantagenet possession of the Norman Vexin. Richard promised that he would finally marry the princess, and he pledged to give Philip 4,000 marks above the 20,000 agreed to by Henry. In exchange, the French king desisted from his demands for Gisors and the Norman Vexin. Richard recovered nearly all the Capetian conquests in Touraine, Maine, Berry and the Vexin that had occurred in the 1188–89 campaign against Henry II except Issoudun and Graçay in Berry, but his recovery of Châteauroux secured Angevin Berry's safety. Farther south, Richard had to surrender his claim to rights over the county of Auvergne.

This final resolution settled a date for departure, which must have pleased Richard, both because it moved the crusade one step closer and because it assured him of Philip's intention to participate. In subsequent meetings at Nonancourt and Dreux, the two kings promised to respect each other's holdings, even defending them as if their own, and their magnates and prelates gave guarantees for upholding the possessions and rights of the two kings while they were crusading. With these treaties, agreements and marriages arranged to secure the borderlands, Richard had restrained Philip as far as possible.

The southeastern flank of Richard's lands remained the last of his security problems in France to which he must attend before departing for the Middle East, 'for there was no threat so serious as that posed by the count of Toulouse'.[34] The Lionheart recognised the possibility that Count Raymond V of Toulouse would take advantage of his absence on crusade to threaten his southern lands, especially attempting to recapture the county of Quercy. Philip Augustus, who had demanded recognition of his right to arbitrate quarrels between Aquitaine and Toulouse, was an ally of Count Raymond, but because he was going to the Holy Land, the threat from his direction was diminished. Richard could not afford to be satisfied, however; and his marriage with Berengaria of Navarre must be seen as part of his plan for stabilising Gascony. The match was 'an ingenious diplomatic device . . . in

---

33 Bertrand de Born describes the two kings: 'King Philip . . . is suspicious of King Richard, who is suspicious of him in turn', quoted by D.D.R. Owen, *Eleanor of Aquitaine: Queen and Legend* (Oxford, 1993), 82.

34 J. Gillingham, 'Richard I and Berengaria of Navarre', *BIHR* 53 (1980), 167.

order to cut his way through a thicket of political problems', although historians have traditionally given Eleanor of Aquitaine credit for negotiating the marriage.[35] It was Eleanor who brought Berengaria to Sicily, where Richard was wintering; and in May 1191, during a stop at Cyprus on the voyage to Jerusalem, the marriage was solemnised.

Berengaria was the daughter of Sancho VI of Navarre (1150–94), a kingdom lying south of the Roncesvalles Pass in the Pyrenees. Navarre and other Christian kingdoms in northern Spain played important roles in the affairs of southwestern France. Henry II had married his daughter, Eleanor, to the king of Castile. The king of Aragon had long nurtured hostility toward the count of Toulouse, having joined Richard in suppressing the Aquitanian rebellion of 1183 to which Count Raymond gave his support. While King Sancho of Navarre did not command the power of the Aragonese or Castilian kings, he was developing closer bonds with Aragon by the late twelfth century in response to the threat posed by expansionist Castile. A marriage alliance with the king of Navarre would protect Richard's possessions in the extreme South by providing an ally to supply assistance to his seneschals in case of noble rebellion. The alliance garnered Sancho VI prestige, but it also served Navarrese foreign policy whereby he gained protection from his greater neighbours.[36]

Two expeditions were made by Richard in 1190 toward the southern border lands, once to La Réole on the Garonne River in February and then into the Pyrenean foothills in May and early June. The presence of Richard's most distinguished subjects at La Réole suggests that a council had been called, where it is not unlikely that Richard's marriage was one of the topics considered. Richard's expedition of May and June took him deep into Gascony. He went as far as Bigorre, high in the Pyrenees, where he attacked, captured and hanged a noble, William de Chisi, for plundering pilgrims who traversed his lands on their journey to Compostella. This military incursion far into the South doubtless had a purpose beyond securing the safety of pilgrims following the route of Saint Jacques. It may have provided Richard with an excuse to return to the region and finalise plans with King Sancho, perhaps in a face-to-face meeting. Possibly it was meant as a warning to Count Raymond V of Toulouse, and it may have strengthened Richard's alliance with the king of Aragon.[37]

The match with Berengaria brought to a head the old problems of Richard's long engagement to marry Alix of France and of the Norman

---

35 Gillingham, 'Richard I and Berengaria', 158.
36 Gillingham, 'Richard I and Berengaria', 157–73.
37 Gillingham, 'Richard I and Berengaria', 161–3; Gillingham, *Richard*, 139–41.

Vexin, which had been assigned as her marriage portion. These problems were resolved in March 1191 at a conference between Richard and King Philip at Messina in Sicily, where the two crusader kings wintered before setting sail for Palestine. Philip agreed to give up Capetian claims to the Norman Vexin and the fortress of Gisors. In return, Richard had to buy off the French king by becoming his liege man and agreeing that any sons succeeding him would hold their lands in-chief of the French crown; he surrendered his claims to the Auvergne and to the lordships of Issoudun and Graçay in Berry, but he kept Quercy by paying Philip 10,000 marks.

Regardless of complications arising from Richard's previous betrothal, the Navarrese marriage alliance served his purposes well. Twice while Richard was absent, King Sancho intervened in Aquitaine to uphold the interests of the king-duke. In 1192 Sancho assisted the Aquitanian seneschal, driving back the forces of Raymond even to the gates of Toulouse, and in 1194 the Navarrese army thrust deep into Angevin territory in response to Augustus's aggressions, joining the forces of Richard for an attack on Loches. Through this marriage alliance, the Lionheart had isolated and restrained Count Raymond so effectively that, had he not been captured on his return from the East, Aquitaine and Gascony would have been largely undisturbed.[38] Not until 1196 when Richard had patched up relations with Raymond VI, the son of his longstanding enemy, via another Angevin marriage did the Navarrese alliance wane in significance.[39]

Regencies were needed capable of preserving all Richard's accomplishments in preparation for his departure. By February 1190 he had named Pierre Bertin to Poitou and Élie de la Celle to Gascony, both experienced administrators drawn from the region's lesser nobility.[40] Two of the three Henrician justiciars or seneschals were removed from office: Stephen of Tours (or Etienne de Marçay) in Anjou was ousted and imprisoned immediately; Ranulf de Glanvill in England was replaced at the Pipewell Council; but William fitz Ralph, longtime seneschal of Normandy, was retained in office. Richard not only imprisoned Stephen of Tours, but forced him to pay £30,000 sterling, and allegedly demanded an additional payment. Roger of Howden, the English chronicler, asserts that Richard went further, arbitrarily demanding that Stephen also separate from his wife on grounds that one of his *bourgeois* background was unworthy of marriage to a woman of superior rank. Another chronicler describes him as mean even to his master, a possible

---

38 Gillingham, 'Richard I and Berengaria', 167–8.
39 Gillingham, 'Richard I and Berengaria', 171–3; R. Benjamin, 'A Forty Years War: Toulouse and the Plantagenets, 1156–1196', *Historical Research* 61 (1988), 282.
40 Landon, 25; Gillingham, *Richard*, 138.

cause of the king's anger, but the *Histoire de Guillaume le Maréchal* records a conversation that provides a more likely reason. Following Henry II's death, William Marshal told Stephen of Tours that he ought to distribute alms to the poor of Chinon from the dead king's treasure, to which Stephen replied that there were none to disperse.[41] An empty royal treasury cannot have pleased the crusader king. Stephen's replacement as seneschal was Payn de Rochefort, a Poitevin, appointed by 11 January 1190.[42]

As Richard set his face toward Jerusalem, he left his empire with no guarantees of his safe return. Historians have attacked Richard for his pre-crusade plans with assaults on his sagacity and personal integrity; their comments on Richard's lack of political sense are unfair, however. The empire's defences were in order; disturbances that did occur in his absence were contained by the arrangements that Richard made before his departure.

---

41 *Gesta Regis*, 2: 71–2; Newburgh, 2: 424–5, describes Stephen as *ex statu mediocri*; also Meyer, *Histoire de Guillaume le Maréchal*, ll. 9173–211; and Devizes, 4, and Appendix A, 85.

42 Gillingham, *Richard*, 138, suggests that Stephen de Marçay regained his office for the duration of the crusade, but evidence of witness-lists does not support this. Payn witnessed as seneschal of Anjou on 11 January 1190 and throughout the spring until at least 25 June; Stephen witnessed one of Richard's charters on 5 May 1190 without any title; J.C. Holt and R. Mortimer (eds), *Acta of Henry II and Richard I: Hand-list of Documents Surviving in . . . the United Kingdom*, List and Index Society, 21 (Gateshead, 1986), no. 354; Landon, 26, 32, 35; BN ms. nouv. acqu. Lat. 1224, ff 226, 227, 245–6, 269, 273. Newburgh, 2: 424, however, seems to indicate that Stephen was seneschal until Richard's return from Germany. A charter of Payn as seneschal depicts him settling a dispute; *Cal. Docs. Fr.*, 385–6, no. 1087, dated 1190.

CHAPTER SIX

Richard's governance of England prior to departure on crusade

While the strategic centre of Richard's inheritance was the Loire valley lands of the counts of Anjou, his financial base lay to the north in England and Normandy. Richard was well aware that within his kingdom of England he possessed powers that he lacked in most of his French possessions, enabling him to raise efficiently revenues for his fighting forces all along his continental 'empire's' long frontiers. Although he had little direct exposure to the Anglo-Norman governmental system, an assumption that his lack of experience with its administrative forms equates to his failure to appreciate or admire its strengths is unjustified.[1] The Lionheart surrounded himself with capable advisers, thoroughly trained in the English administrative system, and he showed confidence in his father's servants by elevating several to positions of power and influence. They were instrumental in ensuring continuity and efficiency in his government, serving as his counsellors, accompanying the royal court and attending the great councils where important decisions were made.

As seen earlier, Richard Lionheart had rewarded his younger brother John, already lord of Ireland, with the county of Mortain in Normandy and with grants of wide lands in England comprising several counties, and scholars have roundly criticised him for his munificence. Having done this, what did the king do to diminish any negative effects that Count John's power might have while he was away crusading? Richard's arrangements required the count to coexist with governments able to protect the absent king's interests. His county of Mortain lay in the west of Normandy, distant

---

1   For this type of criticism, see Bryce Lyon, 'Henry II: A Non-Victorian Interpretation', in J.S. Hamilton and P.J. Bradley (eds), *Documenting the Past: Essays in Medieval History Presented to George Peddy Cuttino* (Woodbridge, 1989), 21–31.

from Capetian territory, and his English shires were surrounded by sheriffs of known loyalty to the crown. William Marshal, one of the associate justiciars, held the shrievalty of Gloucester; and Henry Longchamp, brother of the justiciar, held neighbouring Herefordshire.[2] Within the various honours turned over to John were royal castles that remained in the hands of the government. The Marshal had Gloucester Castle, Roger fitz Reinfrey held Wallingford and the Yorkshire sheriff provisioned Tickhill.[3]

When Count John succeeded in chasing Richard's chancellor and chief justiciar, William Longchamp, out of the country in autumn 1191, he could not prevent Archbishop Walter of Rouen, Richard's representative sent out the previous spring from his Sicilian winter camp, from assuming power as chief justiciar. While John secured the title *rector regni*, it merely put him 'close to the throne . . . , but with no inherent claim on power'.[4] The governments in both Normandy and England steadfastly frustrated and resisted John's advances, pressures and claims.

What if Richard had required that John accompany him on the crusade? This seems on the surface a good alternative to leaving him behind in England with potential for trouble-making, except that it could be argued that taking John to the East would have threatened the Angevin dynasty with extinction. When Richard left England for his crusade at the end of 1189, he was unmarried and childless, but there were two other throne-worthy Plantagenets in his brother John and the son of his deceased brother Geoffrey of Brittany, the child Arthur. It seems unlikely, then, that the king gave serious attention to a threat of Angevin extinction as long as two candidates survived to take up his crown, should he die before fathering a son. Perhaps the larger obstacle to Richard's insisting that John go along on the Third Crusade was the thought of having at his side for so long his brother for whom he had so little respect.[5] Yet Richard's patronage to his brother in the two best governed and wealthiest portions of his empire would have given Count John a strong advantage over young Arthur in the succession stakes, should the king have died on the Third Crusade.[6]

Two final checks that Richard undoubtedly believed would restrict John's power were Eleanor of Aquitaine's influence and John's oath to remain out of England. Neither of these worked as planned. Eleanor, while given no official position in the regency comparable to that of Philip Augustus's

---

2 *PR2RI*, 45, 58.
3 *PR2RI*, 58–9, 159.
4 W. Stubbs, *Historical Introductions to the Rolls Series*, ed. A. Hassall (London, 1902), 448.
5 Gillingham, *Richard*, 136; D. Carpenter, 'Richard by his Contemporaries: Was He a "Model King"? England in 1189', unpublished paper, Colloque aux Archives du Calvados (Caen, April 1999), 15.
6 R.V. Turner, *King John* (London, 1994), 41.

mother in France, none the less was a prominent figure in England and in Richard's counsels. Yet she left England for Navarre in order to deliver the princess Berengaria to her son in Sicily. Tensions had already begun to rise between Count John and William Longchamp when the queen mother returned to England in 1191. From that time on, as Richard had expected, she exerted enough maternal pressure on her youngest son to keep him from joining Philip Augustus in early 1192. In the second instance, at the great council of Nonancourt in Normandy in 1190 Richard had, as an additional precaution, demanded that Count John promise not to return to England for three years. Eleanor was the main instrument in undoing the oath, for her intervention on John's behalf caused Richard to free him from it. This oath, however, remained a problem for John as late as 1193, when recognition of his release from the oath was included in the terms of a treaty that Richard and Philip concluded during the English king's German captivity.[7]

Richard Lionheart took similar precautions with his half-brother, Geoffrey Plantagenet, whom he installed as archbishop of York. He had extracted from Geoffrey, as with Count John, an oath that he would stay out of England for three years, but the king released the archbishop-elect from his oath just prior to sailing for the Levant. Also like John, Geoffrey was positioned in the best governed of Richard's provinces where an administrative apparatus and a powerful justiciar operated. Surrounding Geoffrey were men of known loyalty. The sheriff of Yorkshire was John Marshal, member of the rising Marshal clan, and later Osbert Longchamp, the justiciar's brother.[8] Also Bishop Hugh du Puiset of Durham, originally picked to be co-justiciar during the crusade, controlled County Durham and was strengthened by his recent purchase of the Sadberge wapentake and the earldom of Northumberland in the northern part of Geoffrey's archiepiscopal diocese.[9] Philip Puintel, close associate of William Longchamp, had custody of York Castle, and Newcastle-on-Tyne was held by government men.[10] Furthermore, Richard may have intended to make York Minster a hornet's nest of jealous churchmen by naming his own men to important posts in the cathedral. The raucous history of the archdiocese subsequent to Geoffrey's election clearly shows that these royal appointments were distasteful to the archbishop.[11] Ecclesiastical problems kept Geoffrey distracted and vulnerable to royal pressure.

7   Howden, 3: 32, 217; Landon, 198.
8   *PR2RI*, 58–9.
9   *PR2RI*, 21; Landon, 16.
10 *PR2RI*, 2, 18, 58–9, 75. Hugh du Puiset had Newcastle until it was seized by the justiciar and turned over to Osbert Longchamp.
11 M.B. Lovatt, 'The Career and Administration of Geoffrey Plantagenet, Archbishop of York ?1151–1212', PhD thesis (Cambridge University, 1975), 33, 218; R.V. Turner, 'Richard Lionheart and English Episcopal Elections', *Albion* 29 (1997), 4–5.

Geoffrey's relationship with Richard afforded other means by which to keep him intimidated and subservient. By forcing his half-brother into ordination, Richard had eliminated any hope of secular office for the archbishop, but Geoffrey's temperament meant that the Lionheart had not heard the last of him. He challenged the king on several occasions before Richard left England. Geoffrey objected to Richard's appointments to certain York ecclesiastical posts and attempted to secure his *pallium* from the pope without royal permission. These actions raised the king's temper significantly, requiring the archbishop to contribute £3,000 for the crusade in order to regain his confiscated lands and royal pleasure.[12] Geoffrey's failure to pay his fine and his excommunication of York's treasurer and dean, royal appointees, met with the Lionheart's brief attempt to undo Geoffrey's election. Because of these incidents, the archbishop spent considerable time at court trying to regain favour. Richard's sternness with his bastard brother and his practice of burdening Geoffrey with insurmountable debt helped in two ways. They neutralised this 'prince-archbishop' for much of the reign, and they served notice to all that Richard could be harsh, even with blood-relatives.[13]

Are Richard's actions toward John and Geoffrey the reckless, thoughtless works of a distracted crusader? While it is not possible to enter the Lionheart's mind and discern his motives for acting as he did toward his brothers, he was a ruler with prior experience of treacherous, untrustworthy subjects. Since so much of his career had been spent restoring and preserving peace in Aquitaine, his ability to appreciate the problem may well have been the best of any of the Angevins; as count of Poitou, he knew the ways of the rebel. He also understood that the English administrative system, headed by a powerful justiciar acting in the king's name and buttressed with a staff devoted to royal power, was his best hope of maintaining order while he was far away overseas. Knowing the danger, Richard hedged in his brothers as best he could. Furthermore, his arrangements corresponded with accepted practice as established by the house of Anjou. He had provided for his brothers, John and Geoffrey, at a level due to royalty; and he eventually raised his other brother, William Longsword, to an earldom, albeit a lesser one. In 1189, John and Geoffrey were not over-mighty subjects when compared to the might and resources at the king's disposal; both had the means to contribute to England's stability, but were balanced by sufficient power to prevent disaster. Before making attempts to advance themselves because of their brother's absence, these two would have much to consider.

---

12   Howden, 3: 25–8. *PR2RI*, 74, has Geoffrey owing £2,000; over £1,500 remained at Richard I's death, *PR1J*, 40–1.

13   Lovatt, 'Career and Administration of Geoffrey Plantagenet', 32–3.

But all was not well despite the Lionheart's constructive and promising extra precautions to check his brothers, for recent scholarship on Richard's revenue has brought to light the crippling impact on royal finances of the grants to John and others. The chronicler William of Newburgh describes the kingdom and its wealth after Richard's visit in 1189 as being 'cut up and scattered'.[14] Calculations of the revenue recorded by the exchequer during the early years of Richard's reign point to a catastrophic drop in totals. In Henry II's last full year, 1188, the exchequer gleaned over £21,000 from England; and in 1194, the year that John's counties returned to exchequer supervision, receipts exceeded £25,000. In contrast, the moneys collected by the exchequer between 1191 and 1193 averaged a meagre £11,000 per year. Furthermore, demesne loss as *terrae datae* rose from £3,200 to £4,900. According to Nick Barratt, Richard had reversed his father's lifetime work of restoring royal lands 'virtually overnight'. These losses were compounded by inflation and the extraordinary strains of rebellion, Welsh unrest, a threatened French naval assault, raising the king's ransom and demands of defending Normandy.[15] Richard's ravaging of royal lands and resources in 1189–90 raised the only possible but foreboding scenario: increased taxation on his subjects to fund his numerous conflicts.

Early in Richard's reign, in a gesture designed to secure popular support, Eleanor of Aquitaine implemented his desire that injustices perpetrated at the end of Henry II's reign be reversed. A proclamation, read throughout the English shires prior to the new king's arrival, freed those imprisoned for offences against forest law and those held by word of the late king or his justiciars rather than by lawful procedure. It restored to peace those outlawed under forest law and ordered those misusing the system to depart the land or be jailed. Also it called on all his new subjects to swear homage and fealty to him and promise assistance in the maintenance of order.[16] The proclamation was not a general amnesty that merely emptied the gaols, for the conditions for release were specific and consistent with legal principles and practices. William of Newburgh, however, was disgusted that Richard had unleashed 'these pests' back onto society only to terrorise decent subjects more confidently in the future.[17] Queen Eleanor gloried in it, as she reflected on her own incarceration and the rejuvenating effects of freedom.[18] In her enthusiasm, Eleanor mirrored most closely the reaction of the people.

---

14   Newburgh, 1: 306–7.
15   N. Barratt, 'The English Revenue of Richard I', unpublished paper presented at the Colloque aux Archives du Calvados (Caen, April 1999).
16   *Gesta Regis*, 2: 74–5.
17   Newburgh, 1: 293.
18   *Gesta Regis*, 2: 74.

Richard's arrival in England generated raucous crowds seeking a glimpse of their new sovereign who was already carrying out the promise to give justice that was part of the coronation oath that he would soon take.

In much the same way that the imprisoned were at the king's mercy, so were the Jews. Trouble loomed for them, for Richard's departure for crusade raised the possibility of renewed pogroms against the Jewish community that had accompanied earlier crusades. Their anxiety undoubtedly motivated some of the London Jewish leaders to seek an audience with the king while he banqueted with his barons and bishops. Although Richard had specifically stated that women and Jews were to be excluded from these festivities, the Jewish leaders showed want of wisdom by approaching the banquet hall. A fierce attack on them loosed an ugly episode of anti-Semitism in London, resulting in wanton death and destruction for many in the Jewish community. Richard dispatched Ranulf de Glanvill and an armed contingent to suppress the uprising, but it was beyond their capacity to control. Angry because his celebrations had been sullied and his charges viciously robbed, Richard ordered the perpetrators brought to justice, but to no avail. He instructed the sheriffs of England to prevent all such incidents in the future.

These orders were obeyed while Richard remained in the kingdom, but shortly after his departure, word was received at court that anti-Jewish riots had once again erupted. Townsmen along the eastern coast turned on the Jewish population; some were rescued by flight to royal castles, while others became helpless victims. In York the situation reached its zenith. Urged on by the local nobility, the sheriff and constable, the mob stormed the castle only to find that most of the Jews had committed mass suicide out of sheer fright. This time the king's justice took a greater toll, which William Longchamp exacted in restoring order. The pipe rolls reveal the dispatch of an army to York under command of Longchamp's brother, Henry, removal of the sheriff, the justiciar's personal visitation, confiscation of lands and chattels of those who fled after the assaults, amercement of many and imprisonment of others for whom the justiciar had ordered the purchase of sixty shackles.[19] The financial damage done to the Jews – and ultimately to the king – is seen in the small amounts of money collected from properties of those killed in Norwich and Bury St Edmunds, and the loss in York of all records documenting Jewish loans. After these measures were enacted, violent anti-Semitism did not appear again in England during Richard's reign.

The single most important and potentially destabilising group in the kingdom was the nobility. Although notions of an innate hostility between a

---

19 *PR2RI*, 3, 4, 8, 62, 68–70, 74–5, 116, 134.

monarch and his great men no longer accurately define their relationship, the earls and barons of England had to be considered as Richard planned for his departure on crusade. Collectively this group had enormous wealth and military resources and controlled castles and wide swaths of the English countryside. While many great lords contentedly absented themselves from court and its political manœuvres, preferring to promote their families' landed position, no medieval monarch could disregard with impunity his magnates or mistreat them, for they could mount impressive rebellions as events of 1173 and 1215 clearly demonstrate.

The greatest lay names of England at this time – the earls Ranulf de Blundeville of Chester, William d'Aubigny of Sussex, Hamelin Plantagenet of Surrey, Robert de Beaumont of Leicester and Richard de Clare of Hereford – held lands of between 140 and 200 knights' fees each and numerous castles. Earl Ranulf of Chester's territories were immune to exchequer authority, and he, William d'Aubigny and Robert de Beaumont had extensive Norman holdings as well. Some earls found positions in the king's government, as shown by the earl of Norfolk's judicial record and the shrieval career of the earl of Salisbury. Due to the military threat, lords on the Welsh frontier such as William Marshal, William de Braose and William fitz Alan accumulated unusual power, serving as constables, sheriffs or associate justiciars. Braose and Fitz Alan represent the group of great men who lacked comital title though not power. Men like Robert fitz Walter, Warin fitz Gerold, Humphrey de Bohun, Gervase Paynell, Robert de Gant, Robert de Lacy, Robert de Strafford and Nigel de Mowbray held forty-five or more fees from the king plus some lands held from others. Barons such as Simon de Kyme, one-time sheriff of Lincoln, had few fiefs from the king but many from other lords.

Ecclesiastical lords also counted among the great men of the realm, for they too held lands and castles. In one case, Bishop Hugh of Durham not only exercised spiritual power over large portions of northern England, but was immune from exchequer interference and for a while held the earldom of Northumberland. In general, though, prelates were not of the same stuff as the lay nobility, for most held their posts as rewards for long years of service to the crown. Overall, they were loyal to the monarch and did not represent the political challenge that their lay peers did.

The Angevin interest in preserving a working relationship with the English baronage sprang from the collaboration required to draw out of the kingdom as much wealth as possible. Maintaining this mutually advantageous arrangement had by the late twelfth century become decidedly more difficult. Innovations in governmental structure and practice, reliance on lesser-ranking knights and *curiales*, larger and more frequent financial demands, declining royal dependence on noble martial arts and clashing theories of kingship all elevated tensions between the two sides. Richard appears to have been generally successful in fostering a harmonious relationship between monarchy and nobility, helped undoubtedly by his military reputation and the English governmental machinery which tended to cow his barons. He faced no major noble rebellions in England such as those that had confronted his father and would challenge his brother or that were so frequent in his southern territories. Richard did not hesitate to grant shrievalties and castellanies to earls and barons. To some he granted rights that had long been withheld from them by Henry II, such as custody of the honour of Arundel which William d'Aubigny regained, or full rights over the earldom of Norfolk awarded to Roger Bigod. Richard also wisely added to the ranks of great men by lavish marriages, judicial action and ecclesiastical preferment, as in the celebrated cases of William Marshal, Geoffrey fitz Peter and Godfrey de Lucy. Many of England's great men showed their loyalty to the Lionheart by crossing the Channel to fight in his host in Normandy.

At his coronation Richard had promised to preserve the peace of the Church, a peace that was being disrupted in the early days of his reign. Prelates and their monastic chapters in several English bishoprics had endured strained relationships for a long time, and it now became incumbent on Richard to bring this scandal to a close, especially since a papal legate was *en route* to England with power to impose a permanent settlement. The problem swirled around the authority of the bishops, over chapters that were monastic foundations, and the freedom of their monks, who had enjoyed substantial latitude in their own affairs. Councils had been called, secular colleges of canons had been established at some cathedrals, and violence had erupted as the two sides took matters into their own hands.

Two incidents in October 1189 brought the problem into the limelight: Archbishop Baldwin's nomination of Roger Norreys as prior of Christchurch, Canterbury, without the monks' blessings, and Bishop Hugh de Nonant's expulsion of the monks from Coventry Priory.[20] On 8 November 1189, a delegation of monks was summoned to a meeting of the great council at Westminster to resolve the problem. Little that was constructive could be accomplished initially, but at Canterbury in late November at a final meeting of the great council before Richard left England, the Canterbury monks agreed to allow him to use his own judgment to settle the case if the archbishop would withdraw his appointment of Norreys as prior. This done, the king and his advisers declared that the archbishop did, in fact, have the right to name his own prior and to have a college of secular canons, a decision that was a 'triumph both of Richard's kingly power and of his

---

20   Gervase, 1: 461; Landon, 10–1.

personal tact'.[21] The monks humbly but disingenuously submitted to this decision, quieting the problem only for a time.[22]

Richard also fulfilled his obligations to the church by filling vacancies in bishoprics, abbacies and lesser offices that had been left unfilled during Henry II's last years. At the Council of Pipewell in September 1189, Richard made nominations to these ecclesiastical posts: his half-brother, Geoffrey Plantagenet, to York; his chancellor, William Longchamp, to Ely; and Godfrey de Lucy to Winchester, Richard fitz Neal to London, and Hubert Walter to Salisbury. All these latter three were members of administrative families. Other nominations filled posts in the York chapter, pre-empting the new archbishop's prerogative: Henry Marshal as dean, Bouchard du Puiset as treasurer, William de Chimellé as archdeacon of Richmond, and William de Sainte-Mère-Église as a canon, and also as dean of St Martin's, London. Robert fitz Ralph was named bishop of Worcester; and abbots were also named to Selby, Glastonbury, Sherborne, Pershore, Feversham and Evesham.[23]

Richard's diligence in filling these English religious posts contrasts with his father's tendency to leave them vacant and collect the wealth from attached estates for himself. About to launch an expensive crusade, Richard could easily have continued his father's practices. Whether his motivation was fulfilment of coronation vows or spiritual security, such piety came at significant personal cost. Neither should this be equated to the alienations of royal lands discussed earlier. Kings had long appropriated ecclesiastical lands following episcopal deaths, on shaky grounds that custody of the vacant property was a feudal prerogative, and Richard's work at restoring its possessions was expected and respected. A pattern of filling ecclesiastical vacancies promptly characterised Richard's reign, suggesting Richard's sincere concern about this responsibility. During the 1190s, the average time between an English bishop's death and the elevation of his successor was only seven months. This is all the more remarkable since Richard was far from England most of the time. The king also demonstrated foresight and 'a prudent regard to existing personal and political interests' in his appointments.[24] Hubert Walter, who hoped to acquire the vacant archbishopric of York for himself, and Hugh du Puiset who wanted it for his son, were compensated with Hubert's nomination as Salisbury's bishop and appointment of Puiset's son as York's treasurer, ending their objections to Richard's decision regarding Geoffrey Plantagenet.

21   K. Norgate, *Richard the Lion Heart* (London, 1924), 107.
22   Stubbs, *Historical Introductions*, 406–10.
23   *Gesta Regis*, 2: 85–7; Howden, 3: 15–16; Landon, 7, 18, 22, 35.
24   Stubbs, *Historical Introductions*, 207.

Because a regency capable of functioning effectively during the king's absence was essential, Ranulf de Glanvill's dismissal from the English justiciarship seems, in light of his ability, a surprising move by Richard. Certainly the need for experience and ability was at its height with the king expecting to leave for a long and distant absence. One chronicler states that Richard and Glanvill did not agree on methods of devising a regency, and hence Glanvill resigned.[25] This explains why Ranulf continued to function as justiciar until mid-September 1189. He seemed comfortable enough with his authority to question the king's elevation of Geoffrey Plantagenet to the archbishopric of York.[26] In addition, he had taken the cross, a good excuse for covering any potentially embarrassing reasons for stepping aside.[27]

Another chronicler writes that the king hounded Glanvill and his associates out of office.[28] A third adds more to the story, alleging that Glanvill was imprisoned and fined £15,000 for taking advantage of the late king's trust or for misbehaviour in office.[29] Though not stated, the latter charge could have included complicity with Queen Eleanor's confinement, rapacity as justiciar and sheriff, or inability to quell the anti-Semitic riots that marred the coronation feast. Glanvill's ability to finance a trip to the Holy Land suggests that the fine has been exaggerated, although pipe roll entries show the former justiciar's agents and relatives offering large fines to recover royal favour. Their size shows that Glanvill and his clan had taken care to exploit their positions.[30] Lastly, Richard, considering the attitude of his English subjects toward the old king's servants, may have ousted Ranulf as a means of showing them that a new era of justice had arrived, recalling his great-grandfather Henry I's treatment of the hated justiciar of his predecessor.[31] That Richard used Ranulf de Glanvill in this way explains why he joined the king on crusade; he saw it as a bargaining chip for regaining royal favour.

At Pipewell Abbey in September 1189, Richard and his advisers set out to establish a regency to govern England while he went on crusade. To the office of chief justiciar, two men were named, Bishop Hugh du Puiset of Durham and William de Mandeville, earl of Essex. With these men of social

---

25 Newburgh, 1: 302–3.
26 Gervase, 1: 457.
27 Howden, 2: 302, 3: 16; *Gesta Regis*, 2: 79, 83, 87.
28 *Gesta Regis*, 2: 90–1.
29 Devizes, 5; also Norgate, *Richard*, 103.
30 *PR2RI*, 67–8, 101, 111; *Gesta Regis*, 2: 74–5. The pipe rolls fail to record a fine by Glanvill, although he knew of Angevin willingness to accept promises and their tolerance of delinquent payments; see T.K. Keefe, 'Proffers for Heirs and Heiresses in the Pipe Rolls: Some Observations on Indebtedness in the Years Before the Magna Carta (1180–1212)', *HSJ* 5 (1993), 99–109.
31 F. Barlow, *The Feudal Kingdom of England 1042–1216*, 4th edn (London, 1988), 171.

distinction but of little administrative knowledge were affiliated *appares*, associate justiciars, to assist in the daily routine of governance, aspects of rule for which Puiset and Mandeville likely had little knowledge or disposition. Those named to be *appares* were William Marshal, Geoffrey fitz Peter, William Briwerre, Roger fitz Reinfrey and Robert of Wheatfield, all with the exception of the Marshal experienced in the Henrician system as justices, sheriffs or foresters. Though it was not stated whether one of the co-justiciars was to act as senior member, Puiset's biographer suggests that priority was given to the bishop.[32]

In his book on the English justiciarship, Francis J. West describes the new arrangement as a 'superficial' break from the past, designed to handle the king's long periods of isolation from England's affairs. It could have been seen by Richard as experimental, given the context of crusade and his lack of experience with this form of governance.[33] Infusions into Poitou of English money for mercenaries had earlier acquainted Richard with the wonders of the Henrician system. Now surrounded by English *curiales* as he toured his new kingdom, the king undoubtedly heard it touted by these who had made it work, and he saw its effectiveness in the 100,000 marks found in the English treasury.[34] Regardless of the wisdom of his action, it appears prudent to state merely that Richard consciously chose not to follow precisely the pattern of governance applied by his father in his last years.

Richard I's initial plans for the justiciarship reflect both his experience in Aquitaine and his appreciation of the English administrative system. Historians have noted that the new king had learned his politics in an unruly duchy, where divisions of authority and balance-of-power schemes proved the best means of keeping peace.[35] Illustrative of this thinking is his choice of Puiset, a northern, ecclesiastical magnate, and Essex, a southern, lay magnate. Apparently, politics and administration were to be 'divorced' with associate justiciars or *appares* entrusted with the technical details of daily governance while the two justiciars were to treat great matters of state.[36] Richard's attachment of the *appares* to his regency aimed at stability, for justice and finance would remain in competent hands, though under baronial supervision. Furthermore, the king took care to elevate certain of the *appares* to new social respectability. William Marshal's good fortune has been discussed, but by the time Richard had completed adjustments of the

---

32 G.V. Scammell, *Hugh du Puiset, Bishop of Durham* (Cambridge, 1956), 50.

33 F.J. West, *The Justiciarship in England, 1066–1232* (Cambridge, 1966), 65–6.

34 Howden, 3: 8.

35 Gillingham, *Richard*, 138; Barlow, *Feudal Kingdom*, 351; F.M. Powicke, 'England: Richard I and John', in *Cambridge Medieval History*, 6: 208.

36 West, *Justiciarship*, 66.

regency, he had sold Geoffrey fitz Peter the right to succeed to the earldom of Essex.[37] In the words of the Marshal's most recent biographer, these royal grants conferred on these two 'enough land to give [them] dignity before the other magnates, whom it was [their] duty now to help to control'.[38] Richard's experiment combined the system that he knew with the system that he was learning.

This plan was never fully implemented because one of the co-justiciars, Earl William de Mandeville, died unexpectedly in Rouen before the king left England. At first Richard allowed the vacancy to go unfilled, but added his trusted chancellor and new bishop of Ely, William Longchamp, to the group of *appares* associated with the Bishop of Durham. Gradual intrusion of the chancellor into the surviving justiciar's inner circle indicates some anxiety on Richard's part. An additional sign that the king was looking for substantial alteration in Hugh du Puiset's post of chief justiciar appeared when he gave the Tower of London to the chancellor, who already had custody of the royal seal.[39] With these actions, a power shift toward Longchamp was signalling that the king aimed to restore to the justiciarship some of its administrative focus. It had become apparent that the chief regent's actual power came from control of the administration, and that separating the two left Puiset with high honour but little real authority.[40] Because medieval government was 'a gigantic shakedown', the chief justiciar had to have direct authority over the judicial bench and the exchequer, the means of predation, in order to raise revenues that the monarch required.

Change occurred in March 1190 at a council in Normandy to which Richard had summoned several bishops, his mother and brothers, and Alix, his betrothed.[41] Having taken counsel with this group, including the bishop of Durham, Richard formally elevated Longchamp to *summus justitiarius*, chief justiciar. Bishop Hugh retained a truncated authority over the region from the Humber River on northward, the area of England where his titles as bishop of Durham and earl of Northumberland already gave him vast influence. The *appares* for the second arrangement were Geoffrey fitz Peter, William Marshal, William Briwerre and Hugh Bardolf. By limiting Hugh du Puiset's authority to the extreme north, Richard had given Longchamp the excuse to exclude him from Westminster, by this time the centre of

---

37 *PR2RI*, 111.

38 D. Crouch, *William Marshal: Court, Career, and Chivalry in the Angevin Empire, 1147–1219* (London, 1990), 69.

39 *Gesta Regis*, 2: 101; J.T. Appleby, *England Without Richard 1189–1199* (Ithaca, NY, 1965), 24.

40 West, *Justiciarship*, 68.

41 *Gesta Regis*, 2: 101; Howden, 3: 28; Landon, 26. The issue of Richard's marriage may also have been discussed, as Gillingham has postulated, hence the strong family element and Alix's presence; 'Richard I and Berengaria of Navarre', *BIHR* 53 (1980), 160–2.

English administration, even though Puiset still had the title of justiciar. While Longchamp may have interpreted Richard's commission narrowly in certain circumstances, he saw his authority extending over the North, for example, ousting the Yorkshire sheriff and sending troops to punish the York anti-Semites. Finally in June 1190, from southern Aquitaine, Richard declared Longchamp chief justiciar of all England, the same day that news arrived that the pope had conferred on him legatine authority over the island kingdom. With such power, 'the laity found [Longchamp] more than a king, the clergy more than a pope, and both an intolerable tyrant'.[42]

Chroniclers have given historians of medieval England sources not enjoyed by continental scholars. For instance, while Richard's appointments to the higher offices that he established for his continental provinces are known, only in England do documents survive recording changes at lower levels of government, notably sheriffs, the government's most important local officials in the crucial work of raising money and securing the kingdom. These royal officers had far-ranging duties in the shire covering justice, law enforcement, defence and revenue collection. Debts recorded in the pipe rolls show them energetically sought, often at great cost, for Richard regarded sheriffs' offices as resources to be sold. Sweeping alterations of personnel were made in 1189, resulting in all but five of the sitting sheriffs, including Geoffrey fitz Peter, William Briwerre, Hugh Bardolf and Ranulf de Glanvill, being dismissed or reassigned. Six shrievalties fell away from the exchequer's jurisdiction as the king gave several shires to Count John and one to Bishop Hugh of Durham as palatine grants.[43]

Richard I was personally involved in appointments of sheriffs. Henry de Cornhill's appointment to Surrey was secured by royal charter. Gerard de Camville, through royal charter, obtained the constableship of Lincoln Castle and confirmation of his wife's landed inheritance.[44] While Camville's charter neglects to mention his appointment to the Lincolnshire shrievalty, his

---

42 A.L. Poole, *From Domesday Book to Magna Carta*, 2nd edn (Oxford, 1955), 354, quote from Newburgh, 4: 14.

43 *PR2RI*, 10, 14, 24, 26, 29, 31, 37, 43, 45, 49, 58, 89, 91, 103, 111, 116, 117, 122, 126, 127, 138, 152, 155; *List of Sheriffs for England and Wales: From Earliest Times to A.D. 1831*, Public Record Office Lists and Indexes, 9 (1898; rpt New York, 1963), 72. John received Cornwall/Devon, Lancashire, Nottinghamshire/Derby, and Somerset/Dorset, and Bishop Hugh, Northumberland. How Bishop Hugh governed Northumberland is not known, but evidence suggests that John placed his own men over his shires; R.R. Heiser, 'The Sheriffs of Richard the Lionheart: A Prosopographical Survey of Appointments, Politics, and Patronage, 1189–1199', PhD dissertation (Florida State University, 1993), 240–1.

44 J.C. Holt and R. Mortimer (eds), *Acta of Henry II and Richard I: Hand-list of Documents Surviving in . . . the United Kingdom*, List and Index Society, 21 (Gateshead, 1986), no. 315, 331; J. Hunter (ed.), *The Great Roll of the Pipe for the First Year of the Reign of King Richard the First*, Record Commission (London, 1844), 216; Landon, 2.

700-mark fine was for appointment to the two offices of constable and sheriff.[45] Another indicator that royal participation in shrieval appointments was substantial is found in the pipe rolls. Fines for purchase of sheriffs' offices appear in the pipe roll of 1189–90 under the headings *placita et conventiones* that do not bear the names of regency officials, indicating that they were heard by the king himself. Indeed, J.C. Holt, looking at distribution of patronage in 1189, sees a 'single unique effort' with the king as the driving force.[46]

Royal involvement in shrieval appointments can be inferred from other evidence. For instance, Gerard de Camville's presence at Richard's court undoubtedly worked to his advantage in the rush to acquire privilege and position in the new regime. Generalising from this instance to royal appointments as a whole strongly intimates that those close companions of the new king who were granted shrievalties in 1189 – William Marshal, for instance – received them from the king's own hand. The same principle would pertain to officials of the court, such as the chamberlain William Mauduit.[47] Furthermore, if Richard had delegated to members of the regency council responsibility of filling the shrieval offices, why would they have not taken such lucrative posts for themselves? Geoffrey fitz Peter, William Briwerre and Hugh Bardolf, all three of whom were associate justiciars, came into shrievalties only after the king had departed for crusade once William Longchamp asserted his ascendancy.[48] Finally, the king's military mind would have realised the sheriffs' importance for defence as constables of the shire and custodians of royal castles. Whether Richard had filled every shrieval office before leaving for the Holy Land cannot be known, but it is apparent that he had a high level of interest and involvement in appointments of sheriffs in 1189.

Historians have long identified the office of sheriff as a critical point of contact between local and central government and *curiales* as the link, but a prosopographical survey of Richard's sheriffs and constables shows that he himself did not extensively employ royal intimates in the shrievalties. In 1189 there were only six curial sheriffs. Thus some credence is given to assumptions that posts went to the 'highest bidder', with the king caring little for the buyer's ability, only for his money. Another look at the evidence shows, however, that prudence and foresight characterised Richard's placement of sheriffs, not carelessness and recklessness. Those *curiales* appointed by Richard were positioned strategically – for instance, John and William Marshal,

---

45 *PR2RI*, 89.
46 J.C. Holt, 'Ricardus Rex Anglorum et Dux Normannorum', in *Magna Carta and Medieval Government* (London, 1985), 73.
47 *PR2RI*, 35, 37, 52, 58. Others frequenting the royal court who received shrievalties in 1189 include Bishop Hugh of Coventry and John Marshal.
48 Heiser, 'Sheriffs of Richard I the Lionheart', 113–16.

who held Yorkshire and Gloucestershire respectively, counties where the king's two untrustworthy brothers held their principal lands. Henry de Cornhill and Oger fitz Oger, longstanding civil servants, sat in shrievalties of above-average significance. Cornhill held counties of Surrey and Kent near medieval England's capital city, the Tower of London and Dover Castle on the Kentish coast. Oger fitz Oger's Hampshire shrievalty contained the old administrative centre of Winchester and important coastal castles and ports, such as Southampton and Porchester, essential embarkation points for supplies headed for the continent.

The majority of shires remained, none the less, in the hands of men of local stature and significance. Established in 1189 and held to steadfastly, this practice was basic to Richard's shrieval appointments; even the shrievalties of magnates and some curial servants lay in regions where they exercised significant influence as local or regional landholders. Two points about the king's employment of people of local stature and prominence as sheriffs deserve mention. First, they were subject to the exchequer's management, for sheriffs with limited influence at court tended to be less obstinate toward its demands.[49] Such sheriffs were not weak, however, because they were usually men of distinction and wealth in their home shires. In this way, the central government succeeded in maintaining local strength for sheriffs, but without their counter-productive leverage at the royal court. Second, the king's reliance on local notables was a prudent fiscal action. Money was a major problem for the Lionheart, and he was trapped by the sheriff's fixed farm, which prevented his tapping fully the country's real wealth.[50] Hence, to tap elusive money sources in the shires, Richard imposed entrance fines or gifts and increments; and to state it bluntly, he could extract more from sheriffs whose importance was localised.

Constables of royal castles, like sheriffs, were significant figures in late twelfth-century English political life, as evidenced by William of Newburgh's observation that castles were the 'bones of the kingdom'.[51] Obviously, the daily affairs of a constable/custodian depended on whether he was also sheriff, in which case most of his time was spent fulfilling those functions. Keeping the castle provisioned in a state of readiness and commanding its garrison numbered among the constable/custodian's urgent military responsibilities. Yet few English constables experienced war, and in peacetime, raising revenue from the shire farms and from the treasury for needed repair work consumed much of their energy.

---

49   D. Carpenter, 'The Decline of the Curial Sheriff 1194–1285', *EHR* 91 (1976), 1–7.
50   B.E. Harris, 'King John and Sheriffs' Farms', *EHR* 79 (1964), 532–3; P.D.A. Harvey, 'The English Inflation of 1180–1220', *Past and Present* 61 (1973), 3–12, 15.
51   Newburgh, 1: 331.

Although the chief purpose of castles was military, they fulfilled other functions; St Briavel's in Gloucestershire, for example, developed into a manufacturing centre for crossbow bolts. Some were also preferred royal residences, such as Winchester and Northampton. In many shires, if not most, a royal castle was the sheriff's seat; and from that stronghold, the sheriff executed royal writs, administered justice, incarcerated criminals, collected revenues and stored treasure. The fortresses of the Peak in Derbyshire and St Briavel's were administrative centres for the royal forests in which they sat.[52] Although the posts of constable and forester were not necessarily linked, a royal castle most likely was the centre for forest administration. Early in Richard's reign, William de Beauchamp was sheriff and constable of Worcester and forester of Feckenham.

Approximately half of England's royal castles were held by sheriffs; constable/custodians for the remaining ones were appointed by the king or his justiciar, the commissions of which rarely survive unless monetary considerations were attached. Only a few were hereditary, and the king's advantage in keeping control by avoiding hereditary constableships is obvious. Hereditary claims existed, none the less, such as the two Beauchamp families' claims to Worcester and to Bedford Castles, the Fitz Rualdi post at Richmond Castle, Henry de Oilli's rights to Oxford Castle, and Gerard de Camville's claim to Lincoln's constableship by his marriage to Nichola de la Haye.[53] The archbishops of Canterbury had held custody of Rochester Castle continuously since the time of Henry I.

Like sheriffs, constables in the early 1190s were of utmost significance to the royal government's success in the shires; but unlike sheriffs, who had to account semi-annually at the exchequer, the constable/custodians surface in the records only when receiving payments or reporting expenses. Constables of some castles are never mentioned in the rolls, but other sources fill in gaps, supplying some names. For instance, Matthew de Cleres, constable of Dover and brother-in-law of Longchamp, whose actions against the arch-bishop of York precipitated the chancellor's downfall, is known through chronicle accounts.[54]

A prosopographical study of constable/custodians from Richard's early years reveals that the majority who can be identified were either of baronial or curial stature, indicating the significance of this post. The list includes

---

52 C. Young, *The Royal Forests of Medieval England* (Philadelphia, 1976), 51–3; H.M. Colvin (ed.), *The History of King's Works*, 2 vols (London, 1963), 2: 616–17, 776, 821.

53 Colvin, *History of King's Works*, 2: 558, 771–2, 888; N.J.G. Pounds, *The Medieval Castle in England and Wales: A Social and Political History* (Cambridge, 1990), 78, 96; S. Painter, *The Reign of King John* (Baltimore, 1949), 70; J.H. Round (ed.), *Ancient Charters*, PRS, 10 (1888), 91.

54 Gerald of Wales, 4: 387–93.

such barons as Simon de Beauchamp, William de Braose, Robert fitz Roger and Hugh de Say, as well as familiar curial names such as William Marshal, Geoffrey fitz Peter, William Mauduit, Hugh Bardolf and William Briwerre.[55] Those of knightly rank often had curial or baronial connections, men such as Simon de Pattishall, Richard of the Peak, Matthew de Cleres and Osbert Longchamp.[56] Three were clerics: Bishop Hugh du Puiset of Durham, Bishop Hugh de Nonant of Coventry, and, of course, Bishop William Longchamp of Ely.[57]

The king evidently was not stationing his close confidants in the castles. Charters show that those with high attestation rates for Richard's earliest royal *acta* were not typically custodians of castles. By and large, the constables appointed by the king were unknown to him; he did not fill the castellanies with his household members, at least at this point in the reign, although a few exceptions are noteworthy, notably William Marshal and the bishops of Coventry and Durham. This was a pattern seen also in his appointments to shrievalties and one that Longchamp was to alter, as will be seen.

Perhaps the most distinctive characteristic of Richard's appointees as castellans is the number who proffered money for the post. Nine of the nineteen constable/custodians known to have been royal appointees paid for their posts, often in conjunction with a shrievalty, such as William Marshal's offer of 50 marks for Gloucestershire's shrievalty and castle or Gerard de Camville's 700 marks for Lincoln Castle and shrievalty. Other acquisitions of castles along with the purchase of a shrievalty were not explicitly mentioned; offerings by Bishop Hugh of Coventry and William de Beauchamp are examples. Still others sought a castle by hereditary right, for example, a proffer of £100 for Bedford Castle by Simon de Beauchamp. William Mauduit presented the king with a similar sum for Rockingham Castle and surrounding lands; and Alan fitz Ruald promised 200 marks for the constable-ship of Richmond Castle in Yorkshire.[58] The Lionheart seems to have respected hereditary rights to castles, especially if money was attached to a request for confirmation.

As has been seen, when Richard became king in 1189, with few exceptions, he turned out the Henrician sheriffs and installed new ones. Indications are that constables were ousted as well. For instance, the Glanvill/Valognes

55 Barons, *PR2RI*, 48, 144; *PR3/4RI*, 29, 34, 78, 81; curialists, *PR2RI*, 36, 37, 58; *PR3/4RI*, 24, 92.
56 *PR2RI*, 2, 18, 26; *PR3/4RI*, 29; R.V. Turner, 'Simon of Pattishall, Northamptonshire Man, Early Common Law Judge', *Northamptonshire Past and Present* 6 (1978), 5–14; Gerald of Wales, 4: 387–93; Doris M. Stenton (ed.), *Pleas before the King or his Justices*, vol. 3, Selden Society, vol. 83 (London, 1967), lxi, cxxxvi–cxxxviii; Appleby, *England without Richard*, 47–72.
57 *PR2RI*, 2, 15, 18, 37, 44; *PR3/4RI*, 61, 275.
58 *PR2RI*, 24, 36, 37, 44, 58, 66, 89, 144.

families suffered loss of office, including custodies of Dover and Appleby castles and Newcastle-on-Tyne.[59] At least one curial sheriff was removed, for on Hugh Bardolf's expulsion from Wiltshire and custody of Salisbury Castle, the new constable was Robert de Tresgoz.[60] Other examples are lacking, but it can be assumed that purchase of a particular castle resulted in an unidentified previous holder's removal. This was the case for William Marshal and Gerard de Camville. There was some continuity in the castellanies, especially for those with hereditary claims, for William fitz Aldelin, William de Beauchamp, Simon de Beauchamp, Ralph fitz Guy Extraneus, Turstin fitz Simon and Henry de Oilli all retained their positions.[61]

Richard's roster of constables, as with the shrievalties, consisted typically of men of local stature not frequently found at court. Rarely were constables imposed on a locality, for even the few curial constables fit the pattern of men possessing local significance taking custody of nearby royal castles. Bishop Hugh of Coventry at Montsorrel and Kenilworth castles, Simon de Pattishall at Northampton Castle, William de Braose at certain Welsh castles, Gilbert de Lacy at Scarborough, William de Beauchamp at Worcester and Ralph fitz Guy Extraneus at Church Stretton Castle on Shropshire's Welsh frontier provide examples.[62] Only three of nineteen royal appointees are exceptions to this rule, and they are Bishop Hugh of Durham at Windsor Castle, Robert de Tresgoz at Salisbury Castle and Roger fitz Reinfrey at Wallingford Castle in Berkshire. Even Roger, though not known to have had family connections in the Berkshire area, was known to that community, having held Windsor Castle since the early 1170s and having served there as Henry II's sheriff since 1186.[63] Since castles were key installations for dominating the countryside, the great men of the realm wholeheartedly approved of the king's practice of naming local notables.[64] Furthermore, the investment opportunities that castles represented could only have added to the barons' delight, even though they contracted large debts in the process of purchasing custodies. Baronial names in significant numbers on the roll of constables underscore this.

59 Colvin, *History of King's Works*, 2: 553; *PR1RI*, 232, 240; Richard Mortimer, 'The Family of Rannulf de Glanville', *BIHR* 54 (1981), 4–8.
60 *PR1RI*, 171; *PR2RI*, 117.
61 Pounds, *Medieval Castle*, 78, 96; Colvin, *History of King's Works*, 2: 558, 771–2, 888; *PR2RI*, 45, 124, 144; *PR3/4RI*, 195.
62 Colvin, *History of King's Works*, 2: 583, 888; *PR2RI*, 26, 37, 48, 112, 124.
63 R.V. Turner, *The English Judiciary from Glanvill to Bracton c. 1176–1239* (Cambridge, 1985), 42; *List of Sheriffs*, 6.
64 Matthew Strickland, *War and Chivalry: The Conduct and Perception of War in England and Normandy 1066–1217* (Cambridge, 1996), 204; Stephen Morillo, *Warfare under the Anglo-Norman Kings 1066–1135* (Woodbridge, 1994), 96–7.

While Richard's disruptions in such important posts as sheriff and constable have drawn criticism, three explanations justify his changes of shrieval and castellan personnel: royal right, revenue and rebellion. For these causes, he cannot be criticised. First, Richard handled these local officials in a manner consistent with contemporary practice. As appointed officials, sheriffs and constables held office only during the king's pleasure; for him to depose the shrieval and castellan staff was entirely within his royal prerogative. His sale of offices has often been used to illustrate the depths to which he stooped to wring money out of England, and chroniclers exhibited chagrin that '[the king] put everything up for sale'. Even Richard's champion, Richard of Devizes, warned buyers that they were getting bad deals, and William of Newburgh considered such profit-seeking a sign of bad governance.[65] But the practice was not unique to Richard since medieval monarchs, confusing private and public sectors, viewed government offices as their property to be auctioned off as they pleased. To be sure, what appeared to chroniclers' eyes as auction of offices was viewed by the buyers as opportunities to be seized, not vices to be denounced.[66]

For Richard to replace his local officials was legitimate and wise. Because of their administrative, legal and military importance, their loyalty had to be assured. Moving royal servants from place to place or in and out of office had long been a means of control. Henry I's sheriffs had been 'shuffled constantly', a tactic admired as progressive, and Henry II had removed several sheriffs during and after the rebellion of 1173–74. Richard's contemporary, Philip Augustus of France, also made frequent rotation an important element in the new office of *bailli*.[67] With few exceptions, Richard's appointees remained faithful to him, even though the king was distant or captured and threatened by usurpers.

Abundant evidence of Richard's sale of shrievalties and castellanies points to procurement of cash as one of the purposes for his visit to his new kingdom. Money was a major problem, not only for Richard's voyage to the Holy Land, but also for his 24,000-mark debt to Philip Augustus, and for generous gifts bestowed on his mother, his brother and other favourites. Although Henry II allegedly left a full treasury, normal income generated by royal estates, feudal incidents and profits of justice was no longer sufficient, especially due to recent depletions of royal lands by grants to Count John

---

65 *Gesta Regis*, 2: 90–1; Devizes, 5–6, 9; Newburgh, 1: 306–7.
66 Gillingham, *Richard*, 134; Holt, 'Ricardus Rex', 73–4, 82; Carpenter, 'Richard by his Contemporaries', 2–8.
67 C.W. Hollister and J.W. Baldwin, 'The Rise of Administrative Kingship: Henry I and Philip Augustus', *AHR* 83 (1978), 885; *List of Sheriffs*, 21, 26, 34, 59, 67, 72, 78, 92, 150, 157; Baldwin, 132–3.

and others. Inflation in late twelfth- and early thirteenth-century England was making Richard's fiscal woes all the greater as prices doubled and possibly trebled between 1180 and 1220. Furthermore, whereas English lords made profitable adjustments in their economic relationships with their tenants, the king's income from his estates was part of the sheriff's fixed farm, hampering any rapid increase in his revenues.[68] Finding new sources of income was a necessity for Richard Lionheart.

Both contemporary chroniclers and modern scholars conclude that during Richard's four months in the kingdom he 'engaged in a deliberately exploitative sale of office and privilege'.[69] At least, this policy tapped the deepest wells, sparing the lower ranks of his subjects from imposition of a general tax, but magnates must have resented having to pay for lands that they considered rightfully theirs. Geoffrey de Say offered the staggering sum of 7,000 marks for succession to the vast Mandeville honour late in 1189, following the death of his cousin, the earl of Essex. Such a large fine was necessary because he had a rival claimant to the earldom, a niece who was married to Geoffrey fitz Peter, one of Richard's *appares*. Another large fine was 1,000 marks offered by the newly named bishop of Winchester, Godfrey de Lucy, for his own inheritance plus £3,000 for two manors claimed as estates belonging to his new bishopric.[70] Most common were sales of offices. Aside from numerous examples of sheriffs and constables purchasing offices, Hugh du Puiset, bishop of Durham, offered 2,000 marks for Northumberland and another 1,000 marks for appointment as justiciar and release from his crusading vow.[71] In addition, Richard added to his war chest by forcing royal servants accused of maladministration to offer large sums to regain his favour. Most notable is the fine of his father's justiciar, Ranulf de Glanvill, who, according to one chronicler, was imprisoned and forced to cough up £15,000.[72] The effect of all this is the raising of an enormous sum of money, not through the shire farm but rather drawing deeply from other sources of income such as justice, feudal incidents and forests. Figures for the exchequer year 1190 show the king pulling more money out of England than at any other time of the reign – over £31,000, a total that Henry II never attained and that John would match only once.[73]

---

68 S.K. Mitchell, *Studies in Taxation under John and Henry III* (New Haven, CT, 1914), 2; Harris, 'King John and Sheriffs' Farms', 532–3; Harvey, 'English Inflation', 3–12, 15.
69 Quotation, *PR2RI*, xxi.
70 R.V. Turner, 'The Mandeville Inheritance, 1189–1236: Its Legal, Political and Social Context', *HSJ* 1 (1989), 148–72. For Godfrey de Lucy, *PR1RI*, 182, 186; Devizes, 8–9.
71 *PR2RI*, 21; *PR2RI*, 89; Howden, 3: 16; Newburgh, 1: 304–5.
72 Devizes, 5.
73 Barratt, 'English Revenue of Richard I', Tables 1–4.

On his first visit to England, Richard Lionheart had to see to defence of the kingdom's frontiers, although its insular geography rendered threats from its Celtic neighbors to the West and North far less menacing than threats on the borders of Richard's French teritories. Even so, the Welsh revolted even before Richard had set foot on English soil.[74] He dispatched emissaries to Wales, put the feudal host under the command of Count John, who was assisted by William Longchamp, and levied a scutage for an expedition; but the Welsh capitulated without serious resistance. Indeed, it is believed that most of the money raised by the scutage was spent on crusade preparations. Certain Welsh leaders met the king at Worcester in late September and promised to maintain peace while the king was on crusade.[75] When Rhys ap Gruffudd, leader of the Welsh forces, journeyed to Oxford to make his formal submission, the king did not deign to meet with him.[76] This humiliation gave Lord Rhys excuse to continue to cause problems, but Richard did not leave the regency to the schemes of the Welsh prince. His appointments to shrievalties in the western marches demonstrate a realisation of the need for powerful men with known loyalty and immediate access to resources. William Marshal, Henry Longchamp, William fitz Alan and William de Beauchamp were such men. Richard enabled another great marcher lord, William de Braose, to ready the Welsh castles of Carmarthen, Swansea and Llawhaden, by pardoning him £527 of an oblation of 1,000 marks.[77] By these decisions, the Lionheart had erected the machinery needed to contain the Welsh.

Scotland presented a greater threat than the Welsh, as evidenced by the grave danger that Henry II had faced when the Scottish king, William (I) the Lion, joined the rebellion of 1173–74. Following William's surprise capture by English forces at Alnwick, Henry had extracted a heavy price for the Scottish king's participation in the revolt. By terms of the Treaty of Falaise, William gave liege homage for Scotland and all lands held by the Scottish crown, lords and prelates of Scotland became Henry II's tenants-in-chief, such crucial castles as Edinburgh, Stirling and Berwick were garrisoned by English troops at the Scottish king's expense, and William performed a public ceremony of submission at York before gaining his release. While Henry II squeezed William hard in the treaty, its actual working out was relatively painless, and the relationship between the two monarchs later improved dramatically.[78]

---

74 J. Gillingham, 'Henry II, Richard I and the Lord Rhys', *Peritia* 10 (1996), 231–2; Gervase, 1: 457.
75 Gillingham, 'Henry II, Richard I and Lord Rhys', 231–3; *PR2RI*, xxii; Norgate, *Richard*, 106; Appleby, *England Without Richard*, 25.
76 *Gesta Regis*, 2: 88, 97; Howden, 3: 23; Devizes, 7.
77 *PR2RI*, 48.
78 W.L. Warren, *Henry II* (Berkeley and Los Angeles, CA, 1987), 132–4, 186.

Nevertheless, Richard had no guarantees that William would remain on good terms with him. In November 1189 William and his brother David travelled to Canterbury for an audience with the new king. A treaty was negotiated there that pleased both parties, that captured William's loyalty to Richard, and that has been described as 'the wisest and most statesmanlike' of Richard's pre-crusade actions.[79] In exchange for 10,000 marks, Richard cancelled the obligations required by Henry II, released the Scottish earls and bishops from their liege homage to him, restored confiscated castles and affirmed customs, grants and English landholdings.[80] At a later date, Richard granted the earldom of Huntingdon to William the Lion's brother, David.[81]

The advantages afforded to Richard by his treaty with William the Lion were substantial, as the results indicate. The Scottish king supported Richard's declaration of Arthur as his heir and later refused to join John's attempt to seize the English throne or to allow him to recruit Scottish mercenaries. Richard and William journeyed extensively together in 1194 after the English king's release from captivity, and they talked of a possible marriage between William's daughter and Richard's nephew, Otto of Saxony. Richard even issued a charter detailing proper protocol to be shown to the king of Scotland while he accompanied the English royal court. Also, a large sum of money was delivered to Richard which he otherwise would have had no reason to expect. Earlier, William had asked Henry II to withdraw English garrisons from his castles in exchange for a 4,000-mark payment; but the Scottish nobility refused to go along, and the proposal fell flat.[82] According to Henry's biographer, '[The Treaty of Falaise] was the ransom price for William the Lion's release from captivity; in selling it back to him all that Richard did was realise the asset.'[83] Finally, Richard's treaty with William preserved the English crown's claims to lordship over Scotland without the harsh, alienating and precise terminology found in Henry's settlement; indeed it was 'a formula capable of double interpretation', acceptable to both parties.[84]

Historians' accusations that the Lionheart had undermined his father's firm and orderly government are unfounded for the most part. Internal discontent was pacified by justice for those abused in the previous regime, peace along

---

79 Appleby, *England Without Richard*, 33.
80 *Gesta Regis*, 2: 98; Landon, 21.
81 Landon, 35; an estate was based on the Fotheringay barony with a strong castle and enjoyed exemption from scutage; I.J. Sanders, *English Baronies: A Study of Their Origin and Descent 1086–1327* (Oxford, 1960), 118; Painter, *The Reign of King John*, 22.
82 Howden, 3: 242–5, 247–50, 298–9, 308; Warren, *Henry II*, 186; Norgate, *Richard*, 108.
83 Warren, *Henry II*, 187.
84 Norgate, *Richard*, 111.

England's northern frontiers was uncompromised for the whole of Richard's reign, and the English Church was strengthened by filling ecclesiastical vacancies and by restoring peace between prelates and monks. Royal relatives were accommodated according to contemporary practice, while loyal and capable men were entrusted with authority to guard the interests of the crusader-king until he returned from his crusading mission.

That being so, were there glitches? Richard had alienated valuable demesne lands both to John and other deep-pocketed subjects, seriously jeopardising the government's abilities to generate income the easier, old-fashioned way: from the king's own. And what of the arrangements for the regency, especially the choice of Longchamp as chief justiciar? The chroniclers tended not to be impressed, but the accuracy of their opinions must await later discussion.

CHAPTER SEVEN

The government of England during the Third Crusade and German captivity

Richard Lionheart's departure for the Third Crusade in 1190 presented England with arguably its greatest challenge at any time during the Angevin period. Earlier kings had left the island kingdom under the authority of regents and justiciars, but they had never put such distance between themselves and their thrones as Richard would with his journey to the Holy Land. For months that stretched into years the monarch of England would be beyond the sea, out of reach of effective communication, with little ability to exert leadership over his realm. It is not surprising that the most tumultuous years of the Lionheart's reign were those when he was crusading or languishing in captivity, episodes that posed tremendous challenges to his English regencies, led first by William Longchamp and then by Walter of Coutances, archbishop of Rouen. England, only one province in the larger Angevin empire, was affected throughout this period by events on the Continent. The absence of Philip Augustus on crusade with Richard resulted in fewer continental distractions during Longchamp's justiciarship, but with the French monarch's return to France in 1191, rocks thrown into the Angevin pond by the Capetian soon made waves in England.

William Longchamp, the former ducal chancellor elevated to royal chancellor and bishop of Ely, had been elevated by the king to co-justiciar and finally promoted to chief justiciar, when in June 1190 Richard ordered all to obey him. About the same time, word was received that the pope had made the bishop of Ely his legate for the British isles in the absence of the archbishop of Canterbury on crusade. William exercised unparalleled power, and he 'forged his spiritual and secular authority into a formidable two-edged sword'.[1]

---

1   Devizes, 13, says that Richard refused to go on crusade unless the pope made William legate. Also
    I. Sprey, 'William Longchamp: Papal *legatus a latere* and Faithful Royal Servant', unpublished
    paper presented at the American Historical Association annual meeting (Seattle, January 1998).

The claims of the chronicler that Longchamp had 'three titles and three heads' and that Longchamp had become 'Caesar and more than Caesar' ring true.[2] Furthermore, Richard gave true breadth to the powers assumed in Longchamp's titles. For example, according to Richard of Devizes, the king determined that after Count John's release from his oath to remain out of England, his admission into the kingdom was 'at the chancellor's pleasure'.[3]

Unfortunately, it appears that Richard's trust either fed or created an arrogance and ambition within the chancellor that ultimately brought him ruin. Devizes comments that the chancellor 'made up for the shortness of his stature by his arrogance, counting on his lord's affection and presuming on his good will'. William of Newburgh claims that Longchamp's haughtiness nearly equalled that of royalty. Bishop William Stubbs concurred, describing the chief justiciar, chancellor, bishop of Ely and papal legate as 'elated by the greatness of his position beyond the ordinary exultation of the upstart'. A modern authority on the justiciarship argues that one of Longchamp's points of vulnerability was indeed his prideful personality.[4]

Longchamp's qualities can be no better observed than in his manner of ousting his fellow justiciar, Bishop Hugh du Puiset of Durham, from the government. Puiset had initially been chosen by the Lionheart as one of the co-justiciars, but on the death of his colleague, the earl of Essex, the king began the tinkering that ultimately left Longchamp solely in charge of the kingdom. According to Devizes' chronicle, the stage for a showdown with Puiset was set, for the government of England had already been entrusted to Longchamp when the king sailed for Normandy in December 1189.[5] Puiset himself questioned whether the regency arrangement had been devised in sincerity or merely as a means of picking his deep pockets more thoroughly.[6]

It is commonly construed that Longchamp received his office and power at the great council at Nonancourt in March 1190, but that council's decisions only ratified the *de facto* case in England. Longchamp's power rested on his possession of the royal seal of absence which resulted in handing him control of the administration of the realm. This authority Puiset lacked, as shown by the far fewer writs and charters issued in his name than in Longchamp's during the period prior to Nonancourt. Furthermore, outbursts of anti-Semitism in northern England prior to the Norman council had

---

2   Devizes, 13; Newburgh, 1: 331.
3   Devizes, 13–14.
4   Devizes, 9; Newburgh, 1: 333; W. Stubbs, *Historical Introductions to the Rolls Series*, ed. A. Hassal (London, 1902), 217–18; F.J. West, *The Justiciarship in England, 1066–1232* (Cambridge, 1966), 69.
5   Devizes, 9.
6   Howden, 3: 101.

provided evidence of the ineffectiveness of the bishop of Durham's government. By March 1190, with Puiset's power sinking, needed reforms were implemented that limited his authority to the regions north of the River Humber and entrusted the bulk of responsibility to the bishop of Ely.

Both bishops remained with the Lionheart at the conclusion of the council, Longchamp returning to England after about three weeks and Puiset following about ten days later. Why Puiset allowed his colleague this advantage can only be guessed; perhaps he hoped to convince the king to change his mind once the chancellor's influential voice had been removed, or perhaps Richard forbade him to leave. Regardless, Puiset detected on his return to England a conflict between his vision of the new arrangement and its actual workings. Longchamp seized the moment to exert full power as *summus iustitiarius* by excluding him from the exchequer at Westminster in the chancellor's southern bailiwick and by advancing into Yorkshire, Puiset's northern sphere, to punish those who had violated the king's peace in massacring the Jews. The latter indignity must have stung Puiset deeply, for Longchamp exercised all a justiciar's authority in the north by sending an armed force to York, removing the sheriff and decreeing confiscations, amercements and imprisonments.

Also insulting were ecclesiastical actions taken by Longchamp while in York. Puiset had extended his power in the archiepiscopate during its long vacancy that had lasted since 1181, possibly to the point of exercising spiritual jurisdiction within the cathedral.[7] When Longchamp arrived at York Minster, demanding the respect due a papal legate, the cathedral clergy politely refused because he was not yet formally confirmed in the office. With that, the chancellor placed the great church under interdict, suspended the clergy from their posts and had the bells removed.

Rebuffed by these events, Hugh de Puiset set out from Westminster, 'as though he were expecting to stage a triumph', to confront the chancellor, intercepting him at Blythe, Nottinghamshire.[8] There occurred an exchange between the two men which, according to Puiset's biographer, 'cast a sad light on [Puiset's] political sagacity'.[9] The bishop of Durham improvidently demanded that the chancellor respect his royal commission as justiciar of the North; Longchamp reacted in a measured way, proposing that the two meet again in a few days to discuss matters further. At the second meeting, Puiset was outmanoeuvred by the chancellor who produced documentation proving that he held authority from the king sweeping enough to silence

---

7 G. Scammell, *Hugh du Puiset, Bishop of Durham* (Cambridge, 1956), 172, 176.

8 J.T. Appleby, *England Without Richard, 1189–1199* (Ithaca, NY, 1965), 47–8.

9 Scammell, *Hugh du Puiset*, 52.

and, indeed, to arrest the duped bishop. Longchamp informed Puiset that he was arrested 'not as a bishop seizing another bishop, but as the chancellor seizing a castellan'.[10] Stripped of his recent acquisitions and humbled by a demand to surrender his own son as hostage, Puiset returned to one of his manors where he languished under house arrest; and from there, he launched an appeal for justice to the king. Richard ordered restitution of all his properties save Windsor Castle, but left Longchamp as sole justiciar.

Whether Longchamp forged the document used to subdue Puiset or whether he had an actual royal letter is impossible to know. The calendar of events simply does not have the accuracy or clarity needed to determine what document Longchamp had. Clearly, its power had ended Puiset's aspirations. The interval between the two rivals' meetings gives credence to Longchamp's forgery, allowing him time to generate the necessary documents, but most probable is Longchamp's awareness of the king's designs to make him chief justiciar and papal legate. If documents were forged, they were consistent with royal plans and not products of the chancellor's imagination or naked ambition.

His power as chief justiciar now secure, Longchamp presided over a government that knew no parallel in its day. The development of English governmental institutions has long occupied historians, resulting in countless specialised works. The primary purpose for devising more advanced systems of governing was twofold: expanding royal justice and increasing royal revenues, although the two were not always sharply distinct from one another. In the latter area, the English government operated primarily through the exchequer, an agency that dated at least to Henry I's reign. At the exchequer, the sheriffs appeared twice a year to account for their shire farms; other royal officials and subjects also reported for their debts to the king. Records, meticulous by medieval standards, were kept, pipe rolls preserving a register of moneys owed and amounts paid in. Indicating the close link between finance and justice, the barons of the exchequer served as judges settling disputes and tracked the activities of itinerant justices dispatched periodically from Westminster. The rolls contain accounts of amercements (fines in modern parlance) and fines (proffers for privileges) levied before the justices, which were collected and delivered by the sheriffs. Sources of revenue other than shire farms and profits of justice included debts owed to deceased Jewish moneylenders, tallages of towns on the royal demesne, other tax measures, profits from royal forests and other royal resources, feudal dues such as escheats, reliefs, scutages and wardships, and fines. From the exchequer, treasure was dispatched for the king's use on crusade and throughout his dominions.

10 Devizes, 12.

The exchequer did not account for all royal income, meaning that the pipe rolls are not exhaustive evidence for all royal revenues. Royal debtors could pay money directly into the king's chamber, although in Richard's reign this occurred infrequently due to his extended absences. At times, separate exchequers were set up to handle such extraordinary demands as debts to the Jews and the raising of Richard's ransom. Unfortunately, the accounts of receipts for neither the chamber nor the special exchequers survive.

Angevin government of England has won praise for its judicial innovations. Henry II and his sons were motivated to develop as efficient a legal system as possible to generate new revenue. To that end, justice was made readily available through expansion of the system of royal courts. By Richard's reign, his subjects could settle their disputes before proto-professional judges sitting regularly at Westminster and periodically travelling on circuits through the counties. Additionally, justices were sent to the shires to hear cases dealing with offences against the dreaded forest law. Along with its availability, justice was made less fearful. As a result of Henry II's reforms, juries of peers were made available as alternatives to trial by combat, and lesser freemen could shift their cases from their lords' courts to the royal justices. Royal writs could be purchased from the chancery which ordered sheriffs to investigate claims of forcible dispossession and which provided for restoration of lands to the deprived holder until such cases could be heard and decided by the king's justices. Into royal courts were sent all high crimes, now classed as pleas of the crown or breaches of the king's peace. The English people apparently recognised the judicial system's power, for many sought to protect themselves from law suits by securing royal charters in overwhelming numbers or by having legal decisions recorded on the pipe rolls or feet of fines. Of the surviving charters from Richard's reign, nearly three-quarters were granted to English subjects, suggesting what may have been tantamount to a mad rush for royal charters. Legal documents were becoming the weapons of choice in an increasingly litigious society.

The justiciarship developed in response to the need that the Norman and Angevin monarchs had to leave someone in charge of the realm while they toured their continental holdings. Under Richard, this office reached its pinnacle of power, as he was so seldom in England. This key official, though usually depicted as regent over all the government, technically was head of the exchequer, to which were added judicial duties as royal justice expanded. Expected to extract revenue from the realm and maintain order to sustain an uninterrupted flow of funds, the justiciar exercised broad powers during a royal absence. During Richard's reign, all the justiciars, except Bishop Hugh du Puiset, were men with long records of faithful and able service to the Angevins in administrative rather than military capacities.

Assisting them were others of similar backgrounds who served as sheriffs, constables, foresters and judges.

Although magnates continued to factor large in the political life of England, twelfth-century English monarchs had turned to trained dependents to do the work of governing rather than leaving the task to powerful lords in the localities. By late in the century, the barons were feeling the effects of burgeoning royal power made possible by an increasingly systematic and organised governmental apparatus, operated by an intensely loyal staff. From the baronage were demanded burdensome 'feudal' payments and services, enforced by zealous royal servants. Various types of written records gave added weight to the subordination of the nobility to royal will, whether commands to appear before the king's justices by writ or reminders of crown debts recorded on the pipe rolls. Naturally a divergence of opinion on the nature of government would develop as the magnates witnessed their power diminishing in relation to the king's and lost out to upstart royal servants in the contest for royal patronage.

Having removed Puiset, Longchamp carried out the functions of governance with speed and effectiveness. Few historians doubt the chancellor's abilities; indeed, one scholar considers this the heart of the complaints against him, for 'he was plainly an efficient superintendent of royal business'.[11] Contemporary records indicate that the kingdom's administration continued unabated, though with less spectacular financial reports to show for it. The chancellor commissioned and dispatched a judicial eyre in 1190–91 that blanketed much of the kingdom. Longchamp himself led the 1190 eyre that traversed the counties of the Welsh border.[12] Even during the summer of 1191 when the justiciar was embattled with Count John, justices were sitting in the East Anglian counties and other scattered shires. Several circuits included judges experienced with the Henrician judicial system, although the majority were local notables. At least one justice, John of Kentish, a chancery clerk, certainly came from the chancellor's household.[13] Additionally, the justices at Westminster held regular sessions from February through November 1190 and from January through May 1191, often with the chancellor present.[14] Statistical analysis of Longchamp's presence at court reveals that he witnessed between 20 and 30 per cent of the final concords. While this is unimpressive in comparison to Hubert Walter's near 90 per cent attestation record, it is consistent with the judicial activity of

---

11   West, *Justiciarship*, 70, 72.
12   D.M. Stenton (ed.), *Pleas Before the King or his Justices, 1198–1212*, Selden Society, vol. 83 (London, 1967), 3: lxxxi–lxcxxiv, lxxxviii–lxxxix.
13   *PR3/4RI*, xxi–xxiv.
14   Stenton, *Pleas*, 3: lxxix–lxxx, lxxxv–lxxxvi.

Ranulf de Glanvill and Walter of Coutances.[15] Judicial activity had not yet become the justiciar's central focus, as would be the case under Hubert Walter and his successors.

Shrievalties and castles also received the chancellor's attention. Richard had removed many of Henry II's long-tenured sheriffs during his brief progress through England in 1189, and further changes came with Longchamp. The king had given precious few shires to high-ranking men in the government, but Longchamp reintroduced them into the shrievalties. Geoffrey fitz Peter, William Briwerre and Hugh Bardolf, associate justiciars, had been sheriffs under Henry II but were excluded by the new king. Longchamp not only restored them but gave multiple shires to Briwerre and Bardolf. Not content with that, Longchamp made further adjustments to the shrieval roster by removing sheriffs from eight additional shires and replacing them with men from his own household. Two were his own brothers, Henry and Osbert, and other close associates among his sheriffs included Henry de Cornhill, William de Stuteville and John de Rebez. In the end, men from Longchamp's household occupied thirteen counties, spreading his influence over a sizeable portion of the kingdom.[16]

Similarly Longchamp closely supervised royal castles. As with the shrievalties, many of the constables were his men. His acquisition of Windsor from Bishop Hugh of Durham has already been discussed. Given the keys to the Tower of London and Dover Castle by the king, Longchamp named as constable of the Tower a member of his entourage, William Puintel; and the chancellor's brother-in-law, Matthew de Cleres, was posted to Dover Castle.[17] Other household members were stationed in various castles about the kingdom: Philip Puintel, brother of the constable of the Tower, at York, Hugh Bardolf at Kenilworth, and Osbert Longchamp at Newcastle-on-Tyne. Roger fitz Reinfrey, initially one of the *appares*, is identified as custodian of Wallingford Castle; John de Rebez was constable of Winchester and Porchester castles; Robert fitz Roger, Longchamp's choice as sheriff of Norfolk/Suffolk, had Orford; William Briwerre held Southampton; and Robert de Tresgoz was named sheriff of Wiltshire and constable of Salisbury Castle.[18] Longchamp attempted briefly to replace Gerard de Camville at Lincoln Castle with one of his supporters, but failed when determined opposition arose.[19]

---

15   R.R. Heiser, 'The Households of the Justiciars of Richard I: An Inquiry into the Second Level of Medieval English Government', *HSJ* 2 (1990), 228, 233.

16   R.R. Heiser, 'The Sheriffs of Richard I: Trends of Management as seen in Shrieval Appointments from 1189 to 1194', *HSJ* 4 (1992), 113–15.

17   *PR2RI*, 1, 156, 159; Devizes, 41n.

18   *PR2RI*, 18, 36–7, 44, 58–9, 117–18, 136; *PR3/4RI*, 34.

19   Devizes, 30–1.

Castles factored centrally in Longchamp's strategy for retaining control of the kingdom while it was under his watch, and he spent large sums of money preparing them for conflict. In 1189–90, over £3,900 was spent on fortifications: £2,800 on the Tower and £550 on Dover, and another £660 in the following year. While the sums spent on the Tower are still frequently cited, the chancellor provisioned and repaired castles throughout the kingdom.[20]

Furthermore, those fortifications that received Longchamp's attention support the claim that he aimed his spear at Count John, whose vast holdings given him by Richard made him the greatest lord in England. All the renovated castles were located either in or near John's lands or those of his associates. Longchamp's attacks at Gloucester and Lincoln Castles were obvious strikes against his nemesis, Count John. Longchamp's behaviour toward the king's brother was clearly threatening and aggressive, if not outright provocative, hardly endearing the two toward each other. Evidence from the early 1190s shows the chancellor controlling the Peak and Bolsover, two important Derbyshire strongholds supposedly granted to John. The rolls reveal both in the possession of royal custodians, however, who were in receipt of money *per breve regis* as early as 1190.[21] Indeed, the payments received by these two seem no different from those received by any other constable/custodians reporting to the central government.[22] If they were indeed in Longchamp's employ, he had taken two important castles in direct violation of what John expected by right of the king's own orders. Clearly, Longchamp was not above acting in high-handed ways.

Longchamp, besides overseeing justice, shrievalties and castles, also had to ensure the collection of revenue. Some of this activity coincided with his work in the shrievalties and eyres, as justices levied amercements and sheriffs collected them. A cursory view of entries in the 1191 pipe roll for Yorkshire reveals the pressure applied by the government to collect the financial penalties assessed against those accused of attacking the Jews; most names listed had already paid down or cleared their debts.[23] The 1190 roll begins the Welsh scutage assessment, and the next year's roll shows Longchamp receiving oblations from individuals in nearly every shire.[24] Another lucrative revenue source not overlooked was almost £7,000 owed to the deceased

---

20 N.J.G. Pounds, *The Medieval Castle in England and Wales: A Social and Political History* (Cambridge, 1990), 78; R.A. Brown, 'Royal Castle-building in England, 1154–1216', in *Castles, Conquest and Charters: Collected Papers of R. Allen Brown* (Woodbridge, 1989), 22, 49, 58–9.

21 H.M. Colvin (ed.), *The History of King's Works* (London, 1963), 2: 572, 776; *PR2RI*, 75; *3/4RI*, 29.

22 For example, Walter de Clifford at Knighton Castle and Richard Revel at Exeter Castle, *PR3/4RI*, 81, 281.

23 *PR3/4RI*, 69–70.

24 *PR2RI*, xxii; *PR3/4RI*, xiii.

Jewish moneylender, Aaron of Lincoln. The chancellor established a special exchequer responsible for collecting obligations owed to Aaron, and almost £3,000 was paid.[25] With this activity, it is little wonder that Richard of Devizes compared the movements of the justiciar to 'a flash of dazzling lightning'.[26] The picture of Longchamp travelling to every shire collecting oblations must be understood in the context of diminished royal assets as already discussed. The government under Longchamp had to work extremely hard to scrape together the £12,000 it did.[27] Although the totals for all this activity fell below previous years' by sizeable margins, nevertheless, bullion was sent to the king, and huge sums were spent, such as £2,250 for the crusading fleet.[28] For Devizes, treasure loaded onto ships for transport to Messina 'was exceedingly great and beyond reckoning'.[29]

Longchamp also acted in the capacity of defender of law and order as his decisive action against the anti-Semites in both York and Lincoln indicates. The sheriff, John Marshal, whose failure to give strong leadership resulted in the deadly mêlée, was ousted, and a similar though unsuccessful move was attempted against the sheriff of Lincoln. Long lists of fines are found in the pipe rolls, as are entries referring to confiscations and expenditures for shackles.[30] The Jewish community's safety for the remainder of Longchamp's justiciarship underscores the effectiveness of his measures.

Defending the Welsh frontier presented the justiciar with challenges as well. The Welsh had risen while Richard was in the kingdom, but had been quieted by a show of force. Richard's refusal to meet with the Welsh leader, Lord Rhys, however, undoubtedly resulted in bitterness that boiled over into trouble during Longchamp's justiciarship, although it was probably brief and relatively uneventful. The pipe rolls record castles on the Welsh frontier being repaired and fortified, and perhaps in one case, restored to English castellans. Also clerics holding Welsh churches were sent as emissaries to the Welsh, although nothing is known of the outcome.[31] The host was called out for a military campaign and scutage assessed against those not answering the summons; proof is the earl of Salisbury's pardon from scutage because he had been with 'the army of Wales'.[32]

25 *PR3/4RI*, xii–xiv, 17–24, 135; James H. Ramsey, *A History of the Revenues of the Kings of England, 1066–1399*, 2 vols (Oxford, 1925), 2: 205.
26 Devizes, 13.
27 N. Barratt, 'The English Revenue of Richard I', unpublished paper presented at the Colloque aux Archives du Calvados (Caen, April 1999), Table 1.
28 *PR2RI*, 2–3, 8–9; *PR3/4RI*, 136.
29 Devizes, 15.
30 *PR2RI*, 3, 68–70; *PR3/4RI*, 15–17, 221; *PR5RI*, 72; Devizes, 11.
31 *PR2RI*, 48; *PR3/4RI*, 93, 165.
32 *PR3/4RI*, 121.

Although these many activities of Longchamp are associated with his position as chief justiciar and royal chancellor, he ruled the Church in England with similar vigour through his office of papal legate. The English Church had been disturbed by the conflicts at York and by hostility between cathedral monks and prelates. Longchamp's commitment to exercising his legatine authority over the English Church is manifested in his holding councils and filling vacancies. His leadership does not appear to have been disruptive, for the bishops of England banded together and signed a petition circulated by Longchamp himself, seeking a renewal of his legatine appointment following Pope Clement III's death in the spring of 1191.

Longchamp's only known ecclesiastical council was held in the autumn of 1190 at Westminster. This meeting gave the legate an opportunity to 'satisfy his vanity and display his power', but it appears that the thorny problem of the relationship between monastic cathedral chapters and prelates had surfaced yet again.[33] Bishop Hugh de Nonant of Coventry had proffered 300 marks for recognition of his rights over Coventry Cathedral Priory in 1189.[34] Later that year, a formal complaint came before an assembly of English prelates against the Coventry monks who had allegedly assaulted the bishop. Naturally, the bishops stood in support of their aggrieved brother. At the council of Westminster, the matter was finally resolved, according to papal instructions. It was decreed that the monks of Coventry be expelled and secular canons installed in their place.

Emotions continued to run strong against the monastic community at this council as evidenced by an abortive attempt to limit the number of horses allowed in abbots' entourages. This met with a swift response from Abbot Samson of Bury St Edmunds who declared that thirteen horses would never suffice for him. A final incident in 1190 pitted the abbot of Malmesbury against the bishop of Salisbury, where smouldering conflict regarding the abbot's subordination to the bishop burst into flames. Both parties, however, produced letters from the king that prevented the chancellor from proceeding, and the matter was postponed until Richard returned from crusade.

In ecclesiastical appointments, Longchamp was diligent to fulfil the king's wishes and to win his own family's promotion. The only English bishopric to fall vacant during his period of power was Worcester, when its bishop died in 1190. The canon of Lincoln and archdeacon of Nottingham, Robert fitz William fitz Ralph, son of the seneschal of Normandy, was selected as successor. Longchamp's role in filling this post was probably limited to his consecration of the bishop-elect at Canterbury in May 1191. At the same

---

33 Appleby, *England Without Richard*, 53.
34 *PR2RI*, 43.

time, orders concerning the election of a new archbishop of Canterbury had arrived from the king in Sicily. Richard recommended Archbishop William of Montreale to the vacant see, but the monks declined to accept his letters of instruction, citing the need for more authentic royal directives. That Longchamp wanted this ecclesiastical plum for himself was the rumour.

Monastic vacancies received the chancellor's attentions as well. At Crowland Abbey in Lincolnshire, the legate secured the appointment of his brother, Henry Longchamp, in 1190. He tried with temporary success to install as abbot of Westminster in 1191 another brother, Robert Longchamp, a monk of Saint-Etienne, Caen. An agreement was struck between the chancellor and the Westminster monks regarding Robert's elevation; when the chancellor's fortunes shifted later that year, however, the monks, encouraged by Count John, reneged and elected one of their own. At Muchelney Abbey in Somerset, where Longchamp imposed Abbot Robert of St Guthlac's, Herefordshire, a reaction similar to that at Westminster Abbey followed. The monks unceremoniously ejected Longchamp's appointee, with even his bedding following him out of the door.[35]

The reactions of these monasteries to Longchamp indicate the mood of the kingdom at large by 1191. Richard of Devizes describes the chancellor 'as more savage than a wild beast'; a modern historian writes in a more measured tone, noting that Longchamp employed 'indelicate vigour'.[36] The chief justiciar, though an effective supervisor of England's government, became the lightning rod of dissatisfaction. Causes for his downfall are numerous, many beyond his power to control, but they combined to squeeze him out. A budding English anti-foreign feeling, his innate arrogance and various high-handed actions doomed him, alienating the chancellor from the people he was asked to lead. Richard's absence further undermined Longchamp; had the monarch been closer, royal backing would have provided better cover and preserved his power.

Modern scholars have shown that by the late twelfth century, a strident national feeling was maturing in England that would sever any English sense of kinship with the Normans, and such nativist sentiments were eventually directed at the Norman Longchamp.[37] Clerks at the exchequer mocked

---

35 Devizes, 55.
36 Devizes, 10; Scammell, *Hugh du Puiset*, 53.
37 D. Crouch, *William Marshal: Court, Career, and Chivalry in the Angevin Empire, 1147–1219* (London, 1990), 44, 141; D. Crouch, 'Normans and Anglo-Normans: A Divided Aristocracy?', in D. Bates and A. Curry (eds), *England and Normandy in the Middle Ages* (London, 1994), 66; D. Bates, 'The Rise and Fall of Normandy *c*. 911–1204', in D. Bates and A. Curry (eds), *England and Normandy in the Middle Ages*, 30–5; J.C. Holt, 'The End of the Anglo-Norman Realm', in *Magna Carta and Medieval Government* (London, 1985), 243–54.

him and his brother through comments and markings in the pipe rolls.[38] Manifesting this mockery in its most vitriolic form is a letter written by Hugh de Nonant, bishop of Coventry, at the time of Longchamp's removal from the justiciarship. Bishop Hugh declared that Longchamp's grandfather had been of peasant stock who had fled from French territory to Normandy to escape his servile status. None of this was true, but it was believed by critics of courtiers, who reflected in their writings on the intolerable situation of having a low-born man exalted to high estate.[39]

Longchamp's opponents exploited anti-foreign feelings with the charge that the chancellor ruled England without his royally appointed associate justiciars, all of whom were English natives. Since this charge is patently untrue, it most likely expresses Count John's claims that Longchamp was importing 'foreigners and unknown men' and turning the realm over to them.[40] The question that probably cannot be answered is what exactly was expected of Longchamp relating to this charge of governing without his associates. Longchamp did not violate some royal constitution which the *appares* and magnates of the realm sought to restore, but rather his style and forcefulness in governing raised their hackles. The *appares* can be found serving in shrievalties, participating in eyres, sitting in judgment at Westminster, and accompanying the chancellor about the kingdom. In fact, Longchamp 'co-operated with them in the king's interests, and without them his justiciarship would have been ineffective'.[41] As has been seen, the chancellor did utilise his household dependents alongside the associate justiciars, and it was this practice that his political opponents seized on when making their case for his deposition, for some excuse was needed to remove Longchamp.

Longchamp's arrogance heightened the xenophobia of the English. His progresses through the kingdom produced animosity as he and his entourage descended like swarms of locusts on communities, eating everything and leaving the area utterly ravaged.[42] Additional evidence of his haughty spirit that further alienated the English is his action in 1191, when Walter of Coutances arrived from Sicily with the king's instructions that he should incorporate the archbishop of Rouen into the inner circle of advisers. Longchamp disregarded the order, claiming that his innate knowledge of the king's will was more certain than possibly fraudulent letters. Also boosting Longchamp's confidence in his own knowledge of the king's will were

---

38 *PR2RI*, 116; *PR9RI*, xxvi.
39 Howden, 3: 72, 142; Gerald of Wales, 4: 418.
40 Devizes, 31.
41 West, *Justiciarship*, 72.
42 Newburgh, 4: 14; *Gesta Regis*, 2: 143.

letters that arrived from Richard continually reasserting that 'the chancellor was to be obeyed by all . . . especially . . . his brother John'.[43] Yet popular opinion was rising against him, and his awareness of this could only inflame his suspicion, turning him more and more toward personal dependants.

Inordinate confidence in royal support made Longchamp careless, and he engaged in activity that snowballed into political disaster for him. Longchamp's approach was to take advantage of the free hand that the king had given him 'to swat those he saw as his enemies'.[44] His action against John Marshal in York after the Jewish massacre is explicable on grounds of failure of duty, but his apparent attack on William Marshal's castle at Gloucester, recently purchased from the king, seems pure folly. Marshal, one of the *appares* and recipient of extensive royal favour, was not an overt threat to the chancellor, but his connections to Count John caused the chancellor worry.[45] For the chancellor to resolve in this fashion supposed problems between Marshal and himself was wholly unproductive, however; for it isolated him from those who could be helpful in times of trouble.

Devizes recounts another episode of the chancellor's swatting at prominent persons that alienated rather than endeared the English to him, an account borne out by the pipe rolls. Godfrey de Lucy, nominated at Pipewell to the bishopric of Winchester, had secretly offered the king £3,000 for various confirmations, offices and grants. Longchamp moved against the bishop, however, seizing his recently purchased castles, shrievalty and lands, despite Godfrey's having cleared the entire debt in a year. Godfrey hastened to meet the justiciar and demanded the return of his properties and offices; the chancellor went only part way, however, returning to him his patrimony. If Devizes is to be believed, Godfrey should have been grateful for this gesture, since 'all the others . . . got less than nothing for their pains'.[46]

The aggrieved wasted no time launching appeals to the king before he got too far away; indeed, 'Complaints against Longchamp had been chasing Richard across Europe.'[47] Richard, however, was loath to act against his justiciar, and is even portrayed as defeating his subjects' attempts to obtain justice. On the one hand, Richard 'instructed [the chancellor] very fully in all the things he was to do, thus forestalling the complaints of the envious', and then he feigned to hear their protests and granted them 'whatever letters they wanted'.[48] This can only have emboldened Longchamp; the

---

43 Devizes, 28–30.
44 Crouch, *William Marshal*, 69.
45 Crouch, *William Marshal*, 71–2.
46 *PR2RI*, 131, 136; *PR3/4RI*, 84–5; Devizes, 8, 10, 12–13.
47 F. Barlow, *The Feudal Kingdom of England 1042–1216*, 4th edn (London, 1988), 374.
48 Devizes, 10–11; *Gesta Regis*, 2: 157.

remainder of his justiciarship is a story of one outrage after another until his undoing.

The relentless chorus against 'the tyrant' Longchamp finally penetrated the crusader king's trust. Queen Eleanor, *femina incomparabilis*, is generally credited with achieving the breakthrough when she delivered complaints to Richard in Sicily.[49] It is also said that Eleanor had a moderating effect on her youngest son, for Count John was virtually unseen prior to the conflict with Longchamp in 1191; but as soon as she departed for Navarre, he surfaced 'in active mischief'.[50] Because the queen mother was absent from England between April 1190 and January 1191, both her influence over John and her reports to the king on English affairs are doubtful. She simply could not have brought alarming reports to Richard about his chief justiciar, since she had been far from England, travelling from Navarre with Berengaria. The king's famous letters to Longchamp and William Marshal were composed in February, and Richard did not see his mother until five weeks later.[51] The Lionheart acted out of his own motivation and good sense.

What actions were taken in response to the hue and cry against Longchamp? A twofold strategy appears to have aimed at hemming in Longchamp to a degree without yanking him from power unless the situation proved irredeemable. Although the Lionheart's trust in his chancellor was unshakable, the king plainly saw that if he could not preside over the kingdom in peace and tranquillity, serious ramifications threatening to the crusade were likely. Two clerics were chosen as the king's agents for change: Geoffrey, archbishop-elect of York, and Walter of Coutances, archbishop of Rouen. Geoffrey Plantagenet had never been consecrated, but now he could be useful in England as a counter-balance to Longchamp's ecclesiastical power. Consequently, Eleanor returned by way of Rome to lobby the pope for Geoffrey's swift consecration.

The other prelate, Archbishop Walter of Rouen, was given a satchel of letters from the king that he was instructed to use as he deemed necessary, 'a delicate mission in difficult circumstances'.[52] Letters written in late January gave instructions regarding the election of an archbishop for Canterbury, and directed that the manor of Kirton-in-Lindsey be turned over to William Longsword, Richard's half-brother.[53] Two further letters were composed in

---

49   Devizes, 10, 25; *PR3/4RI*, xv; D.D.R. Owen, *Eleanor of Aquitaine: Queen and Legend* (Oxford, 1993), 81.
50   Stubbs, *Historical Introductions*, 224.
51   Landon, 46–7.
52   S. Painter, *William Marshal: Knight-Errant, Baron, and Regent of England* (Baltimore, 1933), 88; West, *Justiciarship*, 74.
53   Dated just prior to the better known documents, possibly sent ahead or delivered by Coutances; Landon, 46.

February, one addressed to Longchamp and the *appares* and the other to Marshal and his fellow associates. The first commanded that Coutances be admitted into the regency council 'as long as he remains in England and we on crusade' and that the Canterbury election proceed 'just as [Coutances] proposes it to you from our side'. The second instructed William Marshal and the *appares* to act on Archbishop Walter's word, if 'our chancellor does not govern our kingdom according to the counsel of the archbishop, yourself and the other men'.[54] Coutances was first to observe the situation, determining whether the circumstances were as troubling as rumours had suggested. The 'leisurely pace' of Coutances and the queen mother on their return to England is an indication that Richard was far from panicked.[55] Clearly the king was reluctant to move dramatically against Longchamp, an indication that the chancellor's power was not the issue for him, but rather the dangerous political situation.

When Archbishop Walter arrived in England, he found that the situation was indeed critical, for Count John and Longchamp had faced off before the walls of Lincoln Castle. Both had been entrusted with tremendous power and endowed with ambition for still more, and their relationship had steadily deteriorated over the preceding several months. John, remarkably quiet during 1190 and the first months of 1191, was thrust into action by his eroding position regarding succession to the throne, should his brother die crusading. This occurred while Richard was in Messina, Sicily, where he hoped to settle the affairs of his widowed sister, Joan. Richard's aggressive actions and contemptuous attitudes at this time had roused the hostility of the islanders and their leader, Tancred of Lecce. A treaty was signed in 1191, in which Richard received a large sum of money from Tancred and in return agreed to the marriage of Tancred's daughter and Prince Arthur of Brittany, whom Richard now declared to be his heir.[56] That latter provision was of obvious concern to Count John, especially since Longchamp's growing domination of the kingdom had enhanced the odds for the succession of the crusading king's designated heir, should he fail to return to his kingdom. Many castles and shrievalties were in the hands of the chancellor's *familiares*, the king of the Scots' support had been secured, and the archiepiscopate of Canterbury was vacant with the chief justiciar a possible candidate. Should Longchamp have succeeded in obtaining the archbishopric, John's chance of winning England's crown would be lost, and it is not surprising that in May 1191

---

54 Diceto, 2: 90–1; Devizes, 28.
55 West, *Justiciarship*, 69–70; Gillingham, *Richard*, 217–18.
56 E. Jamison, 'The Alliance of England and Sicily in the Second Half of the Twelfth Century', *Journal of Warburg and Courtauld Institutes* 6 (1943), 30–2. Terms of the treaty, Landon, 42–3, Appendix E, 197.

John wrote to the monks of Canterbury, remonstrating with them against electing the bishop of Ely.[57]

Developments such as these pushed matters beyond the breaking point of Count John's tolerance. A meeting between the two chief antagonists at Winchester in March 1191 to discuss custody of castles and John's money grants from the exchequer did not resolve the problems. Devizes describes the kingdom as seething with sedition. John travelling about the country with large retinues, barons fortifying castles and solicitations for support through letter-writing campaigns all characterise the political stage.[58] The homage to Count John by Gerard de Camville, constable of Lincoln Castle, struck Longchamp as 'an offence against the crown'.[59] It sparked the show-down that Archbishop Walter faced when he landed in June 1191.

Archbishop Walter's response to the crisis demonstrated balance and prudence, qualities that he had no doubt exhibited while travelling with the king to Sicily and that had inclined Richard toward sending him to England. Coutances's modern biographer describes the tricky situation, for Walter had 'to restrain Longchamp without playing into John's hands'.[60] It was the chancellor who requested Coutances's services in defusing the incident, and as a result, a second meeting at Winchester was called for 28 July. Tension was high. John, not daring to risk a recurrence of what had happened to Bishop Hugh du Puiset, arrived with 4,000 Welsh soldiers and called on all who would to join him. Longchamp responded in kind, calling out a third of the feudal levy and a supplemental force of mercenaries to escort him. In the historic city, under tremendous pressure, the opponents patched together a treaty that pushed them away from the brink of warfare.

Devizes gives a thorough account of the treaty's provisions. In the first step, three bishops – Bath, Winchester and London – were appointed to select twenty-two arbitrators, eleven from each side, to hammer out an agreement. They swore to act honourably and to reconvene should future conflict arise, and the count and the chancellor promised to abide by whatever decisions were concluded. The resulting treaty's provisions required Longchamp to restore the castle and shrievalty of Lincoln to Gerard de Camville. Count John returned Nottingham and Tickhill castles to the regency; however, their custody went to men affiliated with the count, William Marshal and William de Wenneval. Constables of other castles were changed as well, and hostages demanded of each nominee. Additional

57 W. Stubbs (ed.), *Epistolae Cantuarienses*, RS (London, 1865), 330, 346.
58 Devizes, 26, 29–30.
59 Devizes, 30.
60 P. Poggioli, 'From Politician to Prelate: The Career of Walter of Coutances, Archbishop of Rouen, 1184–1207', PhD dissertation (Johns Hopkins University, 1984), 59.

agreements provided for key castles to revert to Count John, should the king die overseas, and allowed John to change castellans within his lands if he could show adequate justification. Most damaging to the chancellor's cause were his agreements to abide by the counsel of the king's associates and barons, to cease land seizures without due process and to recognise his opponent as Richard's heir.[61]

The treaty of Winchester served as a powerful indictment of Longchamp's methods as justiciar. Although the treaty clearly worked to Longchamp's disadvantage, John left Winchester with no more role in the government than before. By checking both the chancellor and the count and restoring some semblance of order in the kingdom, Walter of Coutances bought the time that he needed 'to assess Longchamp's viability', the purpose of his dispatch from the king.[62] Within days, it became apparent that a change was required.

Two days after the Winchester conference, Longchamp sent orders to the coastal authorities forbidding Archbishop Geoffrey Plantagenet's landing, beginning the terrible blunder that made his position in England untenable. Longchamp also decreed that letters from the pope, rumoured to give the archbishop of York freedom from his legatine authority, were not to enter the kingdom, and he sent emissaries to the continent to prevent Geoffrey's embarkation from Flemish ports. Apparently, Count John had also recognised the usefulness of Geoffrey's presence in the kingdom in his contest with the chief justiciar, for he had been encouraging the archbishop to come to England.[63] An often overlooked proviso was attached to Longchamp's orders to his men in the Channel ports; according to Devizes, Geoffrey was to be arrested and held unless the twenty-two arbiters declared that he be released.[64] The terminology is in stark contrast to that used by Longchamp when he had declared that he knew the king's will better than anyone. Perhaps he was not chastened enough to realise the need to live under the terms of the treaty of Winchester. Whatever the circumstances, the zeal with which the authorities at Dover, most of them intimately connected with the chancellor, carried out his instructions cost him the justiciarship.

Chroniclers portray the September 1191 episode in Dover as an outrage that rivalled other infamous attacks on clerics. The scene of the archbishop fleeing to Dover Priory for safety and being unceremoniously dragged by Longchamp's men from sanctuary to imprisonment exhausted the patience of the English with their chief justiciar. Although Longchamp strenuously

---

61 Devizes, 33–4; Howden, 3: 135–7.
62 Poggioli, 'From Politician to Prelate', 66.
63 Devizes, 39.
64 Devizes, 40.

declared that the injustices suffered by Geoffrey had gone far beyond his orders, irreparable damage had been done. In Gillingham's words, 'From that day there was no act of tyranny, no offense . . . of which they did not think him capable.'[65] The opposition now possessed an envious advantage, an excuse for acting against the chancellor that cloaked personal ambitions and individual resentments.

The outrages committed against the archbishop of York both energised and united Longchamp's opponents and neutralised his supporters. The bishops of Lincoln, Norwich and London issued ecclesiastical sanctions against those involved in this deed. Bishop Hugh of Coventry, more a man of direct action than mere words, turned to Count John, the one person who could lead a united front against the chancellor, and prodded him to swift and forceful action. Rising to the occasion, John summoned a great council at Marlborough, where he made serious complaints before the bishops and barons of the kingdom, charging that the peace of Winchester had been broken and his brother unlawfully seized. As a result, Longchamp was ordered to meet the council at Loddon Bridge near London to answer these indictments.

At Loddon Bridge, John and his followers heard the charges against the chancellor who, stricken by fear, was not present but sent a representative. Archbishop Walter added to Archbishop Geoffrey's obvious complaints the accusation that Longchamp had obstructed him in carrying out royal orders regarding the Canterbury election and had excluded him from decision-making, charges that the *appares* echoed. Walter of Coutances read the royal letters authorising Longchamp's deposition, should he refuse to rule in accordance with the king's men, and on the basis of that document the council was urged to remove the chancellor from office. All that remained was to inform Longchamp of his misfortune. This was a significant point in the episode, not because it ousted Longchamp, but because it made Coutances spokesman of the opposition in place of Count John, who had been asserting himself as the victims' champion.[66]

Events unfolded rapidly from the Loddon Bridge meeting until Long-champ's flight to the Continent. On hearing rumours that John had dispatched troops to London, Longchamp fled there to fortify the city and to find safety in the Tower. Beseeching the Londoners to shut their gates to the count and his forces, he received their derision and insults, shouts that he was a traitor and disturber of the kingdom. This response was the product of careful work by the archbishop of York who had visited London

---

65 Gillingham, *Richard*, 218.
66 Poggioli, 'From Politician to Prelate', 70–1; Stubbs, *Historical Introductions*, 238, 246.

before meeting his half-brother. He used his time to inflame the Londoners' opposition to the chancellor, reminding them of the horrors that he had endured.

The great men assembled in St Paul's chapter house and again in open air before the Tower to rehearse the chancellor's crimes and to arouse further the people of London. Bishop Hugh of Coventry launched a scathing attack on Longchamp, drawing from the assembled crowd the cry, 'We will not have this man to reign over us!'[67] With a re-reading of the king's letters, he was deposed. After several days' delay, Longchamp surrendered to John and the council. He defended his work and called on the *appares* to speak to the legitimacy of his actions. His concluding remarks describe the situation as he had created it: 'You, being many, have beset one man. You are stronger than I and I . . . give way to stronger men because it is necessary.'[68] Giving hostages, two of his brothers among them, and surrendering the king's seal and all castles save three, Longchamp travelled to Dover where he suffered additional indignities before his flight across the Channel at the end of October.

It has been argued that Longchamp's political demise was the result of Count John's combined power and ambition, which were too great for a single justiciar lacking a proximate king.[69] Longchamp's problems did not originate with John, however; for Richard's absentee government earlier had contained the count, and Coutances would continue to frustrate his efforts to exercise any real power. Longchamp's problems were of his own making; his alienation of large segments of the kingdom's powerful people left him with no depth of support. The chancellor failed to build a foundation of loyalty, and he fell, not in the face of an overwhelmingly superior foe, but because he faced his enemies alone. Longchamp possessed authority and ability, but he had not used his assets in a politically astute way.

It can be argued that Richard bears blame for his favourite's fall, that his appointment of Longchamp as chief justiciar was a grievous error, counting against his historical reputation. Clearly, William Longchamp was the wrong man for the job, something that the Lionheart should have foreseen. Longchamp mistreated the king's subjects in ways that were inexcusable, and consequently Richard, responsible for his installation as justiciar, missed the mark on one of his coronation vows, that of caring for his people.[70] The abilities of Richard's later justiciars – Walter of Coutances and Hubert

---

67 Devizes, 48.
68 Devizes, 52.
69 West, *Justiciarship*, 73.
70 D. Carpenter, 'Richard by his Contemporaries. Was He a "Model King"? England in 1189', unpublished paper, Colloque aux Archives du Calvados (Caen, April 1999), 12.

Walter – are counted as evidence for the king's administrative aptitude; yet here the verdict must go against him. To his credit, Richard did remove the chancellor, although he was painfully slow in doing so.

Scholars have found grounds for arguing that the experience of ousting Longchamps reflects the magnates' political maturity that had burgeoned since the anarchy of Stephen's reign.[71] The barons and prelates had gathered to address a menace to the realm's safety and well-being and had resolved the problem without resorting to violence. The great council acted for Richard in his absence and on behalf of his subjects suffering from injustice at the chancellor's hands, and 'No more striking testimony could be given to the sense of collective responsibility for the good order and government of the kingdom . . . .'[72] This practical experience in governance may have provided the baronage with a precedent for the collective action that they would take in 1215 against King John and still later against Henry III, strengthening their notion of themselves as spokesmen for the common good of the kingdom.

On the other hand, the great council acted in ways that accepted royal supremacy. When Longchamp was summoned to Loddon Bridge, he was told that he must answer charges arising out of terms of the treaty of Winchester and not ill-defined ambiguities. The final act against the justiciar was predicated on the royal letters that Coutances had brought from Sicily. Neither did the council act beyond royal directives, but exactly as the king had designed, with lords, prelates and *appares* working in concert to maintain peace and tranquillity in the kingdom. It should be remembered that the leading voices were by and large those of royal agents, such as William Marshal, William Briwerre, Geoffrey fitz Peter and Archbishop Walter of Coutances. What role they played in bringing balance and measured responses to the process is unknown, but clearly the council's behaviour reflected more the spirit of administrative monarchy than baronial oligarchy. Finally, the council neither proposed nor adopted any significant reform programme. It was content to remove a bad justiciar, a necessary but not notably progressive step, demonstrating 'moderation and good sense'.[73]

The assembly that deposed Longchamp had now to determine his successor. In an arrangement similar to that established by Richard between Puiset and Longchamp, Count John won recognition as heir and the title

---

71 For example, Appleby, *England Without Richard*, 67–87; B. Wilkinson, 'The Government of England during the Absence of Richard I on the Third Crusade', *Bulletin of the John Rylands Library* 28 (1944), 485–509; F.M. Powicke, 'England: Richard I and John', in *Cambridge Medieval History* (Cambridge, 1929), 6: 211.

72 Appleby, *England Without Richard*, 87.

73 Barlow, *Feudal Kingdom*, 376, 384.

of *summus rector totius regni* but no meaningful role in government, while Coutances received the chief justiciarship with actual authority. Nevertheless, John was given great latitude in the kingdom, as when he 'turned over all the fortified places of the land . . . to whomever he pleased and most trusted'.[74] Obviously it would have been foolish to frustrate him, a potential heir, holding much power and vast tracts of English land; and he enjoyed the support of London, having promised them a commune in exchange for their assistance against the chancellor. Nevertheless, John remained at the fringe of governing, unable to dominate Coutances or manipulate the regency unduly. This aggravation must have motivated his subsequent behaviour against the regency.[75]

Further troubles for the new justiciar would come with Philip Augustus's return to France from the Holy Land. While Longchamp was losing power in England, the crusade was enjoying great successes. Richard Lionheart left Sicily in the spring of 1191 and sailed first to Cyprus, which he captured for use as a supply depot, and then to Acre on the Palestinian coast, where he joined the crusading host besieging the walls of this important Muslim city. The lacklustre Philip Augustus had reached Acre first and was delaying a final assault until Richard's arrival. Landing in June, Richard soon over-shadowed Philip in the siege operations, and he continued to upstage the French king throughout the entire crusade. Philip Augustus left Palestine prematurely, at the end of July 1191, using illness as a pretext. More likely his departure was due in large part to frustrations over his rivalry with Richard which dated to their encampment at Messina.

The Capetian ruler's trials on crusade had sharpened his hostility toward Richard Lionheart, and he returned to harass the lands of his Plantagenet rival. Although he had sworn to protect Richard's lands while he was away on crusade, he was determined not only to seize large chunks of Normandy, but to enforce his lordship over all the Plantagenets' French possessions. Indeed, in the view of some scholars, Philip's 'supreme task on his return from the crusade was to dislodge the Angevins from their continental possessions'.[76] Philip's return was a foreboding development for the English regency, as he caused additional tensions by testing Count John's loyalty and pressuring Norman defences.

Coutances's justiciarship brought about a dramatic difference in the kingdom's management; the writs that he issued bore the king's name rather than his own. He governed 'by the will and consent of his associates and by

---

74 Devizes, 52; Turner, *King John*, 44.
75 Poggioli, 'From Politician to Prelate', 71, 73; Gillingham, *Richard*, 219.
76 Baldwin, 87; and earlier, Kate Norgate, *England under the Angevin Kings* (London 1987; rpt New York, 1969), 2: 363.

the counsel of the barons of the exchequer'.[77] It was not difficult for the archbishop to see that his predecessor's approach was counter-productive in gaining the support and cooperation of the powerful. Sharing power and delegating responsibility resulted in heightened morale and deeper loyalty toward the regency. Abandoned was the chancellor's authoritarian model, and adopted was a collegial style of governance revealed in Coutances's letter to the Canterbury monks shortly after Longchamp's removal. Reminding them of the recent strife, the archbishop of Rouen announced that 'royal mandates concerning the business of the realm [will] be decided commonly and run under the seal of the lord king'. Walter could act in this fashion because of his familiarity with his colleagues in the government, alongside whom he had laboured at the court of Henry II, an advantage that Longchamp did not have. A result of Coutances's manner of governing was the loyalty of the baronage during John's revolt later in his justiciarship.

A central figure in Walter's counsels was Queen Eleanor, who exerted powerful influence in the kingdom. Although Coutances bore the king's commission to replace Longchamp, the energy of his justiciarship has been credited in large measure to the credibility that came to it through the person of the queen mother.[78] She, however, did not arrive in England until February 1192, having spent the autumn and winter in Normandy, to which she had retired after visiting Richard in Sicily. In January, she had an exchange with King Philip of France, recently returned from the Holy Land, who was demanding the return of Princess Alix. Eleanor returned to England to alert the regency and to intercept her son before he sailed for the French king's court after she learned of his intrigues with Philip Augustus. In England she dominated in other arenas as well. For instance, she was a prime mover in forcing Coutances and Longchamp to patch up their quarrels, so that their respective ecclesiastical sanctions would no longer have detrimental effects on innocent people.[79]

Count John and Walter, of course, had a stormy affiliation. At first it seemed as if problems could be avoided, as they presided together at a judicial proceeding in November 1191.[80] John's adviser, Bishop Hugh de Nonant of Coventry, filled several offices in Coutances's government, notably sheriff, justice and possibly even keeper of Jewish debts.[81] Otherwise,

---

77   Stubbs, *Epistolae Cantuarienses*, 348–9; Howden, 3: 141.
78   West, *Justiciarship*, 75; A.L. Poole, *From Domesday Book to Magna Carta*, 2nd edn (Oxford, 1954), 363–4.
79   Devizes, 59–60.
80   Stenton, *Pleas*, 3: lxxxvii.
81   D.E. Desborough, 'Politics and Prelacy in the Late Twelfth Century: The Career of Hugh de Nonant, Bishop of Coventry, 1188–98', *Historical Research* 64 (1991), 4.

nothing indicates cooperation, and John continued his scheming to bring all royal castles under his control. Philip Augustus's presence in western Europe, constantly tempting the count to betray his brother, was undoubtedly a primary cause of John's disaffection, and he was frustrated by his failure in obtaining a greater role in the regency.

Archbishop Walter of Coutances's government faced challenges similar to those confronting Longchamp, such as justice, shrievalties, castles, revenue, the Welsh, and ecclesiastical appointments. Judicial activity continued both at Westminster and on eyres. While men of local renown such as Bishop William of Hereford, William de Stuteville and Richard of the Peak are found among the itinerant justices, men more experienced on the bench appear more frequently. Geoffrey fitz Peter, Hugh Bardolf, Bishop Godfrey of Winchester, Bishop Richard of London and William Marshal are examples. Walter usually sent these judges to their regions of greatest influence, for example, the bishops of Hereford and Coventry to the Midlands and marcher counties, Geoffrey fitz Peter to Northamptonshire and surrounding areas. The archbishop himself conducted a tour through the home counties in 1192–93. At Westminster, justices tended to be such longstanding associates in legal affairs as Roger fitz Reinfrey, Robert of Wheatfield, Master Thomas of Hurstbourne and Michael Belet. Walter's name is found often at the head of the list of justices sitting at Westminster.[82]

Shrievalties and castles received Coutances's attention as well. With the chancellor's deposition, numerous sheriffs were changed, most of them Longchamp's men. Eight of the eleven shires receiving new sheriffs previously had Longchamp associates as sheriffs; the dispossessed were Longchamp's two brothers, John de Rebez, the Tresgoz knights and Henry de Cornhill. Others were restored to their shrieval offices, including Oger fitz Oger, Earl William of Salisbury and Bishop Hugh of Coventry. Coutances's justiciarship has been described as the golden age of the curial sheriff for the reign of Richard, for during his tenure no fewer than eight shrievalties were held by *familiares*, several of whom held multiple shires, a pattern never repeated during the reign.[83] Clearly, the previous justiciar's practices had been reversed, for none of the Longchamp shrieval appointees continued in office except Robert fitz Roger in Norfolk/Suffolk and the *appares*.

The principle operating in shrievalties was undoubtedly replicated with castellanies, although not all castles appear in the rolls, making a listing of new castellans difficult. At the beginning of Coutances's justiciarship, Count John had been given considerable latitude, enough to elicit Devizes' rather

---

82 Stenton, *Pleas*, 3: xcii–xciv; Heiser, 'Households of the Justiciars', 224–5, 228; *PR5RI*, xxv, 152, 157, 161, 171.

83 Heiser, 'Sheriffs of Richard I', 116–18.

ominous remark that the count of Mortain entrusted castles to whomever he pleased. Nevertheless, the picture drawn by the chronicler was not longlasting, for the pipe rolls show the kingdom's major fortresses in government agents' custody: for example, Roger fitz Reinfrey at the Tower and Wallingford, Geoffrey fitz Peter at Northampton, and William Briwerre at Oxford, Southampton and Sherbourne.[84]

The government's choice for constable of Knighton and Norton on the Welsh border was William de Braose. Security on the frontier with Wales remained a concern, and Coutances, like Longchamp, had to deal with a rising there. When the Welsh leader Rhys ap Gruffudd attacked the castle at Swansea in the summer of 1192, Coutances showed similar energy and vigour in thwarting this menace to the peace of the kingdom. Large sums of money were spent on numerous castles in the region, and an army and fleet, under the command of William Marshal and Geoffrey fitz Peter, were dispatched to relieve the garrison at Swansea. Count John may also have assisted in the military action. A difference between the two justiciars is that whereas Longchamp appears to have led forces against the Welsh personally, Coutances delegated the duty to his associate justiciars.[85]

In all these administrative matters, the archbishop of Rouen demonstrated an 'efficient supervision of the technical detail of government'.[86] Revenue was collected, justice served, the borders defended and officials appointed. Evidence of the energy that Coutances exerted for the king is found in the pipe rolls, where almost every county's entry lists oblations offered before him. He is found as far north as York as late as 1193, even in the midst of the turmoil and threats caused by Count John.[87] Because of Coutances's practice of delegating responsibility, council meetings factored large in his style of governance. Nevertheless, someone provided initiative and leadership for the regency's smooth operation, and it is reasonable to assume that it was the chief justiciar.

Fulfilling royal mandates concerning ecclesiastical elections also occupied the chief justiciar. One of Richard's desires frustrated by Longchamp was the election of the archbishop of Montreale, Sicily, to Canterbury. With Longchamp's departure, Walter made the election a priority, calling the monks of Canterbury to London in October 1191 to proceed. The monks once again rejected the royal nominee as a foreigner, returning to Canterbury to await divine inspiration in the matter. A subsequent letter arrived at Christchurch informing the monks that the justiciar and council were

---

84 *PR3/4RI*, 149, 258–9, 268, 293; *PR5RI*, 83, 87, 134.
85 Poggioli, 'From Politician to Prelate', 90–1.
86 West, *Justiciarship*, 77.
87 *PR3/4RI*, xxv; *PR6RI*, 160.

coming to oversee an election on 2 December. A companion letter was sent to the bishops of the province instructing them to assemble at Canterbury to participate, a sore spot with the monks who claimed an exclusive right to archiepiscopal elections. The monks, suspecting the worst, rushed forward with the election of Bishop Reginald fitz Jocelin of Bath, an action that deeply agitated Archbishop Walter and the suffragan bishops, who appealed the election immediately. In addition, Coutances called the monks and their nominee, Reginald fitz Jocelin, before his court to answer for their actions; but they stoutly insisted on their rights and denied the royal court's jurisdiction. The justiciar, however, found the procedure faulty on grounds that no representatives from either the king or the bishops had been present. As a result, the archbishopric's temporal powers and rights were withheld, although nothing could keep Reginald from assuming his spiritual duties. The crisis soon blew past, when Reginald died shortly after Christmas 1191.

Gervase of Canterbury explains the force of Walter's reaction to the election as motivated by frustrated ambition, but Coutances always acted in concert with the king's mandates and was more worried about accomplishing the royal will than following clerical traditions or achieving personal agendas.[88] Coutances's concern to protect the royal role in episcopal nominations is seen in other elections. Soon after the Canterbury election, Savaric, archdeacon of Northampton, was elevated to the Bath vacancy created by Reginald fitz Jocelin's translation. Because Savaric possessed a royal charter allowing him election to any vacant see that would have him, Coutances did nothing to impede his election and consecration. When the bishop of Exeter died in 1191, Henry Marshal, dean of York, was the candidate proposed; Walter hesitated, however, until he received permission to proceed from the king in Germany. Consequently, not until November 1193 was Henry elected to Exeter. Similarly at Worcester, when the bishop died in the summer of 1193, the justiciar waited until word came from Richard sanctioning an election; and Henry de Sully, Richard's choice as Glastonbury's abbot in 1189, was elected bishop.

The final ecclesiastical election under Archbishop Walter occurred in May 1193, when Hubert Walter, bishop of Salisbury, was translated on the king's orders to the archbishopric of Canterbury. Hubert's experience on the Third Crusade changed the course of his life, for close association with the king won him Richard's undying trust.[89] Again Coutances acted in response to royal directives. In March 1193 Richard communicated his wishes to his mother, the justiciar and the regency council, and the monks

88 Gervase, 1: 510; Poggioli, 'From Politician to Prelate', 76–80.
89 C.R. Cheney, *Hubert Walter* (London, 1967), 44.

of Christchurch, both by letter and the word of his clerk. Richard's urgency can be seen in subsequent letters dated 8 June 1193, in which he urged Eleanor to resolve the matter quickly by going to Canterbury herself. Although the monks and suffragans continued their rivalry, the royal instructions were carried out without a hitch and confirmed by the justiciar.

After assuming the justiciarship, Coutances faced three major crises during his justiciarship, all occurring within a span of approximately twenty-four months, and all threatening to throw the realm into turmoil again. Longchamp returned, seeking to resume the justiciarship, Count John schemed with Philip Augustus to acquire the English throne for himself, and King Richard was captured by the Austrians and held for an enormous ransom by the German emperor. The realm remained secure under Coutances, revealing his effective leadership of the government.

By the beginning of 1192, Longchamp, bishop of Ely, and Walter, archbishop of Rouen, commenced a 'resounding series of excommunications'.[90] The chancellor's crossing to Normandy resulted in confiscation of his episcopal revenues. What Devizes calls an 'ominous contest of the strong' erupted as Longchamp placed his diocese of Ely under interdict and threw anathemas at his attackers, and Coutances responded in kind by ordering that Longchamp be treated as an excommunicant in Normandy.[91] Having appealed to the papacy for redress, Longchamp won letters from the pope that brought down thunderings and curses on his enemies. The chancellor sent these missives to Bishop Hugh of Lincoln, asking that he carry out the sentences against, among others, Count John, Archbishop Walter, Bishop Hugh of Coventry and the *appares*, but the English clergy ignored the papal letters. This situation was not reversed until the queen mother intervened on behalf of the stricken people of Ely in the spring of 1192. Moved to pity by their troubles, Eleanor insisted that the archbishop of Rouen restore Longchamp's holdings and repay his losses, and she persuaded the bishop of Ely to revoke his excommunications. While Eleanor's actions relieved the suffering of the innocent, they did not produce personal reconciliation, for Devizes notes that 'the habits of thought contracted through an old hatred could not be changed'.[92]

Soon after the sentences of excommunication were lifted, Longchamp returned to England, seeking to resume power. His appearance in the kingdom in March 1192 coincided with a meeting of the great council at London, summoned to deal with Count John's occupation of the royal castles of

---

90 Appleby, *England Without Richard*, 99.
91 Devizes, 54.
92 Devizes, 59–60.

Wallingford and Windsor. Longchamp's presence at Dover aroused added alarm, and his desire 'to carry out his orders to the very last clause' only heightened anxieties. With the chancellor back in England, he was perceived as the greater threat, and again the regency government looked to John for leadership against him. He responded that the chancellor had promised him £700 and that if the council were wise, it knew what to do for one in need of money. The council knew what to do, and the count was given £500; in return, John denounced the chancellor. The archbishop and the council also surrendered to John the two castles that he had seized in order to win his support. Strengthened by John's support, the council urged Longchamp to make haste across the Channel 'for his own safety'.[93] The council also attempted to keep the king informed of events as they unfolded. By May letters arrived in the Holy Land from the regency, outlining the intrigues of John and the French king.[94] It was these communiqués from England that convinced Richard to treat with the Muslim leader, Saladin, for a truce and make preparations for a rapid return to the West.

The council at London had originally convened to address the problem of Count John, who had begun to menace the regency soon after Philip Augustus's return in summer 1191. The Capetian monarch had designs on Richard's French territories that only his barons' refusal to fight against a crusader prevented. John had no such scruples, and his flirtation with Philip was only circumvented by Eleanor's insistence that he remain in England. Even at that, to prevent his leaving required the council's threat to seize his castles. John consoled himself by taking into his custody two royal castles, Wallingford and Windsor, and Walter of Rouen responded by calling the council to London to discuss possible sanctions. Much equivocation occurred at the council, for the magnates, fearing Count John, recoiled from taking strong measures. By the time that the council finally decided to call the count for questioning, Longchamp had landed at Dover, diverting its attention.

John remained quiet for a time, and a precarious peace prevailed until word reached England that the Lionheart had been captured by the Germans. On his way home from the Holy Land and in order to avoid the lands of the French king, Richard attempted to sneak through the territory of Duke Leopold of Austria, whom he had humiliated at Acre. In December 1192 he fell captive to the Austrian duke, who delivered his prisoner to the German emperor, Henry VI, on 6 January 1193. John saw his elder brother's captivity as an opportunity to strengthen his position as heir to the Plantagenet domains; indeed, he acted as if he assumed that Richard would

---

93   Both quotations, Devizes, 61–3.
94   Landon, 64.

never leave Germany alive. John rushed to France in early January 1193, making straight for the Capetian court.

Thus began the greatest crisis that the English regency would face at any time in the 1190s. The need to learn of Richard's fate and to communicate with him and to safeguard the realm led the justiciar to call a great council in February 1193. There it was decided to renew oaths of fealty and send the abbots of Robertsbridge and Boxley to locate the captive king. Philip's invasion of Normandy, following Count John's flight to Paris in January, was expanded to preparation of an invasion fleet to assist in John's attempt to usurp the English throne. The justiciar and council, therefore, summoned the militia and began strengthening defences, while John busied himself hiring mercenaries from Wales and Scotland. The Scottish king, however, still grateful for the Lionheart's magnanimous gesture in 1189, refused the count his kingdom's support.

With John's mercenaries in the castles at Wallingford and Windsor securing his back, he appeared before the council at London demanding its allegiance, claiming that Richard was dead. Following the council's flat refusal to support him, hostilities broke out. John's Welshmen began plundering the countryside near Windsor, an occurrence that was particularly frightening since it took place so near the administrative centre at Westminster, and it required prompt action by the regency.[95] Its prompt attention to strengthening the garrisons and weaponry of castles all over the kingdom, especially the coastal and Welsh castles, succeeded in stopping defections to John's cause; even such known associates of the count as Gerard de Camville and Bishop Hugh de Nonant shied from supporting him openly.

The regency's strategy to contain John was to attack two of his principal fortresses, Tickhill and Windsor. Coutances took command of forces laying siege to Windsor Castle and commissioned northern barons, most notably the bishop of Durham, to invest Tickhill. No expense was spared in the attack against Windsor as the rolls indicate over £700 spent there.[96] The siege lasted until late April when Hubert Walter arrived at Windsor with letters directing the regency to begin raising the king's ransom. The expense of fighting Count John could no longer be borne once news arrived of this more extensive demand on funds, making a truce with him a necessity. Here may well be the premier example of the effects of the government's diminished resources following Richard's generosity toward his brother in 1189, for the regency could not ransom its king and suppress rebellion simultaneously. The truce also relieved some political pressure, for if Richard's freedom

---

95   J. Gillingham, 'The Beginnings of English Imperialism', *Journal of Historical Sociology* 5 (1992), 399; *PR5RI*, xv–xvi.
96   Scammell, *Hugh de Puiset*, 57; Poggioli, 'From Politician to Prelate', 95; *PR5RI*, xviii–xix.

could be secured, John would cease to be a problem; if not, a humiliated heir would be uncomfortable for the regency to face. With both castles on the verge of collapse, a truce was negotiated that was to last until 1 November 1193. John surrendered the two castles plus a third, the Peak, to his mother, but he retained Tickhill and Nottingham and the promise that the others would be returned, should Richard not be freed.

One chronicler suggests that Coutances acted with less vigour than was appropriate because John might become king and because his kinsmen numbered among the count's supporters. Another notes that the barons shied away from directly confronting John at the council called to answer his seizure of Wallingford and Windsor. Even the *appares* are suspect. A recent biographer of William Marshal suggests that the Marshal was a member of the count's affinity, and Hugh Bardolf refused to attack John on the grounds that he was John's vassal for lands around Tickhill.[97] Certainly prudent and measured action by Coutances's government was essential to handling this crisis, but had not those qualities earlier found expression during Coutances's dealings with Longchamp? Careful and thorough, Walter of Coutances did nothing rashly, but effectively cut John off from reinforcements, mercenary or baronial. When the truce went into effect, only two royal castles remained in John's hands. Furthermore, anticipation of the king's release once the ransom was raised diminished the threat that John posed. Through Richard's correspondence, the regency knew that they had his support in blocking his brother's attempts to take power. Many historians credit Hubert Walter, recently arrived from the king, with suggesting a truce and winning its approval in the council. Even so, Coutances cannot be described as indecisive or lethargic; his action was consistent with conciliar decision, his preferred manner of governing.

Meanwhile in Germany, Richard's negotiators had concluded a ransom deal that had as its centrepiece the enormous sum of 150,000 silver marks (about £100,000 sterling). Hubert Walter's arrival from Germany redirected the regency from John's rebellion to collection of a 100,000-mark downpayment to purchase Richard's release. To raise the money, a levy of 20 shillings was exacted from each knight's fee; all property and income of both laity and clergy were taxed at a rate of 25 per cent; all churches were stripped of their altar plate; and the Cistercians' wool crop was confiscated, since they possessed no gold or silver vessels. Furthermore, all normal sources of revenue were tapped as fully as possible. Exemptions from taxation, even the clergy's, were nullified by the urgency of the situation; complaints fell on deaf ears, for additional levies were decreed when initial collections failed to

---

97   Gervase, 1: 515; Devizes, 61; Crouch, *William Marshal*, 64, 71–2; *PR5RI*, xix.

meet the need.[98] The king communicated with his kingdom regarding the ransom, petitioning the prior of Canterbury in March 1193 to lend him money from the Church's treasury. In another letter, Queen Eleanor and the regency were encouraged to begin raising the ransom as soon as possible, and they were informed that Longchamp would arrive shortly to escort hostages as pledges to the emperor for full payment. Instructions were attached about proceeding with this monumental task, urging leaders to set an example of generosity, and compiling a registry of donations 'so that we may know by how much we are beholden to each of them'.[99]

A council convened in June 1193 at St Alban's to discuss matters related to the ransom. A special exchequer of the ransom was established, and treasure was stored in St Paul's Cathedral under the justiciar's and the queen's seals. As Coutances's biographer has remarked, 'Walter had taken a revolutionary step in the transformation of the taxation system.'[100] His government's efficiency in collecting the ransom was realised, for the emperor announced in December 1193 that his demands had been met and that Richard would be released early in the new year.

Prior to this, Richard had languished in captivity with his enemies working overtime to prolong his captivity. Philip Augustus did all that he could, sending agents to offer the emperor large sums in the hope of preventing the Lionheart's release. The English king's capture added to Philip's opportunity to make trouble on the Norman frontier and to conspire with Count John. Desperate to keep damage to his possessions to a minimum, Richard dispatched William Longchamp to the French court to work out an agreement at almost any cost. On 9 July 1193, the chancellor and Philip Augustus negotiated a truce at Mantes that negated any Capetian plans for invading England, although at heavy cost in cash and land.[101] The benefit to Coutances and the regency was relief from the threat of a French invasion, although raising the 20,000 silver marks promised to Philip presented a great challenge.

Richard Lionheart summoned Eleanor of Aquitaine and Archbishop Walter to Germany, and they arrived in time to celebrate Christmas with him. John, having learned of his brother's good fortune, fled to Paris where he waited for the inevitable. Toward the end of December 1193, the king appointed as chief justiciar Hubert Walter, who has overshadowed his predecessor. Walter of Coutances's accomplishments are significant, however. Having assumed the justiciarship under far from favourable conditions, he ruled the kingdom through the council with wisdom and balance, keeping

---

98   Newburgh, 1: 399–400.
99   Appleby, *England Without Richard*, 112–13; Howden, 3: 208–11; Landon, 74–5.
100 Poggioli, 'From Politician to Prelate', 100.
101 Landon, 78–9.

John restrained and raising what money he could in an unbelievably short time. Hubert Walter's reputation has largely and justifiably been built on his talents as an administrator, talents that more easily find expression in a period of peace and security and a proximate king. These were not conditions under which Coutances and the *appares* laboured, and they must be judged in that light. Perhaps the importance of Coutances's justiciarship is best seen in his biographer's statement, 'His political acumen had quietly saved Richard's throne.'[102]

---

102 Poggioli, 'From Politician to Prelate', 102.

CHAPTER EIGHT

The government of England under Hubert Walter and Geoffrey fitz Peter

W.L. Warren's survey of English government during the Anglo-Norman and Angevin periods finds that the justiciarship reflected the unity of mon-archical power, for the justiciar 'conducted all aspects of government'.[1] Perhaps at no other time is that ideal realised more fully than during the latter half of Richard's reign, especially the justiciarship of Hubert Walter. One of Hubert Walter's biographers declares that 'the whole burden of English government fell on the justiciar'.[2] Possessed of administrative skill that knew few parallels in the medieval period, Hubert Walter managed the kingdom with decisiveness, efficiency and balance. The king reluctantly accepted Hubert's resignation in 1198, and installed a friend and associate of the great justiciar, Geoffrey fitz Peter, who carried on the tradition established by his predecessor. Unlike the first justiciars of the Lionheart's reign, Hubert Walter and his successor had the advantages of a chastened Count John, peace within the kingdom and the proximity of the king, although war raged on the Continent, a reality that affected England directly and deeply. As a result, predominant in England's government during the late 1190s are administrative developments that expanded the business of government to facilitate collection of huge sums of money for Richard's overseas wars.

Hubert Walter's career as chief justiciar began in late 1193 when Archbishop Walter of Rouen was called to the king in Germany, but the appointment did not herald his first appearance in places of power. Hubert Walter had worked under his uncle, Henry II's chief justiciar Ranulf de

---

1 W.L. Warren, *The Governance of Norman and Angevin England, 1086–1272* (Palo Alto, CA, 1987), 128.
2 C.R. Cheney, *Hubert Walter* (London, 1967), 90.

Glanvill; and at the Council of Pipewell, where many decisions were made in preparation for the crusade, Richard had named him bishop of Salisbury. Hubert spent little time in his diocese as he accompanied the crusading host to the Holy Land where he distinguished himself in the king's entourage, on the battlefield, at the negotiating table and in pastoral duties of various kinds.

Having passed through what one historian calls his 'trial by battle', Hubert Walter gained the respect of the Lionheart, a trust and admiration that could only have intensified when he appeared at the king's side soon after Richard was taken captive in Germany.[3] *En route* to Germany from Sicily, the bishop of Salisbury, aware of the political disaster that had befallen his sovereign, lobbied in Rome for Pope Celestine III's support. His talents, however, could be put to better use in England, and to that end Richard I dispatched him to England in late April 1193 to assure the king's subjects of his well-being and to commence the task of raising the ransom. Although he was not a member of the regency, Hubert's authority, nevertheless, emanated from the fact that he had visited the king and bore his words of instruction.

Chief among Richard's concerns at this point, of course, was his release from German bondage. He and the German emperor, Henry VI, had agreed upon initial terms for release by March 1193, which Richard promptly communicated to the English government. In England, Count John had seized the moment of his brother's distress to advance his own ambitions, but the government took strong measures to pacify the kingdom and to strengthen English defences. With arrival of news from the king that terms had been set, expending resources fighting John became a distraction, and a truce was made. Historians have generally credited Hubert Walter with suggesting this course of action, demonstrating that his arrival in England entailed far more than simply the coming of a royal messenger.[4] The truce permitted the English regency to concentrate its energies on raising the ransom, about which additional details and instructions were arriving in Richard's letters to his mother and to others, and by emissaries, such as the chancellor, William Longchamp.

The logistics of collecting the ransom remain mysterious. A *scaccarium redemptionis* was established to supervise the collection process, most likely at the council at St Albans in June 1193. It was an *ad hoc* arrangement, separate from regular exchequer functions, and the pipe rolls provide next to no clues regarding this collateral exchequer. The 1193 roll records the assessment of two tallages and the disbursement of moneys for the transport of treasure *ad deliberationem domini R.*[5] At St Albans, Hubert Walter, Bishop

---

3 C.R. Young, *Hubert Walter, Lord of Canterbury and Lord of England* (Durham, NC, 1968), 42.
4 For example, Cheney, *Hubert Walter*, 78; Young, *Hubert Walter*, 43; Gillingham, *Richard*, 230.
5 *PR5RI*, 37, 69, 73, 78.

Richard fitz Neal of London, the earls of Arundel and Warenne and Henry fitz Ailwin, mayor of London, were appointed custodians of the ransom, which was to be locked in a chest and stored in St Paul's Cathedral, London, under the queen's and justiciar's seals.

When Hubert Walter returned to England from Germany, his travelling companion, William de Sainte-Mère-Église, bore letters from the king to the regency and the monks of Christchurch, declaring the royal wish to see the bishop of Salisbury translated to the vacant archbishopric of Canterbury. These letters do more than merely communicate the Lionheart's desires; they give reasons that the king so admired Hubert. By the king's account, he had endured 'pains and perils . . . for the sake of God's name', had performed 'many services . . . pleasing to God . . . and ourselves', and had demonstrated 'discretion, loyalty, and constancy, and . . . sincere love . . .'.[6] To Eleanor, Richard recounted Hubert's work at the Roman *curia* and the emperor's court in seeking his release; indeed, nothing except his own freedom was of greater urgency to the captive king than installing Hubert Walter at Canterbury. With such accolades preparing the way, the election was accomplished on 29 May 1193, with only the perennial spat between the prelates of the province and the monks of Christchurch over the right of election marring the festivities.

Hubert Walter's nomination as archbishop placed him among the elite of the king's men and established him as an individual of power and influence in the kingdom's administration. The province of Canterbury spread over the larger and wealthier portions of England and included Wales, and the archbishops had long claimed primacy over all England. Tradition dictated that the archbishop held a ministerial post at the king's side. Indeed, political rather than spiritual considerations were instrumental in Richard's decision to back Hubert's nomination. With Hubert Walter, the Angevins again attempted to forge the power lock over Church and state that William I had achieved with Archbishop Lanfranc and that Henry II had sought with his nomination of Thomas Becket. The success of Richard Lionheart's attempt is apparent.

Richard completed creation of a new regency when he called Walter of Coutances to Germany and installed his new archbishop of Canterbury as chief justiciar, at Christmas 1193. Richard had moved in the direction of placing into one person's hands the reins of power over both Church and state when he secured the papal legateship for Longchamp, but by granting Hubert Walter the posts of archbishop and chief justiciar, the king entrusted him with unparalleled power. A study of the justiciarship finds that Hubert

---

6   W. Stubbs, *Epistolae Cantuarienses*, RS (London, 1865), 363; Cheney, *Hubert Walter*, 39.

Walter enjoyed 'unequalled importance and prestige', and that he 'had a much wider discretion in matters of government than his predecessors'.[7] Richard's appointment of Hubert Walter was in recognition of his knowledge of the king's will, his influence as archbishop, and his role in ransom collection that had already placed him at the centre of government.

The Herculean efforts that were exerted to raise the ransom bore fruit by December 1193 when Henry VI announced that Richard would be released on 17 January 1194. On the appointed day, however, the emperor delayed because he had received from Philip Augustus and Count John proposals that he needed time to consider. Of course, those propositions offered Henry VI significant sums of money to keep the English king in confinement or worse, turn him over to them. Richard launched an impressive appeal to those German lords and prelates present, and they prevailed upon the emperor to stay true to his word. By week's end, the crusader-king had been released to begin the last leg of his journey, bound for England. Foiled in the attempt to extend Richard's hard luck, Philip Augustus came to agreement with a desperate Count John, extending him aid at a high price. He extracted John's promise to cede all Normandy east of the Seine except for Rouen and its surroundings, plus three strong points commanding access to Berry from Touraine.

The new justiciar's wielding of power passed through a preliminary phase – the months before the king's release and return to England – that were times of stress for him. Foremost among the challenges was Count John's rebellion which had matured from the threats of the previous year to full-blown treason. The government became aware of this early in February 1194, when John's messenger to his castellans was arrested in London after brazenly bragging of the count's good relations with the French king. A council was convened shortly afterwards, where it was announced that John's lands were to be seized, his castles besieged, and he and his followers excommunicated for their actions against the unfortunate crusader-king. The earls of Salisbury and Derby were installed in John's lands as sheriffs. The archbishop-justiciar personally led an assault on John's position at Marlborough, and after its fall received the surrenders of Lancaster and St Michael's Mount. Meanwhile, the indomitable bishop of Durham besieged Tickhill Castle in Yorkshire and several earls attacked Nottingham. Upon hearing that the Lionheart had landed, the archbishop hastened to greet him, joining him on the road from Rochester to London; and then he returned to join the assault on Tickhill, arriving there as the garrison surrendered.

---

7 F.J. West, *The Justiciarship in England, 1066–1232* (Cambridge, 1966), 79.

The king took command of the forces arrayed against Nottingham Castle, and by the last week of March all was quiet. He then called a great council at Nottingham to punish those who had recently risen against him and to prepare for the coming struggle to drive Philip Augustus from Plantagenet territory in France. This council charted the course for England for the remainder of the reign; Hubert Walter sat at Richard's right hand. Money was of paramount importance both for redeeming the hostages who remained in Germany and for arms and men to fight the French. Also of significance was ensuring the integrity of royal officials, especially local officers, after the rebellion. These two concerns collided in the shrievalties and castellanies, as Richard changed many sheriffs and constables and made monetary arrangements with them.

During the king's visit to England in the spring of 1194, two-thirds of the shrievalties received new sheriffs, several receiving royal appointees for the first time in the reign due to the confiscation of Count John's shires. Richard's involvement in the 1194 appointments of sheriffs is less discernable than in 1189, but scraps of evidence that survive point to substantial royal participation. For instance, Roger of Howden's account of the Nottingham Council has the king dealing directly with the Lincolnshire and Yorkshire shrievalties, and the new sheriffs' first appearance in the pipe roll is at Easter term, the time that Richard was in England.[8] The return of William Longchamp's relatives to shrieval offices can only be explained by royal decision, given the depth of hostility felt by the English toward this family. Motives for the king's actions range from punishment for adherents to Count John's cause, such as Bishop Hugh of Coventry and Gerard de Camville, to patronage for close associates, such as Longchamp's kin, to strategic concerns, such as William de Braose in Welsh border counties, to administrative considerations, such as Hugh Bardolf in counties previously exempted from the central government's jurisdiction.

Richard did more than simply settle the kingdom by these appointments; he also used them as sources of revenue. In the second round of shrieval appointments, the king still intended to sell shrievalties and still primarily utilised men of local stature, but his methods of raising money had changed. Now, Richard employed smaller entry fines, but added in most cases sizeable annual increments. The largest was the £200 required annually of Simon de Kyme from Lincolnshire. Initial returns from this policy change were less than spectacular, but in the long run, increments proved an improved revenue-raising method which produced larger and steadier sums. The money

---

8   Howden, 3: 240–2; R.R. Heiser, 'Richard I and his appointments to English Shrievalties', *EHR* 112 (1997): 4–7.

collected by 1199 on increments alone more than doubled that collected under the previous method of large fines and proffers.[9]

Other important local officials receiving attention during the king's visit were the constables of castles, although it is more difficult to discover their names than those of sheriffs. None the less, changes in the roster occurred, although how sweeping and at what cost to individual constables is unknown. Dover Castle returned to the custody of Matthew de Cleres, brother-in-law of William Longchamp, who had been ousted when the chancellor lost his justiciarship. The earl of Salisbury purchased in 1194 the vill, shrievalty and castle of Salisbury for 40 marks which ended for a time Robert de Tresgoz's custody of the castle.[10] Nottingham, Tickhill, Wallingford and Windsor, previously granted to Count John, now received royal constables, but their new constables are unnamed in the pipe rolls. William Briwerre, sheriff of Berkshire and Nottinghamshire/Derbyshire where three of these castles were situated, likely held them as part of his shrieval duties; a similar scenario prevailed at the Yorkshire castle of Tickhill, where Archbishop Geoffrey Plantagenet was sheriff. Clearly Richard installed new constables and probably did so in exchange for cash.

The Nottingham Council's action in stripping Count John of all his lands and castles and its subjection of his lands to royal sheriffs and constables indicates that punishment was also the order of business. Even with Hubert Walter pleading for mercy on behalf of the rebels, the king exacted a terrible price for their folly. Robert de la Mara was fined only 10 marks, although Gerard de Camville and Bishop Hugh of Coventry were saddled with fines of 2,000 marks each. The lands of Ralph Murdac and William de Wenneval, John's constables at Nottingham Castle, were seized and overseen by William de Sainte-Mère-Église, royal escheator, and lists of other confiscated properties of the king's enemies can be found on the pipe rolls. The sheriff of Cornwall delivered several fines paid to him by men who had been in St Michael's Mount *contra Regis*. Even Count John's wife was forced to pay £200 to protect her dower and marriage portion from the vengeful king.[11] According to Ralph of Coggeshall, Richard reserved his cruellest punishment for his prisoner Robert Brito, whom he ordered starved to death.[12]

---

9 *PR6RI*, 103; Heiser, 'Richard I and Shrievalties', charts on 14, 15, 16, 18.
10 *PR6RI*, 196, 202, 242.
11 *PR6RI*, 84–5, 118, 120, 218, 238; *PR7RI*, 191. Howden gives Coventry's fine as 5,000 marks; 3: 287. For Nottingham castle, *PR6RI*, 15, 18; *PR7RI*, 44–5. For Cornwall fines, *PR6RI*, 174; the countess of Gloucester, *PR6RI*, 193. Another example is the wife of William Blanchard, who lost her dower *quia vir suus fuit cum comite Johanne*; *PR6RI*, 118.
12 Coggeshall, 63; Brito's lands were still in the king's hands after Richard's death; C.T. Flower (ed.), *Curia Regis Rolls* (London, 1923–), 1: 207–8, 245, 264–6.

Changing sheriffs and constables and fining and punishing rebels settled the kingdom, and Richard's actions after this rebellion were hardly unique, although starvation seems cruel and unusual. Once those matters had been addressed, however, he turned his attention to the issue of money more directly. Before the king stood the challenge of ejecting Philip Augustus from lands he had treacherously seized while his Angevin vassal was crusading and languishing in prison. Richard called out a third of the English feudal host to join him in Normandy, which provided him with resources in several ways. Those answering the summons obviously added to his manpower, and they were often rewarded by exemptions from the ransom scutage. Others offered fines for not answering his call to arms, funds that could be used to hire mercenaries. The 1194 pipe roll also indicates that a twenty-shilling scutage and hidage at a rate of two shillings per hide had been collected.[13]

Towns also contributed to the revenue-raising effort. London presented 1,500 marks for its portion of the ransom, for its liberties and for the king's goodwill. The people of York gave 200 marks in celebration of the king's safe return, and the citizens of Lincoln proffered 500 marks for confirmation of their charter of liberties. Other towns, such as Doncaster, Norwich and Gloucester, purchased the right to have their towns at farm.[14] Few indeed were the sources of funds that went untapped, and significant sums were collected, for the pipe roll records men, money and equipment following the king to France when he departed England in May.[15]

Evidence from the pipe rolls indicates that Richard I husbanded his resources somewhat better in 1194 than in 1189. The shires that had fallen away from the exchequer during the king's first visit to England were restored, helping to produce the dramatic rebound in annual receipts for his final years which ran fully £10,000 per year ahead of totals in the first half of the reign. Royal lands were not reclaimed, however, as revenues from *terrae datae* continued their pitch into lower returns. Whereas Henry II was able to realise about 60 per cent of the real value of the royal demesne, by 1198 Richard had alienated so extensively that the percentage had dropped to 39 per cent. It was left to Hubert Walter to exploit other sources of revenue, such as feudal incidents, profits of justice and patronage, in order to make up the difference.[16]

---

13 *PR6RI*, xxiv, 65, 85, 66, 120, 130, 135, 192–4; H. Hall, (ed.), *Red Book of the Exchequer*, RS (London, 1896), 1: 79.
14 London, *PR6RI*, 182; York, 118; Lincoln, 163; other towns, 64, 161, 238.
15 *PR6RI*, 141, 176, 212, 213.
16 Barratt, 'English Revenue of Richard I', Colloque aux Archives du Calvados (Caen, April 1999), 8, 10.

Richard's only diplomatic business while in England was a meeting with the king of the Scots, William the Lion, who had contributed generously to the ransom. The Scottish king had long harboured a wish to regain the northern English shires of Westmorland, Cumberland and Northumberland lost on account of his support for Henry II's rebellious sons in 1174, but through diplomatic missteps and blunders he had failed. Richard's magnanimous treatment in 1189 sparked hope within King William, and with the path prepared by his sizeable gift toward the ransom, he asked for the three counties. The king ducked this request by saying that such a huge petition required the advice of his council, which turned it down. William made another bid, this time sweetening the deal by offering 15,000 marks; and the council, reluctant to reject a financial boon, agreed to allow him Northumberland without its castles. Far from satisfied, the Scottish king withdrew his offer. A couple of days later, William tried one last time to get something from Richard, but he left frustrated by another denial.

Richard's policies toward the Scottish king in 1189 have been praised as prudent and timely, but had he undone the good work by his intransigence in 1194? The English king needed two things: money that these counties could produce and peace on the Scottish border, making this a tricky diplomatic situation. An irate Scottish king could be courted by Philip Augustus and persuaded to cause trouble in the north of England while Richard was pinned down on the Continent. The Lionheart showed political savvy by deferring to the council, dodging the grim task of declining William's request personally. The council tried to appease the Scottish king by confirming privileges that he would enjoy when visiting with the English court. That Richard valued good relations with the Scottish ruler is seen in his later attempt to marry his nephew, Otto of Brunswick, to William's daughter, Margaret. Although this match never occurred, it indicates that the Scottish king had not abandoned his favourable policy toward Richard. The Lionheart could leave England confident that William would not defy him.

Before the king left England in April, a grand ceremony was held at Winchester Cathedral. Often described as his second coronation, this event is better understood as a traditional crown-wearing, a reminder to his English subjects that, captivity and rebellion aside, the Lionheart remained enthroned as the realm's sovereign. A king could no more be crowned a second time than a prelate could be reconsecrated, but 'the king's person was regarded with an awe that Richard's crown-wearing would naturally increase in the minds of the spectators'.[17] Richard himself was reluctant to endure this

---

17 Gillingham, *Richard*, 242; J.T. Appleby, *England Without Richard, 1189–1199* (Ithaca, NY, 1965), 138–9.

spectacle, but his leading men and advisers prevailed, and the ceremony was held on 17 April. Surrounded by the kingdom's great men, both lay and ecclesiastical, by Queen Eleanor and by the Scottish king, Richard Lionheart was presented in full regalia to the assemblage in the cathedral.

With the technicalities of pacifying England behind him, the king turned his attention to his French holdings suffering under the assaults of the Capetian ruler. After waiting impatiently at Portsmouth for the weather to clear, he sailed from England on 2 May, leaving its care to Hubert Walter. This time, the Lionheart left England in a stable state, having restored order after John's rebellion, punished those who had foolishly joined in it, and secured the border regions. He had appointed many new sheriffs and constables, implemented improved revenue-raising methods, installed an able chief justiciar, and reminded all of his undiminished authority by his crown-wearing. Richard had also filled his war chest with funds necessary to start the work of driving his enemy from his cross-Channel lands. As in 1189, he sold what people would buy, but avoided or reversed many of the errors of his first visit to his English kingdom.

Hubert Walter's justiciarship, though dated from Christmas 1193, actually began with the king's departure. For the archbishop, the king was not too distant and John had been eliminated as a political force within the kingdom. Prior to this time, Hubert had not had opportunity to mould the administration into the finely tuned machine that would characterise his justiciarship. A description of his mode of governing best begins with his incredible level of activity. To quote one biographer, 'Whatever else Hubert Walter may have been, he was industrious', and that applied to both Church and state. Another remarks on his 'remarkable vigor and enterprise', observing his mental acumen and his personal participation in the actual business of governance.[18] His primary concern was supplying the king financially, unlike Longchamp and Coutances, whose principal duty had centred on preserving the kingdom for the king. As a result, Hubert had the time, interest and reason to regularise the administrative system. His legacy to medieval English government was a veritable overhaul of the administrative apparatus, all of it driven by 'hard-headed, fair-minded, practical, and down-to-earth' thinking.[19]

Observable in Hubert Walter's justiciarship is a notable change in style of governance. Whereas Archbishop Walter of Rouen had worked by way of consensus with the queen, nobility and *appares*, Hubert Walter abandoned that practice almost completely. The number of magnates holding office as

---

18   Young, *Hubert Walter*, 166–7; Cheney concurs, *Hubert Walter*, 95–6; West, *Justiciarship*, 94–5.
19   Appleby, *England Without Richard*, 198–9; West, *Justiciarship*, 94–5; Young, *Hubert Walter*, 125.

sheriffs and constables steadily declined during the latter half of the 1190s, although the justiciar did not work actively to disadvantage the nobles, for 'he had the political wisdom to avoid the kind of confrontation that would unite them in opposition to him'.[20] Rather, Hubert Walter built up England's administrative system without unduly encouraging the arbitrary nature of Angevin government. Even his hard-bitten critic, Gerald of Wales, calls the justiciar the bridle of princes and obstacle of tyranny.[21] That is not to say that Hubert Walter did not wield a powerful sword; his brutal dealings with William fitz Osbert in London are evidence that the English government under Hubert would act energetically against those threatening the peace of the realm. Some historians have applied such terms as ruthless and oppressive to Hubert Walter's justiciarship. While these terms may accurately represent how English subjects felt during these days of unfathomable taxation, they are not descriptive of the justiciar himself.[22]

Unlike his predecessors, whose primary concerns were survival, uppermost in Hubert Walter's mind was efficiency in government's functioning to facilitate the raising of fighting funds. In creating an administrative machine that smoothly carried out orders, Hubert Walter, it is argued, turned to men experienced in government. A look at the offices of sheriff and constable and their holders recommends a less hasty conclusion. In the shrieval office, for instance, Hubert Walter made no attempt to subvert the settlement established by the king; he no doubt had taken part in the appointment process and was pleased with the result. In this regard he stands in contrast to Richard's previous justiciars. Vacancies occurring after 1194 were usually the result of sheriffs' deaths or political necessity, such as the passing of William fitz Aldelin in Cumberland and the earl of Salisbury in Wiltshire, or the patronage extended to Robert de Harcourt, or Simon de Kyme's failure to pay outstanding debts. Where Hubert Walter differed from the king is in his preference for using lower-level servants. By the end of his justiciarship, the number of counties under such officials had tripled, but this hardly heralded the formation of a professional shrieval class, involving only four men in six shires.

If professionalism did not come with Hubert's appointments of sheriffs, how did it occur in local administration? The creation of professional bodies of servants has at its centre specialisation of task and personnel, but the sheriff, because of his wide-ranging duties, was an omnicompetent officer among

---

20 Young, *Hubert Walter*, 113–14.
21 Young, *Hubert Walter*, 168–70; Gerald of Wales, 1: 247.
22 F. Barlow, *The Feudal Kingdom of England 1042–1216*, 4th edn (London, 1988), 388; Cheney, *Hubert Walter*, 91. See also D. Carpenter, 'Abbot Ralph of Coggeshall's Account of the Last Years of Richard and the First Years of John', *EHR* 3 (1998), 1210–30.

the king's civil servants. Hubert Walter's approach reflects his mental agility and his creativity in addressing administrative challenges. Instead of developing a corps of professional sheriffs, the justiciar removed many of the duties that had formerly belonged to sheriffs through such specialised offices as the escheators and coroners, such groups as the knights of the shires, and regulations forbidding sheriffs from serving as justices within their own shrievalties. No longer juggling so many different tasks, the sheriff was left primarily with criminals, revenue and castles. David Carpenter, in an important article on thirteenth-century curial sheriffs, sees this trend and concludes that the sheriff had become the crown's chief fiscal officer in the localities.[23]

Administrative records during Hubert Walter's justiciarship suggest that custody of royal castles again became a primary task of the sheriff as in previous reigns. Royal castles had played a major role in Longchamp's and Coutances's justiciarships, and they appear to have named numerous constables who were not sheriffs, but the number of non-shrieval constables named during Walter's justiciarship is considerably smaller. Usually these few were well known to the government, such as Hugh Bardolf, William de Sainte-Mère-Église or the earl of Salisbury, but they did not hold multiple castles or enjoy long tenure of those they held. Sheriffs accounted for castle expenditures from their annual farms, and it may have been that Hubert Walter was combining the two posts in a more deliberate fashion. Whatever the case, the evidence does not support the development of a group of professional constables.

The office of royal justice, unlike that of sheriff and constable, follows the traditional line of argument regarding growth of a professional judiciary, and historians have used this royal official as proof that Hubert Walter was creating a corps of professional administrators. Exercise of justice moved toward ever-increasing specialisation, signalled by written records begun under Hubert's supervision: plea rolls, coroners' rolls and feet of fines (copies of agreements ending property disputes). Less than twenty people served Hubert Walter regularly as judges, most with ample judicial experience; and the older omnicompetent officers of the realm, such as Geoffrey fitz Peter and Hugh Bardolf, are no longer found among them. Furthermore, these trends apply to the bench at Westminster as well as eyres, and justices' employment appears connected more to ability than to family or patronage. The confining of personnel to those of known legal expertise is also seen in the small number of justices recruited from either the royal or archiepiscopal households.[24]

---

23   D. Carpenter, 'The Decline of the Curial Sheriff 1194–1285', *EHR* 91 (1976), 4.
24   R.R. Heiser, 'The Households of the Justiciars of Richard I: An Inquiry into the Second Level of Medieval English Government', *HSJ* 2 (1990), 223–31.

Part of Hubert Walter's strategy for improving the government's efficiency included specialisation in departments as well as personnel. The pipe rolls indicate that the exchequer was swamped in the latter half of Richard's reign due to the 'strenuous financial effort necessitated by the king's ransom ... and the war with France'.[25] At least two secondary exchequers were created to ease the workload of the main accounting body. The first, the *ad hoc* exchequer for the ransom, has already been discussed; another is the exchequer for Jewish debts. The justiciar had not put forward a serious effort to collect outstanding Jewish debts, many of which were owed since the death of Aaron of Lincoln late in Henry II's reign. By 1198, however, an exchequer of the Jews was operational, entrusted with clearing the slate of debts that had been uncollected for years. Those appointed to accomplish this task were Simon de Pattishall, Henry de Whiston, Benedict de Talemont and Joseph Aaron.[26] These changes did not create a revolution within the English administrative system, but they lightened the workload of the barons of the exchequer and forced a division and specialisation of labour previously unknown.

Under Hubert Walter, the office of royal escheator was placed on a firmer footing. Earlier in Richard's reign, John Marshal had held an office akin to what was to be formed in 1194, but with a far less elaborate accounting procedure. The 1194 roll reveals that Hugh Bardolf had been installed as royal escheator for the northern counties and William de Sainte-Mère-Église for the southern counties. Holding escheated lands as guardians rather than farmers, these men provided the exchequer with detailed accounts of the lands they supervised. For some reason, the office was phased out by 1198 when escheats were restored to the sheriffs.[27]

Similar professionalism was introduced in administering the kingdom's mines. Hubert Walter's interest in the proceeds that mines could produce became evident soon after he took the justiciarship. His clerk, Joseph Aaron, received payment for services rendered at the Careghofa silver mine, and by 1195 Joseph was reporting for its earnings.[28] The same year the justiciar was dealing with the tin trade in Cornwall and Devon. These mines had usually been farmed by the sheriff, resulting in small sums entering the treasury, but by Easter 1195 they were removed from the sheriff and given to Master Philip de Hawkchurch and Hervey de Helyon. In 1198 the

---

25 *PR9RI*, xiii.
26 *PR9RI*, xxi; *PR10RI*, xxix, 210, 214.
27 *PR3RI*, 60, 198, 254; *PR5RI*, 14; *PR6RI*, 1–27; *PR7RI*, 26–62. *PR9RI*, xxv; R.V. Turner, *The English Judiciary from Glanvill to Bracton c. 1176–1239* (Cambridge, 1985), 83; *Men Raised from Dust: Administrative Service and Upward Mobility in Angevin England* (Philadelphia, 1988), 23.
28 *PR6RI*, xxxiv; *PR7RI*, xxv.

justiciar installed an associate of Geoffrey fitz Peter, William de Wrotham, as custodian of the mines. Contained in documents related to William's installation were detailed instructions for the accuracy of measuring instruments and for disposing of profits. Profits from these mines increased dramatically due to Hubert's measures, surpassing those of the county of Cornwall itself.[29]

A new office, that of coroner, was a product of the general eyre of 1194. The coroners' duties were carried out by three knights and a clerk who were elected by the shire court. Possessing county-wide jurisdiction and free from shrieval authority, these officials removed from the sheriffs the duty of gathering and preserving criminal evidence in preparation for the testimony of juries of presentment before the itinerant justices. The duties performed by these elected servants fulfilled tasks essential for the functioning of justice in England. Warren has called the coroner 'a piece of administrative tidying', for it removed from the sheriff a time-consuming responsibility at a time when he was being called upon to produce more revenue.[30] Coroners also represent the central government's growing dependence on local men for performance of administrative tasks.

The eyre of 1194 represents the justiciar's determination to acquire information and deliver the message that ordered government had returned to England. In September 1194, the justiciar, following the pattern that general eyres visit the shires once every four years, sent delegations of justices to every shire save Bedfordshire and Buckinghamshire. The itinerant justices received instructions in the form of twenty-five articles covering five categories: the hearing of pleas, investigations into escheats, promulgation of regulations, enquiries into local officials' conduct and enquiries into special non-recurring matters, such as issues arising from Count John's rebellion.[31] Preparations for this eyre likely resulted in the creation of the office of escheator, and instructions guiding the itinerant justices contained directives instituting the coroners' office. Other matters within the itinerant justices' jurisdiction related to criminals, methods of electing juries and a tallage. Although the inquisition into royal officers' activities was postponed by Hubert Walter, the articles reflect his wide-ranging efforts to secure royal rights and revenue. A similar eyre was launched in 1198, consistent with the four-year schedule, and it resembled the 1194 eyre in scope and breadth.

---

29 W.R. Powell, 'The Administration of the Navy and the Stannaries, 1189–1216', *EHR* 71 (1956), 179–80; Young, *Hubert Walter*, 125; *PR7RI*, 126–35; *PR9RI*, 15–16; *PR10RI*, 181; *PR1J*, 242.

30 Warren, *Governance*, 135–6.

31 Warren, *Governance*, 137–8.

Hubert Walter issued in 1195 an *edictum regium* that revised machinery for keeping the peace in the shires. Local knights were selected to extract from all males over the age of 15 an oath promising to preserve and enforce the king's peace by denouncing criminals in their communities and joining in their pursuit. Violators of the peace were turned over to knights of the shire who would hand them over to the sheriff for safekeeping until justice could be administered. This measure takes on importance for future administration of justice, for the knights appointed to take the oaths were forerunners to the keepers of the peace who eventually evolved into the justices of the peace. The employment of knights of the shire is noteworthy. Here, as with the coroners and juries of presentment, local men with no direct link to the central administration, not even a salary for services rendered, were drawn into the king's service. Warren underscores the importance of this decree, stating that the 'device of locally appointed officials acting in the interests of the community but strictly accountable to the king's justices for the enforce-ment of the king's law forged a new kind of link in the chain of government, and a new relationship between the crown and its subjects'.[32] Being drafted to perform these tasks delighted few knights, if historians' terms of 'drudgery' and 'onerous' are to be accepted; yet research shows that those possessing the social or economic clout to evade these duties made little effort to do so.[33]

How do these developments reflect on the contention that one of Hubert Walter's primary achievements was professionalising Angevin England's administrative system? Local officials, whose role in royal government was growing substantially, cannot be categorised as possessing the skills and talents demanded by a sophisticated governmental machine. The picture of increasing professionalism and specialisation must be modified to reflect the dual nature of Angevin administrative development by the 1190s. Indeed, government was becoming more and more dependent for the performance of its duties, especially judicial, upon local men of stature. While it is true that Hubert Walter created a body of professional justices, that fact is balanced by a corresponding rise in recruitment of knights of the shires to do the king's bidding. Looking down through the corridor of English history, the latter trend prevails as the preferred method of governing the realm, for English monarchs never developed the elaborate and extensive bureau-cratic systems found in continental kingdoms. None of this is to say that the government had turned to buffoons, for the men found serving in the shrievalties and courts were men of standing in the community.

---

32 Warren, *Governance*, 134; also Barlow, *Feudal Kingdom*, 387–8.
33 Hugh Thomas, 'The Knights of the York County Court in 1212', in E. King and S. Ridyard (eds), *Law in Mediaeval Life and Thought* (Sewanee, TN, 1990), 137–50; Appleby, *England Without Richard*, 217; Warren, *Governance*, 136.

Among the articles of the eyre of 1194 is a directive for a tallage that reveals the emphasis on raising money for the king's wars in France. This search for money became the hallmark of Hubert Walter's justiciarship. As has been stated, the kingdom of England had been put on a war footing, not for self-preservation but for defence of the Angevin empire on the Continent. Because money from England purchased the extra men and supplies needed by Richard for Normandy's defence, Hubert Walter had to raise unprecedented sums. Indeed, recent scholarship on Richard's and John's finances reveals Hubert Walter wringing more money out of the English than even John did prior to 1204. So onerous was the tax burden in the late 1190s that a pipe roll editor concluded that England was reaching the breaking point.[34] Contributing to the urgency was inflation in late twelfth-century England, which multiplied the costs of waging war. If Richard of Devizes described William Longchamp as a lightning bolt, to what would he have compared Hubert Walter? A nuclear blast, had he known of it? Ralph of Coggeshall considered the endless demands for more money Richard's greatest sin, for his exactions were greater than those of any king before him.[35]

Few were the sources of revenue overlooked, including an attempt at imposing general taxation on the English. An experiment with reviving the old geld, a land tax called the carucage took place in 1198, with the assessment based on the carucate or a measure of ploughland. Again local knights played key roles in assessing the tax, but the experiment failed to take root, for many shires offered fines to be free of the obligation. Besides new initiatives, old obligations were revived. For instance, the bishop of Lincoln was compelled to fulfil the ancient but lapsed tradition of supplying the king with fine furs, an obligation that was repealed after the bishop's offering of 2,000 marks.[36] In 1194 Richard I lifted the ban on tournaments in England, and Hubert Walter appointed his brother, Theobald, as collector of admission fees. Figures for other areas of royal finance such as justice, scutage, debt collection, tallage and other miscellaneous items saw marked increases as the government pounded harder and harder to squeeze out revenue wherever it might be found.[37]

Richard, like his father and his brother John, had to resort to exploitation of his lordship over the English baronage for raising money, eventually fuelling baronial resentment over feudal payments and services. Heirs to

---

34 Turner, *King John*, 87–114; N. Barratt, 'The Revenue of King John', *EHR* 111 (1996), 835–55; N. Barratt, 'The English Revenue of Richard I', table 1; *PR9RI*, xiii.
35 Coggeshall, 93.
36 Appleby, *England Without Richard*, 183–4; *PR7RI*, 159.
37 Barratt, 'The English Revenue of Richard I', table 4.

baronies found that they had to offer reliefs or fines for succession to their predecessors' property greater than the £100 that was coming to be seen as customary. Records for Richard's reign reveal at least thirty-seven relief payments for baronies, and the amounts varied greatly: only one below 100 marks, six (16 per cent) at 100 marks, seven (19 per cent) at 200–300 marks, eleven (30 per cent) at £100, and eleven at 500 marks or more. Baronial heirs' offerings had to increase with inheritances more complicated than simply a son's succession; the largest was Roger de Lacy's 1195 fine of 3,000 marks for Pontefract, which he claimed by right of his mother through a series of females. In addition to Lacy's fine, Ralph de Somery first sought his uncle's barony of Dudley, Worcestershire, with an offering of 300 marks, which grew to 400 marks when he met with the king in Germany. Similarly, Harvey Bagot offered 200 marks for the barony of Stafford by right of his wife, sister of the deceased baron, but later Hubert Walter required an additional 100 marks.[38]

Another case that shows Richard Lionheart personally involved in a baronial inheritance is Roger Bigod's quest for the earldom of Norfolk. He paid 1,000 marks in 1189 for the earldom, which Henry II had withheld from him since his father's death in 1177. Soon after paying, his right was challenged by his younger half-brother's claim to the inheritance, and Roger offered 100 marks that he not be disseized of lands that his half-brother was claiming except by judgment of the *curia regis*. The king by a writ *de ultra mare* intervened, informing the exchequer that Roger, fighting at his side in Normandy, had increased his proffer to 700 marks.[39]

Several recent studies detail ways in which royal lordship had become 'truly mercenary' by Richard's later years. Thomas K. Keefe, for example, finds an increase of over 1,000 per cent in baronial oblations under Richard I: from average annual fines of £104 in Henry II's reign to £1,248 in Richard's.[40] Other papers detail the Angevin kings' treatment of women in

---

38 Lacy, *PR7RI*, 98; I.J. Sanders, *English Baronies: A Study of their Origin and Descent 1086–1327* (Oxford, 1960), 138; W.E. Wightman, *The Lacy Family in England and Normandy* (Oxford, 1966), 86; Somery, *PR6RI*, 74; *PR9RI*, 143; Bagot, *PR5RI*, 85; *PR6RI*, 41.

39 J.C. Holt, 'Ricardus Rex Anglorum et Dux Normannorum', in *Magna Carta and Medieval Government* (London, 1985), 75; R.A. Brown, 'Framlingham Castle and Bigod, 1154–1216', in *Castles, Conquest and Charters: Collected Papers of R. Allen Brown* (Woodbridge, 1989), 199–200.

40 Quotation from S.L. Waugh, *The Lordship of England: Royal Wardships and Marriages in English Society and Politics, 1217–1327* (Princeton, NJ, 1988), 158; T.K. Keefe, 'Proffers for Heirs and Heiresses in the Pipe Rolls: Some Observations on Indebtedness in the Years Before the Magna Carta (1180–1212)', *HSJ* 5 (1993), 99–109. In another paper, Keefe identifies ten men in Richard's first years as members of a '£1,000 Club', i.e. those whose fines for favours had indebted them to the king for at least £1,000; 'Counting Those Who Count: A Computer-assisted Analysis of Charter Witness-lists and the Itinerant Court in the First Year of the Reign of King Richard I', *HSJ* 1 (1989), 139, table 2.

their custody, widows and heiresses of barons. Scott Waugh's study of Angevin wardship policies finds under Henry II relatively modest fines for wardships, but which increased under Richard from an average of 176 marks to 1,158 marks.[41] Janet Loengard's study of widows' payments for freedom from remarrying turned up few such fines under Henry II, but Richard I's 1198 command for a 'sweep of eligible widows' by the itinerant justices 'appears to have been little less than an act of extortion'. While widows had proffered a total of 2,096 marks in Henry II's entire reign, they offered his successor 1,689 marks in 1198 alone.[42] Not only noblewomen had to offer fines in order to marry freely, but also male heirs in royal custody. Ralph Musard, minor heir to the barony of Stavely, Derbyshire, at the beginning of Richard's reign, offered a sixty-mark fine 'for marrying where he should wish'. The king, after his return from Germany, would not accept sixty marks from Ralph and demanded a hundred instead.[43]

The 1198 pipe roll shows the king and the justiciar exploring every possible source of revenue. A new royal seal was commissioned in 1198 with orders that all documents authenticated with the previous seal be resealed; attached, of course, were markedly higher fees to the chancery for the resealing. Alongside all this, a general forest eyre commenced in 1198, which became still another drain on an already drained kingdom, as forest proceeds rose from £22 in 1197 to £748 in 1198.[44]

Barons and curialists were willing to offer large fines for such profitable favours as wardships of minor heirs. Hubert Walter played this game, offering 500 marks in 1194 for the heir to the barony of Odell. In 1197, William de Stuteville offered 1,000 marks for custody of two boys, one of them the heir to the earldom of Lincoln.[45] They were gambling that they could pay off their fine out of profits from their wards' lands, paying the exchequer in extended instalments or perhaps never paying. Such gamblers ran the risk of encountering the exchequer as a collection agency for crown debts, following an

---

41 And to 3,068 marks under John; Waugh, *Lordship of England*, 157–8.
42 Thirty-nine fines were recorded in 1198; and 3,411½ marks in fines for the years 1189–98; *PR10RI*, xxviii, 16, 107, 125. See J.S. Loengard, ' "Of the Gift of her Husband": English Dower and its Consequences in the year 1200', in J. Kirshner and S.F. Wemple (eds), *Women of the Medieval World* (Oxford, 1985), 234–5; Waugh, *Lordship of England*, 159–60; also S.S. Walker, 'Feudal Constraint and Free Consent in the Making of Marriages in Medieval England: Widows in the King's Gift', in T. Cook and C. Lacel (eds), *Historical Papers, Saskatoon, 1979*, Canadian Historical Association (Ottawa, 1979), 97–109.
43 Sanders, *Baronies*, 83; *PR2RI*, 58; *PR6RI*, 235; *PR7RI*, xxix.
44 *PR10RI*, xix–xxx. Appleby, *England Without Richard*, 214–17, 220; Young, *Hubert Walter*, 125–6; Landon, 173–80; Barratt, 'The English Revenue of Richard I', table 4.
45 Hubert Walter; H.G. Richardson, *Memoranda Roll 1 John* [Originalia Roll 7 Ric. I], PRS, ns. 21 (London, 1943), 86; *PR6RI*, 209; Stuteville, *PR9RI*, 62; for other examples, *PR6RI*, xxii.

administrative law – the *lex scaccarii* – that could result in loss of their lands, should the king insist on payment of their fines.

These actions by the king and his justiciar in demanding more and more from the baronage did not always meet with quiet acceptance, although complaints were relatively rare. The Lionheart was no longer content that simple scutage payments and fines should exempt barons from a royal summons to overseas service.[46] At a great council in December 1197, Hubert Walter presented to the assembled magnates the king's demand for 300 knights to serve for one year. While the majority of barons, lay and ecclesiastical, were prepared to submit to this exaction, Bishop Hugh of Lincoln, perhaps still smarting from the fiscal shakedown he had received earlier, refused on the grounds that he owed no military obligation outside England. He was joined in his defiance by the bishop of Salisbury. The justiciar's and king's response was to order these prelates' lands confiscated, which occurred in the case of the Salisbury estates, but no one dared touch the holdings of one so holy as Hugh of Lincoln. Later Hubert demanded one-tenth of the feudal levy which nearly equalled the 300 knights originally demanded, though without the year's service.

The justiciar's episode with William fitz Osbert epitomises the unrest kindled among the lower orders over the relentless taxation. The poorer citizens of London rallied in early 1196 to Fitz Osbert's banner to protest demands levied by the city's magistrates. They had burdened London with promises to the king that it could not meet, such as 1,500 marks for royal favour and confirmation of liberties, 500 marks in gift, and £40 scutage. Inflammatory language sparked a riot that ended with the rabble's leaders barricaded in a church. Efforts at peaceful resolution gave way to more forceful measures when the church's tower was set afire, driving Fitz Osbert and his companions into the authorities' hands and eventually to the gallows. Because the justiciar acted decisively, 'The city elders could sleep again quietly in their beds.'[47]

One other incident pointing to the extent and intensity of exactions during Hubert Walter's justiciarship is the rather odd episode involving Abbot Robert of Saint-Etienne, Caen, and the bishop-elect of Durham whom Richard sent to investigate charges of embezzlement allegedly occurring on the chief justiciar's watch. The abbot had managed to convince the king that as much as half of the revenue raised from his island kingdom was not making its way into the royal coffers. An inquiry was ordered, and the sheriffs were summoned for interrogation, but the scheme fell flat with Robert's sudden

---

46 That is, *ChanR8RI*, 117, 141, 186, 271.
47 Quotation, Cheney, *Hubert Walter*, 93–4; Young, *Hubert Walter*, 127–9; Appleby, *England Without Richard*, 191–2.

death soon after his arrival in England. Hubert Walter was offended at the thought that Richard would question his and his officials' integrity, and the king hastened to alleviate the justiciar's distress by claiming that the inquest was intended only for learning who had contributed to his cause. Unappeased, the archbishop temporarily sought release from his post, but not before reminding the king of how much money he had raised for him in the previous two years.

The problem of Wales festered throughout much of Hubert Walter's justiciarship. The king's concern for this region can be seen in his exemption of the Welsh border lords from answering the summons to arms.[48] Powerful men, William de Braose and William fitz Alan, retained custody of shrievalties; and royal agents were rebuilding castles in the region: Cymaron Castle by Roger de Mortimer and Bleddfa Castle by Hugh de Say.[49] The first military expedition led by Hubert Walter against Wales occurred in 1196, when a successful attack was made at Welshpool against the rising leader, Gwenwynwyn of Powys. Sums spent for this military effort suggest that it was a substantial showing by the English.[50] The justiciar installed trusted agents as custodians of Welshpool and Denbigh Castle, to the north.[51] Shortly afterward, Hubert Walter settled a succession dispute among Rhys ap Gruffudd's sons, declaring in favour of Gruffudd. Welshpool was apparently invested again by the Welsh in 1197 as the pipe rolls record moneys being sent to its constable in order to lift a siege. The situation still later that year was troublesome enough for the justiciar to visit the Welsh border, where he installed new constables at Bridgnorth, Ludlow and Hereford.[52] As one of Hubert Walter's last acts as chief justiciar, he helped to organise in the summer of 1198 yet another expedition against Gwenwynwyn, who had besieged William de Braose at Painscastle. It fell, however, to Geoffrey fitz Peter as the new chief justiciar to lead this force.

Records suggest that the Welsh were far from unified in their struggle against English encroachment. Mercenaries for the war in France were hired in large numbers from among them, and the pipe rolls contain numerous references to Welshmen receiving compensation for services rendered to the king. Cadwallon, brother of Gwenwynwyn and son of Rhys ap Gruffudd, was taken to meet the justiciar in 1195 and by 1197 held Church Stretton Castle in Shropshire.[53] Gerald of Wales, of mixed Norman and Welsh

---

48 *ChanR8RI*, xvii.
49 *PR7RI*, 107, 243, 244; *ChanR8RI*, 41, 87; *PR9RI*, 9, 108, 156, 194; *PR10RI*, 108, 211.
50 *ChanR8RI*, 17–20.
51 *ChanR8RI*, xxiv, 42; *PR9RI*, 156.
52 *PR10RI*, xxvii, xxxi.
53 *PR7RI*, xxvi–xxvii, 244, 254; *ChanR8RI*, xxiv; *PR9RI*, 156.

ancestry, remained in receipt of government wages throughout Walter's justiciarship. Frustration at his continual attempts to become bishop of St David's had not yet turned Gerald against the Plantagenet line.[54]

Hubert Walter's justiciarship had two bedrock foundations, king and Church, the latter being far more than ornamental. In 1195 Richard I petitioned the pope and received for his chief regent and archbishop of Canterbury the legateship of all England. Recent research into the legateship of another of Richard's justiciars, William Longchamp, indicates that Richard, in contrast to his father's experience, was remarkably successful in combining secular and religious powers in one faithful servant, thereby 'harnessing legatine authority to the royal cause'.[55] Providentially, Hubert Walter faced no royal–papal conflicts during his justiciarship or archiepiscopacy that might have forced him to choose between king and pope.

As primate of the English Church, Hubert Walter was responsible to promote its spiritual vitality. This required, among other things, convening ecclesiastical councils, conducting visitations and hearing appeals. Another key was ensuring that vacancies were filled. Recent research has shown that in this matter Hubert Walter was not the prime mover; rather it was the king, who moved quickly, nominating mainly curial favourites. Even though Richard was hard pressed for money, he preferred to fill vacancies rather than let them serve as cash cows for the royal government, as Henry II had done. During the latter years of the Lionheart's reign, bishops were placed in Durham, Ely, London, Worcester and Coventry; and monastic houses receiving new abbots included Chertsey, Eynshem, Glastonbury, and St Mary's York.[56]

As archbishop and papal legate, Hubert Walter carried out visitations, for example, to York Minster to settle affairs there. Archbishop Geoffrey was with the king in France, and Bishop Hugh of Durham was dead, leaving the northern Church in dire need of leadership. The long-running argument about primatial authority, often manifested in the two archbishops' staging of processions with erect crosses in each other's province, was averted as Hubert Walter conscientiously warned York officials of his coming. They proved willing to receive him as legate rather than archbishop. He removed abbots from Thorney and St Mary's York for inability to carry out their duties; he arbitrated in various cases affecting Church property and practice, and he sat as judge over other issues. In 1197 he helped the pope to organise another crusade, a project that would not bear fruit until the pontificate of Innocent III.[57]

---

54   *PR5RI*, 88; *PR6RI*, 136; *PR7RI*, 108; *ChanR8RI*, 88; *PR9RI*, 195; *PR10RI*, 211.

55   I. Sprey, 'William Longchamp: Papal *legatus a latere* and Faithful Royal Servant', unpublished paper presented at the American Historical Association annual meeting (Seattle, January 1998).

56   R.V. Turner, 'Richard Lionheart and English Episcopal Elections', *Albion* 29 (1997), 1–13.

57   Young, *Hubert Walter*, 131–2, 141.

The archbishop also settled two old arguments relating to monastic cathedral chapters and their prelate-abbots, who preferred secular canons. Bishop Hugh de Nonant had ousted the monks at Coventry Cathedral earlier in the reign, but Hubert Walter, acting on papal directive, reinstalled the monks in January 1198. Similarly, Hubert made peace with the monks of Christchurch, Canterbury, who had fought hard against his scheme to establish a house of canons at Lambeth. The archbishop tried to assure the monks that he meant them no harm, but they were not assuaged, and by 1199 he had begun demolishing buildings at Lambeth. While these are only examples of Hubert Walter's ecclesiastical activities, they demonstrate the breadth of his concern for the Church, making accusations of neglect misleading.

In 1198 Hubert Walter resigned from the justiciarship, and opinion is divided about why he quit his post. He may have left office because of the workload's adverse effects on his health, or because he had tired of clerics' raised voices against his involvement in secular affairs. Hubert Walter did not leave the king's service, however, for he joined the royal entourage on the Continent. As a fitting summation of the career of this great man, Francis West wrote '[T]he administration performed well enough to raise unprecedented amounts of money while at the same time securing and maintaining the safety and good order of the kingdom.'[58]

The government of the realm fell to Geoffrey fitz Peter, who had been closely associated with the great justiciar-archbishop. Installed in July 1198, Fitz Peter served Richard for only nine months before John acceded to the throne. During this brief period, a general eyre and forest eyre were launched, the former following the pattern established for the eyre of 1194. The justiciar rode to the relief of William de Braose who was trapped by Gwenwynwyn in Painscastle on the Welsh frontier, and he won there a dramatic victory over the Welsh. Geoffrey appeared no less determined in revenue-raising than his predecessor, and he was instrumental in keeping the kingdom quiet during the transition of power following Richard's death. The change in chief justiciars made little difference in the government's smooth functioning because Hubert Walter and Geoffrey worked closely together, the former writing often with advice on matters relevant to the justiciar's office.[59]

Although policies established in the previous justiciarship continued uninterrupted, Geoffrey fitz Peter did make personnel changes among sheriffs, justices and constables. At the Michaelmas 1198 session of the exchequer, ten shires received new sheriffs. Two counties, Staffordshire and Yorkshire,

---

58 West, *Justiciarship*, 96.
59 R.V. Turner, *Men Raised from the Dust* (Philadelphia, 1988), 44–55.

went to the justiciar himself, which was the first instance in Richard's reign of a sitting justiciar holding shrieval office. This likely can be explained by Fitz Peter's status as the Lionheart's first lay justiciar, although clerics holding secular and ecclesiastical office never seemed to bother him. The number of shires with curial sheriffs increased somewhat, but Geoffrey continued to employ men of local stature. Alterations in the roster of those dispensing justice occurred as such judges as John of Guestling, Henry de Whiston and Eustace de Fauconberg joined the core of professionals at Westminster recruited by Hubert Walter. A few constables were changed also. John fitz Godfrey had held Colchester for much of Richard's reign, but now it was turned over to William de Lanvaley, lord of the Walkern barony in Hertfordshire.[60] John de Torrington, newly appointed sheriff of Cornwall and Devon, was given custody of Carmarthen Castle in Wales; and Alan fitz Oger took possession of Winchester Castle, previously held by Oger fitz Oger.[61] It is likely not coincidental that Geoffrey held lands near those of both Lanvaley and Torrington and that Alan bears an old curial name.

During the five years before Richard's death at a distant castle in south-western France, the government of England carried out its duties with swiftness, efficiency and productivity that enabled him to prosecute effectively his wars on the Continent. With few exceptions, the justiciars of the latter half of the reign – Hubert Walter and Geoffrey fitz Peter – preserved order in the kingdom and succeeded in binding baronial support to the government despite their ever-increasing financial demands.

---

60 Sanders, *Baronies*, 92; *PR1J*, 87.
61 *PR1J*, 1, 182, 187.

CHAPTER NINE

The duchy of Normandy

Richard I and his father, Henry II, both spent more time in Normandy than they did in England or in their possessions to the south. The Lionheart spent a month there on his accession in July 1189 and again on his return from England in December. After his two-month visit to England in the spring of 1194 following his release from captivity, he was busy in Normandy defending the duchy against Philip Augustus almost continuously until February 1199.[1] Although the amounts of time that Richard spent on the two sides of the English Channel differed greatly, Normandy shared with England such similarities in administrative structures and sometimes in personnel that scholars often have treated them together as a single 'Anglo-Norman realm'. Recently, however, historians have expressed doubts about the Anglo-Norman king/dukes' or their Angevin successors' attempts to mould their duchy and their cross-Channel kingdom into a single Anglo-Norman *regnum*.[2] All agree, however, that Richard, his father and his brother John had in their two northern domains more efficient machinery for exercising power than farther south. Both territories had effective governments, capable of functioning in Richard's absence and of raising vast revenues.

1　For Henry, T.K. Keefe, 'Place–date Distribution of Royal Charters and the Historical Geography of Patronage Strategies at the Court of Henry II Plantagenet', *HSJ* 2 (1990), 179; for Richard, Landon, *passim*.

2　Supporting the concept of a single 'Anglo-Norman realm', see Hollister, 'Normandy, France, and the Anglo-Norman *Regnum*', in his *Monarchy, Magnates and Institutions in the Anglo-Norman World* (London, 1986), 17–58; and J. Le Patourel, *The Norman Empire* (Oxford, 1976). Critics include D. Bates, 'Normandy and England after 1066', *EHR* 104 (1989), 851–76; J. Green, 'Unity and Disunity in the Anglo-Norman State', *Historical Research* 63 (1989), 115–34; D. Crouch, 'Normans and Anglo-Normans: A Divided Aristocracy?', in D. Bates and A. Curry (eds), *England and Normandy in the Middle Ages* (London, 1994), 51–67.

The 'feudal transformation', usurpation by castellans of public authority in much of eleventh-century France, was averted in Normandy, and its government continued to maintain an 'essentially Frankish character'. The early dukes had kept much of their public authority, preserving 'to a remarkable degree' prerogatives inherited from their Frankish predecessors.[3] Doctrines of royal or ducal power stretching back from the Carolingians to Rome, coupled with the duke's superior material resources, permitted frequent interventions in the fiefs of tenants-in-chief, 'overturning the principles and functioning of a feudal regime of the classic type'.[4] Consequently, the Norman and Angevin dukes took direct management of much of the work of governing that was left to localities and landlords in other French principalities.

Just as in the Carolingian kingdoms, the early Norman dukes maintained monopolies over mints and fortifications that were two essential traits of sovereignty and of public authority. The 'peace of the duke' gave him authority to regulate his nobles' construction of castles, to protect merchants and peasants and to curb to some extent private warfare. Most obvious is nobles' submission to judgments of the ducal court; as the *Très ancien coutumier* stated, 'Let no man dare wage war against another man, but bring his complaint to the duke or his justice about any injury borne by him.'[5] Ducal jurisdiction extended to all serious criminal offences or 'pleas of the sword'; an 1174 list included murder and manslaughter, mayhem, robbery, arson, rape and premeditated assault. Henry II initiated new civil actions, possessory assizes for settling property disputes similar to those that he introduced into England. These assizes, affording litigants who purchased a writ the sworn inquest as a more rational mode of proof, soon proved more popular than the traditional proofs by duel or compurgation. With Henry, the ducal judicial system 'overshadowed nearly all private jurisdiction', and this near-monopoly over justice generated revenues that compensated for a decline in income from the ducal demesne.[6] Indeed, Norman profits of justice were

---

3   D. Bates, *Normandy before 1066* (London and New York, 1982), 173, 238.
4   J. Boussard, 'Aspects particuliers de la féodalité dans l'empire Plantagenêt', *BSAO*, 4th ser., 7 (1963), 34; also Powicke, *Loss*, 59, '[I]t seems to me impossible to believe that the dukes were able to achieve all this [authority] simply in virtue of their feudal lordship. Their position implied an element of sovereignty.'
5   E.J. Tardiff (ed.), *Le Très ancien coutumier*, c. 31, p. 27, in *Coutumiers de Normandie*, 1 (Rouen, 1881); cited by P. Poggioli, 'From Politician to Prelate: The Career of Walter of Coutances, Archbishop of Rouen, 1184–1207', PhD dissertation (Johns Hopkins University, 1984), 195.
6   C.H. Haskins, *Norman Institutions* (Cambridge, MA, 1918), 187, 196–212; Tardiff, *Coutumiers*, 64–5; Powicke, *Loss*, 63; F.M. Powicke, 'The Angevin Administration of Normandy II', *EHR* 22 (1907), 17.

proportionately greater than similar income from England, mainly due to a better rate of debt collection in Normandy.[7]

The Norman dukes combined Carolingian traditions of public authority with newer concepts of military lordship to create a more authoritarian and hierarchical structure of 'feudal' government than elsewhere on the Continent. Castles were key to Normandy's defence, and the dukes took care to regulate their nobles' construction of new fortifications and to enforce their 'rendability', the ducal right to occupy and garrison them when military necessity dictated. When Count Geoffrey le Bel of Anjou occupied the duchy, he took control of a number of private castles, and his son Henry II continued this policy of confiscating castles. According to Roger of Howden, Henry took in his hand all the castles of England and Normandy in 1176, installing his custodians in them.[8] Although Howden may have overstated Henry II's control over castles, he and his sons did continue to build new fortifications and to strengthen old ones, consuming large sums on castle works. Yet Richard Lionheart's expenditures for building Château-Gaillard outranked all other castle works, totalling almost £46,000 *angevin* (over £11,250 sterling).[9]

Soon after the conquest of England, the Anglo-Norman king/dukes had succeeded in forcing their Norman vassals to accept fixed quotas of knights to provide for the feudal levy, as two documents show: the Inquest of 1133 for the bishopric of Bayeux's fiefs and the Inquest of 1172. The latter is comparable to the English Inquest of 1166, listing ducal tenants-in-chief, the number of their knights enfeoffed, and the number owed to the duke. They include about sixty lay barons, the seven Norman bishops, ten abbots and one abbess.[10] Generally, Norman barons owed only a small portion of their enfeoffed knights to the duke; the bishop of Bayeux, for example, owed only a sixth of his knights, 20 of 120.[11] The dukes of Normandy did not depend solely on the feudal levy for raising a military force, however; in an emergency, they could proclaim the *arrière-ban*, mobilising all their barons' knights regardless of the number assigned as *servitium debitum*. More significant were the mercenary soldiers that the dukes' cash revenues enabled them to hire and the contributions of militias organised by communes.[12] Normandy

---

7 V. Moss, 'Normandy and England in 1180: Pipe Roll Evidence', in D. Bates and A. Curry (eds), *England and Normandy in the Middle Ages* (London, 1994), 194.

8 Howden, 2: 105.

9 Powicke, *Loss*, 186–90, 205–26; see Boussard, 252, n. 4, on castle expenditures for 1180 and 1184, citing Stapleton, 1: 29, 50, 52, 56.

10 H. Hall (ed.), *Red Book of the Exchequer*, RS, 3 vols (London, 1896), 2: 624–45, 1172 Inquest.

11 S.E. Gleason, *An Ecclesiastical Barony of the Middle Ages: The Bishopric of Bayeux, 1066–1204* (Cambridge, MA, 1936), 50, 72–3.

12 Powicke, *Loss*, 211–12.

had its counterpart to England's Assize of Arms, specifying the military obligations that the various classes of society owed.

Norman nobles, in addition to supplying quotas of knights, had to pay a variety of feudal dues that enhanced ducal income. The strong ducal government made possible imposition on the nobility of payments of relief, custodies of minor heirs and widows, and assessments of scutage just as in England. Norman financial records – incomplete compared to England's, but voluminous compared to those of Greater Anjou and Aquitaine – record numerous fines offered for such favours as custodies of minor heirs and marriage of heiresses. For example, the county and city of Evreux were in ducal hands after Count Amaury III died on the Third Crusade, leaving a minor son as heir. Even though the boy's mother had offered £2,000 *angevin* (£500 sterling) in 1195 for custody of her son's lands, she evidently acquired possession of only part of them, and the county remained in Richard's hand for the rest of his reign.[13] This contrasts with custom in Anjou and Aquitaine, where custody was claimed by family members.

Although 'feudal' revenues were significant under the Angevin king/dukes, their local agents – *baillis* – continued to collect public revenues surviving from the Carolingian period as part of their farm of the *prévôté*. Even early dukes had taken care to prevent their magnates from usurping the public obligations owed by ordinary freemen.[14] Although the precise composition of the farms is unclear, they chiefly represented an amalgamation of rights and revenues, most descending from the Carolingian *fisc*. They included a variety of imposts on land and agricultural produce collected from an early date in coin. Some of these had fallen to seignorial lords as customary dues owed by their peasants; but others continued to be general taxes collected by the *baillis*, for example, the *graveria* or viscount's aid and the *fouage* or hearth tax. The latter was levied only triennially, but it substantially increased ducal revenues every third year. Also various tolls on commerce collected at ports, along the Seine and on roads survived from the pre-Norman period, known by the ancient names of *theloneum, passagium, pedagium, pontagium*. By the twelfth century, the Norman towns' expanding commerce provided income from taxes collected at fairs and markets, or at Rouen, a levy of a portion of the wine sold. They apparently produced ducal revenues averaging about £20,000 *angevin* (£5,000 sterling) annually, but Richard was willing to grant

---

13 D. Power, 'The Norman Frontier in the Twelfth and Early Thirteenth Centuries', PhD thesis (Cambridge, 1994), 180–81, 191, 193; citing Stapleton, 1: 139 (widow's fine); 2: 151 (1195); 413, 462–4 (1198); similarly, Stapleton, 1: 40, Clementia, widow of Robert de Montfort, rendered account of £500 remaining of her fine from custody of the land of her son.

14 Powicke, *Loss*, 210.

away a high proportion of this inelastic income. He granted income of some farms to his mother, Eleanor of Aquitaine, and to his brother, Count John.[15]

Reliance upon aids or tallages and forced loans grew as the pressures increased for more money for Normandy's defence during Richard's last years. As in England, aids, tallages or *tailles* not limited to the three or four so-called 'feudal aids' – for example, *auxilium exercitus* or *tallagium servientium* recorded on the 1198 pipe roll – raised substantial revenues both from urban and rural communities on the ducal domain. The nature of the tallage on towns varied; some negotiated lump-sum payments, others imposed forced loans on leading families, and occasionally ducal officials assessed individuals. In 1180, no loans are recorded and tallages of only two towns, raising £66 *angevin*. By 1198, however, tallages and loans were the chief fiscal resource, producing slightly less than half the duchy's revenue. Richard's tallages *per preceptum regis* appear to have been an assertion of the Angevins' arbitrary will, perhaps essential for raising his ransom.[16]

By the time of Richard's accession, Rouen was well on the way to becoming a 'capital' comparable to Paris; it was the largest city in France after Paris with a population of 30,000–40,000 in the early thirteenth century. Henry II had granted Rouen a charter of liberties, the *Etablissements de Rouen*, as early as 1150–51 which became a model for the privileges that Richard and John granted other towns within their 'empire'.[17] Rouen's charter freed its citizens from tallages, 'unless they should wish to give it to us by their free will'.[18] In 1195, the farm of the *prévôté* of Rouen brought in £3,200 *angevin* (£800 sterling), and additional revenues increased the duke's total income from the city to more than £7,000 *angevin* (£1,750 sterling).[19] Normandy's Jewish community was centred in Rouen, and as in England, the

---

15 Powicke, *Loss*, 234. Various estimates of the *prévôts'* total farm include Moss, 'Normandy and England in 1180', 195, who estimates 1180 income at £12,488 *parisis* or £18,365 *angevin* (£4,591 sterling); V. Moss, 'Normandy and the Angevin Empire: A Study of the Norman Exchequer Rolls 1180–1204', PhD thesis (University of Wales College, Cardiff, 1996), 65, estimates 1198 farm revenue at almost £13,000. L. Delisle, 'Des revenues publiques en Normandie au 12ᵉ siècle', *BEC*, 2nd ser., 5 (1848–49), 287, gives a higher figure of 12,000 marks (£7,850 sterling). See Moss, 'Normandy and the Angevin Empire', 68–9, for the decline in farm revenue by almost half through alienation by 1198.

16 C. Stephenson, 'The Aids of the French Towns in the Twelfth and Thirteenth Centuries', in B. Lyon (ed.), *Medieval Institutions: Selected Essays* (Ithaca, NY, 1954), 15–16; Moss, 'Normandy and the Angevin Empire', 65, 69–79.

17 D. Bates, 'Rouen from 900 to 1204: From Scandinavian Settlement to Angevin "Capital",' in J. Stratford (ed.), *Medieval Art, Architecture, and Archaeology at Rouen, British Archaeological Association, Transactions*, 12 (1993), 1–11.

18 Stephenson, 'Aids of French Towns', 10.

19 Bates, 'Rouen from 900 to 1204', 6 and n. 58, citing Stapleton, 1: 70–1; 2: 154–5, 304–5, 306–8. Boussard, 254, n. 1, citing Stapleton, 1: cxlvi–cxlvii, gives lower numbers: £2,200 and £3,000.

Jews formed a valuable resource for the king/duke, enjoying his protection and enduring his often oppressive supervision. For example, the 1195 pipe roll records a tallage of 10,000 marks imposed on the Jews of Normandy, probably toward payment of Richard's ransom.[20] While commercial centres were generating thousands of pounds for the duke, income from his rural bailliages and *prévôtés* raised only hundreds. A recent study of Norman ducal finances estimates revenues from towns at perhaps 25 per cent of the total by the end of Richard's reign.[21]

Despite the growth of towns and trade, Normandy's forests continued to be an important source of revenue for Richard Lionheart. Not all areas under forest jurisdiction were actual woodlands, but cleared land was still subject to special forest regulations, enforced by local assizes, not by English-style forest eyres. Unlike in England, the duke's forest income came chiefly from sale of forest products, not from enforcement of forest law. Richard doubled the 1180 figure of some £2,000 *angevin* for revenue from forests. This was not achieved by new methods of exploitation, but from sales of forest land, an alienation similar to that in England with short-term benefits but long-term liabilities.[22]

Normandy had an exchequer, a central financial office where local officials presented their accounts for auditing; with it, more effective exploitation of monetary rights of ducal lordship over the baronage was possible. Like its English counterpart, the Norman exchequer produced written records, the pipe rolls; but unfortunately, far fewer of the Norman rolls survive, only those of 1180, 1195 and 1198, and fragments from 1203. Not even these surviving rolls present a complete picture of Norman finances, since they are chiefly accounts for income of the ducal domain. They fail to include profits from mints, offerings placed directly in the king/duke's hands, and other miscellaneous payments that supplied substantial revenues, for example, collection of Richard's ransom. Since Richard Lionheart was continuously present in Normandy from 1195 to 1199, funds could have flowed directly into his chamber. None the less, recorded revenues from Normandy under Henry II and Richard I reveal a rapid increase, rising from about £27,000 *angevin* (or £6,750 sterling) in 1180, to more than £42,000 *angevin* (£10,500 sterling) in 1195, and to almost £100,000 *angevin* (£25,000 sterling) by 1198. Such figures compare favourably with annual revenues during the same period from the larger English kingdom that were averaging almost

---

20 Powicke, *Loss*, 241; Moss, 'Normandy and the Angevin Empire', 73, citing Stapleton, 1: 134–35, 229.
21 Moss, 'Normandy and the Angevin Empire', 79–81; also Powicke, *Loss*, 56.
22 Moss, 'Normandy and the Angevin Empire', 17–18, 66; Powicke, *Loss*, 57–8.

£25,000 sterling.[23] They indicate that the Norman exchequer was either growing more efficient or more rapacious, or both.

A viceroy in Normandy, the seneschal – also called justiciar after 1176 – headed the exchequer and the central government, concentrating in his hands administrative, financial and judicial activities. Described in an 1179 letter as *princeps omnium et magister*, he was the king/duke's chief agent, much like the English justiciar, giving the Normans effective government in the duke's absence. The seneschal/justiciar had charge of the ducal castles, keys to his control of the duchy. His headquarters were at the Norman exchequer, located at Caen, which became, along with Rouen, the centre of most routine business of ducal government. Treasuries were located at Caen and Rouen, with other deposits of funds at Falaise and at Argentan.[24]

Richard inherited his Norman seneschal from his father: William fitz Ralph, member of a Derbyshire family, whose 'entire professional formation took place in England'. He held the post from 1177 until his death in 1200, literally 'the head of the State' during Richard's absences.[25] A number of household officers such as the constable or marshal had assisted the seneschal; while most tended to become hereditary and honorific offices, held by members of noble families, the Norman constable remained active in the duchy's affairs. Richard in June 1190 confirmed William de Hommet as his father's successor in the office of constable.[26] He and William fitz Ralph were among the most frequent witnesses to the new king/duke's charters during the months before his departure for the Holy Land (December 1189–June 1190), and third was the archbishop of Rouen, Walter of Coutances. No other Norman official approached their frequency as charter witnesses in that period before the Crusade.[27] Assisting the seneschal at the exchequer was Robert, abbot of Saint-Etienne, Caen. Richard Lionheart sent Robert to England in spring 1196 to conduct an investigation of Hubert Walter's financial administration, but he died soon after arriving in London, and the inquiry was abandoned. Also active in financial affairs was a money-lender of Rouen, Geoffrey Cambiator or Geoffrey du Val Richer. He did not hold any official title, but acted throughout Richard's reign in financial matters, especially in collection of the king's ransom and funds for construction of

---

23 Moss, 'Normandy and the Angevin Empire', 63, citing J. Ramsey, *A. History of the Revenues of the Kings of England, 1066–1399* (Oxford, 1925), 1: 191, 227. For another calculation, N. Barratt, 'The English Revenue of Richard I', unpublished paper presented at the Colloque aux Archives du Calvados (Caen, April 1999), table 3.

24 Powicke, *Loss*, 52; C.H. Haskins, *Norman Institutions* (Cambridge, MA, 1918), 176, n. 115.

25 J. Le Patourel, 'Henri II Plantagenêt et la Bretagne', app. 2, in *Feudal Empires, Norman and Plantagenet* (London, 1984), 119–20; Powicke, *Loss*, 52.

26 *Cal. Docs. Fr.*, no. 536.

27 R.R. Heiser, 'The Royal *Familiares* of Richard I', *Medieval Prosopography* 10 (1989), 40.

Château-Gaillard. He may also have acted as one of the custodians of the treasury at Rouen.[28]

The key local officials were the *baillis* whom Geoffrey Plantagenet had introduced from Anjou after his conquest of Normandy on behalf of his son Henry. They largely replaced the earlier *vicomtes*, although the two terms continued to be used interchangeably. These officials, like many of the Angevins' servants, were recruited from the middling ranks of the knightly class, and they came mainly from native Norman families. Only a few, such as Robert de Tresgoz, *bailli* of the Cotentin 1195–1202, had personal ties to the Lionheart.[29] The duchy had about twenty-eight *baillis* responsible for districts variously known as *bailliages* or *vicomtés*, but in some areas smaller districts known as *prévôtés* survived primarily as units of financial administration, although the office of *prévôt* did not. Norman administrative units tended to remain fluid, never as firmly fixed as the English counties.[30] *Baillis* usually served also as castellans of a ducal castle that served as their base. In many ways, they were counterparts of the English sheriffs, exercising judicial and military responsibilities as well as accounting for revenues. Just as periodic general inquests in England scrutinised the sheriffs' performance of their duties, inquiries in Normandy checked on the *baillis*' conduct.[31] The farm of the *prévôté*, a fixed payment comparable to the sheriff's farm of the county in England, was the responsibility of the *bailli* at the exchequer, along with profits of justice and other ducal income.[32]

The seneschal (or justiciar) presided over the exchequer's twice-yearly sessions at Caen, auditing the *baillis*' accounts. He and his fellow barons of the exchequer also sat as a tribunal before which litigants could bring their suits.[33] Just as in England, many religious houses, prominent persons and ducal officials received charters or writs of protection, granting them the privilege of having their pleas heard only before the king/duke or his chief justiciar, that is, at the Norman exchequer. Twenty-seven of Richard Lionheart's charters placed Norman religious houses under his special protection.[34] Between exchequer sessions, the seneschal organised yearly

---

28 Moss, 'Normandy and the Angevin Empire', 44–5, 121, 130.
29 For names of *baillis*, Moss, 'Normandy and the Angevin Empire', app. 2, 248–56.
30 See the list in Powicke, *Loss*, 68–78; Moss, 'Normandy and the Angevin Empire', 134, lists 6 new *bailliages* formed in the 1190s.
31 For example, Stapleton, 1: 146, John de Préaux rendered account of over £600 following an investigation of all the Norman *baillis*, cited by Powicke, *Loss*, 64, n. 140.
32 Boussard, 335; Powicke, *Loss*, 52–6, 103–16; Powicke, 'Angevin Administration II', 22–6.
33 Haskins, *Norman Institutions*, 184; for a survey of Norman justice, S.R. Packard, 'The Judicial Organization of Normandy, 1189–1204', *Law Quarterly Review*, 40 (1909), 442–64.
34 C. Fagnen, 'Essai sur quelques actes normands de Richard Coeur-de-Lion', *Ecole nationale des Chartes, Positions des thèses* (Paris, 1971), 72.

circuits of royal justices that took the new possessory assizes, carrying ducal justice from the exchequer to the *bailliages* and forming a link between the centre of government and the localities. In the Middle Ages, justice was a source of profit for the prince; and the duchy of Normandy was no exception, producing revenues ranging from over 10 per cent of the total in 1180 to little more than 4 per cent in 1198.[35]

Only a few records of pleas before the seneschal's court survive, scattered among exchequer rolls and cartularies. This lack of evidence makes it less easy to know the personnel of the ducal *curia* than the English royal justices. The ducal justices, however, appear to have been professional royal servants, as likely lay as clerical, similar to those in England. An example is Ralph l'Abbé, a bourgeois of Sées, farmer of ducal revenues at Alençon by 1180 and *bailli* at Argentan for twenty years. He appears as a justice late in Richard's reign, served John on the bench, and continued to be a judge under Philip Augustus after 1204.[36] Another sign of professionalism at the seneschal's court is the composition of the first part of the *Très ancien coutumier* about the time of Richard Lionheart's death; apparently the work of a clerk in the seneschal's service, it shows the influence of the English treatise on common law, *Glanvill*.[37]

Normandy's strong government compared to Anjou or Aquitaine is reflected in the number of Richard's writs and charters concerning the duchy. Although the Lionheart's surviving *acta* overwhelmingly treat English topics, Norman documents far outnumber those dealing with the rest of his continental territories combined: 142 (19 per cent) Norman and only 65 (8 per cent) treating the rest of the Angevin 'empire'. As J.C. Holt points out, 'The distribution of the surviving documentation almost certainly reflects that of the jurisdictional system of assizes and writs which England and Normandy alone shared within the Plantagenet domains.'[38]

---

35 Moss, 'Normandy and the Angevin Empire', 65.

36 For an account of his career, see Power, 'The Norman Frontier', 341, n. 135. Another example is Henry de Pont-Audemer, an administrator who heard assizes at Falaise in 1200 and at Pont-Audemer in 1203. He is unique in continuing his judicial career in England; see R.V. Turner, *The English Judiciary from Glanvill to Bracton c. 1176–1239* (Cambridge, 1985), 148–9.

37 P. Orliac, 'Législation, coutumes et coutumiers au temps de Philippe Auguste', in R.-H. Bautier (ed.), *La France de Philippe Auguste: le temps de mutations* (Paris, 1982), 482–3. For dates, Baldwin, 226.

38 J.C. Holt, 'The Acta of Henry II and Richard I of England 1154–1199: The Archive and its Historical Implications', in P. Rück (ed.), *Fotografische Sammlungen mittelalterlicher Urkunden in Europa* (Sigmaringen, 1989), 139, gives 433 English, 117 Norman, and 40 for other domains of 590 total. I have replaced Holt's Norman figure with 142, adding charters collected in Fagnen's work, 'Essai sur quelques actes normands de Richard Coeur-de-Lion', and those collected by Deville, BN ms. nouv. acq. lat. 1244.

Except for its sea coast, Normandy had no natural boundaries, and its frontiers were 'zones' rather than sharply drawn borders that required measures for defence.[39] The early dukes had created counties as marcher lordships to protect the duchy's frontiers, but by the Angevin period all Norman counties had come into Richard Lionheart's hand except the county of Alençon on the southern frontier with 111 knights' fees. At the beginning of his reign, the Lionheart carried out his father's wishes in granting to his younger brother, John, the county of Mortain at the corner of Brittany, Maine and Normandy. In the counties of Aumâle and Eu on the northeastern frontier, he installed loyal supporters through marriages of heiresses. Before departing on crusade, he married the widowed countess of Aumâle to one of his Poitevin warriors, William de Forz; on William's death in 1195, he gave the countess in marriage to his companion on crusade and in captivity, Baldwin de Béthune. Some time before August 1194, Richard gave the heir to Eu in marriage to Ralph of Exoudun, a member of the Lusignan family of Poitou which had proven its loyalty to him in the Holy Land. Since Philip Augustus had made rival grants of these two counties to his allies, Ralph of Exoudun and Baldwin de Béthune proved to be 'keen protagonists of the war [against Philip] in north-eastern Normandy'. Unhappily for Baldwin, Aumâle fell to the French in August 1196, and he never regained it.[40] As noted above, a fourth frontier county – Evreux – fell into ducal hands due to Count Amaury III's death on the Third Crusade, leaving an under-age son as heir. [See Map III]

West of Normandy, jutting into the Atlantic, lay the peninsula that formed the county or duchy of Brittany, a savage land isolated by language and geography. The Norman dukes had long seen potential danger in a weak and disunited Brittany that might offer rebel Norman nobles support or sanctuary, and the counts of Anjou also had a strategic interest in one Breton territory, the county of Nantes, for within its boundaries Greater Anjou's link to maritime commerce, the River Loire, emptied into the sea.[41] Magnates along Brittany's frontiers such as the lords of Fougères often held estates in neighbouring principalities, just as nobles of Normandy, Anjou, Maine and Poitou held lands on the Breton side of the frontier. Breton families were eager to expand from the rocky, isolated interior into Normandy and Maine, or to migrate farther afield, and they had enlisted in the 1066 Norman invasion of England.[42]

---

39   D. Power, 'What did the Frontier of Angevin Normandy Comprise?', *ANS* 17 (1995), 181–5.
40   Quotation, Gillingham, *Richard*, 257; see Powicke, *Loss*, 109–10.
41   Le Patourel, 'Henri II Plantagenêt et la Bretagne', *Feudal Empires*, 99–101.
42   P. Galliou and M. Jones, *The Bretons* (Oxford, 1991), 187–90; A. Chedeville and N.-Y. Tonnèrre, *La Bretagne féodale xiᵉ-xiiiᵉ siècles* (Rennes, 1987), 21.

Brittany assumed more and more the status of a satellite of the Plantagenets, when Duke Conan IV (d. 1171), also earl of Richmond in England, acknowledged the lordship of Henry II in his capacity as duke of Normandy. Since Conan was unable to control his turbulent nobles, the Angevin ruler betrothed his third son, Geoffrey, to Constance of Brittany, daughter and heir of the Breton duke. Henry entered Rennes in July 1166 to take direct control of the duchy on behalf of his young son, and the following autumn, he took the homage of the Breton baronage.[43] As part of the peace settlement between Louis and Henry in 1169 at Montmirail, the French monarch accepted the homage of Young Henry for Brittany as well as for Normandy and Anjou, thus acknowledging the Norman dukes' lordship over Brittany. After this act, the young king as duke of Normandy took the homage of his younger brother, Geoffrey, as duke of Brittany.

Although Angevin government in Brittany may have lacked the refinements of England or Normandy, it clearly followed the administrative model similar to Normandy's.[44] Henry selected a loyal Breton baron to serve him as the principal Angevin agent in the duchy; he also installed regional seneschals, directly answerable to him, who supervised territories or *baillies* as judicial and executive officers, a pattern that continued in Richard's time. Once installed as lawful lord over Brittany, Geoffrey created a new office, seneschal of Brittany, instituted largely to enhance the young duke's dignity. His choice, Ralph of Fougères, was comparable to the seneschals or justiciars of other Plantagenet princes.[45]

Geoffrey died in August 1186 at the court of his friend and his father's enemy, Philip Augustus, leaving his wife Constance with two young daughters and carrying his unborn son, Arthur of Brittany. The name chosen for Geoffrey's heir appealed to the Bretons' pride in their Celtic past, recalling the promise of the legendary King Arthur's return related in several twelfth-century poems and in the prophecies of Merlin, recorded in Geoffrey of Monmouth's *History of the Kings of Britain*.[46] The name, supposedly suggested

---

43 Galliou and Jones, *The Bretons*, 171, 194–5; W.L. Warren, *Henry II* (Berkeley and Los Angeles, CA, 1987), 99.

44 B.-A. Pocquet du Haut-Jussée, 'Le grand fief breton', in F. Lot and R. Fawtier (eds), *Histoire des institutions françaises au moyen âge* (Paris, 1957–62), 1: 272; Le Patourel, 'Henri II Plantagenêt et la Bretagne', 110–11.

45 Pocquet du Haut-Jussée, 'Le grand fief breton', 272; Le Patourel, 'Henri II Plantagenêt et la Bretagne', 105–13; also J. Everard, 'The "Justiciarship" in Brittany and Ireland under Henry II', *ANS* 20 (1998), 90–8.

46 L. Thorpe (trans.), *Geoffrey of Monmouth: The History of the Kings of Britain* (Harmondsworth, 1966), 175; for references to poems, see K. Carter, 'Arthur I, Duke of Brittany, in History and Literature', PhD Dissertation (Florida State University, 1996), ch. 4, n. 3.

to Constance by her barons, presaged the Bretons' opposition to Plantagenet domination that would inspire their alliance with the Capetian monarch against Richard by 1196. From Henry II's death until the mid-1190s, however, Constance of Brittany had remained in her duchy, separated from a second husband selected by Henry and ruling for seven years relatively free from interference by Richard.

Once Richard's grandfather had joined Greater Anjou and Normandy under Plantagenet rule and his father had subjected Brittany to Normandy, the threat to Lower Normandy's frontiers seemed less severe than that to Upper Normandy's border adjoining Capetian territory. Yet Richard Lionheart tried to bind to him some of the nobles along the duchy's southern boundaries who had ties with the Capetians or with other nearby noble houses. An example is his marriage of Matilda of Saxony, his niece, to Count Geoffrey III of Perche, but the marriage failed to secure his loyalty.[47] Another important lord of the southern marches was Robert III, Count of Alençon, through whose lands ran the route from Normandy to Le Mans and the South. The region's strategic significance had led Henry II to seize Alençon Castle, and Richard kept it in ducal hands throughout his reign.[48]

Norman lords along the frontiers with the Ile de France held some estates lying within Capetian territory, and warfare between the Plantagenets and the Capetians enabled such marcher lords to seek redress of their grievances by playing one lord off against another, especially after 1193. Among the tenants of both the French king and the Norman duke was Robert IV, count of Meulan, also lord of Beaumont-le-Roger in Normandy, who constantly oscillated between his two lords.[49] The lords of Tillières and of l'Aigle were also among such marcher nobility. Tillières, key to the Avre valley on the southeastern march, was in ducal hands during most of Richard's reign; its lord, Gilbert, died during the Third Crusade, and his son was still under age in 1198.[50] The l'Aigle lordship was 'a rather motley collection of lands, assembled over a period of time and held from a number of lords'; yet Gilbert III de l'Aigle had important English holdings, including the ancestral honour of Pevensey, Sussex, and the Yorkshire inheritance of his wife, Isabelle de Warenne. While his English lands held him firmly in Richard's

---

47   Power, 'The Norman Frontier', 326–7.
48   K. Thompson, 'William Talvas', in D. Bates and A. Curry (eds), *England and Normandy in the Middle Ages* (London, 1994), 169; Powicke, *Loss*, 182.
49   For an account of his career, S. Mesmin, 'Du Comté à la commune: le léproserie de Saint-Gilles de Pont-Audemer', *Annales de Normandie* 37 (1987), 30–40.
50   Power, 'The Norman Frontier', 317–22; Powicke, *Loss*, 182, 353.

ranks, he and other cross-border Norman nobles sooner or later would prove susceptible to 'Capetian blandishments'.[51]

A most vulnerable marcher territory was the Vexin in the upper Seine Valley, often an invasion route for Capetian forces striking from Paris toward Rouen. The River Epte, a tributary of the Seine, divided the Vexin into Norman and French parts that were constantly contested by the dukes and their Capetian lords. A complication in the contest was the Norman Vexin's designation as the dowry first of Louis VI's daughter Margaret, the bride of Henry the Young King, then after his death the dowry of another daughter, Alix, the betrothed of Richard. Because noble families in the two Vexins were likely to hold lands on both sides of the Epte, their interests were largely local with little loyalty to the duke of Normandy.

Examples of such families are the lords of Gisors or of Guitry, each of which was essentially 'a French family with some Norman estates'. The lords of Gisors, despite their title, did not hold Gisors Castle, which was a ducal fortress until it fell to Philip Augustus in 1193.[52] Another typical lord of the Vexin was Hugh de Gournay, the dominant lord in the Pays de Bray, whose changeability won him a reputation as 'a man of both sides'. Less typical was Richard II de Vernon, whose seat stood on the upper Seine near the mouth of the River Epte. After the loss of Vernon to Philip Augustus, he retained Nehou in the Cotentin, a lordship of thirty knights. Richard Lionheart managed to install in the Vexin one of his stalwarts, Stephen Longchamp, brother of another of the king's 'new men', William Long-champ, royal chancellor and English justiciar. On the death of Osbert de Baudemont, Richard married his daughter and heir to Stephen. The Baudemont lordship passed under Capetian control, however, and in an 1193 treaty between the English and French rulers, it was stipulated that Longchamp should hold the lordship of the Capetian king.[53]

Because Richard could not count on the lords of the Vexin, he had to turn to military means of asserting his control of the region, relying upon ducal castles. The presence of these castles so near their own must have rankled the nobles of the Vexin, wearing away what little loyalty they held

---

51 On l'Aigle, K. Thompson, 'The Lords of the Laigle: Ambition and Insecurity on the Borders of Normandy', *ANS* 18 (1995), 192, 196. Quotation, D. Crouch, 'Normans and Anglo-Normans: A Divided Aristocracy?', in D. Bates and A. Curry (eds), *England and Normandy in the Middle Ages*, 61–3.

52 J. Green, 'Lords of the Vexin', in *War and Government in the Middle Ages* (Woodbridge, 1984), 59.

53 Powicke, *Loss*, 109, 348. See also D. Power, 'Between the Angevin and Capetian Courts: John de Rouvray and the Knights of the Pays de Bray, 1180–1225', in Keats-Rohan (ed.), *Family Trees and the Roots of Politics*, 373–4. On Stephen Longchamp, Green, 'Lords of the Vexin', 56–7.

for the Plantagenet dynasty. Such cross-border nobles were among the first Normans to defect to Philip Augustus, for warfare between their two lords enabled them to seek remedy from the French king for their complaints against Richard, and later against John Lackland.[54]

While most English or Norman nobles' possessions were concentrated on one side of the Channel by the late twelfth century, several great barons still had substantial holdings in both the kingdom and the duchy. The earls of Arundel held the Norman honour of Saint-Martin d'Aubigny; the Beaumont earls of Leicester were major Norman lords with their honour of Breteuil, totalling over 120 knights' fees; the Welsh marcher family of Braose still held the lordship of Briouze in Normandy; and the earls of Chester held over fifty scattered Norman fees plus the hereditary title of *vicomte* of the Avranchin, the Bessin and the Vau de Vire. Royal servants acquired Norman holdings through their marriages to heiresses: Geoffrey fitz Peter won the lordship of Mandeville, along with the earldom of Essex; and William Marshal took the lordship of Longueville with nearly 100 knights' fees in addition to the earldom of Pembroke.[55] Another royal servant was Robert Marmion, who served Henry II as sheriff of Worcester, but lost royal favour on Richard's accession. He held Fontenai-le-Marmion, a major fee of the honour of Beaumont-le-Roger, and the honour of Tamworth, Nottinghamshire. Roger IV de Tosney, a faithful fighter for the Angevin king/dukes, held the barony of Flamstead, Hertfordshire, in addition to ancestral lands on the Seine and Eure above Les Andeleys that were important for Normandy's defence. The Tosney family's lands also included estates in the forest of Conches, west of Evreux.[56]

Normally, the bulk of an Anglo-Norman baron's holdings lay largely on one side of the Channel with only a few estates on the opposite side. An example is Roger Bigod, earl of Norfolk, whose family seat lay in Normandy, but whose landholdings there were insubstantial.[57] Excluding great lords on the duchy's marches, the largest Norman landholder without substantial English holdings was William de Tancarville, hereditary chamberlain of Normandy, with about 95 fees. He had minor holdings at Hailes, Gloucester.[58] The remaining Norman barons were such second-rank lords as Fulk Paynell or Ralph Tesson. In the Cotentin, Fulk Paynell was lord of Hambye

---

54 Green, 'Lords of the Vexin', 61; Power, 'The Norman Frontier', 374.

55 Powicke, *Loss*, 331–58.

56 For Marmion, Gillingham, *Richard*, 133; Powicke, *Loss*, 339; Sanders, 145. For Tosney, G.E. Cokayne, *Complete Peerage*, new edn. 12 vols (London, 1910–59) 13: 765–69; Powicke, *Loss*, 193–4 and 355–6.

57 L. Loyd, *The Origins of Some Anglo-Norman Families*, ed. C.T. Clay and D.C. Douglas, Harleian Society, 103 (1951) (rpt Baltimore, 1975), 14, 32.

58 Powicke, *Loss*, 353.

and Bréhal, holding in part of the abbot of Mont-Saint-Michel; and he held English manors at Bingham, Nottinghamshire, and Drax, Yorkshire. Tesson held the honour of Thury in the Bessin, a holding of 33.5 fees; he also held 15 fees at Saint-Sauveur-le-Vicomte. Sometime after 1190–91, he married the co-heir to Patricksbourne, Kent, gaining half an English barony.[59]

Emblematic of the Angevin kings' control over Normandy was their supremacy over the Norman Church, which corresponded roughly to the ecclesiastical province of Rouen and consisted of seven dioceses. Henry II and Richard dominated it more effectively than any of their other Churches on the Continent. Their ducal ancestors had exercised 'quasi-religious authority' over the Church derived from Carolingian tradition,[60] and the French king could not claim any jurisdiction over Norman bishops or religious houses. Perhaps the most striking symbol of ducal authority was the king/duke's assignment to abbots and bishops of fixed quotas of knights for his feudal host, just as in post-Conquest England. The bishops of Bayeux, for example, owed 20 knights from their 120 knights' fees, the largest number of fees held by any of the duke's ecclesiastical barons.[61]

Duke William II had presided over ecclesiastical councils. At Caen in 1047, he and his bishops had established the Truce of God, which they enforced by excommunication and exile of offenders. As ducal power grew, however, the ducal peace overshadowed the Truce of God, and the episcopal role became merely financial. Richard Lionheart confirmed in 1190 bishops' right to a share of the profits of justice; they received seven pounds of the money belonging to convicted homicides with the remainder going to the duke.[62] The Council of Lillebonne in 1080 had defined the duke's relationship with the Norman Church, asserting ultimate ducal authority. Lillebonne's canons, reissued by Henry II in 1162, approximated what he hoped to achieve in England with his Constitutions of Clarendon.[63] The canons of Lillebonne sanctioned ducal regulation of the Norman Church's relations with the papacy; also the canons conceded that prominent laymen could not be excommunicated without the duke's or his justiciar's consent; and they reserved for the ducal courts jurisdiction over 'criminous clerks'. Eventually, the Norman clergy objected to the duke's right to try clerics accused of secular crimes or 'pleas of the sword'; and in 1190, while the Lionheart was away on

---

59   For Paynell, S. Painter, *The Reign of King John* (Baltimore, 1949), 26, 150; Powicke, *Loss*,
      342. For Tesson, Sanders, 135; Loyd, *Anglo-Norman Families*, 101–2.
60   Bates, *Normandy before 1066*, 191–2, 227–8.
61   Gleason, *Ecclesiastical Barony*, 72–3.
62   Fagnen, 'Essai sur quelques actes normands', no. 39; *Cal. Docs. Fr.*, no. 55.
63   Torigny, (ed.), Howlett, *Chronicles* . . . RS, (London, 1890), 43, 212; see Poggioli, 'From
      Politician to Prelate', 163, 278–9.

crusade, the seneschal of Normandy gave way. Richard eventually confirmed his concession in 1198.[64]

Little evidence shows ducal efforts to interfere in monastic elections, and the seneschal's 1190 agreement with the Norman clergy confirmed bishops' right to supervise elections of abbots and abbesses, priors and prioresses. Episcopal elections were another matter, however; and the dukes of Normandy continued to control them tightly long after the eleventh-century Investiture Contest.[65] When Richard became duke in 1189, six of the province's seven prelates had close ties to his father, four of whom continued in office throughout his reign. Most prominent was the archbishop of Rouen, Walter of Coutances, a longstanding royal clerk of Henry II, actually a native of Cornwall despite his toponymic. Henry II had him translated from the bishopric of Lincoln to Rouen in 1184. Bishop Henry of Bayeux (d. 1205) also had belonged to the king/duke's household before his election in 1165, and he continued to serve his Angevin masters in secular affairs, accompanying Richard on his first visit to England in 1189. John fitz Luke (d. 1192), bishop of Evreux since 1182, was another of Henry II's clerks; he accompanied the Lionheart to the Holy Land, where he witnessed many royal charters. Ralph de Varneville (d. 1191) had headed Henry II's chancery before his nomination to Lisieux in 1182 to replace Bishop Arnulf, whom the king had forced into retirement.

The English and Norman Churches shared much of the same personnel, with English-born clerics named to ecclesiastical benefices in Normandy and Normans taking posts in England. Every Norman or Angevin monarch before 1200 made cross-Channel episcopal appointments, for example, Walter of Coutances, archbishop of Rouen. Four of Richard's nominees for English bishoprics had Norman connections. The interchange of clergy between the two Churches was so significant that they can be said to have formed 'a unique ecclesiastical entity' that 'reinforced the political underpinnings' of the Angevin empire.[66]

Four episcopal elections took place in Normandy during the decade of Richard's rule: two at Avranches, and one each at Evreux and Lisieux. Named bishop of Avranches in 1196 was William de Chemillé, whose toponymic shows that he came from a prominent Angevin family. Richard had earlier named William to the lucrative post of archdeacon of Richmond, Yorkshire.

---

64 Poggioli, 199–203.

65 See R.V. Turner, 'Richard Lionheart and the Episcopate in his French Domains', *French Historical Studies* 21 (1998), 524–6; D. Spear, 'The Norman Empire and the Secular Clergy, 1066–1204', *JBS* 21 (1981–82), 7.

66 Spear, 'Norman Empire and Secular Clergy', 4, 10.

William witnessed royal charters as bishop-elect of Avranches in early autumn 1197. Before William could be consecrated bishop of Avranches, however, the chapter of Angers, where he had been a canon and school-master, elected him their bishop. No doubt, they reached their choice through Richard's inspiration, and William abandoned Avranches for Angers in 1198. Pope Innocent III objected to his translation and suspended him in May 1198, but absolved him by the end of the year. A second election at Avranches to replace William de Chemillé resulted in the elevation of William Toleran, clerk of the seneschal of Normandy. His election aroused an unsuccessful appeal to Rome by the master of the schools of Avranches who labelled William Toleran *illiteratus* and complained of irregularities in the election.

Less is known of the two other Norman episcopal elections, both held during Richard's absence. No details are known of the election at Evreux in 1193, during the duke's captivity in Germany, other than Richard's nomination of Guarin de Cierrey, who was consecrated as bishop of Evreux the following year. Whether or not Guarin had previously served the king/duke as a clerk, he proved to be 'King Richard's close collaborator', supporting him in his quarrel with Archbishop Walter of Rouen over Les Andelys, one of Walter's most profitable manors, seized by Richard as the site for his stronghold on the Seine, Château Gaillard. Even less is known about the election at Lisieux that replaced Ralph de Varneville with William de Rupière. William's career as bishop shows him to have been devoted to the king, representing Richard at the papal court in his 1196 dispute with the archbishop of Rouen and acting again as a royal agent at Rome in 1198.

In Richard's last years, both Norman clerics and laity grew alienated from Plantagenet rule under the pressures of chronic warfare. The combatants came to consist largely of non-natives, foreign mercenaries and English knights. This meant that the warfare became more ferocious, threatening the civilian population and the Church's property. A sign of the damage inflicted upon northeastern Normandy, roughly the region of the diocese of Rouen, is its decline as a source of ducal revenues and a shift of effective fundraising to central Normandy.[67] Some English chroniclers began to doubt Norman loyalty as early as the time of Richard's German captivity, due to the treacherous surrender of Gisors Castle to Philip Augustus by its castellan, Gilbert de Vascoeuil, in 1193. About the same time, another Norman lord, Hugh de Gournay, temporarily abandoned the Angevin cause for the Capetians.[68]

---

67 Moss, 'Normandy and the Angevin Empire', 79.
68 Powicke, *Loss*, 96; Power, 'Between the Angevin and Capetian Courts', 374; for a lesser figure, John de Rouvray, see Power, *ibid.*, 378.

With the widespread use of mercenaries came also a militarisation of government, a relegation of all other administrative matters to a place secondary to the supplying of fortresses and armies. The Normans were experiencing arbitrary measures that the Angevins' harsh critic, Gerald of Wales, associated with Angevin rule over England.[69] At the same time, Richard's rule over Normandy was coming to resemble Aquitaine, where military might had maintained authority over unruly vassals. The difference was an efficient exchequer in Normandy extorting an ever larger portion of the population's wealth that had no counterpart in Richard's southern duchy, making his rule appear more oppressive to his Norman subjects.

---

69 Powicke, *Loss*, 178, also 297–9, citing Gerald of Wales, 8: 258, where he wrote that 'the violent despotism which the dukes had practised as kings of England, had been extended to their Norman subjects'. Earlier, Ralph of Diss, commenting on the rebellion of 1173–74, had written that Henry II 'was trampling upon the necks of the proud and haughty, was dismantling or appropriating the castles of the country, and was requiring . . . those who occupied properties which should have contributed to his treasury, to be content with their own patrimony'; Diceto, 1: 371, translation of Warren, *Henry II*, 124.

CHAPTER TEN

Greater Anjou

Greater Anjou (Anjou and Maine, plus the Touraine) was the geographical centre of the collection of territories that constituted the Angevin 'empire'. Lying in the Loire valley, it served the Plantagenets as a base of operations for mercenaries to be dispatched to the north into Normandy or to the south into the duchy of Aquitaine to counter Capetian invasions or rebel uprisings. It was also crucial for Richard Lionheart's defence of his possessions against the Capetians. A treasury at Chinon, a centre for paying and supplying armies, attests to the region's strategic importance. Yet the degree of Richard's authority in his Loire valley principalities falls midway between two extremes, less effective than in Normandy or England, but stronger than in Aquitaine or Gascony.

The county of Anjou was one of the strongest small principalities to arise on the Carolingian Empire's ruins. Since the rise of the counts in the tenth century, they had worked to expand territorially with Fulk Nerra (987– 1040) acquiring the small county of Vendôme and the larger one of Maine, while his son Geoffrey Martel took the county of Touraine from the count of Blois. Henry II's great-grandfather, Fulk Rechin (d. 1109), is usually depicted as ineffectual, yet he succeeded in reasserting control over Maine and marrying its heiress to his son.

A fundamental question regarding Anjou under Henry II and his sons is: how 'feudal' was it? While Anjou is usually seen as a successful small feudal state, and its early counts as pioneers constructing a government based on private, feudal arrangements to replace the late Carolingians' ineffectual authority,[1] they more likely considered themselves lawful continuators of the

---

1 For example, R.W. Southern, *The Making of the Middle Ages* (London, 1953), 80–90.

work of Frankish or even Roman public officials. Indeed, Bernard Bachrach emphasises 'the neo-Roman facade that adorned the Angevin state' under Fulk Nerra, depicting eleventh-century Anjou as a true state in which the direct ruler–subject relationship outweighed the lord–tenant relationship. Bachrach finds the counts continuing Carolingian patterns of taxation, regularly collecting taxes on land (*census*), on agricultural produce (*consuetudines*) and tolls on traders (*theloneum* or *pedagium*), as well as levying supplies of goods and labour services that can be classified as public obligations, not feudal services. Most significant, Bachrach finds the counts demanding military service from all their subjects as a universal obligation owed to the state, not as a tenurial obligation of a feudal vassal.[2] Moreover, the early counts of Anjou controlled nominations to the see of Angers and to most abbeys in their county; at Saint-Aubin, Angers, they held the title of *archiabbas* or lay abbot.[3] Geoffrey Martel continued this strong government, exercising direct power over comital castles and asserting authority over lords outside his own domain.[4]

It must be asked, then, whether the counts succeeding Fulk Nerra and Geoffrey Martel preserved some idea of the public interest and asserted the authority of royal officials over the castellans in the disintegrating West Frankish kingdom. In an age when 'public' power supposedly had disappeared, the counts were working out a theory of princely power from surviving Roman principles of *potestas publica*; and comital charters still expressed some sense of 'the public role of the state', styling the counts as *principes*.[5] Yet scholars have viewed Anjou's comital control in feudal terms as a result of the counts' ties of lordship with the castellans and their own castles that protected frontiers against aggressive neighbours.[6] Is it necessary, then, to follow tradition in ascribing the strong government of Anjou primarily to the personal bonds of vassalage and fiefholding?

Anjou's 'feudal transformation' customarily is dated in the late eleventh century after Geoffrey Martel died childless, and uncertainty over the

---

2 B. Bachrach, *Fulk Nerra, a Neo-Roman Consul 987–1040* (Berkeley and Los Angeles, CA, 1993), who strongly rejects Southern's view, xii and 286 n. 31; Bachrach, 'The Angevin Economy 360–1060: Ancient or Feudal', *Studies in Medieval and Renaissance History*, new ser. 10 (New York, 1988); also on the economy, Bachrach, *Fulk Nerra*, xiii–xiv, 191–6, 255–9.

3 K.F. Werner, 'Kingdom and Principality in Twelfth-century France', in T. Reuter (ed.), *The Medieval Nobility* (Amsterdam, 1978), 284, n. 46.

4 O. Guillot, 'Administration et gouvernement dans les états du comte d'Anjou au milieu du XIe siècle', *Beihefte der Francia* 9, *Histoire comparée de l'administration (IVe–XVIIIe siècles)*, ed. W. Paravicini and K.F. Werner (Munich, 1980), 311–26.

5 Bachrach, 'The Angevin Economy', 32; O. Guillot, *Le Comte d'Anjou et son entourage*, 2 vols (Paris, 1973), 1: 350–70, depicts Geoffrey Martel (1040–60) seeking to rule as a Carolingian territorial prince, over a *regnum*, 'a territorial entity submitted to a quasi-royal type of government, assumed by the prince'. On Fulk Nerra's and the title *princeps*, see Bachrach, *Fulk Nerra*, 199.

6 Most influential on English speakers, Southern, *Making of the Middle Ages*, 81–9.

succession provoked turmoil. At the same time that William the Bastard was asserting his supremacy over the nobles of Normandy, family rivalries were enfeebling the counts of Anjou. Civil war between the brothers Geoffrey le Barbu and Fulk Rechin, *c.* 1060–68, enabled castellans to take advantage of the confusion to usurp castles, to divert resources to themselves, converting traditional comital levies on the peasantry into seignorial customs, and to assume comital authority over rural villages, compromising jurisdiction of the count's court. Over forty castles, the 'repositories of lordship', became hereditary possessions of the castellans' families, enabling them to dominate the surrounding countryside in defiance of their count.[7] Fulk Rechin after 1067 presided over a looser, less centralised comital regime than his more authoritarian Norman neighbours. Yet complete localisation of authority hardly seems to have been the case; Fulk retained resources for unseating disloyal nobles, resisting Norman expansion and securing possession of Maine.[8]

From his accession in 1109, Fulk V (abdicated 1129) was rebuilding public power, and then his son Geoffrey le Bel, and after him Henry Plantagenet, continued to assert their rights as public authorities. Geoffrey le Bel, after facing several revolts by Angevin barons, had restored comital power by his death in 1151, suppressing the nobility's private warfare, demolishing their castles, and forcing them to submit to his lordship. Once Henry had cemented his hold on Greater Anjou by 1152, he reimposed a measure of authority approaching that of his ancestors. He continued the work of his father and grandfather in Anjou, recovering lands, castles and privileges previously usurped or granted away.[9] Henry II's coronation as English king in 1154 had enhanced his personal authority in Anjou, giving the force of the *imperium regis* to his commands. Indeed, the court held by his Angevin seneschal was sometimes called the *curia regis*.[10] A traditional regalian right of Henry's comital predecessors that he exercised was a monopoly on the coining of money, and he closely controlled mints at Angers and Le Mans. The *denier angevin* circulated throughout Henry II's 'empire', and when he

---

7 Phrase of R.C. Smail, *Crusading Warfare 1097–1193* (Cambridge, 1956), 214; numbers from Guillot, *Le Comte d'Anjou et son entourage*, 310, 316.

8 W.S. Jessee, 'Count Fulk Rechin of Anjou and the Acquisition of Maine: A Reassessment', unpublished paper presented at the International Congress of Medieval Studies (Kalamazoo, MI, May 1996).

9 J. Chartrou, *L'Anjou de 1109 à 1151: Foulque de Jerusalem et Geoffroi Plantagenêt* (Paris, 1928), 1–35, 161; J. Boussard, *Le Comté d'Anjou sous Henri Plantagenêt et ses fils 1151–1204* (Paris, 1938), 64, 105–7; J. Boussard, 'Aspects particuliers de la féodalité dans l'empire Plantagenêt', *BSAO*, 4th ser., 7 (1963), 38; and F.M. Powicke, 'The Angevin Administration of Normandy II', *EHR* 22 (1906), 36.

10 J. Avril, *Le Gouvernement des évêques et la vie religieuse dans le diocèse d'Angers (1148–1240)*, 2 vols (Paris, 1984), 1: 226–7, also 230; and Delisle/Berger, 1: 278, no. 131, 334–6; no. 200; 408–10, no. 263.

introduced a new coinage to England in 1180, he sent for *cambitores regis* from Le Mans, Tours and Rouen.[11]

According to Jacques Boussard, a fully feudal society in twelfth-century Anjou strengthened the count's hands. Through union of vassalage and fief, castellans performed homage and feudal services to him as vassals and tenants instead of allegiance and public services as subjects of a prince. In short, the territorialisation of feudal obligations had been accomplished.[12] Boussard's view owes more to longstanding assumptions about 'feudalism' than to documentary evidence, and new scholarship now requires another look at this received view of the growth of Greater Anjou.

It is likely that in much of the twelfth century, nobles' oaths of fealty and ceremonies of homage still were meant 'to acknowledge and symbolize political subjection', not signifying recognition that they held their estates as comital fiefs.[13] It is far from certain that the Angevin aristocracy acknowledged holding all their lands as comital fiefs, although the count doubtless granted them some estates as feudal tenures. Only occasionally do comital charters show men performing homage to the count in return for grants of land or revenues. Given the persistence of alodial holdings in the twelfth century, it is unproductive to speculate on whether twelfth-century Angevin lords of castles and peasant villages thought that the count exercised authority over them because they were his subjects, his vassals or his fiefholders.

No records survive outside Normandy to illuminate Geoffrey le Bel's, Henry II's or Richard Lionheart's success in imposing feudal military and financial obligations on their nobles of Anjou equivalent to those owed by their English or Norman barons. Angevin sources give no evidence for quotas of knight-service, relief, the 'gracious aids' or the 'feudal incidents' defined by scholars as basic obligations of nobles to their lords. Boussard wrote that Henry would not have dreamed of seeking to impose such concrete burdens.[14] Most surviving comital charters record grants of rights to religious houses that scholars would classify as 'seignorial' dues or 'public' obligations rather than as 'feudal' payments and services.

Charters reveal, however, that whenever the counts granted land to a church or a lay lord, they took care to preserve their right to raise armed men from the land, the ancient military responsibility of all subjects known as *ost et chevauchée*.[15] Aristocratic landlords of the Loire valley principalities

---

11 Boussard, 300–5.
12 J. Boussard, 'Les institutions de l'empire plantagenêt', in F. Lot and R. Fawtier, *Histoire des institutions françaises au moyen âge*, 3 vols (Paris, 1957–62), 1: 44, 49–50.
13 S. Reynolds, *Fiefs and Vassals* (Oxford, 1995), 130.
14 Boussard, 241, 377. Also J. Boussard, 'La diversité et les traits particuliers du régime féodal dans l'Empire Plantagenêt', *Annali della Fondazione italiana per la storia amministrativa* 1 (1964), 178.
15 Chartrou, *L'Anjou*, 157, 287.

fought in their lord's host, but no prescribed or specified military obligation was owed from landed property. Evidence for castle-guard as an obligation to the count of Anjou, however, dates from the eleventh century.[16] Indeed, Henry II saw military service as a general obligation of his subjects, indicated by his 1180 decree specifying the military obligations of all freemen, varying according to their wealth. Although the Plantagenet monarchs' Norman ancestors had assessed quotas of knights on their English tenants following the Conquest, Henry II and his sons relied heavily on mercenary soldiers and paid knights in their military households for a fighting force. No Angevin aristocrats were among the 'military nucleus' that dominated Richard's witness lists during his last years, spent fighting in Normandy and Poitou.[17]

Richard, as count of Anjou, could not impose on Loire Valley nobles the feudal payments that he exacted from his English and Norman barons. Anjou is unlikely to have differed much from the Mâconnais, where lords gained few revenues from their knightly tenants; for example, a new tenant on succession to his fief paid only token relief, perhaps a palfrey.[18] Although so-called 'feudal' aids were known in Anjou, in some parts of France they were collected chiefly from commoners, not from fiefholders. All classes everywhere paid in one way or another, for an aid was accompanied by a tallage, assessed on all the lord's subjects – knights or *bourgeois*, free or servile.[19] Those paying would not have appreciated modern scholarly distinctions between 'feudal' aid, servile *taille* and communal *donum*.

In Anjou, wardship of minors usually fell to family members, not to the lord, as in England. When Maurice II de Craon died in July 1196, custody of his minor son Maurice III went, not to the king/count, but to the boy's mother *sicut jus est et consuetudo in Andegavia*.[20] Surviving records from King John's time show him controlling some custodies and marriages; for example, his command to the seneschal of Anjou to give two daughters in his custody for marriage to the son and nephew of one of his men. Probably these maidens were residents of the comital domain.[21]

---

16 Reynolds, *Fiefs and Vassals*, 131, 307.

17 R. Heiser, 'The *Familiares* of the Court of King Richard I', Florida State University M.A. thesis (Tallahassee, 1988), 125.

18 G. Duby, *La société aux XIe et XIIe siècles dans la région mâconnaise* (Paris, 1971), 424–5; T. Evergates, *Feudal Society in the Bailliage of Troyes under the Counts of Champagne, 1152–1284* (Baltimore, 1975), 128, on the rarity of relief to the count in Champagne.

19 Reynolds, *Fiefs and Vassals*, 299–300; also C. Stephenson, 'Origins and Nature of the *Taille*', in B. Lyon (ed.), *Medieval Institutions: Selected Essays* (Ithaca, NY, 1954), 41–103.

20 C.-J. Beautemps-Beaupré, *Coutumes et institutions de l'Anjou et de Maine antérieures au xvie siècle*, 8 vols (Paris, 1877–97), pt 1, vol. 3: ciii–cv, testament of Maurice de Craon.

21 *Rot. Norm.*, 51; also *Rot. Chart.*, 72b–73.

The twelfth-century counts saw clearly the importance of castles, and they sought to assert the old precept of their 'rendability', or their right to occupy and garrison them with their own soldiers when necessary. Henry II, like his father, insisted that his nobles turn over their fortresses to him in wartime. Indeed, this Angevin castle policy has been described as the implementation of 'prerogatives of monopolistic and imperial type . . . using force, fear and not a little fraud'.[22] Loss of comital control over numbers of castles in Greater Anjou alarmed Henry II, and he moved to assert control; in 1156, for example, Henry besieged and occupied Chinon and Loudun, and he forced the lord of Mirebeau Castle to acknowledge his lordship. A few years later in 1162, he forced the lord of Mayenne to surrender castles on the marches separating Maine from Normandy held by his family for a generation; they would remain in comital hands until 1199.[23]

Aiding Henry II and later his son Richard in controlling their Loire principality was the paucity of large territorial lordships among the aristocracy; apart from such family lands as Craon, Laval, Mayenne and Sablé, most holdings were relatively modest in extent. Also many Angevin nobles were growing poorer in the course of the twelfth century, overspending on military expeditions and pilgrimages and pledging their property to monastic houses in return for loans.[24] In Anjou proper, the most powerful nobles were the lords of Craon. Maurice II de Craon (d. 1196) loyally supported Henry, and he went on crusade with Richard Lionheart. Another great house of Anjou was the Chemillé family, centred in the extreme southwest. The most powerful nobles in Maine belonged to the house of Mayenne, holding possessions in Maine that bordered on Brittany and Normandy; in the Lionheart's time, it was headed by Juhel III (1161–1220?). Along Maine's frontier with Normandy lay the lands of the viscounts of Beaumont-sur-Sarthe, who were descended from an illegitimate daughter of Henry I of England. Also prominent in the Sarthe valley was Robert de Sablé. When he did not return from the Third Crusade, his possessions passed to his son-in-law, William des Roches, a 'new man' who had served Henry II and continued in Richard Lionheart's service, and who eventually became seneschal of Anjou after Richard's death. The house of Laval, headed by Guy VI (c. 1194–97), dominated the western part of Maine. Amboise constituted the most important lordship in Touraine; its lords were also lords of

---

22 C. Coulson, 'Fortress-Policy in Capetian Tradition and Angevin Practice: Aspects of the Conquest of Normandy by Philip II', *ANS* 6 (1984), 15.

23 Annales de Saint-Aubin in L. Halphen (ed.), *Recueil d'annales angevines et vendômoises* (Paris, 1903), 14; also W.L. Warren, *Henry II* (Berkeley and Los Angeles, CA, 1987), 95; citing Howlett (ed.), Robert of Torigny, RS, 211–12.

24 Boussard, 'Aspects particuliers', 38–9; Avril, *Le gouvernement des évêques*, 1: 66.

Chaumont, which they held of the counts of Blois.[25] Lying on the borders of Anjou, Maine, and Blois-Chartres was the county of Vendôme, a fief of the counts of Anjou held by Bouchard IV (1192–1202). [See Map IV]

Within Greater Anjou, Henry II and his sons did not have the benefit of the 'administrative monarchy' with fine-tuned mechanisms that they enjoyed in England. The seneschal of Anjou, originally a household officer, first began to play an important governing role in the time of Geoffrey le Bel, who needed a representative at home while he was subduing Normandy. The only local officials over whom the counts had effective authority were the dozen or so *prévôts*, removable agents dating from the eleventh century. Headquartered at one of the count's castles, they held power only within the count's domain, where they presided over courts trying serious crimes committed on comital lands, collected customary payments due from domanial estates that constituted the count's chief source of income, and in time of war raised and led the count's host.[26]

Yet Richard I inherited from Henry II an administration capable of enforcing comital authority in his absence, guided to some extent by the model of administrative machinery in the Anglo-Norman domains. The great rebellion of 1173–74 taught Henry that he could not enforce his will over his far-flung territories simply by 'hard riding',[27] dashing from one province to another; and beginning after 1175, he had given each of his empire's constituent parts its own regional governor. Like the English justiciar, who exercised authority during the king's absences from the kingdom, the seneschal in Anjou became 'master of the county'; he was authorised to act in the count's name, supervising the *prévôts*, commanding military forces and controlling the treasury at Chinon Castle and other fortifications.[28] While the seneschal played some military role, Henry II had to turn to more skilled warriors to defend Anjou in times of crisis. In his sons' 1173–74 rebellion, he had relied militarily on Maurice de Craon, and in Richard's final rebellion of 1188–89, he turned to his bastard son, Geoffrey Plantagenet.[29]

Henry's pattern for Anjou's administration continued to serve Richard Lionheart well, although one of his first moves as count was to dismiss his father's seneschal, Etienne de Marçay or Stephen of Tours. Richard

25 Boussard, 99–100; Boussard, *Comté d'Anjou*, 40, 42, 59, 62. On William des Roches, G. Dubois, 'Recherches sur la vie de Guillaume des Roches, seneschal d'Anjou, du Maine et de la Touraine', *BEC*, 6th ser., 5 (1869), 384–5; Baldwin, 234–7.
26 Boussard, 'Les institutions de l'empire Plantagenêt', 1: 41; Boussard, 321–3; Chartrou, *L'Anjou*, 115–17; and Werner, 'Kingdom and Principality', 257–8.
27 Phrase of M.T. Clanchy, *England and its Rulers 1066–1272* (London, 1983), 114.
28 J. Boussard, 'Les influences anglaises dans le développement des grandes charges de l'empire plantagenêt', *Annales de Normandie* 5 (1955), 224.
29 Boussard, *Comté d'Anjou*, 85, 126.

imprisoned him, allegedly made him pay £30,000 sterling, and demanded an additional £15,000. Payn de Rochefort, a Poitevin, was appointed by 11 January 1190 to replace Stephen.[30] By January 1195, however, Robert of Thornham, an English knight, was seneschal, and he held the post for the remainder of the reign.[31] Robert was one of the Lionheart's crusading companions whom he entrusted with office on his release from captivity in Germany. Having distinguished himself as a naval commander during the conquest of Cyprus, Robert had won the post of governor of the island; later he went to Germany as a hostage for Richard's ransom. Robert was frequently in the Lionheart's company during the last five years of his reign; he was the eleventh most frequent attestor of royal charters. He was with the king at Chinon in mid-March 1199 just before his departure for his ill-fated campaign in the Limousin.[32]

A significant measure of the counts' public power is their role in justice, for settlement of disputes remained an important duty of French territorial princes even in the tenth and eleventh centuries. Fulk V, Geoffrey le Bel and later Henry II followed their ancestors in asserting their rights as public authorities to remedy unjust judgments or defaults of justice. Doubtless, this represented a survival or revival of Roman and Carolingian doctrines of the ruler's responsibility to amend wrongful judgments and defects of justice. Surviving charters from Henry II's reign indicate an active comital court, often with the king personally present, but sometimes with the seneschal presiding in his place.[33] Holding a general and permanent delegation of

---

30 Gillingham, *Richard*, 138, suggests that Stephen de Marçay regained his office for the duration of Richard's crusade, but Payn witnessed as seneschal of Anjou on 11 January 1190, and throughout the spring until at least 25 June; Stephen witnessed one of Richard's charters on 5 May 1190 without any title; J.C. Holt and R. Mortimer, *Acta of Henry II and Richard I: Hand-list of Documents Surviving in . . . the United Kingdom*, List and Index Society, special ser. 21 (Gateshead, 1986), no. 354; Landon, 26, 32, 35; BN ms. nouv. acqu. Lat. 1224, ff 226, 227, 245–6, 269, 273.

31 Boussard, *Comté d'Anjou*, 114–17.

32 Heiser, M.A. thesis, 136–7; Landon, 50, 98, 100, 144–5.

33 Delisle/Berger, 1: 113–14, no. 19, *c.* 1156, *coram me in curia meo apud Andegavim*; 1: 238–9, no. 131, April 1159, *coram Henrici, regis Anglie et comite Andegavorum*; 1: 212–13, no. 107, *c.* 1156–59, *in presencia mea*; 1: 223–4, no. 118, *c.* 1156–59, *per judicium curie mee*; 1: 321–2, no. 190, *c.* 1156–61, *coram me*; 1: 333–34, no. 199, *in curia mea Andegavis*; 1: 414–15, no. 267, 24 March 1168, *in aula mea*; 2: 227–9, no. 618, dated 1182, *coram me consilio et assensu meo in curia mea*; 2: 262, no. 648, dated 1185, *coram nobis*; 2: 391–2, no. 749, *c.* 1182–89, *coram me*; Bertrand de Broussillon (ed.), *Le Cartulaire de Saint-Aubin d'Angers* (Paris, 1903), 2: 339–40, no. 806, *per judicium curie mee*, undated charter. For references to disputes settled before the seneschal's court: Delisle/Berger, 1: 197, no. 91, dated 1158, *in curia mea coram Josleno de Turuonis dapifero meo*; 2: 135, no. 555, *c.* 1180, letter of Stephen, seneschal of Anjou; *Cartulaire de Saint-Aubin*, 2: 287–8, no. 808, *c.* 1165–9, the court at Angers 'in the hall of the lord king'; 2: 320–2, no. 851, *c.* 1160–80; 2: 387–8, no. 913, *c.* 1157–89, 'court of

the count's judicial authority, the role of the seneschal's tribunal in Anjou resembles that of the bench at Westminster, headed by the justiciar. The seneschal disposed of disputes to which litigants came by written summons, no longer simply a place selected by the parties for settling their disputes by arbitration or negotiation.[34] Henry's seneschal, Etienne de Marçay, left an account of his difficulties in forcing one recalcitrant noble to appear in court. He failed to respond to the seneschal's letters delivered by 'two prudent men', and finally judgment was pronounced against the noble in his absence.[35] Nothing suggests that the comital court was a 'feudal' body; it was ready to hear cases 'without any legal theory of appeals from his vassals' courts'.[36] It settled disputes brought both by lay tenants and religious houses, although most surviving accounts of litigation before the seneschal's court are – not surprisingly – disputes involving the property of religious houses.

Several charters show the seneschal holding sworn inquests or assizes, proceedings much like the jury recognitions so common in England and Normandy.[37] Indeed, it appears probable that Geoffrey le Bel brought the jury to Normandy from Anjou. Evidence survives of his father, Count Fulk V, rejecting seventy-seven compurgators supporting a litigant's claim, and instead commanding an inquest of twelve men chosen by the court to swear to the truth in order to settle a dispute with one of his tenants.[38] Rolls that chance to survive from John's short period as ruler over Anjou record writs to the seneschal and constables that read much like English kings' peremptory orders to their sheriffs. Although about eighty writs concerning Anjou survive, almost double the number surviving from Aquitaine, the scarcity of surviving records from Anjou signals an administration still lagging behind that of England and Normandy.[39]

Lord Stephen, seneschal of the English King'. *Cal. Docs. Fr.*, 385–6, no. 1087, a charter of Payn de Rochefort, seneschal of Anjou, describes settlement of a dispute before him and Queen Eleanor in 1190.

34 Boussard, 287, 357–9; Chartrou, *L'Anjou*, 126.

35 Delisle/Berger, 1: 334–6, no. 200, Marmoutier Abbey versus Hamelin de Autenoria.

36 F.M. Powicke, 'The Angevin Administration of Normandy I', *EHR* 21 (1906), 648; Chartrou, *L'Anjou*, 107.

37 Delisle/Berger, 2: 164–5, no. 580, an assize taken at Mayet, Sarthe, to determine whether land granted to the abbey of St Pierre de la Couture, Le Mans, was a fee of Henry II: *utrum elemosina illa de feodo meo esset*; 1: 431–2, land admeasured by *juratis regis*; 2: 135, no. 555, proof *per chartam suam et per vivas voces legitimorum testium* that Walter de Mayenne owed the priory of St Etienne, Mayenne, £100 in tithes.

38 Chartrou, *L'Anjou*, 274–5, *pièces justificatives*, no. 42. Also Chartrou, *L'Anjou*, 299, no. 168 (1144–45), a sworn inquest into property of the bishop of Bayeux ordered by Duke Geoffrey; and 301–2, no. 177, another Norman inquest under Geoffrey.

39 *Rot. Norm.*, 49, acquittal of a debt to Jews of Saumur; 52, grant of money fee; 66, exchange of land; 68, grant of La Chartre Castle; 77, grant of land; 83, custody of land in the king/count's hand.

Less evidence for the criminal jurisdiction of the seneschal's court survives; doubtless, seigneurial courts often usurped the privilege of punishing criminals within their own domains. In a case before Fulk V's court, the claimant retained jurisdiction over cases of *sanguinem et latronem et duellum*. Yet Geoffrey le Bel, in a settlement restoring rights to certain churches, retained for himself responsibility for three crimes: homicide, rape and arson.[40] Charters of Henry II and Richard Lionheart show duels still belonging to private jurisdictions. In an agreement made before Henry between William de Montsoreau and Fontevraud Abbey, William surrendered his court's right to preside over most duels involving the abbey's men. Richard's charter for the monks of Saint-Nicholas, Angers, specifies that duels of their men were to take place in the monks' court; however, 'If one of their men provokes one of the count's men to *bellum*, it will be settled in our court.'[41]

Another indicator of the Plantagenet rulers' authority within Greater Anjou is their control over the Church. It was less sure than in England or Normandy but firmer than in Aquitaine, as evidenced by episcopal nominations.[42] Henry II sought to extend to Anjou the ecclesiastical privileges that he enjoyed in England and Normandy, just as he was seeking to expand his secular authority on the Anglo-Norman model. By the mid-twelfth century, however, the churches of the Loire region had grown accustomed to the freedom won during the Gregorian reform movement, freely electing their prelates. While early counts had exercised regalian rights over vacant bishoprics and abbacies, no surviving evidence shows Henry or Richard profiting from the temporalities of vacant churches.

At Angers, 1153–56, Henry II had sought to revive an old custom of the count's choosing the new bishop from three nominees of the cathedral chapter. When the canons resisted, Henry unwisely appealed to Pope Adrian IV, naively expecting him to support ancient custom; not surprisingly, such a proposal outraged the English pontiff. None the less, comital influence over elections continued to be strong, and those prelates elected proved satisfactory to the king/count. Succeeding Geoffrey la Mouche, one of Henry II's chancery clerks, in 1177, and serving during most of Richard's reign was Raoul de Beaumont-Neufbourg, a courtier at the Angevin court and the king's cousin. On Raoul's death in 1197, Richard named as his successor William de Chemillé, already bishop-elect of Avranches.

---

40   Chartrou, *pièces justificatives*, 374–5, no. 42; Delisle/Berger, 1: 23–5, no. 18; dated 1151.
41   Delisle/Berger, 2: 227–9, no. 618, at Chinon, 1182; BN MS. nouv. acq. Lat. 1224, ff. 164–5.
42   See R.V. Turner, 'Richard Lionheart and the Episcopate in his French Domains', *French Historical Studies* 21 (1998), 526–9; Avril, *Le gouvernement des évêques*; D. Walker, 'Crown and Episcopacy under the Normans and Angevins', *ANS* 5 (1982); O. Pontal, 'Les évêques dans le monde Plantagenêt', *CCM* 29 (1986); I.P. Shaw, 'The Ecclesiastical Policy of Henry II on the Continent', *Church Quarterly Review* 151 (1951).

At Le Mans, free elections appear to have been the rule. The canons had elected one of their number, Reginald, only a few years before Henry II's death. His successor, elected in 1190 apparently with Richard's acquiescence, was Hamelin, an aged master of the schools at St Martin of Tours with relatives among the canons.[43] His election cannot have aroused much enthusiasm from Richard, for Capetian-nominated canons of St Martin's had long acted as eyes and ears for Louis VII and Philip II in the Loire valley, reporting on Angevin activities. None the less, Richard evinced some support for Hamelin; the king complained to papal representatives about extortions exacted by the Roman *curia* to secure his consecration at Rome.

While the Plantagenet monarchs could influence the election of bishops at Angers, they had less luck with the archbishops of Tours, whose province covered the Angevin heartland plus the nine Breton dioceses. The town of Tours consisted of two urban settlements centred around rival churches, the *cité* surrounding the cathedral and Châteauneuf ringing the collegiate church of St Martin. Although the counts of Anjou had long claimed authority over the two churches, both had close ties to the French monarchy that Louis VII and Philip Augustus sought to encourage and to exploit, using Tours as a forward post within Plantagenet territory. Frequent conflicts between the archbishop, the canons of St Martin's, the townspeople of Tours, Richard Lionheart and Philip Augustus resulted. The citizens of Tours remained faithful to Richard, giving him a gift of 2,000 marks in June 1194, following his release from captivity in Germany.[44]

In March 1190, Richard and the archbishop, Bartholomew of Vendôme, made an agreement defining their respective rights at Tours. Bartholomew, archbishop throughout Richard's reign, is said to have 'served Philip Augustus better than he had served the Angevins until his death in 1206'.[45] Although the Capetians presented themselves as protectors of the metropolitan see, in February 1199, Philip was willing to hand over to Richard his patronage [*donatio*] of the archbishopric as part of a proposed peace settlement.

Also poisoning the Angevins' relations with the archbishops of Tours was their support for the separation of Brittany from the ecclesiastical province of Tours. As part of Henry II's subjection of Brittany, he had sought metropolitan status for the archbishopric of Dol as a means of strengthening his control over Brittany by exercising control over the Breton

---

43 N. Ogé, 'Hamelin, évêque du Mans, 1199–1214', *La Province du Maine*, 96, 5th ser., 8 (July–September 1994), 233–49; (October–December 1994), 347–60.

44 For the Tours burgesses' gift, see Howden, 3: 252; Diceto, 2: 117.

45 Quotation, Shaw, 'Ecclesiastical Policy of Henry II', 147; Q. Griffiths, 'The Capetian Kings and St Martin of Tours', *Studies in Medieval and Renaissance History*, new ser. 9 (New York, 1987), 96.

church.[46] This struggle over Dol became an aspect of the Capetian–Plantagenet conflict, for the French kings saw their support for Tours' opposition to Dol's claims as essential for cementing the archbishopric's loyalty to the French royal house and for frustrating Angevin attempts to gain influence at Tours. Through Henry's influence, the English pope, Adrian IV (1154–59), confirmed Dol's status; and throughout the second half of the twelfth century, the conflict between Dol and Tours continued.

Archbishops of Dol continued to assert their independence from Tours despite lack of support from succeeding popes, and the Plantagenets continued to assert their domination over the archiepiscopate by naming Normans to vacancies. Under Henry II, prelates at Dol were Roger de Hommet (1171–75), a chancery clerk and relative of the constable of Normandy; Roland of Pisa (1177–87), former dean of Avranches; and Henry fitz Harding (1187–88), former dean of Mortain in Normandy, and a member of a family that had risen to prominence in western England through financial services to the Angevin monarch. A long vacancy lasted until 1194, when the petition to Rome for the pallium by the archbishop-elect was rejected. Pope Innocent III ended the controversy with a bull on 1 June 1199, reducing Dol to merely another Breton diocese under the archbishop of Tours' authority.

At Tours, the counts of Anjou had to contend with the French monarchs' authority over the collegiate church of St Martin. While the Capetian kings held the title of lay abbots at St Martin's, the Plantagenet counts were mere canons; and Richard quarrelled bitterly with his fellow canons, for the deans and treasurers of the chapter were either the Capetian king's clerks or cousins. These Capetian-nominated canons assisted the French monarchs by reporting on Angevin activities. Early in Richard's reign, on 4 July 1190, he met with Philip Augustus to end his conflict with the canons. An inquest sorted out the rights of the count of Anjou and of the French king and the rights of the canons and the citizens in the town of Tours; the results proved satisfactory to both monarchs. The 1190 agreement did not hold, however; for following Richard's return from Germany, strife with the canons broke out again. The new dean of St Martin's, elected in 1192 with Philip Augustus's support, refused to swear fealty to Richard. Fearful of Philip's influence among the canons, Richard expelled them, forcing some to flee to the countryside and others to take refuge in Capetian territory. Philip Augustus in reprisal sequestered the revenues that the archbishop of Rouen collected

---

46 G. Conklin, 'Les Capétiens et l'affaire de Dol de Bretagne 1179–1199', *Revue d'histoire de l'Eglise de France* 78 (1992), 241–63; B.-A. Pocquet du Haut-Jussée, 'Les Plantagenêts et la Bretagne', *Annales de Bretagne* 53 (1946), 15–20; Shaw, 'Ecclesiastical Policy of Henry II', 148–9; Turner, 'Richard Lionheart and the Episcopate in his French Domains', 326.

from his French territories. By autumn, however, the Lionheart had restored the canons' goods to them.[47]

The counts of Anjou were founders and patrons of a number of important religious houses in the Loire valley. Doubtless, their generosity toward Fontevraud Abbey, the burial place of Richard Lionheart and his parents, is the best-known example. At the comital foundation, the abbey of Saint-Aubin, Angers, Richard's ancestors had held the title of *archiabbas*. Richard, at the beginning of his reign, found himself involved in the troubles of Saint-Aubin. As its protector, he intervened in the dissension between the abbot and his monks in July 1189, ejecting Abbot William and naming a new head, Jacquelin. The conflict ended when the old abbot died a few days after his deposition.[48] Toward the end of his reign, Richard again thrust himself into a monastic election, directing the seneschal Robert of Thornham to make an inquiry into the election of the abbot of Noyers.[49] The counts were traditionally *domini et abbates* of another house at Angers, Saint-Laud, and their hereditary title of seneschals of the French monarchs carried with it custody of the abbey of Saint-Julien of Tours.[50] The abbey of La Trinité, Vendôme, was a comital foundation that continued to enjoy Henry II's protection, illustrated by the peace settlement between the abbot and the count of Vendôme concluded before him in 1185.[51]

A key factor of Angevin history in the mid- and late twelfth century is the region's robust economic growth. Reclamation of arable land from forests and from low-lying areas along the Loire was under way, as was a shift from grain fields to vineyards. Symptomatic of the Loire region's prosperity is the rise of Saumur as a centre for markets and fairs, where Henry II shared revenues with the abbot of Saint-Florent. Another indicator of the region's economic strength is the wide acceptance of its monetary unit, the *livre angevin* (worth a quarter of a pound sterling), as the semi-official currency of the Angevins' continental possessions.[52] This revival of trade and towns meant that lords who controlled urban centres – such as the counts of Anjou – were becoming much richer than those whose incomes came only from the countryside.

Although signs of Greater Anjou's prosperity are abundant, record evidence that would depict Richard and his father harvesting greater riches is

---

47 Landon, 94, 99; Griffiths, 'Capetian Kings and St Martin of Tours', 98.

48 For Saint-Aubin, see Werner, 'Kingdom and Principality', 284, n. 46. Halphen, *Recueil d'annales angevines et vendômoises*, 17; April, 1: 438.

49 Beautemps-Beaupré, *Coutumes et institutions*, pt 2, 1: 285.

50 For Saint-Laud, Chartrou, *L'Anjou*, 388; for Saint-Julien, Delisle/Berger, 1: no. 87.

51 Delisle/Berger, 2: no. 648; P. Johnson, *Prayer, Patronage, and Power: The Abbey of La Trinité, Vendôme, 1032–1187* (New York, 1981), 83–4.

52 F. Dumas, 'La monnaie dans les domaines Plantagenêt', *CCM* 29 (1986), 53–9.

wanting, for Anjou lacked an advanced financial system similar to the English and Norman exchequers. England and Normandy were unique in northern Europe before the last decades of the twelfth century for requiring that local officials present their accounts for periodic auditing and for preserving the records in writing. Probably Anjou's pattern remained more primitive, resembling that of the French royal domain before the 1190s: largely oral checks on the *prévôts*, based on inventories of comital estates and crude *memoranda*.[53]

While the extent of the comital domain cannot be estimated, it lay scattered throughout the three counties of Anjou, Maine and Touraine.[54] Although nothing is known of the management of comital estates, the Loire valley's growing prosperity should have generated increased domanial income. The Plantagenets' domination of cities lying on the Loire River and its tributaries produced easily collected taxes. Possibly something of early counts' efficient exploitation of their estates had survived into the twelfth century. Certainly John Lackland's *prévôts* later raised substantial sums from lands under their management.[55] It is likely that Henry II and Richard levied tallages of their comital domain, both rural and urban. Tallages of towns could have yielded substantial sums, since the communal movement for urban liberties lagged behind in the Loire valley. While a commune possibly appeared at Le Mans as early as the late eleventh century, evidence elsewhere in Greater Anjou is problematic, and other towns continued to be in the counts' hands throughout the twelfth century.[56]

Richard's demand in 1194 that all his Angevin agents (*baillivi*) repurchase their offices represents an attempt to increase comital income from the *prévôts'* farm, comparable to the increments in the sheriffs' farms that he demanded in England.[57] While the farm of the *prévôté*, tolls and customs duties provided regular income, other revenue sources added to the count's resources – for example, licences sold to moneyers or levies on Jews. No doubt, emergencies led to extraordinary demands – for example, special

---

53 T. Bisson, 'Les comptes des domaines au temps du Philippe Auguste: Essai comparatif', in R.-H. Bautier (ed.), *La France de Philippe Auguste: le temps des mutations* (Paris, 1982), 275–6.

54 Boussard, *Comté d'Anjou*, 16–21.

55 For example, *Rot. Norm.*, 39, an oblation of £200 offered by the *prévôt* of Segré on the Anjou–Maine border.

56 Supporters of an early date include R. Latouche, 'La commune du Mans (1070)', *Mélanges d'histoire du moyen âge dédiés à la mémoire de Louis Halphen* (Paris, 1950); and H. Miyamtsu, 'A-t-il existé une commune à Angers au xiie siècle?', *JMH* 21 (1995), 117–52. Neither Boussard, 184, nor Avril, *Gouvernement des évêques*, 1: 56, find traces of urban organisation at Angers in the twelfth century; and J. Mallet, 'Une capitale militaire aux origines incertaines (jusqu'en 1475)', in F. Lebrun (ed.), *Histoire d'Angers* (Toulouse, 1975), 23, finds Angers in the counts' hands.

57 Howden, 3: 267.

levies for crusades. At a council at Le Mans in 1188, Henry II levied the Saladin tithe, with the concurrence of bishops from England and Normandy as well as from Anjou and 'the barons of Anjou, Maine, and Touraine'.[58] Another extraordinary tax was levied for Richard Lionheart's ransom. Nothing is known of Greater Anjou's contribution, however, other than a chance statement in a chronicle from Tours that the ransom was raised 'with infinite exactions'.[59]

Earliest surviving financial records from Anjou and Touraine date from Philip Augustus's occupation, and the 1221 accounts show revenues of £2,856 *angevin* (£714 sterling) from Touraine alone.[60] Otherwise, only charters by Henry II or Richard giving away revenues to religious houses disclose some hint of comital income – for example, grants of revenues from *prévôtés*, rents, customs duties or tolls. Henry II made annual cash grants to Fontevraud Abbey of £50 *angevin* from the revenues of the *prévôté* of Angers and another £50 from Loudun, and Richard Lionheart granted his share of the tolls at Angers to Marmoutier Abbey, a sum of £150 *angevin* (£37½ sterling) annually.[61] The Plantagenet lands, lying athwart the River Loire, could produce significant amounts in bridge tolls. Although such sums appear small, multiplied several times they could have resulted in substantial income.

In the absence of any records of comital resources, an estimate of Richard's income from Greater Anjou appears impossible. John W. Baldwin estimates that the bulk of Philip Augustus's increased revenues after his occupation of the duchy of Normandy and the Loire valley came from Normandy, not from Greater Anjou.[62] A useful figure for comparison with the income from the Angevin *prévôtés* is the farm of the Norman *prévôtés*, which produced about £4,600 sterling. Also provocative are figures for the French royal domain before Philip Augustus's financial reforms of the 1190s dramatically increased his revenues. Income from the Capetian *prévôts'* farms then totalled £18,000–20,000 *parisis* annually (roughly £5,625–£6,250 sterling). The *prévôts'* farm could have produced at most £5,000–£7,000 sterling

---

58   *Gesta Regis*, 2: 30.

59   A. Salmon, *Recueil de chroniques de Touraine*, Société archéologique de Touraine (Tours, 1854), 144, *Magnum Chron. Turon.*

60   J.W. Baldwin and P. Nortier, 'Contributions à l'étude des finances de Philippe Auguste', *BEC* 138 (1980), 26; Baldwin, 236, 247, table, 244–5. Philip had turned over substantial Angevin revenues to his seneschal.

61   Delisle/Berger, 2: 157–8, no. 57; *Cal. Docs. Fr.*, 428, no. 1188. Also confirmation by Henry II to Fontevraud of toll on grain, from Angers and Saumur, Delisle/Berger, 1: 541, no. 413; Henry II's gift of £40 *angevin* annually to Saint-Julien, Le Mans, 1: 172–3, no. 70; his grant of tolls on the bridge at Saumur to Saint-Florent, 1: 364–7, no. 226; Henry's concession of tolls from the bridge at Pont-de-Cé to Fontevraud and of customs duties levied at Brissac Castle, 2: 53–7, no. 503.

62   Baldwin, 239–48.

annually from Greater Anjou; collection of aids, tallages or similar arbitrary levies occasionally increased comital income, but could not have doubled it.[63] The *prévôts'* farm plus other sporadic exactions likely produced totals adequate for internal administration, for donations to religious foundations, for construction of castles and churches, and for other expenditures essential to display the Plantagenets' superiority. Lavish building projects such as Henry II's rebuilding of the palace at Angers, 'adorned with splendour befitting a king', attest to the considerable wealth raised from the Loire region,[64] as does the huge fine of Richard's dismissed seneschal.

This income from the comital domain was not nearly as profitable to the Angevin monarchs for extraordinary expenses of warfare as the vast sums that they extracted from England and Normandy, as much as £25,000 from each territory in Richard's last years. It is 'feudal' revenues from the Anglo-Norman realm, 'the incidents of tenure by knight service'[65] and the enormous fines (or bribes for favours) inscribed on the pipe rolls that have most impressed historians of the Angevin 'empire'. With money raised from scutages and other cash payments by the barons of their northern domains, Henry II and Richard I could hire mercenaries outstripping the resources of any of their Angevin or Aquitanian subjects, imposing their will on them through military strength.[66] Anjou, Touraine and Maine may have produced substantial though undocumented revenues, but no evidence shows surplus funds available for transfer from the Angevin treasury for Normandy's defence. Indeed, cash flowed in the other direction; most money deposited in the treasury at Loches for paying mercenaries was shipped from England and Normandy.[67]

After the 1173–74 revolt by Henry's sons, Greater Anjou remained calm until the summer of 1189, when Richard Lionheart and Philip Augustus invaded. Anjou's aristocracy, enjoying more autonomy within their domains than did the nobility of the Norman dukes or English kings, generally refused to join in the periodic rebellions that punctuated Henry's reign. In the 1173–74 revolt by his sons, only a handful of major Angevin barons had taken up

---

63   Vincent Moss's figure is £12,488 *parisis*, in 'Normandy and England in 1180: Pipe Roll Evidence', in D. Bates and A. Curry (eds), *England and Normandy in the Middle Ages* (London, 1994), 195; he estimates £4,000 for Anjou proper, in 'Normandy and the Angevin Empire: A Study of the Norman Exchequer Rolls 1180–1204', PhD thesis (University of Wales College, Cardiff, 1996), 215. For Capetian figures, see Baldwin, 54.

64   K. Norgate, *England under the Angevin Kings*, 2 vols (London, 1887; rpt New York, 1969), 2: 196, citing Diceto, 1: 292.

65   J.O. Prestwich, 'War and Finance in the Anglo-Norman Realm', *TRHS*, 5th ser., 4 (1954), 82.

66   Boussard, *Comté d'Anjou*, 105–8.

67   J.C. Holt, 'The Loss of Normandy and Royal Finance', in *War and Government in the Middle Ages* (Woodbridge, 1984), 104–5.

arms alongside his rebel sons, while the most powerful of all, Maurice de Craon, served him faithfully.[68] In the years following his sons' rebellion, Henry encountered little difficulty in the Loire valley, and he spent little time there. He passed 80 per cent of his reign in the Anglo-Norman realm that he had inherited from his mother.[69] Despite his long absences, his Angevin subjects would look back on his rule as 'a reign of peace'.[70]

During the decade of the Lionheart's rule, fighting was almost endemic, but it was concentrated chiefly in the Seine valley against Philip Augustus and in rebellious regions on the southern fringes of Poitou, leaving the Loire valley on the sidelines of the main events. Because Anjou lay between these two trouble-spots, Richard passed through the region every year of his reign except during his crusade and captivity, 1191 through 1193. Only in the summer of 1194 did warfare draw Richard into Greater Anjou. Following his return from Germany and a visit to England, he marched into the Touraine to reassert his authority. On 6 July, he confronted Philip Augustus near Vendôme, forced him to flee and captured the French baggage train. Returning from Aquitaine to Normandy later that summer, the English king stopped in Anjou to shore up his authority there. He summoned his magnates to an assembly at Le Mans and apparently sought to shame them into stronger support by a speech commending to them the deeper devotion displayed by his English subjects.[71]

Yet no serious revolt threatened the region again until Richard's death in 1199, when a disputed succession gave Angevin nobles an excuse to defy John. Richard seems to have shown little interest in Anjou, and he rarely stopped there for extended stays; his longest sojourns were in the summer of 1194 and early 1195, from late January to mid-May.[72] The Lionheart's government made so little impression on the Angevin annalists that they treat him 'as if he were a stranger to the land'.[73] Charter evidence strengthens this impression. Of his surviving *acta*, an overwhelming majority treat English and Norman matters, and only 27 (3 per cent) out of some 750 concern

---

68 Norgate, *England under the Angevin Kings*, 2: 136–7; Boussard, 478.

69 T.K. Keefe, 'Place–Date Distribution of Royal Charters and the Historical Geography of Patronage Strategies at the Court of King Henry II Plantagenet', *HSJ* 2 (1990), 179.

70 Norgate, *England under the Angevin Kings*, 2: 195–6, discusses chronicles and annals.

71 Norgate, *England under the Angevin Kings*, 2: 367; and Diceto, 2: 119.

72 Landon, 101–2.

73 Avril, *Gouvernement des évêques*, 1: 365; they almost appear to have viewed Richard as an alien: Annales de Saint-Aubin in Halphen, *Annales angevines et vendômoises*, 19, notes without comment the death of Richard, 'most illustrious king of the English', while in recording Henry II's death, it describes him as 'famous and most powerful from sea to sea'. *Chron. magnum turon.* in Salmon, *Chroniques de Touraine*, 144, is more effusive in its obituary of Richard, noting that 'his wars and deeds are recorded in the book of days of the English kings'.

Anjou. Even when Richard was resident in Anjou, most of the charters issued there concerned either England or Normandy. This signifies the higher value that the Anglo-Normans, especially heads of religious houses, attached to his confirmation of their property or privileges. Apparently, numerous possessory and proprietary actions in the royal/ducal courts made them more eager to petition him for charters than his Angevin subjects.[74] Also noticeable is the smaller number of charters issued to Loire valley religious houses that granted them the privilege of having their pleas heard 'before us or our chief justiciar'.[75] No doubt, the smaller number of *acta* from Anjou points to the count's weaker position as patron there, since surviving charters chiefly record confirmations of earlier royal/comital favours along with a few cash grants to favoured religious houses.

Angevin barons' quiescence under Richard is more likely explained by apathy than by enthusiasm for the Plantagenet line, for expansion of their lord's rule had brought them no great advantage. No natives of Anjou figure among the most frequent witnesses to Richard's charters.[76] Their absence points to the Plantagenets' failure to recruit a corps of Angevin-born *familiares* reaping rewards through service to the king/count and remaining loyal because of the expectation of additional favours. The only Loire valley native to gain prominence in the Angevin monarchs' central administration in England was Peter des Roches, a Tourangeau. He entered Richard's service by April 1197, and a little over a year later, he was a chamber clerk; however, his period of power and influence in England only began after King John's loss of Anjou in 1204.[77] In Normandy, Garin de Glapion, a native of Maine, won high office under King John. He attested Richard's charters as early as 1189, and he was the farmer of a Norman *prévôté* in 1195; and in 1200–01, he briefly served as seneschal of Normandy. Two years later, he joined other nobles of Maine in abandoning John and transferring allegiance to Philip Augustus.[78]

Equally telling is the Lionheart's appointment of non-natives as seneschals: first a Poitevin, then an Englishman. Only in 1199 did a native of Greater

---

74 J.C. Holt, 'Ricardus Rex Anglorum et Dux Normannorum', in *Magna Carta and Medieval Government* (London, 1985), 72–3.

75 J.C. Holt, 'The Acta of Henry II and Richard I of England 1154–1199: The Archive and its Historical Implications', in P. Rück (ed.), *Fotografische Sammlungen mittelalterlicher Urkunden in Europa* (Sigmaringen, 1989), 139–40, based on Landon, who collected 590 *acta* for Richard, with 433 for England, 117 for Normandy, and only 15 for Anjou. We have found 10 more for Anjou. None the less, there is a great disproportion that cannot be entirely due to the chances of survival.

76 R.R. Heiser, 'The Royal *Familiares* of Richard I', *Medieval Prosopography* 10 (1989), 39–50, tables.

77 N. Vincent, *Peter des Roches: An Alien in English Politics 1205–1238* (Cambridge, 1996), 19.

78 Powicke, *Loss*, 173–4; Heiser, M.A. thesis, 154, 171.

Anjou, William des Roches, become seneschal, first appointed by Richard's nephew, Arthur of Brittany, then John's rival for the succession; John recognised William des Roches's title by October 1199. His career epitomises the Angevin nobles' lack of commitment to the Plantagenet line. After young Arthur's capture by John at Mirebeau in 1202, William went over briefly to the English king's side and retained his office; but he soon shifted his allegiance to Philip Augustus, bringing with him a number of leading Loire valley lords. He ended his career as the French monarch's seneschal of Anjou.[79]

---

79 On William des Roches, see Vincent, *Peter des Roches*, 22–5; also Baldwin, 233–6.

CHAPTER ELEVEN

The duchy of Aquitaine

The marriage of Henry Plantagenet to Eleanor of Aquitaine in 1152 achieved a long-sought goal of the counts of Anjou, bringing into their orbit the possessions of the counts of Poitou, who were also dukes of Aquitaine and dukes of Gascony. Within the Angevin hegemonic 'empire', Henry II viewed his queen's patrimony as a secondary zone, where he saw his rule not so much as direct occupation and administration as indirect exploitation with local leaders remaining in charge, who could be cowed by periodic displays of military force. Richard Lionheart served as his father's agent in Aquitaine and Gascony for most of the period 1175–89, and he did not accept Henry's relegation of Aquitaine to a secondary position. Richard saw the duchy as his own legacy to rule directly, and he expended much energy – eventually his life – defending it.

Richard Lionheart spent most of his youth in Poitou, serving a long apprenticeship alongside his mother and later alone. Henry II first had tried direct rule over Eleanor's possessions, seeking to impose his will by harsh repression, but his rule aroused powerful resistance from some of the great nobles. A rebellion in 1168 led by the lords of Lusignan resulted in an ambush that took the life of his lieutenant, Earl Patrick of Salisbury; but problems elsewhere forced the Angevin prince to abandon attempts to take revenge. By 1169, he had given up any idea of imposing direct rule and placed his queen in charge of her possessions along with their second son, Richard; within a few years, Richard was acknowledged as *dominus Pictavie* and installed as count in 1172. Yet Henry II continued to bear the title 'duke of Aquitaine' throughout his reign, and Richard bore the lesser title 'count of Poitou' during his father's lifetime.[1] Soon after the great rebellion

---

1 Delisle/Berger, 2: 82–3, no. 519, dated 1172–78, confirmation of La Rochelle's liberties conceded *Richardo filio meo presente, herede meo Pictavie*; also R.V. Turner, 'The Problem of

of 1173–74 and Eleanor's banishment to England, however, Richard was acting as veritable viceroy in Aquitaine and Gascony.

The imprecise nature of Richard Lionheart's authority over Aquitaine or Guyenne corresponds closely to another aspect of the area, for it was hardly a clearly defined geographical unit in the twelfth century. The duchy was a confusing collection of a dozen or so counties including Poitou and Berry in the north, La Marche, the Limousin, Angoumois, Périgord, Saintonge and Aunis, and Uzerches in the centre, and in the south, Agenais, Quercy, Rouergue and Auvergne. [See Map V] Constant warfare had characterised the reigns of Richard's eleventh- and early twelfth-century predecessors. The aristocracy of the south had a reputation for endless strife with each other and with their duke, attested by both contemporaries and modern writers. Earl William Marshal, that paragon of chivalric honour, considered the Poitevins to be scheming traitors.[2]

In the eleventh century, the counts of Poitou lost their military, judicial and financial powers outside their ducal or comital demesne during the 'feudal transformation', and they only held on to full authority within their own lands. Some of the powerful barons of Richard's day were descended from castellans who had first become visible in the early decades of the eleventh century, holding one or two castles. In the course of the twelfth century, they were bringing neighbouring castellans under their control, creating large regional lordships that formed an intermediate level between the count and his castellans. Such lordships acted as checks on the count's authority, much as in late eleventh-century Normandy before William the Bastard imposed order there or in Anjou in the late eleventh century before Fulk V and Geoffrey le Bel restored comital authority. The most dangerous nobles were those who controlled important towns, such as Angoulême or Thouars, that could provide them with substantial cash incomes; those whose chief town was under the local bishop's control, such as Limoges or Périgueux, posed a lesser threat.[3]

The number of castles in the count/duke's own hand was steadily decreasing. Even castles theoretically held for him in custody were falling under permanent control of the custodians' families. Richard Lionheart controlled directly only fourteen castles out of about ninety in Poitou, and he held hardly any in neighbouring territories such as Périgord, the Limousin

---

Survival for the Angevin "Empire": Henry II's and his Sons' Vision versus Late Twelfth-Century Realities', *AHR* 100 (1995), 85.

2   P. Meyer (ed.), *L'Histoire de Guillaume le Maréchal*, Société de l'histoire de France, vols 255, 268, 304 (Paris, 1891–1901), ll. 1577–80, 12,521–50.

3   M. Garaud, 'Les Châtelains de Poitou et l'avènement du régime féodal, XIᵉ et XIIᵉ siècles' MSAO, 4th ser. 1964, 22; Boussard, 146, 379.

or Angoumois. While both Richard and his father sought to reclaim for themselves or to raze many of their rebellious subjects' fortifications in Poitou, they seldom accomplished long-lasting results, for defeated castellans soon rebuilt their demolished fortresses and reinforced their walls.[4] For example, Richard captured and destroyed the supposedly invincible castle of Taillebourg in 1179, yet he had to besiege the reconstructed stronghold again in 1188 and in 1194. The Lionheart did seize several castles in Poitou and Aunis on his return from captivity in 1194, and he held onto them until his death in 1199.[5]

The dukes of Aquitaine since 1058 were also dukes of Gascony, the territory lying between the Garonne River and the Pyrenees. While the dukes themselves held the county of Bordeaux, effective control over the remaining counties and viscounties of Gascony lay with numerous lords, practically independent of ducal authority. The great size of Gascony alone, a sort of federation of thirteen counties, complicated construction of adequate administrative structures, and the count/duke appears among its nobility as little more than first among equals. Richard largely limited his ambition to preserving a hold on Gascony's richest portions, Bordeaux and the Garonne valley.

Both Aquitaine and Gascony might be defined as 'rather a loose union of principalities than a single one'.[6] Within his two duchies, Richard could not assert the public powers that he would enforce effectively in the Anglo-Norman lands and to some extent in greater Anjou. Richard's predecessors had ruled their two duchies separately, summoning their nobilities to meet with them in two separate councils meeting at Poitiers and at Bordeaux. Poitou and Gascony had little in common, not even language, for one province spoke the northern French dialect and the other spoke langue d'oc. Each province had a port important for wine exports – La Rochelle and Bordeaux – but this fostered economic competition instead of common interests.

The entire eastern frontier of the two duchies was in dispute throughout Henry II's and Richard I's reigns. Adjoining Poitou was the county of Berry, divided into Plantagenet and Capetian halves: in the north, the viscounty of Bourges that had passed into the French royal domain in 1101; and lower Berry with its leading lordship of Châteauroux held by the house of Déols, falling under Plantagenet influence. The two royal houses continually

---

4 Robert Hajdu, 'Castles, Castellans and the Structure of Politics in Poitou, 1152–1271', *JMH* 4 (1978), 27–54.

5 P. Marchegay (ed.), 'Chartes de Fontevraud concernant l'Aunis et La Rochelle', *BEC*, 4th ser., 19 (1858), 333, castle of Marans returned to William de Mauzé following Richard's death.

6 C. Stephenson, *Medieval Feudalism* (Ithaca, NY, 1942), 83.

challenged each other for Graçay and Issoudun, two Berry lordships lying between Bourges and Châteauroux.[7] The county of Auvergne's position was always puzzling, as the dukes of Aquitaine, the counts of Toulouse and the Capetians all laid claim to its lordship. Next to Gascony lay the county of Toulouse, which Eleanor's grandfather Duke William IX had sought to subject to his lordship, and to which Henry II had laid claim on behalf of his wife as early as 1156. For forty years conflict continued, involving the kings of Aragon in shifting enmity and alliance with Richard Lionheart and Raymond V of Toulouse.

The Capetians' ambitions contributed to the Angevins' difficulties in the south, for their Aquitanian subjects soon learned to play the two rival powers against each other. The duchy of Aquitaine descended from one of the *regna* into which the Carolingian Empire was partitioned, and the duke of Aquitaine was one of the great lords of France. For much of the post-Carolingian period, however, the relationship of Aquitaine to the French monarchy had remained ill-defined; and Gascony's status was even more problematic. Although ceremonies in churches at Poitiers and Limoges for Richard Lionheart's 1172 investiture conferred on him something of the sacred character of kingship, he did homage on two occasions to the French monarch.[8] The Capetian monarchs claimed a right to intervene in cases of default of ducal/comital justice. As early as 1166, when Henry II claimed jurisdiction over a dispute between the count of Auvergne and his nephew, the count had appealed to Louis VII's court at Paris.[9]

In the spring of 1196, Richard named his nephew, the German prince Otto of Brunswick, count of Poitou, acting without Philip Augustus's consent. This action is difficult to explain, for it seems to contradict the Lionheart's earlier tenacity in seeking to hold on to his southern inheritance. Some scholars attribute the grant to Eleanor of Aquitaine, who was increasingly concerned about the succession to her duchy in case Richard died without a direct heir. Otto returned to Germany by the spring of 1198, however, to pursue his candidacy for the imperial crown. It seems unlikely that he was ever formally invested with the comital title, as Richard had been in

---

7   G. Devailly, *Le Berry du Xe au milieu du XIIIe siècle* (Paris, 1973), 351–426, 438.

8   P. Chaplais, 'Le Traité de Paris de 1259 et l'inféodation de la Gascogne allodiale', *Le Moyen Age* 61 (1955), 127–8, 133; rpt in *Essays in Medieval Diplomacy and Administration* (London, 1981). Also J. Martindale, 'Eleanor of Aquitaine', in *Richard Coeur de Lion in History and Myth*, rpt in *Status, Authority and Regional Power* (Aldershot, 1997), 28–31, who finds Aquitaine under Louis VII 'an autonomous political entity which could not be conceptually absorbed into a pre-existing scheme of political or juridical views on the character of royal power'.

9   A. Richard, *Histoire des Comtes de Poitou*, 2 vols (Paris, 1903), 2: 142. In 1196, when Richard I began proceedings against the lord of Vierzon in Berry, he appealed to Philip Augustus's court; Devailly, *Berry*, 424–5.

1172.[10] Neither does it appear that young Otto exercised independence of action in Aquitaine or Gascony, for Richard's seneschals in the two regions continued to administer their duchies. Furthermore, the Lionheart left two of his men, Andrew de Chauvigny and Gerard de Furnivall, as tutors and guardians for his nephew.

Henry II and Richard I never found a political solution to the problem of asserting authority over the local leaders in Eleanor's lands who showed an independent spirit tending toward anarchy. Without strong administrative machinery, they could not impose the 'feudal' obligations on the Aquitanian nobility that their English or Norman barons owed, and they lacked the resources in the region with which to bind their nobles to them with ties of patronage. Only mutual friendship, shared respect and compromise between the count/duke and the aristocracy could have provided peace and harmony, but neither Henry II nor Richard I had such amicable relations with their southern nobles. They had to face numerous rebellions in the region, and annals and chronicles are filled with accounts of Richard Lionheart's punitive campaigns as count of Poitou, punishing rebellious nobles in the Angoumois and Limousin. Yet his reliance upon military force proved counter-productive. The more ruthless his punitive expeditions and the more rapacious his mercenaries' plundering, the more hostility he aroused. Even English chroniclers commented on the hatred aroused among Richard's Aquitanian subjects by his excessive cruelty.[11]

Ninth- and tenth-century counts of Poitou had delegated authority to several viscounts, but in Richard Lionheart's time only three survived. Aimery, viscount of Thouars, was the most important Poitevin noble with over a dozen castles to dominate the northern and western part of the county. His territory stretched from the ancient fortress of Thouars, guarding the Poitevin frontier south of Saumur on the Loire, to the Ile d'Oléron off the Atlantic coast.[12] The viscounty of Châtellerault constituted another powerful lordship along the northern border, lying athwart the route from Poitiers to Tours. Eleanor of Aquitaine's mother had belonged to the family of the lords of Châtellerault, and Eleanor showed devotion to her maternal uncles, one of whom, Ralph de Faye, ranked among her most trusted household officials.[13]

---

10   Richard, *Histoire des Comtes*, 2: 300–2; E.-R. Labande, 'Pour une image véridique d'Aliénor d'Aquitaine', *BSAO*, 4th ser., 2 (1952), 225–6; J.C. Holt, 'Aliénor d'Aquitaine, Jean sans Terre et la succession de 1199', *CCM* 29 (1986), 97–9.

11   For example, Diceto, 2: 20; *Gesta Regis*, 2: 34; Gervase, 2: 332.

12   Boussard, 115; J. Martindale, 'Aimeri of Thouars and the Poitevin Connection', *ANS* 7 (1985), 234–8.

13   Chamard, 'Chronique historique de Châtellerault avant la fin du XIII\u1d49 siècle', *MSAO* 35 (1970–71); S. Painter, 'The Houses of Lusignan and Châtellerault', in F.A. Cazel Jr. (ed.), *Feudalism and Liberty* (Baltimore, 1961), 82–3.

A third viscounty belonged to the De Brosse family; it protected the frontier between Poitou and Berry below the River Creuse.[14] Close behind them in resources was the Archevêque family of Parthenay, descendants of an early eleventh-century castellan. From their castle lying to the south of Thouars, they dominated the Gâtine and ranked among the most significant mid-level Poitevin nobility, exercising almost complete independence before the Capetian conquest in the thirteenth century. They held lands not only of the count of Poitou, but also of the counts of Anjou and of the abbey of Saint-Maixent.[15] Guarding the frontier between Touraine and Poitou just north of the River Vienne, perhaps as much a Tourangeau house as Poitevin, were the lords of Sainte-Maure.

In the Aunis and Saintonge, no count or viscount survived to dominate the region, but some powerful barons could make trouble. Geoffrey II de Rancon, the dominant lord in Aunis and Saintonge, proved to be one of the Plantagenet dukes' bitterest enemies, often joining such lords of lower Aquitaine as Adémar of Angoulême in rebellion against Richard.[16] Three less powerful noble families – Mauléon, Maingot of Surgères and the Portclie of Mauzé – proved loyal servants to the Plantagenets, holding posts as *prévôts* and seneschals.[17] The Mauléons, centred at Châtillon-sur-Sèvre, had holdings along the Atlantic coast of Poitou and Aunis; they were hereditary custodians for the counts of the Poitevin lordship of Talmont. One of the strongest lordships in the Aunis, Châtelaillon, master of the Ile de Ré and one of four lords on the Ile d'Oléron, also passed to the Mauléons.[18] The Maingots were hereditary custodians of the castle and castellany of Surgères until 1199, when Eleanor of Aquitaine rewarded William III Maingot with outright lordship.[19] East of Poitou lay Berry, where no magnate held the comital title; and instead, several noble families divided the territory. By Henry II's time, however, the house of Déols had come to the fore in Berry; they became lords of Châteauroux and absorbed smaller lordships to create a sizeable dominion.[20]

Below Poitou proper, yet supposedly subject to the count, were a number of powerful and turbulent noble houses in the Limousin, Angoumois and Périgord separating Poitou from Gascony, all of whom were linked through

---

14 S. Painter, 'Castellans of the Plain of Poitou in the Eleventh and Twelfth Centuries', in F.A. Cazel Jr. (ed.), *Feudalism and Liberty* (Baltimore, 1916), 21; Devailly, *Berry*, 424.
15 Boussard, 101; Painter, 'Castellans of the Plain of Poitou', 34; G. Beech, *A Rural Society in Medieval France: The Gâtine of Poitou in the Eleventh and Twelfth Centuries* (Baltimore, 1964), 42–70.
16 Painter, 'Castellans of the Plain of Poitou', 37.
17 R. Favreau, 'Les débuts de la ville de La Rochelle', *CCM* 30 (1987), 9.
18 Boussard, 117, 125; Painter, 'Castellans of the Plain of Poitou', 34.
19 *Rot. Chart.*, 25.
20 Boussard, 'Diversité et les traits particuliers du régime féodal', 177; Devailly, *Berry*, 438.

marriage. Their castles could become barriers blocking Richard's route between his two capitals, Poitiers and Bordeaux. Among the most quarrelsome were the lords of Lusignan, whose expansion from their early eleventh-century castles of Lusignan and Conché in southern Poitou into a major regional power is a striking illustration of the growth of castellans' power. They were prominent in the crusading movement and also conspicuous participants in all the revolts against the Plantagenets. Yet Hugh IX le Brun proved faithful to the Lionheart, winning glory on the Third Crusade; and Richard, on his release from captivity, compensated the Lusignan family for its failure to secure the county of La Marche. Part of the settlement was the marriage of Hugh's younger brother, Ralph of Exoudun, to the heiress to the county of Eu, Normandy, and the barony of Hastings in England.[21]

Other unruly nobles included the hostile counts of Angoulême and Périgord, and the four viscounts of the Limousin: Limoges, Comborn, Ventadour and Turenne. Presenting a threat equal or greater than the Lusignan lords were the Taillefer counts of Angoulême, for their territory constituted the nucleus of a state, securing them the wealth needed to construct a network of castles and to hire mercenary forces.[22] Count Adémar of Angoulême, after his defeat in 1194, sought to strengthen his position by allying with the Lusignans; the betrothal of his daughter, Isabelle, to Hugh IX sealed the alliance. The counts of Périgord consistently joined their more powerful neighbours in revolts against the Lionheart both before and after he succeeded his father, although they generally give an impression of 'absolute impotence'. The viscounts of Limoges maintained 'only a vain title', controlling little more than the castle of Saint-Martial at Limoges and land surrounding the town. Yet they habitually allied with the counts of Angoulême against the Plantagenets, and after Richard's return from captivity in 1194, Viscount Adémar V renounced Plantagenet lordship in favour of Philip Augustus.[23]

Still farther south, Gascony had a number of great barons whose power matched that of the lords in the Limousin. Gascon nobles felt pulled in two directions out of the Angevin orbit: those in the shadow of the Pyrenees were attracted toward the Spanish kingdoms of Aragon and Navarre, and those farther east tended to fall under the influence of the counts of Toulouse.[24] While narrative accounts have made much of the Gascon

---

21 S. Painter, 'The Lords of Lusignan in the Eleventh and Twelfth Centuries', in F.A. Cazel Jr. (ed.), *Feudalism and Liberty* (Baltimore, 1961) 67–81; Painter, 'Lusignan and Châtellerault', 73–89; Boussard, 'Diversité et les traits particuliers du féodal', 177–8.

22 For example, Diceto, 1: 407, Count Vulgrin in 1176 invaded Poitou, *stipatus cohorto nefaria Brabentinorum*. Also Debord, *La Société laïque dans les pays de la Charente X^e–XIIe siècles* (Paris, 1984), 392–6.

23 Boussard, 135, 146, 228.

24 P. Courteault, *Histoire de la Gascogne et de Béarn* (Paris, 1938), 54.

nobility's rebellious spirit, they appear to have proven more loyal to Eleanor, Henry II and Richard I than the nobles on Poitou's southern borders. None seems to have participated in the great 1173–74 revolt. The magnates of Gascony had small reason to feel discontentment with Angevin leadership, since it was so ineffectual that they felt little burdened by it.

The only major rebellion faced by Richard in Gascony was that of Pierre III, viscount of Dax, allied with Centule, count of Bigorre, in 1177–78. Richard confiscated the lands of the viscount of Dax, took control of the town of Dax, and declared it a regalian city. He brought the young viscount of Béarn, Gaston VI, under his control by 1187, seeking to pull him from the orbit of the kingdom of Aragon.[25] Soon after Richard succeeded his father as king in 1189, he marched almost to the Pyrenees to punish Gascon robber barons who had been attacking pilgrims en route to Compostella; perhaps his campaign also served as a warning to neighbouring Spanish princes.

In addition to the large regional lordships in the south, a number of local lords holding only one or two castles acknowledged no immediate lord, only the distant authority of the duke. Typical of such anarchical figures was the troubadour Bertrand de Born, castellan of Hautefort in southwestern Périgord. This petty Aquitanian noble cultivated a chivalric ethos as propaganda for the warfare that provided him with a livelihood. Bertrand revelled in war and brigandage, and he actively fomented conflict through his verses. Drawn to Young King Henry, an attractive though irresponsible youth, Bertrand tried to fan the boy's jealousy toward his brother Richard Lionheart as an excuse for combat in 1182–83. After the Lionheart's return from the crusade, however, Bertrand became his admirer and wrote poems celebrating his prowess before retiring to a monastery in 1196.

In the south of France in the twelfth century, castellans, viscounts and counts did not yet acknowledge that their homage to the duke committed them to perform any defined duties, unless they had received an estate from him as a fief.[26] Regional lords in Poitou and farther south might do homage to their Plantagenet lord after he had defeated them on the battlefield, but that did not stop them from promptly rebelling on his departure. Not surprisingly, the Plantagenets sought to use northern feudal terminology to strengthen their control over the southern nobility, as revealed by the peace settlement with Count Raymond V of Toulouse in February 1173. The count became the man of Henry II, Henry the Young King and Count

---

25   Howden, 2: 117, 170; *Gesta Regis*, 1: 131–2; Boussard, 148–55, 186; Courteault, *Gascogne et Béarn*, 78–9.

26   A. Debord, 'The Castellan Revolution and the Peace of God in Aquitaine', in T. Head and R. Landes (eds), *The Peace of God: Social Violence and Religious Response in France around the Year 1000* (Ithaca, NY, 1992), 138–9.

Richard of Poitou; he acknowledged that he held Toulouse of them *in feudo et hereditate*; he agreed to forty days' military service at his own cost and additional service at their expense; and in addition, he promised tribute of 100 silver marks annually.[27] Of course, this truce proved shortlived, a sign of the frailty of such ties of fealty. The peace treaty of 1174 between Henry II and his sons acknowledged the return of rebel barons and men *in hominium et liganciam domini regis*, and Henry II, following his purchase of the county of La Marche in 1177, took the *homagium et fidelitas et ligantia* of his new county's barons and knights.[28] A later use of feudal terminology is seen in Eleanor's 1199 charter ceding Poitou to John; the bishops and lay nobility of the county owed him as lord their homage, fealty and service.[29]

In general, references to fiefs or vassals were infrequent and imprecise in southwestern France. Richard's Aquitanian charters use the terms *feodum* or *fevum* infrequently and imprecisely, not necessarily meaning tenure by knight service.[30] Perhaps revealing of the minor status that fiefholding connoted in the region was Count Richard's grant of his kitchen as a fief in 1175 to his cook, Alan, and his heirs. Another indicator is Richard's grant in 1190 of land near Niort in Poitou and ovens at Niort to one of his mercenaries, William Cook, 'having and holding for homage and service'. The charter recognised that William should henceforth have the rank of serjeant.[31] In Poitou, and even more so in Bordelais and farther south, a large proportion of land continued to be held as alods. Throughout Gascony, most possessors of castles held them as alods throughout the twelfth century and alodial holdings predominated, although some tenants in the Bordelais held fiefs of the dukes of Gascony.[32]

---

27 Howden, 2: 45; *Gesta Regis*, 1: 36.
28 Howden, 2: 148.
29 *Rot. Chart.*, 30b. Also *Cal. Docs. Fr.*, 389–90, no. 1099, April 1199, Ralph de Mauléon did liege homage to Eleanor when she granted Talmont to him.
30 For example, BN ms. lat., nouv. acq. f444–5, Richard's protection for any land *de feodo nostro* acquired by the abbot of Lieu Dieu; *ibid.* f283, also D. Sainte-Marthe (ed.), *Gallia Christiana*, 16 vols (Paris, 1739–1877), 2: col. 388, charter confirming his gifts to the abbey of Charron uses the term *ex feodo nostro*. In a charter *c.* 1155–83, the abbot of Sauve Majeure granted a *fevum* for a *cens* of twelve measures of grain; C. Higounet and A. Higounet-Nadal (eds), *Grande Cartulaire de la Sauve Majeure*, Etudes et documents d'Aquitaine, 8, 2 vols (Bordeaux, 1996), 1: 277, no. 480. A 1229 charter describes a landholder, owing a *cens* of grain, who *fecit se hominem ligiam* of Sauve Majeure, *ibid.* 1: 227–8, no. 371.
31 *Cal. Docs. Fr.*, 467, no. 1286; also BN ms. lat. nouv. acq. 1244, f304; Richard, *Histoire des Comtes*, 2: 267. P. Boissonade, 'Administrateurs laïques et ecclésiastiques Anglo-Normands en Poitou à l'époque d'Henri II Plantagenêt (1152–1189)', *BSAO* 3rd ser. 5 (1919), 165, identifies William Cook as one of Richard's mercenary captains.
32 J.A. Brutails, 'Les fiefs du roi et les alleux en Guyenne', *Annales du Midi* 29 (1917), 58, 65, 83–4; C. Higounet, 'En Bordelaise: "Principes castella tenentes",' in P. Contamines (ed.), *La Noblesse au moyen âge, xie–xve siècles: Essais à la mémoire de Robert Boutruche* (Paris, 1976), 102.

Although the southern nobles were willing to acknowledge the prince's pre-eminence, they resisted his attempts to expand his lordship over them into the effective rights over their lands associated with feudal tenures in the Anglo-Norman realm.[33] A hint of the Angevins' inability to collect feudal incidents is the absence of references to relief payments in Richard's *acta* from Aquitaine, although occasionally mention is made of *sporla*, a similar, smaller payment.[34] The nobility's power within their territories made it impossible for Henry or Richard to enforce the control over castles, inheritances and various financial perquisites that they enforced fully in their Anglo-Norman lands and somewhat less effectively in Anjou. They proved unable to halt a process of consolidation of power by the castellans of Poitou, who were converting scattered holdings surrounding a single castle into large lordships protected by strings of fortifications.[35]

While princes of Aquitaine and Gascony recognised an obligation to join their duke's host in time of war, it is not at all certain that they considered such military service to be a 'feudal' obligation due from their lands. Earliest Poitevin evidence for grants of knights' fees, lands held in return for definite quotas of knight service, comes from King John's 1214 campaign.[36] Just as in Anjou, ducal grants farther south often retained the traditional public obligation of *ost et chevauchée*; sometimes townsmen owed the duke such military service.[37] The impossibility of raising an effective host locally forced the Angevin rulers to rely upon foreign mercenary forces or, occasionally, on allies from across the Pyrenees. Roger of Howden reports that in 1176 Richard raised a large force from Poitou and surrounding regions 'by means of the stipends that he gave them'.[38] As in other hegemonic empires, Plantagenet authority was enforced in this secondary zone by military forces dispatched from the central zone of Normandy or Anjou, in Richard's case, mercenaries paid with funds raised in England.

---

33 Debord, *La Société laïque*, 381.
34 Bemont, *Recueil d'actes relatifs à l'administration des rois d'Angleterre en Gascogne*, no. 495, 217; Higounet and Higounet-Nadal, *Grande cartulaire*, 1: 277, no. 480; 1: 356, no. 646; 2: 618–19, no. 1116.
35 Hajdu, 'Castles, Castellans', 36.
36 *Rot. Chart.*, 196, Payn de Rochefort granted the castellany of Rochefort as a fee of two knights. An undated twelfth-century charter describes the lord of Sainte-Hermine as holding his fee of the abbot of Saint-Maixent's for service as standard-bearer in the count's host, A. Richard (ed.), *Chartes et documents pour servir à l'histoire de l'Abbaye de Saint-Maixent*, 2, Archives historiques de Poitou, 18 (1886), no. 400.
37 For example, a 1200 charter of Eleanor to Saint-Maixent; Richard, *Chartes de Saint-Maixent*, no. 402; grant of the services of foresters of Savra. Also F. Villard (ed.), *Recueil des documents relatifs à l'Abbaye de Montierneuf de Poitiers (1076–1319)*, Archives Historiques de Poitou, 59 (1973), no. 112, 4 May 1199, exemption from *ost et chevauchée* for men of Montierneuf, except in war (*bellum*) by the duke.
38 Howden, 2: 47; *Gesta Regis*, 1: 120.

Feudal bonds proved 'decidedly ineffectual' in uniting the duke of Aquitaine and his castellans before the Capetian annexation of Poitou.[39] The military aristocracy of Aquitaine and Gascony recognised few obligations other than their personal service as warriors in Richard's host, attendance at his court, and the rendability of their castles in emergencies. In short, minor landlords of the south enjoyed the freedom to do largely as they pleased so long as they showed some minimal loyalty to their own lords. For example, they continued to assert their right to wage private warfare among themselves, contributing considerably to the region's turbulence. While Richard frequently confiscated the lands and castles of rebellious nobles in Aquitaine and Gascony, such forfeitures need not be placed in a feudal context of dependent tenures; they are simply the traditional punishment for treason.

While Henry and Richard sought on occasion to impose the 'feudal incidents' on their southern nobility, the sporadically documented instances do not indicate wide success. Weakening any Angevin efforts to enforce rights of wardship was the chaos of lordships with their own laws, with no single legal tradition dominating the region. One Gascon landlord making his will stated that he held some lands following written law, others following the custom of Bazadais, and still others following the custom of Landes or of Bordeaux.[40] This led to wide variations in inheritance customs, as families decided successions without the pressure for male primogeniture that bore down on the nobility of northern France or England; and in rare cases of a single female heir, relatives normally claimed custody. In Poitou, for example, the family inheritance was held jointly by all the male siblings of each generation under the leadership of the eldest brother.[41] Such shared inheritances afforded fewer opportunities for ducal intervention than did the stricter male primogeniture of the north, and evidence for the feudal rights of wardship and marriage surfaces only rarely.

Yet the Plantagenets attempted to grab custodies of rich heirs. In 1156, Henry II claimed guardianship of the minor viscount of Limoges, despite the claims of the boy's paternal uncles. Later, when Henry claimed custody of the heiress to the lordship of Déols, Berry, following her father's death in 1177, he had to contest by force the claim of an uncle to the girl's wardship. Richard Lionheart, as duke, took custody of Angoulême on the death of Count Vulgrin III on behalf of his daughter; but inheritance patterns gave rights to the late count's brothers, and by 1188, Richard had to abandon

---

39 Beech, *A Rural Society*, 78.
40 P. Orliac, 'Législation, coutumes et coutumiers au temps de Philippe Auguste', in R.-H. Bautier (ed.), *La France de Philippe Auguste: le temps de mutations* (Paris, 1982), 484–5.
41 Painter, 'Castellans of the Plain of Poitou', 27–8.

his attempt to have her recognised as countess.[42] Richard does not seem to have played any role in Joscelin de Motoiron's custody of the children of the viscount of Châtellerault (d. 1188); apparently, Joscelin's marriage to the viscount's widow secured him his step-sons' custody.[43] Only seldom were the Angevin count/dukes able to arrange heiresses' marriages. Henry II arranged the marriage of Adémar V, viscount of Limoges, to a daughter of Earl Reginald of Cornwall. Later he married the Déols heiress to Châteauroux to Baldwin de Redvers, earl of Devon (d. 1188); and then Richard married her to Andrew de Chauvigny, one of his Poitevin soldiers.[44] Also Richard gained custody of the daughter and heir of the lord of Cognac, whom he married to his bastard son, known henceforth as Philip of Cognac.[45]

The Plantagenet count/dukes never attempted to create any central administrative agencies for Aquitaine or Gascony, and their overall authority remained spotty at best. The lack of record evidence from the two duchies reflects the rudimentary quality of government in the south. The overwhelming majority of Richard Lionheart's surviving *acta* concern England, even though he rarely visited his island kingdom. Only 37 of some 750 documents treat Aquitanian or Gascon matters, and many of these were confirmations of grants by his predecessors. Even when Richard was in the south, he issued as many charters for English beneficiaries as Aquitanian ones.[46]

The small number of surviving charters from the southern territories reduces chances for identifying Richard's comital *curia* or household before his accession to the English throne. His chief regional and local agents in Poitou, Aquitaine and Gascony were the traditional officials found elsewhere in France, *prévôts* and seneschals. As in Anjou, the *prévôts* had responsibility for administering the comital/ducal domain. Poitou proper was divided into five *prévôtés*, plus three in Aunis and two in Saintonge. Important towns or castles served as their centres, for example, Bordeaux as headquarters for the *prévôt* of the Bordelais.

---

42 Debord, *La Société laïque*, 381; Devailly, *Berry*, 438; Gillingham, *Richard*, 86, 114.

43 Chamard, 'Chronique historique de Châtellerault', *MSAO* 34 (1970–71), 111; J. Duguet, 'Notes sur quelques vicomtes de Châtellerault', *BSAO*, 4th ser. 16 (1981–82), 266–8.

44 J. Le Patourel, 'The Plantagenet Dominions' in *Feudal Empires, Norman and Plantagenet* (London, 1984), 293; Devailly, *Berry*, 423, 438.

45 F.M. Powicke and E.B. Fryde (eds), *Handbook of British Chronology*, 2nd edn (London, 1961), 33.

46 J.C. Holt, 'The Acta of Henry II and Richard I of England 1154–1199: The Archive and its Historical Implications', in P. Rück (ed.), *Fotografische Sammlungen mittelalterlicher Urkunden in Europa* (Sigmaringen, 1989), 139; also J.C. Holt, 'The Writs of Henry II', in J. Hudson (ed.), *The History of English Law: Centenary Essays on 'Pollock and Maitland'* (Oxford, 1996), 47–64, where he gives a figure of 25 (4 per cent) of 590 acts in Landon.

Once the 1173–74 uprising was crushed, Henry II gave each part of his 'empire' its own viceroy, or justiciar for England and elsewhere seneschals overseeing the *prévôts* and garrisoning castles. In Aquitaine and Gascony, the number of seneschals varied, although after 1182, the normal practice was to appoint two: one for Poitou and another for Gascony. Seneschals of Poitou during the 1180s were Guillaume Chapon, then Robert de Montmirail and finally Pierre Bertin.[47] Richard's seneschal for Poitou in 1189 and throughout his reign was Pierre Bertin, a former serjeant-at-arms, a man of the lesser nobility, who had gained administrative experience as *prévôt* of Benon. During Richard's absence on crusade, in captivity, 1190–94, and later while fighting in Normandy, the seneschals became more important, more equivalent to the Anglo-Norman justiciar. While the king was away in the Holy Land, Pierre Bertin led a campaign to crush a rebellion by the count of Périgord and the viscount de Brosse; he crushed the rebels, confiscated their lands and added them to the ducal domains.[48] Serving as seneschals in Gascony were two members of a notable administrative family: Elie de la Celle, and later his relative Geoffrey de la Celle, who seems to have served for a time simultaneously as seneschal for Poitou and Gascony (*c*. 1197).[49]

Another great official was the constable, although his name is rarely recorded; it is assumed that he had important military responsibilities. Richard's chief military lieutenant in the 1170s, Theobald Chabot, lord of Vouvent, performed the functions of constable, whether or not he held the formal title.[50] No doubt an Aquitanian treasury supplied funds for the Angevin princes' expenses, functioning much like the treasury at Loches Castle farther north, but no evidence for a treasurer exists. Possibly the treasurer of the collegiate church of Saint-Hilaire, Poitiers, often an absentee royal clerk, played some role in ducal financial affairs.[51]

Few documents depict the eleventh- and early twelfth-century dukes of Aquitaine hearing pleas, and lawsuits before Henry II, Richard, John or their seneschals were also uncommon.[52] Probably petitions by one of the

---

47 Boussard, 353–6, 510–18. Debord, *La Société laïque*, 399–401.

48 Richard, *Histoire des Comtes*, 2: 263, 279, 291; Debord, *La Société laïque*, 402.

49 Debord, *La Société laïque*, 375–6, 399–402.

50 Boussard, 356–7; Diceto, 1: 407, describes Chabot in 1176 as Richard's *princeps militiae*.

51 For example, Richard of Ilchester under Henry II, and Peter des Roches under King John. See N. Vincent, *Peter des Roches: An Alien in English Politics 1205–1238* (Cambridge, 1996), 17.

52 Two suits settled before Henry II: December 1156, Delisle/Berger, 1: 120, no. 25; *c*. 1163, *Cal. Docs. Fr.*, 452, no. 1250. Richard's judicial activity as count of Poitou: July 1182, Debord, *La Société laïque*, 379, citing *Chartes de l'abbaye de Nouaille* (ed.), Dom P. de Monsabert, Archives historiques du Poitou, 49 (1936), 344; 1187/89, R. Poupardin (ed.), *Recueil des Chartes de l'Abbaye de Saint-Germain-des-Prés*, 2, *1183–1216*, Société de l'histoire de Paris et de

parties initiated these rare suits before the duke, just as petitioners seeking justice had sought out earlier rulers on their intermittent progresses about the provinces. Although the Angevin dukes occasionally gave justice, acting on petitioners' appeals, they afforded their subjects no routine means for redress of grievances at fixed meetings of ducal courts. Neither did they make themselves keepers of the peace, responsible for suppression of crime; for example, charters confirmed religious houses their rights to jurisdiction over the four capital crimes of homicide, theft, rape and arson.[53]

No more than a handful of ducal charters of special protection or confirmations of property for southern monastic foundations survive. In Gascony, such grants were extremely limited geographically; the beneficiaries lay along the strategic Garonne and Adour rivers. Religious houses in neither Aquitaine nor Gascony found such ducal charters as useful as did English or Norman monasteries, which valued them as evidence for suits before the royal or ducal courts. Southern grants of such privileges were more vaguely worded, imprecise guarantees of general protection, not specific licences for having their pleas heard before Richard or his seneschal.[54]

The Plantagenets did not introduce a writ system to make ducal justice readily available to suitors, as in lands north of the Loire. Most property disputes were settled by arbitration, with the parties choosing the site, sometimes the local bishop's court or other times informally outside any tribunal.[55] Aquitanian ecclesiastical foundations proved more likely to look to Rome than to the ducal court for protection of their properties, and appeals from Poitevin religious houses to the pope or to papal legates were

---

l'Ile de France (Paris, 1930), 30. Eleanor of Aquitaine heard a few cases during Richard's reign: G. Pon (ed.), *Recueil des documents de l'Abbaye de Fontaine-le-Comte (xii'–xiii' siècles)*, Archives historiques du Poitou, 61 (1982), no. 24, dated 1189–99 at Poitiers; P. Marchegay (ed.), *Cartulaires du Bas-Poitou* (Les Roches-Baritaud, 1877), Marmoutier Cart., 1; 431, *c.* 1195? at Poitiers; *Cal. Docs. Fr.*, 388, no. 1092, at Fontevraud, 1196.

53 Henry II to the abbey of Notre-Dame de Saintes, Delisle/Berger, 2: 15, no. 465, dated 1174; John's confirmation, *Rot. Chart.*, 7b; also immunity for the men and women of Saint-Maixent from the *prévôt's* jurisdiction, Richard, *Chartes de Saint-Maixent*, 2: no. 394.

54 For example, Count Richard's charter, *c.* 1180, for the priory of St-Pierre, La Réole, *Cal. Docs. Fr.*, 452, no. 1249; A.W. Lewis, 'Six Charters of Henry II and his Family for the Monastery of Dalon', *EHR* 110 (1995), 662–3, no date; Cirot de la Ville, *Histoire de l'abbaye et la congrégation de Notre Dame de La Grande-Sauve*, 2 vols (Paris/Bordeaux, 1844–45), 2: 123–4, 1190, for La Sauve-Majeure; Villard, *Recueil des documents de Montierneuf*, 175, no. 107, for Montierneuf, 1190; BN ms. lat. nouv. acq. 1244, f407, 1195?, the abbot, monks and bourgeois of Sarlat; ff444–5, 1197, for Locus Dei.

55 Garaud, 'Châtelains de Poitou', 22, 29, 109. For example, L. Redet (ed.), 'Documents pour l'histoire de Saint-Hilaire de Poitiers', *MSAO* 14 (1847): no. 164, in 1178 the bishop of Saintes gave judgment in his own dispute with the Saint-Hilaire chapter, by counsel of *dilectorum filiorum nostrorum*; no. 182, an 1198 agreement between St-Hilaire and a knight made by two teams of arbitrators, nominated by the two parties.

not infrequent. The papacy took Saint-Hilaire, Poitiers, under its special protection as early as 1074, despite its traditional protection by the count of Poitou, its lay abbot.[56] Charters only infrequently give evidence of Richard's seneschals or *prévôts* settling disputes at his command.[57] The charters of Saint-Hilaire, for example, rarely reveal the canons bringing suits before Richard Lionheart's court, despite their longstanding ties to the counts. Charters record the canons' cases submitted to the papal *curia*, to the bishop of Poitiers, to neighbouring bishops, or to the archbishop of Bordeaux. Only an 1199 charter records a Saint-Hilaire case settled in the presence of Richard's seneschal, Pierre Bertin, in the king's hall at Poitiers.[58]

It was regional truces – the Church's Peace, the peace of the pope and bishops sworn by knights at ecclesiastical councils – that prevailed. The absence of ducal machinery for justice comparable to that in the Anglo-Norman realm is illustrated by Richard's sanction of a ten-year peace association or commune for the barons, knights and *prud'hommes* of the Bordelais *c.* 1189–95. This was part of a revived peace movement in southern France to be financed by special levies, including a poll tax and a tax on livestock.[59] Later John's confirmation of the liberties of the archbishop of Bordeaux included sweeping immunity from *nullum judex publica* for all the prelate's possessions and dependents.[60] None the less, the peace association at Bordeaux did recognise that complaints of lords' defaults of justice should be

---

56 Redet, 'Documents pour l'histoire de Saint-Hilaire', no. 123.

57 Debord, *La Société laïque*, 378–9: 7 July 1182, Pierre Bertin, *prévôt* of Benon, heard on Count Richard's order a dispute between the abbey of Nouaillé and a layman; 1187/89, Pierre Bertin, seneschal of Poitou, heard on Richard's order a complaint by the abbot of St-Germain-des-Prés about land in Saintonge. A judgment was made by Richard's seneschal in La Marche 'by our authority and command' in a conflict between the abbot of St-Martial, Limoges, and his *prévôt* versus the citizens of La Souterraine, 25 March 1196, BN ms. lat. nouv. acq. 1244, f425. 'Documents pour l'histoire de St-Hilaire de Poitiers', *MSAO*, 14 (1847), 212–13, no. 183, 1199 agreement between the chapter of St-Hilaire and the lord of Ringères, before Pierre Bertin, seneschal of Poitou and La Marche. Pierre Bertin, seneschal of Poitou, gave notification of an agreement made at his court, 1 January 1191, Pon, *Recueil des documents de l'abbaye de Fontaine-le-Comte*, no. 22. Richard, *Histoire des Comtes*, 2: 302, citing *Arch. Hist. Saintonge*, 1: 28, a dispute between Notre-Dame de la Garde and La Couronne, on which Otto of Brunswick as count of Poitou, in counsel with the bishop of Poitiers, ordered his two seneschals to give judgment.

58 For cases before bishops, R.V. Turner, 'Richard Lionheart and the Episcopate in his French Domains', *French Historical Studies* 21 (1998), 530, n. 64. Case before the seneschal, Redet, 'Documents pour l'histoire de Saint-Hilaire', no. 183, dispute with the lord of Ringères.

59 J.-A. Brutails (ed.), *Cartulaire de l'église collégiale de Saint Seurin de Bordeaux* (Bordeaux, 1897), 177–9, no. 204.

60 Brutails, *Cartulaire de Saint-Seurin*, 345–6, no. 349. Similarly Eleanor's 1199 confirmation of the charters of Montierneuf, 'Quarrels between our men and the men of the monks should not come before the court of our *prévôt*, but be heard in the monks' court'; Villard, *Recueil des documents de Montierneuf*, no. 112.

heard *in curiam domini Regis* and that the king should benefit financially with a payment of sixty-five shillings for infringements of the peace. Earlier, Henry II's grant of a commune to La Rochelle had provided that any 'great offense' – otherwise undefined – should be heard 'before himself or his heir, the lord of Poitou'.[61]

An English chronicler described Aquitaine as 'abounding in riches of many kinds . . . one of the happiest and most fertile among the provinces of Gaul'. Poitou had been experiencing a commercial revolution since the mid-eleventh century, with increasing traffic at a number of ports in both coastal and oversea trade.[62] In the interior, Poitiers was a thriving market town that held an annual fair featuring cloth from Flanders, Ile de France and elsewhere. Added evidence for an advanced commercial economy in Poitou is the presence of Jewish moneylenders at La Rochelle, Niort, Oléron and Saintes.[63] The pilgrimage routes of St Jacques criss-crossed the region, attracting visitors in a medieval version of the tourist trade. More than once, Richard Lionheart led expeditions to the Pyrenees to protect pilgrims journeying to Compostella. To the south, the towns of Gascony, especially those such as Bayonne on the coast, were growing wealthy. Bayonne, although a centre for shipbuilders, sea captains and sailors, never became a commercial centre comparable to Bordeaux or La Rochelle.[64] Bordeaux was an expanding port, but it had not yet eclipsed La Rochelle as the premier centre of the wine trade; its peak came a century after Richard Lionheart's time, during the reigns of Edward I and II.[65]

It is impossible to estimate the extent to which the ducal treasury profited from this economic growth, for Aquitaine and Gascony have left no clues in the form of official records. This is not surprising, for the earliest central financial accounts outside England are the Norman exchequer rolls of 1180. The earliest surviving accounts from Poitou date from the mid-thirteenth century in the time of Alphonse of Poitiers, Louis IX's brother who held the county as an apanage.[66] In the absence of financial records from the Angevin

---

61 *Cal. Docs. Fr.*, 453, no. 1251.

62 Diceto, 1: 293; cited by K. Norgate, *Richard the Lion Heart* (London, 1924), 3; O. Jeanne-Rose, 'Ports, marchands et marchandises: aspects économiques du littoral poitevin (IXᵉ–XIIᵉ siècles)', *MSAO*, 5th ser. 4 (1996), 115–42.

63 Richard, *Histoire des Comtes*, 2: 161: 89; for cloth fair, BN ms. lat. nouv. acq., f4, dated 1188; also R. Favreau, 'Les Juifs en Poitou et dans les pays de la Charente au moyen âge', *Revue des études juives* 147 (1988), 6–9.

64 M. Vale, *The Angevin Legacy and the 100 Years War 1250–1340* (Oxford, 1990), 149.

65 J.-P. Trabut-Cussac, *Bordeaux sous les rois d'Angleterre, Histoire de Bordeaux* (ed.), Y. Renouard, 3 (Bordeaux, 1965), 60; Vale, *Angevin Legacy*, 141. R. Stacey, *Politics, Policy and Finance under Henry III 1216–1245* (Oxford, 1987), 175, estimates Bordeaux's farm in 1238 at £700 sterling.

66 F. Hartigan, *The Accounts of Alphonse of Poitiers 1243–48* (Lanham, MD, 1984).

period, it is impossible to ascertain Richard's income from his southern lands. Evidence reveals his revenues only indirectly through charters recording his own or his mother's gifts to religious houses.[67] Many times the first report of levies on towns and individuals dates from the time of John Lackland's accession, when Eleanor was busily surrendering ducal resources as a means of purchasing support for him.[68]

Without machinery for enforcement of feudal financial obligations, the duke was dependent upon his own demesne lands for income, consisting mainly of seignorial dues that his *prévôts* collected from tenants of his estates. Coupled with this were such surviving Carolingian taxes as tolls on roads and bridges, levies on markets, import and export duties collected at ports, and profits from mints. Unfortunately, many of these revenues were incorporated within the traditional 'farm' of their *prévôts*, a fixed sum that was steadily being diverted from the ducal coffers in the form of cash grants to religious foundations, friends or allies.

It is impossible to map the ducal domain, for it was a collection of non-contiguous territories, rights and privileges. It seems, however, to have been most extensive in Poitou, Aunis and Saintonge, Bordelais and the adjacent Bazadais. In Poitou, the comital domain lay around Poitiers's environs and westward to the region of the Sèvre Niortaise and the Vendée, and the coast in the Olonnais and Talmondais. Elsewhere the duke held little direct domain, for example, none in the Limousin outside the town of Limoges.[69] Most of the ducal domains were fertile lands with fruitful vineyards and an expanding wine trade from such Atlantic ports as La Rochelle and Bordeaux. Alongside wine, salt needed for the fishing industry, panned from the salty marshes of the Poitevin coast, some of which lay within the comital domain, was a major element in Poitou's commerce.[70] The duke's demesne lands abounded in forests that generated funds through sale of timber and other resources, as well as rents from forest dwellers. Ducal grants to religious houses of wood and other forest products were not uncommon with a

---

67 Also a grant of rents from comital vineyards in the lordship of Benon, Marchegay, 'Chartes de Fontevraud concernant l'Aunis et La Rochelle', pt ii, 330–1, 337–8; *Cal. Docs. Fr.*, no. 1101. The Poitevin pound apparently had a value similar to the Angevin pound, 25–28 per cent of the silver content of the pound sterling; F. Dumas, 'La monnaie dans les domaines Plantagenêt', *CCM* 29 (1986), 54.

68 For example, grants of communes, *Rot. Chart.*, 4b, 5b, July 1199; or grants of money fiefs to Poitevin knights, 25b, October 1199.

69 Boussard, 'Diversité et les traits particuliers du régime féodal', 175–6.

70 For example, BN ms. lat. nouv. acq. 1244, f11, abbey of Grandselve granted the privilege of sale of salt; King Richard delivers salt to the abbey of La Sauve-Majeur, Cirot de la Ville, *Histoire de . . . La Grande-Sauve*, 2: 122; *Rot. Chart.*, 62, King John's renewal of Richard's grant to the Grandmont monks of salt from his *salinum* at Bordeaux; *Rot. Chart.*, 110, John's confirmation of Richard's charter concerning a saltwork at Oléron.

number from 'the Countess's Land', part of the comital honour of Talmont and one of Richard's favourite hunting grounds.[71] A valuable addition was made to the ducal domain in 1177, when Henry II purchased the county of La Marche for some 5,000 marks from its last count, the childless Adalbert V, who aimed to retire to the Holy Land in atonement for murdering his wife's paramour. La Marche would remain in Plantagenet hands for twenty-one years, until John granted it to the Lusignans in 1199.[72]

Several commercial centres that lay within the ducal domain doubtless yielded the major portion of domanial income; for example, Poitiers was subject to tallages, as most likely were other towns. La Rochelle was, by the last quarter of the twelfth century, the centre for a notable wine trade, linking Poitou and the British Isles, including Ireland, where wine was traded for leather. In 1175, Henry II and his son Richard confirmed La Rochelle's liberties, granting it a commune, the first in that region. Henry confirmed rights of justice to the new commune, reserving only serious crimes for his court; he granted its citizens the right to bequeath their property freely; and later Richard granted them free marriage rights for their sons, daughters and widows. Yet the king continued to exercise considerable control over La Rochelle with his seneschal garrisoning the castle and a *prévôt* collecting import and export duties. King John's confirmation of La Rochelle's liberties did not exempt its citizens from their service of *ost et chevauchée*.[73] Indications of the town's wealth are the 10,000 shillings *angevin* (£125 sterling) from its revenues that John granted annually to the Mauléons to purchase their support and his agreement in 1200 to forego for a year his revenues of 40,000 shillings (£500 sterling) and 20 silver cups from the town.[74]

In Gascony, the ducal domain outside Bordelais and Bazadais had never been large, and even less survived by the end of the twelfth century. Yet the surviving Gascon domain included prosperous grape-growing territories, with Bordeaux producing hundreds of pounds sterling each year in customs duties, and another substantial part of domanial income was levies on Richard's immediate subjects, 'king's men', paid in kind, mostly wine to be

---

71 For example, Richard, *Chartes de Saint-Maixent*, 2: no. 401, mentions the forest of La Sèvre; *Rot. Chart.*, 35, forest of Bordeaux; 147b, forest of Branchin outside Bordeaux; L. de la Boutière (ed.), *Cartulaire de l'Abbaye d'Orbestier*, Archives historiques du Poitou, 6 (1879), 6–10, no. 4, forest of Orbestier or Talmont; BN ms. lat. nouv. acq., f5, wood of Benon (or *Argentario*); f283, forest of Argenchum; f280–1, wood of La Roche, near Talmont; f444–5, wood of Jart, also near Talmont. Forest revenues were still important in the mid-thirteenth century; Hartigan, *Accounts of Alphonse of Poitiers*, 11.

72 Richard, *Histoire des Comtes*, 2: 192–3; Diceto, 1: 425.

73 Favreau, 'Les débuts de La Rochelle', 9–10, 16, 24, 29; *Rot. Chart.*, 137b, 27 September 1204.

74 *Rot. Chart.*, 58b; also 24.

sold or given away.[75] Ducal control of shipping on the Gironde and Garonne meant larger sums collected as tolls with the expansion of trade. Richard and John were both prodigal in giving exemptions, however, frequently granting free passage for ships of favoured religious houses.[76]

Richard Lionheart profited from control of mints at Poitiers and Bordeaux and possibly elsewhere, which struck pennies and half-pennies under his name. Large quantities of tin were shipped from England to La Rochelle and Bayonne, apparently to dilute the silver content of his coins.[77] Unlike in England and Normandy, Richard had to share his rights over some mints in Aquitaine and Gascony with various local lords, depriving his treasury of full earnings. Even at Bordeaux, he granted one-third of the revenues of his mint to the archbishop; and at Poitiers, the post of master of the mint was hereditary in the Mauléon family.[78]

No doubt Richard Lionheart sought to increase his income from Aquitaine through sales of offices and arbitrary exactions, just as he did in England. Certainly exploitation of the Jewish communities within Aquitanian cities with tallages would have proven profitable for him.[79] The region contributed to his ransom, for the Saint-Martial chronicle reports that all monastic houses were compelled to pay an aid and that Saint-Martial's contribution was 100 marks.[80] When Eleanor of Aquitaine visited her domains in 1199, the people of Bordeaux petitioned her to abolish 'certain evil impositions, unheard of and unjust', imposed by Richard.[81]

Evidence from the mid-thirteenth century after the Capetians had taken control of Poitou shows Alphonse of Poitiers collecting periodic aids and *dona*, and he maintained that he was asking nothing that his predecessors had not obtained. On the occasion of his knighting in 1241, La Rochelle paid him £1,000 (presumably *tournois*, almost £300 sterling) and Niort, Poitiers and Saint-Jean-d'Angely £500 *tournois* each; and in 1249, the towns

75 Trabut-Cussac, *Bordeaux sous les rois d'Angleterre*, 60.
76 Martindale, 'Eleanor of Aquitaine', 26. For alienation of tolls, see BN ms. lat. nour. acq. 1244, f10, Count Richard's grant of free passage for ships of Grandselve Abbey; grant of free passage to boats of Saint André, Bordeaux, Sainte-Marthe (ed.), *Gallia Christiana*, 2: 285; confirmation of La Sauve-Majeur's right to tolls on ships passing before Bordeaux; Cirot de la Ville, *Histoire de . . . La Grande-Sauve*, 2: 122.
77 *PR&RI*, xix.
78 Dumas, 'La monnaie dans les domaines Plantagenêt', 53–9. For Bordeaux, BN ms lat. nouv. acq. 1244, f29; for Poitiers, *Rot. Chart.*, 11.
79 T.D. Hardy (ed.), *Rotuli Litterarum Clausarum*, 2 vols, Record Commission (London, 1833–44), 1: 397; *Patent Rolls*, 1, 1216–25, Public Record Office (London, 1901), 357–8, 366; W.W. Shirley (ed.), *Royal Letters, Henry III*, 2 vols, RS (London, 1862–66), 1: 206–7, no. 185.
80 Duplès-Agier (ed.), *Chroniques Saint-Martial*, 192.
81 *Bordeaux sous les rois d'Angleterre*, 23.

of the Auvergne gave him £7,500 (about £2,200 sterling). When Alphonse later raised funds for his second crusade, he levied a double *cens* in Poitou and Saintonge on all non-nobles, which was described as a customary *gracia liberalis*.[82] Since these payments are dated after King John's grants of communal privileges to the cities of Aquitaine, Richard Lionheart's financial demands could well have been harsher.

Although Richard doubtless collected greater revenues in Aquitaine than his brother, he lacked both the power and the expertise to profit from the expanding economy in his southern domains. He is unlikely to have reaped the additional coin needed to cover the costs of Aquitaine's defence. Once financial records begin to survive, they show Richard dependent on funds from the English and Norman treasuries for paying mercenaries. The Norman pipe rolls reveal southward transfers of funds in the 1180s, and an English chronicler reports that Henry II gave Richard *infinitam pecuniam* in 1186 for an army against the count of Toulouse.[83] Perhaps a hint of Richard's straitened finances is his 1190 letter to the citizens of Saint-Macaire in the Bordelais, seeking a loan of £50 *bordelais*. He asked them even though they were not his men, 'But because he trusts in them and has need of their help.'[84]

Richard Lionheart could not even count on the support of the Church in his southern domains.[85] Although Richard's Aquitanian ancestors usurped from the Capetians the Carolingian monarchs' authority over the episcopate within their lands, they soon lost any decisive voice in the nomination of bishops. Local lords contended with them for control in the tenth century, and the eleventh-century ecclesiastical reforms challenged all lay domination of the Church. An Angoumois chronicle, discussing twelfth-century episcopal elections, describes post-Gregorian reform procedures as *electione cleri, petitione populi, principi assensu*.[86] Louis VI of France, on the occasion of his son's

---

82   C. Stephenson, 'The Aids of the French Towns in the Twelfth and Thirteenth Centuries', in B. Lyon (ed.), *Medieval Institutions: Selected Essays* (Ithaca, NY, 1954), 20–5.
83   *Gesta Regis*, 1: 345; for transfers of funds from Normandy to Poitou, Stapleton, 1: 92 (1180); 113–15 (1184).
84   BN ms. lat. nouv. acq. 1244, f408; also, *Cal. Docs. Fr.*, 450, no. 1247.
85   See Turner, 'Richard Lionheart and the Episcopate in his French Domains', 529–35; D. Walker, 'Crown and Episcopacy under the Normans and Angevins', *ANS* 5 (1982); O. Pontal, 'Les évêques dans le monde Plantagenêt', *CCM* 29 (1986); I.P. Shaw, 'The Ecclesiastical Policy of Henry II on the Continent', *Church Quarterly Review* 151 (1951); P. Imbart de la Tour, *Les Elections épiscopales dans l'Eglise de France du IXe au XIIe siècle* (Paris, 1891); R. Foreville, 'Innocent III et les élections épiscopales dans l'espace Plantagenêt', *Cahiers des Annales de Normandie* 23 (1990); B. Guillemain, 'Les moines sur les sièges épiscopaux du sud-ouest de la France au xie et xiie siècles', *Mélanges E.-R. Labande* (Poitiers, 1976); R. Favreau, *Le Diocèse de Poitiers* (Paris, 1988); B. Guillemain, *Le Diocèse de Bordeaux* (Paris, 1974); R. Limouzin-Lamothe, *Le Diocèse de Limoges des origines à la fin du moyen âge* (Paris, 1951).
86   J. Boussard (ed.), *Historia Pontificum et comitum Engolismensium* (Paris, 1957), 44.

marriage to Eleanor of Aquitaine in 1137, had renounced any ducal claim to regalian rights over the province of Bordeaux, allowing its churches free episcopal elections. He also surrendered ducal rights to the homage and fealty of newly elected bishops, and he allowed them to keep their predecessors' possessions.[87] Ducal domination over the Church in Poitou, Aquitaine and Gascony never approached that in Anjou, much less Normandy or England, where royal/ducal influence over ecclesiastical affairs was decisive.

Because of Louis VI's concession, the Plantagenet dukes' part in episcopal elections in Aquitaine and Gascony's two archbishoprics of Bordeaux and Auch was minor compared to their role in the North. That did not prevent Henry II and Richard from trying to exert influence, however; and they had occasional successes. A chronicle account of the 1159 archiepiscopal election at Bordeaux depicts Henry intimidating the electors in person, seeking to impose his candidate. One bold bishop dared speak out, protesting his presence; and Henry withdrew in great anger, having failed to impose his choice on the episcopal electors. They proceeded to elect the bishop of Périgueux, and Henry's candidate for Bordeaux received Périgueux as a consolation in 1160.[88] None the less, Henry succeeded shortly afterwards in promoting two of his choices: the dean of Le Mans to Bordeaux and the abbot of Reading, England, to Bordeaux. The archbishop of Bordeaux throughout Richard's reign was Elie de Malemort (1188?–1206), member of a noble Limousin family. He was apparently freely elected, and Richard championed his archbishop in a dispute at the papal *curia*. Yet they quarrelled over the episcopal election at Poitiers, 1197–98, when Elie was willing to acknowledge the archbishop of Bourges' primacy over the province of Bordeaux in order to thwart Richard and his mother's imposition of their own candidate.

Most twelfth-century prelates at Poitiers were sons of local nobility, although Henry secured the bishopric for an English cleric, Jean des Bellemains, in 1162. Richard Lionheart sought to impose his own candidate at Poitiers in 1197–98, when the cathedral canons elected one of their own. Richard's nephew Otto of Brunswick, then titular count of Poitou, managed to stop his consecration by the archbishop of Bordeaux in November 1197. One faction within the chapter promoted the candidate favoured by Richard and Eleanor of Aquitaine, their relative, Maurice de Blazon, a noble of Mirebeau and already bishop of Nantes. Young Otto warned the assembled clerics that they must not proceed with consecration of their nominee because he had failed to seek the count's approval. The clergy's response was that it

---

87 Higounet and Higounet-Nadal, *Grande cartulaire de la Sauve Majeure*, 2: 729–30, no. 1278; followed by Louis VII's confirmation, 2: 730–1, no. 1279.

88 Boussard, *Historia . . . Engolismensium*, 44–5.

was not the custom of the Church of Poitou for bishops-elect to seek the count's approval; they cited Louis VI's grant of free elections to the bishops of the province of Bordeaux.

The bishop-elect, along with Archbishop Elie of Bordeaux, proceeded to Bourges, where they sought the intervention of the archbishop as metropolitan with authority over Aquitaine. They petitioned him to consecrate the bishop-elect because Richard was preventing the archbishop of Bordeaux from convoking his suffragans. The archbishop of Bourges, however, declined to act because of a prior appeal to the papal *curia*.[89] By the spring of 1198, the embattled bishop-elect had travelled to Rome and secured papal confirmation of his election, but he died on the return journey. Richard and his mother continued to press Maurice de Blazon's candidacy, and since the canons could find no candidate to oppose him, they elected him unanimously. Late in 1198, Pope Innocent III approved his translation from Nantes to Poitiers.

At Angoulême the prelates throughout Henry II's and Richard's reigns were monks from local religious houses under the protection of the counts of Angoulême. The bishopric of Limoges, lying within the province of Bourges, did not benefit from Louis VII's grant of free elections. Its bishop was one of the great lords of the Limousin, possessing castles and the homage of major nobles. With such means, he was a source of trouble for the Angevins in that troublesome zone separating Poitou from Gascony. Like Tours, two settlements made up Limoges: the fortified *cité* of the bishop and the community surrounding the great monastery of Saint-Martial, containing the viscount's castle.

Henry II and Richard Lionheart, as his father's viceroy, tried – unsuccessfully – to impose their candidate on the church at Limoges, 1178–79. They engaged in a long struggle against a Poitevin noble, Sébrand Chabot, archdeacon of Thouars. His election as bishop without ducal knowledge or consent in February 1178 spurred Henry's order for a punitive expedition by Richard, confiscation of the canons' property and their expulsion. Despite this savage opposition, Sébrand secured consecration at Rome in 1179, and after denying him entry into his cathedral for twenty-one months, Henry finally accepted him. According to an English chronicler, resolution of the dispute was due to posthumous mediation by the archbishop of Bourges; the pope had called on him to settle the conflict, and the archbishop's death apparently shocked the contending parties into a settlement.[90] Years later, Sébrand found it prudent to visit Richard Lionheart in Germany in January 1194, just before his release.

---

89 Bourges, Arch. Dépt. Cher, G28, no. 4, s. xiii in, part of a deposition on Bourges's claims to primacy over Bordeaux.

90 Richard, *Histoire des Comtes*, 2: 194–5, 201; Vigeois, 324–5; Diceto, 2: 4.

Another conflict followed Sébrand's death in March 1197, when the canons of Limoges elected their dean, Jean de Vierac, a Limousin noble. Two Poitevins who were archdeacons of the diocese contested the election: one was the late bishop's nephew; and the other, Hugh Saldebreuil, was a kinsman of Eleanor of Aquitaine's former constable. As soon as Jean's election was announced in June 1197, Hugh rushed off to Richard to protest; but according to the chronicler's account, 'By just judgment of God, he died on the way.' Soon the other challenger died as well, and Jean de Vierac became bishop of Limoges without opposition. In 1204, he would turn toward the Angevins' adversary, Philip Augustus, and place his see under Capetian protection.[91]

Although little is known of elections of the eleven bishops in the province of Auch, almost contiguous with Gascony, it appears that mostly men from local noble families were elected. The canons of Bazas apparently freely elected their bishops, mostly selecting candidates of local origin, although the duke did control the bishopric of Bayonne. Dax and Oloron, however, followed an old tradition of electing monks. None the less, these Gascon prelates apparently had good relations with Richard. Two of them – Gerard de la Barthe, archbishop of Auch, and Bernard de la Carre, bishop of Bayonne – accompanied the king on the Third Crusade; and in 1190, he named them commanders of his fleet before it set sail for the Holy Land. The bishop of Bayonne was often in the king's company during the long stopover in Sicily, witnessing charters.

In his southern churches, Richard had no more success in imposing his nominees on episcopal electors than his father or his maternal ancestors. Only at Poitiers and Limoges in 1197–98 did King Richard seek to force the election of his own candidate. In both instances, he had to contend with the claims of Bourges, a French royal see, to authority over disputed episcopal elections within Aquitaine. The Angevin monarchs' failure to forge close links with the bishops of Aquitaine and Gascony had serious consequences, contributing to their inability to construct a lasting political structure for their 'empire'. One authority points out that their failure denied them 'a powerful element in formulating and publicising ducal policy'.[92] Curial bishops – literate and learned in the law – could have helped create administrative structures for asserting ducal authority.

Instead, the southern bishops remained 'essentially local figures working for their own interests', rarely recruited from the royal *familiares* and rarely attending the royal court.[93] This deprived Richard of bishops and abbots'

91 Vigeois, 324–5; Diceto, 2: 4; *Chroniques de Saint-Martial*, 193; Baldwin, 312, 418.
92 Walker, 'Crown and Episcopacy', 232.
93 Walker, 'Crown and Episcopacy', 232.

assets that were potential sources of strength for the king/duke. Aquitanian prelates had long played an important role in peacekeeping; and many litigants, in the absence of functioning ducal courts, turned to episcopal courts for settlement of secular disputes. Control of fortifications, both urban citadels and rural castles, gave prelates prominence in military matters, for example, the fortified *cités* of the bishops of Angoulême and Limoges or several Poitevin castles held by the bishop of Poitiers's vassals.

Only rarely did English or Norman clerics find preferment in the south, and even more rarely did a southern cleric secure an English or Norman benefice. During the two reigns, 1154–99, no more than three Aquitanian bishops came from England or Normandy.[94] The only bishop who came to England from the southern domains was Master Philip of Poitiers, nominated as bishop of Durham in 1195. He was Richard's vice-chancellor, who had accompanied the king on the voyage from Palestine and had remained with him during his German captivity. When the Angevin kings did attempt to install agents, their heavy-handedness may have backfired, as at Limoges. The contrast of their brazen interference with subtler Capetian ecclesiastical policy likely contributed to clerics' lukewarm backing for continued Angevin rule.

At the lower levels of the ecclesiastical hierarchy, Richard and his father had little patronage to distribute to favoured clerics. Lay patronage of parish churches in Poitou had passed into the hands of monastic foundations early in the twelfth century. This left the dukes of Aquitaine without means of providing livings for clerks who served them as administrators. Failure to recruit an administrative class or *curiales* drawn from the Church, with an interest in preserving and expanding ducal power, reinforced the hegemonic nature of Henry II's and Richard's rule over Aquitaine and Gascony. The Plantagenet dukes' inability to plant in key posts their own clerks, bound to them in personal allegiance, deprived them of administrators committed to the cause of an Angevin 'empire'.

A lack of professional servants linking the localities to the ducal court denied Richard's southern possessions the strong government prevailing in England and Normandy, leaving his subjects living outside the ducal domain exposed to domination by their lords, who were restrained only by an occasional ducal show of force. Unlike in England, where the Angevins cultivated the support of the knightly class with judicial protections for tenants against their lords, Richard had little success in forging a partnership with local elites in Aquitaine and Gascony to contest regional princes' power.

---

94 William le Templier, archbishop of Bordeaux (1173–*c.* 1188); Jean de Bellesmains, bishop of Poitiers (1162–88); and possibly Pierre Minet, bishop of Périgueux (1169–82), a cousin of Peter of Blois, not a native Anglo-Norman, but doubtless in Henry II's service in the North.

Without effective control of the countryside, brute force was Richard's only means for imposing order on his southern provinces; as Kate Norgate wrote, 'The Aquitanians discovered that if [Henry II] had chastised them with whips, the son of their own duchess was minded to chastise them with scorpions.'[95] Richard's preoccupation with punitive warfare hampered cultivation of any strong sense of dynastic loyalty, impeded growth of new administrative organs, and induced a political vacuum that regional lords – especially in southern Poitou and beyond – rushed to fill.

Because of ineffective revenue-gathering machinery, financial burdens of Richard's southern subjects were lighter than those of his Anglo-Norman subjects, yet they paid a heavy price for the absence of effective central power. Periodic revolts and the heavy-handed Plantagenet response caused physical destruction and damage to the economy. Without local officials to requisition supplies, bands of foreign mercenaries often went unpaid and turned to pillaging. Following rebellions, the notorious *Brabançons* frequently ravaged the countryside. More than once, Aquitanian bishops had to raise forces to drive these freebooters out of their dioceses.[96]

Aquitaine and Gascony were a financial liability for the Angevins, sucking funds from England and Normandy, and cultural contrasts with the Plantagenets' northern domains hindered growth of any imperial consciousness. Richard, his father and his brother did not aim at integrating these territories into a single political entity. Neither did they look at those possessions with an eye to monetary profit or loss, and they made no attempt to institute new administrative agencies. In their view, holding those ancient lands, home of a rich culture, enhanced their family's prestige, linking them to another prestigious dynasty, Eleanor's ancestors. For the Lionheart, Aquitaine was his homeland, the land of his youth, where he had learned the arts of war and government. His southern domains gave him political clout, making him a powerful player in the diplomacy of southern France and extending his influence all the way to the Mediterranean Sea.

One of history's ironies is that the one southern region to remain under Plantagenet rule was Gascony. The explanation for Gascony's continued loyalty to its English kings/dukes doubtless lies in the ineffectiveness of Angevin rule beyond the Garonne River. Gascon nobles had little incentive to exchange a Plantagenet lord for a Capetian one because rule from far-away England rested so lightly on them, limiting their own authority hardly at all.

---

95   Norgate, *England under the Angevin Kings*, 2: 208–9.
96   *Chroniques de Saint-Martial*, 190, 193; Limouzin-Lamothe, *Diocèse de Limoges*, 91–2. Also during an 1176 invasion of Poitou by the count of Angoulême and his *Brabançons*, the bishop of Poitiers and Theobald Chabot, Duke Richard's *princeps militiae*, had to organise defence; Diceto, 1: 407.

CHAPTER TWELVE

Richard's warfare following the crusade, 1193–99

Richard Lionheart would spend the years following his return from captivity defending his duchy of Normandy and his county of Poitou from the Capetian king. As Hubert Walter explained to the English magnates in 1198, their lord was struggling against a very powerful ruler, well financed and determined to destroy him. Many scholars agree that Richard's – and later John's – defence of his possessions required more and more revenues in the face of Philip's expanding power. In England and Normandy, the two territories where taxation was most efficient, Richard and, after him, his brother John put the economy on a wartime footing, and their rule took on more and more a military tone. Yet no medieval state could manage a mass mobilisation. As Kate Norgate maintained long ago, neither Richard Lionheart nor his Capetian antagonist could afford to mount campaigns massive enough to bring their war to a decisive conclusion; in the late 1190s, the struggle in Normandy consisted of series of raids and counter-raids.[1] Yet the fighting was more cruel than ever, made so by both sides' large-scale hiring of mercenary captains and their companies.[2]

Once Philip Augustus returned from the Crusade in 1191, he charted steps that would ultimately drive his over-mighty Angevin vassal out of all Plantagenet possessions north of Gascony. Philip found himself in a stronger position on his return, for the death of Philip, count of Flanders, without direct heirs gave him control of much of the upper Somme valley, including the towns of Amiens and Arras and the fortress at Péronne, and threatened to hamper contacts between Normandy and Flanders. As a result, Capetian

---

1   K. Norgate, *Richard the Lion Heart* (London, 1924), 322; a similar view is expressed by F. Barlow, *The Feudal Kingdom of England 1042–1216*, 4th edn (London, 1988), 364.
2   J. Bradbury, *Philip Augustus: King of France 1180–1223* (London, 1998), 116.

power would more closely approximate that of the Angevins north of the Loire, enabling Philip to intensify his pressure on Normandy. [See Map VI]

Warfare between the armies of Richard and Philip would centre chiefly on two theatres: the Vexin of Normandy and the border between Poitou and Berry. Contention over the Norman Vexin, a heavily fortified region lying between the rivers Seine and Epte, had long inflamed relations between the Capetians and the Plantagenets, and neither the marriage arrangements between the two royal houses nor the 1191 Messina settlement ended the conflict. Without control of the Vexin, Rouen and the upper Seine valley could never be secure in Angevin hands. Shortly after Philip returned to France, he met with William fitz Ralph, the Lionheart's seneschal of Normandy in January 1192; and he demanded that the Norman Vexin be turned over to him, since it was his sister Alix's dower and Richard had married another. When the seneschal and the Norman barons refused to accede to his demand, he invited Count John to Paris to offer him recognition as Richard's replacement as ruler of the Plantagenet possessions in France and the hand of Richard's rejected fiancée Alix in marriage. Before John could accept Philip's invitation, however, his mother, Eleanor of Aquitaine, rushed to England to stop his embarkation from Southampton.[3] The French king would have to try to wrest the Vexin from Richard by force.

On the Berry–Poitou frontier, Philip Augustus would repeat the tactic that he had pioneered in 1189 against Henry II, driving a wedge to split the Plantagenet domains. Farther south, he would continue to foment rebellion against Richard by the perpetually troublesome nobility of the Angoumois, Limousin and Périgord, the region separating southern Poitou from Gascony. Whenever warfare broke out, the Capetian ruler had the advantage of a compact core centred on his royal demesne in the Ile de France. This simplified Philip's dispatch of forces to various Angevin weak points: the upper Seine valley, leading to Rouen; Berry, bordering on Poitou; or the cluster of counties separating Poitou proper from Bordeaux and Gascony: the Angoumois, La Marche, the Limousin and Périgord. Richard, however, suffered the handicap of defending a frontier that extended from the English Channel to the Pyrenees, stretching lines of communications and dispersing resources among widely scattered fortresses.

The French monarch had some success in prying the nobility of Aquitaine away from their allegiance to their Plantagenet lord. In 1192, after Philip Augustus's premature return from the Holy Land and before Richard's return, a revolt broke out in the South. As usual, the rebels were nobles of the region lying between Poitou and Gascony, chiefly Elie, count of Périgord,

---

3 Gillingham, *Richard*, 219–20.

and Bernard, viscount de Brosse. Doubtless doing all that they could to foment the rebellion were the Lionheart's enemies, the Capetian king and the count of Toulouse. With Pierre Bertin, seneschal of Aquitaine, lying ill, Richard's marriage alliance with the king of Navarre worked as he had anticipated. His new ally, his brother-in-law Sancho, son of the king of Navarre, came to the rescue with a large band of Navarrese knights; together, Sancho and the seneschal took the offensive, invading Toulouse and pushing up to the city's walls. The viscount de Brosse paid for his rebellion by having his lands confiscated.[4]

By the spring of 1192, messages from England had convinced Richard Lionheart that he must conclude his crusade and return to the West as soon as possible. He agreed with the Seljuk sultan, Saladin, on a three-year truce reserving for the Latin Christians a narrow strip along the Palestinian coast and guaranteeing pilgrims safe passage from the port cities to Jerusalem. Having accomplished all that he thought possible to secure the kingdom of Jerusalem, the English king sailed for the West in October, only to fall captive in Germany at the end of 1192. This aroused fears for Richard's safe return, and he remained the emperor's prisoner until February 1194, when terms for a ransom of 150,000 silver marks were settled.[5] Philip Augustus did all that he could to prolong Richard's captivity, sending first his cousin, the bishop of Beauvais, and later his uncle, the archbishop of Reims, to the emperor's court.[6]

The English king's capture added to Philip's opportunity to make trouble on the Norman frontier and to conspire with Count John, Richard's sole surviving brother. Philip now returned to a technique that he had perfected in Henry II's last years: playing off one Plantagenet against another. By the spring of 1193, while negotiations for Richard's release from his imprisonment were dragging on, war broke out in three different parts of the Angevin 'empire'. In Aquitaine, Count Adémar of Angoulême transferred his allegiance from Richard to Philip Augustus, admitting that he held his county as a fief of the French king. Adémar began to raid ducal estates in Poitou, but officials loyal to the Lionheart succeeded in defeating his force and captured him; he remained a captive until the treaty of Mantes, July 1193, provided for his release.[7] In England, the 'uneasy peace' between Count John and England's regency government had collapsed when word of

---

4   Gillingham, 'Richard I and Berengaria of Navarre', *BIHR* 53 (1980), 167; Gillingham, *Richard*, 219–20.
5   Landon, 71–83.
6   Baldwin, 88.
7   A. Richard, *Histoire des Comtes de Poitou*, 2 vols (Paris, 1903), 2: 279; Landon, 78, for treaty of Mantes.

Richard's capture by the Germans arrived, and a civil war was under way between Count John and the government headed by Archbishop Walter of Rouen.[8] Most serious of the three wars that broke out in 1193 was a French invasion of Normandy that got under way in the spring under Philip's direct command, and afterwards invasions of the duchy became almost annual events.

In 1193, a number of castles protecting the Norman frontiers fell to Philip Augustus's forces: Gisors, Neaufles, Châteauneuf and Gournay, in the Vexin, Aumâle and Eu in the extreme northeast, also Ivry and Pacy in the Eure valley. Philip did not have to take Gisors Castle by siege, for it fell into his hands through treason, when its castellan, Gilbert de Vascoeuil, surrendered it without a fight. The Capetian king's invasion of Normandy inspired a rebellion by Norman nobles, especially those on the frontiers. Warfare between the Angevins and Capetians typically presented frontier lords with an opportunity to seek redress for long-held grievances over loss of lands or castles by switching to Philip Augustus's side. Even barons loyal to Richard had to face the possibility that he would never win release from captivity and that his brother John, with the assistance of Philip, would become their duke. Gilbert de Vascoeuil was not the only one to lower his castle's drawbridge to Capetian forces; others included the counts of Aumâle, Eu, Meulan and Perche.[9] Philip and his ally, Baldwin VI, count of Flanders, reached Rouen with a large army and siege machinery, but they withdrew after two weeks without entering the city. Philip even contemplated an invasion of England, perhaps only half-seriously. He assembled a naval force at Wissant for sending Flemish troops across the Channel to aid his ally, Count John; but no invasion fleet ever set sail. Meanwhile, John returned to England with a force of Flemish mercenaries, announced that his brother was dead, and demanded recognition as monarch. Richard's mother and the agents in charge of England's administration refused to accept as accurate this news of the king's death, however; and by April 1193, word of his capture arrived from Germany.[10]

On 9 July 1193, the Capetian monarch and Richard's chancellor, William Longchamp, negotiated a truce at Mantes that negated any plans that Philip Augustus might have had for invading England. It was agreed that Richard would pay 20,000 silver marks, and several castles were surrendered to be held as security for payment: Arques and Drincourt (or Neuchâtel-en-Bray) in Normandy, Loches and Châtillon-sur-Indre in Touraine. Philip

---

8   *PR3 / 4RI*, xx.
9   Gillingham, *Richard*, 231; D. Power, 'The Norman frontier in the twelfth and early thirteenth centuries', PhD thesis (Cambridge, 1994), 349, 374.
10 Gillingham, *Richard*, 227, 232.

was to keep whatever territories he pleased that he had seized, and the English king was to do homage for all his French possessions. After this, the earlier 1189 Norman frontier was never restored; Richard after his release in January 1194 would find it impossible to retake castles of the Eure or Avre valleys that had fallen to his Capetian foe.[11]

In January 1194, about the time of Richard's release by the German emperor, Philip Augustus came to agreement with a desperate Count John, extending him aid at a high price. He compelled John to cede all Normandy east of the Seine except for Rouen and its surroundings, plus three strong points that commanded access to Berry from Touraine: Loches, Buzançais and Châtillon-sur-Indre. By the 1191 treaty of Messina, Philip already held the lordships of Issoudun and Graçay on the Berry–Poitou border. In short, John was willing to cripple the defences of the Angevin 'empire' by surrendering crucial frontier territories in order to buy Capetian support against his brother. Philip's control of eastern Normandy, coupled with his recognition of Renaud of Dammartin as count of Boulogne, gave him control of much of the Channel coast, including the port of Dieppe. Not long afterwards, Philip gained advantage in the South, when some of Richard's most turbulent nobles of Aquitaine did homage to him, promising that they would remain his men unless he should consent to their becoming men of Count John.[12] Richard Lionheart would face an enormous challenge in restoring his authority and regaining territory following his release from his captivity and his return to his own domains.

Agreement with Emperor Henry VI on Richard's ransom was finally reached in early February 1194, and the Angevin monarch was freed on making a massive preliminary payment and giving hostages for the remainder. He began a leisurely journey back to his own lands. As Richard travelled down the Rhine toward the Flemish coast, he worked to construct alliances with princes of the lower Rhineland that could prove useful in the approaching conflict with Philip Augustus. He promised pensions to courtiers and officials in an attempt to purchase influence in the region.[13] During negotiations for Richard's release from captivity, he had sought to prevent an alliance between his Capetian nemesis and his Hohenstaufen gaoler, sending ambassadors to Paris to obtain a peace with Philip at almost any price.[14] Not until mid-March did the Lionheart reach England, landing at Sandwich. He remained there until early May, crushing Count John's rebellion, restoring

11 Power, 'The Norman frontier', 344; treaty terms, Landon, 78–9.
12 Landon, 85; Gillingham, 'Richard I and Berengaria', 168.
13 Terms of Richard's release, Landon, 82–3; for Flemish pensions, *PR6RI*, xxxii; *PR9RI*, xxiii.
14 Norgate, *Richard the Lion Heart*, 281.

his own authority, raising revenues for his ransom and garnering resources for his combat with the Capetian ruler on the Continent. He celebrated a ceremonial crown-wearing at Winchester Cathedral on 17 April, a symbolic expression of his full restoration to royal authority.

Shortly after Richard's release, Philip launched another attack on Normandy, occupying castles below the Seine promised him by Count John. He took Neubourg, Evreux and Le Vaudreuil, 'the key fortress on this border, controlling access to the Seine bridge at Pont de l'Arche, only ten miles south of Rouen';[15] and he besieged Verneuil, a crucial castle for control of the Avre valley lying along the southeastern frontier. On 12 May 1194, however, Richard Lionheart landed at Barfleur on the Cotentin peninsula; his march across Normandy toward his enemy's army at Verneuil was 'a triumphal progress'.[16] His brother, John Lackland, promptly defected to him, betraying the fortress of Evreux to his brother; and he continued to serve energetically as a soldier in Normandy during the last five years of Richard's life. At Richard's approach, the French king withdrew from his siege of Verneuil, and his besieging force soon followed him in flight. Richard's forces then took Beaumont-le-Roger, seat of Robert of Meulan; and Philip moved on to Evreux, which he forced Count John to abandon. After a diversion to encounter Richard in the Touraine in early July, Philip Augustus turned his attention again to Normandy. Count John, now fighting for his brother in company with the earl of Arundel, was besieging the castle of Le Vaudreuil; but Philip rushed to its defence, staged a surprise attack, and captured most of John's infantry and siege equipment. This striking Capetian success revealed what difficulties awaited Richard in the Norman theatre; warfare there would be for the rest of his reign 'a hard slogging match'.[17]

Richard had moved south from Normandy in mid-June to restore his authority in the Loire Valley and in Aquitaine. He aimed at recovering his castles of Loches and Châtillon-sur-Indre that his agents had surrendered to Philip Augustus while he was a captive.[18] He occupied the town of Tours, and advanced to Beaulieu on the border of Touraine; then he besieged the castle of Loches, taking it with the aid of *Brabançons* and his brother-in-law, Sancho of Navarre, who led a large force from Navarre, including 150 crossbow men.[19] Sancho had to withdraw from Loches to return to Spain on account of the death of his father, but Richard arrived shortly afterward to complete the task of taking the castle. During this campaign, Richard

15 Gillingham, *Richard*, 252.
16 Norgate, *Richard the Lion Heart*, 294.
17 Gillingham, *Richard*, 252–3.
18 Powicke, *Loss*, 99.
19 Howden, 3: 252–3.

pursued Philip Augustus toward Paris, winning an impressive victory on 6 July; at Fréteval near Vendôme, he forced the French king to retreat to Châteaudun.[20] Following in pursuit of the fleeing French force, Richard seized Philip's baggage train with the royal chancery and treasury. Captured documents revealed the extent of his southern nobles' treasonous conduct; in March 1194, Bernard de Brosse and Geoffrey de Rancon had renounced their homage to Richard and become Philip's men.[21]

Having restored his authority over the Loire valley, Richard turned south to reassert control over his traitorous Aquitanian nobles. He brought to heel Adémar, count of Angoulême, occupying the city of Angoulême; and he also subdued the count's half-brother Aimar V, viscount of Limoges, and Geoffrey de Rancon, lord of Taillebourg. On 22 July 1194, the English king proudly announced in a newsletter addressed to his justiciar, Hubert Walter, that he was master of all the strongholds of the Angoumois and of all Geoffrey de Rancon's lands and that he had taken up to 300 knights and 40,000 men at arms.[22]

Richard's rapid string of victories convinced his Capetian rival to agree to a truce at Tillières, Normandy, on 23 July 1194. The settlement was based on a temporary acceptance of the *status quo*; each side was to keep the territories and castles that it held on the day of the truce. It left Philip Augustus in a strong position in Normandy, retaining possession of Le Vaudreuil and its dependent fortifications, Gisors and other castles of the Norman Vexin, while lordships such as Eu, Arques, Aumâle and Mortemer, in extreme northeastern Normandy, and Beauvoir and Neufmarché in the Norman Vexin remained in the hands of Philip's partisans. Richard was stripped of a large part of eastern Normandy and could rebuild only four castles that French forces had demolished: Drincourt in the northeast, and Neubourg, Conches, and Breteuil west of Evreux.[23]

Although the truce was supposed to last until All Saints' Day 1195, conflict in Normandy was renewed in the summer of that year. Richard likely had viewed the truce as only temporary, a means of freeing himself from fighting on his Norman frontier while he pacified his rebellious nobles in Aquitaine. Once fighting began around Gisors, Philip Augustus undertook to demolish the fortress of Le Vaudreuil, apparently aware that his garrison

---

20 Diceto, 2: 117; also A. Salmon, *Recueil de chroniques de Touraine*, Société archéologique de Touraine (Tours, 1854), 144.

21 Gillingham, 'Richard I and Berengaria', 168; Richard, *Histoire des Comtes*, 2: 293. Their chronology differs somewhat. Baldwin, 410, notes that de Brosse's and Rancon's letters of homage were *not* among the documents taken at Fréteval.

22 Howden, 3: 256, 257.

23 Terms in Landon, 96–7.

could no longer control the surrounding territory and fearful that it would fall to Richard; for the English king was busy strengthening his castle of Pont de l'Arche, only a few miles away. Once the French king withdrew, the Lionheart occupied the damaged castle and began rebuilding its walls. At some point during the summer of 1195, Richard turned his attention away from Normandy long enough for a campaign in Berry, along with his mercenary captain Mercadier. Richard's army took the town and lordship of Issoudun, which Philip abandoned to him along with Graçay; and Mercadier then moved on to the Auvergne, where he took prisoner the count's brother, Guy. Although the French king would seize any opportunity to create trouble for the Lionheart in the South, Normandy remained his priority; the Seine valley, leading directly to Paris, had enormous strategic and economic importance for him. Indeed, the struggle between the two monarchs during Richard's last four years, 1195–99, would centre upon the castles of the upper Seine valley between Paris and Rouen.

In August 1195 discussions, the two kings came at last to a final agreement concerning the fate of Alix, Richard's long-suffering former fiancée. She was returned to her brother's custody in return for his renunciation of the northeastern Norman coastal counties of Eu and Aumâle, the castle of Arques, and other Norman castles seized while the English king had been held prisoner in Germany. A marriage was proposed between Philip's son and heir, Louis, and Richard's niece, Eleanor of Brittany; and Richard would grant that couple disputed borderlands, including the Norman Vexin.[24] As soon as Alix was in Philip's custody, however, he married her to William, count of Ponthieu, and granted her as a marriage portion the Norman lordships of Eu and Arques; and a struggle for the two towns of Dieppe and nearby Arques followed.[25] The projected marriage of Louis and Eleanor of Brittany never took place.

The two monarchs reached a settlement to end their fighting in January 1196 with the Peace of Louviers (or Gaillon). It acknowledged the gains made by Richard Lionheart since the truce of Tillières in July 1194; Philip Augustus surrendered a number of the conquests that he had made during Richard's captivity.[26] Philip was to keep all the Norman Vexin, except the archbishop of Rouen's manor of Les Andelys and much of the southeastern march of Normandy; and he could occupy a number of frontier castles: Gisors, Neaufles and Neufmarché along the River Epte; below the Seine, Vernon, Pacy and Ivry along the Eure, Nonancourt on the Avre; and

---

24 Landon, 103.
25 J. Gillingham, 'Richard I, Galley Warfare and Portsmouth: The Beginnings of a Royal Navy', *Thirteenth Century England* VI (Woodbridge, 1997), 9.
26 Terms, Landon, 106–9.

Gaillon on the Seine, only miles from the site for Richard's new fortress at Les Andelys. Philip surrendered to Richard Le Vaudreuil and Evreux, and all his conquests northeast of the Seine, including the county of Aumâle, except for those in the Norman Vexin. Despite the French monarch's concessions, he could take satisfaction in preserving frontiers with Normandy that pushed him closer to Rouen; the old Epte frontier of the Norman Vexin had drifted upwards toward the River Andelle, and the River Iton replaced the Avre as Richard's frontier below the Seine.[27]

A second region where military operations had taken place was on the frontiers of Poitou, and the Treaty of Louviers strengthened Richard's position in those southern Plantagenet possessions. In Berry, he regained a number of castles, but he quitclaimed the county of Auvergne to Philip; and farther south, the Lionheart gained the French monarch's recognition that the troublesome count of Angoulême, viscount of Brosse, and count of Périgueux were his vassals, owing him homage and service. This treaty also settled Richard's relations with the count of Toulouse; Philip agreed to abandon his alliance with the count, if he did not wish to be a party to the peace.

The peace of Louviers was 'merely an expedient for giving both parties a breathing-space',[28] and both rulers began to build up alliances in preparation for a revival of fighting. Richard Lionheart had greater success in the contention for allies. Richard's marriage to Berengaria of Navarre had brought him an alliance with her father, Sancho VI, and then her brother, Sancho VII (1194-1234), which protected his southwestern flank. That alliance began to lose its usefulness after 1194 with the death of Richard's old enemy in that region, Raymond V of Toulouse, followed by the death of Richard's old ally, Alfonso II of Aragon in 1196. The Lionheart precipitated a diplomatic revolution, abandoning the longstanding hostility between the dukes of Aquitaine and the counts of Toulouse that the Plantagenets had inherited. Richard made an alliance with the new Count Raymond VI; he renounced his ancestral claims to lordship over the county of Toulouse and restored Quercy to Raymond. This 1196 agreement was sealed by Raymond's marriage to Richard's sister Joan, widow of the king of Sicily. Richard granted Raymond the county of Agen as his bride's dowry, and in return, Raymond agreed to send 500 knights to fight for a month in case of war in Gascony. This new alliance, reversing forty years of rivalry between the house of St Gilles and the Plantagenets, helped stabilise the situation in

---

27 D. Power, 'What did the Frontier of Angevin Normandy Comprise?', *ANS* 17 (1995), 191, n. 41; F.M. Powicke, *Cambridge Medieval History*, 8 vols (Cambridge, 1929), 6: 306.

28 Norgate, *Richard the Lion Heart*, 305.

the South.[29] Yet abandonment of the Angevins' forty-year struggle for domination over the county of Toulouse is a strong signal of Richard's shift from his father's expansionist posture to a defensive one.

Philip Augustus found valuable allies in the princes of the Low Countries, whom he aimed to bring closer to him in order to threaten Normandy's northeastern frontier. In 1195, he had married his sister Alix, Richard's former fiancée, to William, count of Ponthieu. He won over Baldwin IX, the new count of Flanders and Hainault, whom Richard had recruited in 1194; and he also allied with Renaud of Dammartin, whom he recognised as count of Boulogne. They did homage to the French monarch in June 1196. Elsewhere Philip kept the loyalty of the count of Blois and Chartres, who had gained Vendôme through Count John's treachery.[30]

Also a danger to Richard was the defection of the Bretons, for their hostility could threaten western Normandy and Maine as well as the sea route from England around the peninsula of Brittany to the ports of Aquitaine.[31] In April 1196, Richard sought to reassert his control over the duchy of Brittany, which seems to have fallen away from Angevin authority after the death of his younger brother, Duke Geoffrey, in 1186. During Richard's absence on crusade and in captivity, his brother's widow, Constance of Brittany, had remained in her duchy, savouring seven years of rule relatively unconstrained by Angevin interference, keeping her young son, Arthur, by her side. The Lionheart summoned Constance to his court in Normandy to surrender into his custody Arthur, heir to the duchy. On her way to Richard's court, her second husband – Earl Ranulf of Chester, from whom she was estranged – abducted her; but young Arthur's tutor escaped with the boy, and the Breton nobility refused to turn him over to Richard.

The Bretons renounced Richard's lordship, and their defiance led in spring 1196 to his invasion of Brittany, a campaign that was so cruel that he did not even declare a truce on Good Friday. French operations in Normandy forced Richard to withdraw from Brittany, and after Easter, the Bretons made peace. The Lionheart compelled them to acknowledge his lordship over their duchy, but a long-term result was to alienate them more fully from the Angevins and to affix them firmly to the Capetian side.[32] In the summer of 1196, Richard sent a force into Brittany under the command

---

29 Gillingham, 'Richard I and Berengaria', 172; R. Benjamin, 'A Forty Years War: Toulouse and the Plantagenets, 1156–1196', *Historical Research* 61 (1988), *passim*.

30 Landon, 113; Norgate, *Richard the Lion Heart*, 313.

31 Gillingham, 'Richard I, Galley Warfare and Portsmouth', 10–11.

32 H.-F. Delaborde (ed.), *Oeuvres de Rigord et de Guillaume le Breton*, Société de l'histoire de France, 2 vols (Paris, 1882–85), 2: 130, 131; Gillingham, *Richard*, 260, for fighting on Good Friday.

of Mercadier, his stalwart mercenary captain, with the aim of capturing young Arthur; but the Bretons succeeded in defeating Mercadier and his troops and spiriting the boy off to Paris to the court of Richard's arch-enemy, Philip Augustus.

By late June 1196, Philip broke the peace of Louviers, when he undertook a siege of Aumâle in the northeastern corner of Normandy with support from Baldwin of Flanders. The county of Aumâle had been in the hands of two of Richard's stalwarts: first William de Forz, one of his Poitevin soldiers; then Baldwin de Béthune, his companion on crusade and in captivity. Capetian capture of Aumâle shifted westward the duchy's northeastern frontier from the River Bresle toward the Béthune valley. Richard reacted by attacking the castle of Nonancourt on the southeastern march of Normandy; it fell promptly, surrendered by its garrison without a fight. After this success, however, the summer campaign went badly for the Lionheart. He turned north to relieve Aumâle, but his attempt resulted in a defeat, and Aumâle surrendered to the French forces in August. Philip promptly razed the castle, and Richard had to pay 3,000 marks to ransom its garrison. Philip then moved on to retake Nonancourt, which fell to him after a few days. Next Richard suffered a wound in his knee during his unsuccessful siege of Gaillon Castle on the Seine. The single Angevin success of the summer was his brother John's capture of Gamaches, a castle in the Norman Vexin.

Shortly after negotiating the Peace of Louviers, Richard began construction of Château-Gaillard to strengthen the Angevin position in that critical region for control of Normandy, the Seine valley between Rouen and Paris. The Norman capital was now vulnerable to a Capetian army's advance from the Ile de France, since Richard was deprived of the line of the Epte River and of Gisors Castle. Château-Gaillard was to be 'the most spectacular castle in western Europe', and its dramatic location on a cliff three hundred feet above the Seine upriver from Rouen made it not only a vital site for Rouen's defence but also a useful staging point for Richard's planned reconquest of the Norman Vexin. Most of his warfare with Philip in his last years revolved around castles and bridges near his new stronghold in the upper Seine valley, and a fleet of galleys ferried treasure across the Channel from the English king's new port of Portsmouth and up the Seine to Château-Gaillard.[33] Richard personally supervised the construction of his new fortress which he rushed to completion in only two years. Its mighty walls provide evidence for 'his deep practical knowledge of the craft of siege warfare'.

---

33 Gillingham, *Richard*, 252; Gillingham, 'Richard I, Galley Warfare and Portsmouth', 12–14.

Richard himself boasted that its design was so nearly perfect that he could defend it even if its walls were made of butter.[34]

Construction of Château-Gaillard was a clear violation of the January 1196 peace settlement, which had specified that Les Andelys was to remain unfortified; furthermore, it alienated a stalwart servant of the Plantagenets, Archbishop Walter of Rouen, whose manor Richard seized as the site for his fortress. The king and his archbishop quarrelled fiercely over Les Andelys, one of his most profitable manors; and Walter placed Normandy under an interdict and fled to Rome in November 1196. They settled the dispute only under papal pressure, and it left an irreparable breach between the Lionheart and his long-serving official.

Warfare between the Capetian and the Plantagenet resumed in April 1197, when Richard subjected to a severe sack the town of Saint-Valéry-sur-Somme, a Channel port belonging to the count of Ponthieu, burned the ships in its harbour and devastated the surrounding countryside. English chroniclers lamented the fury of the fighting and destruction brought upon Normandy after this resumption of fighting. William of Newburgh wrote of 'the provinces so lately flourishing [that] were devastated by fire and the sword', and Roger of Howden complained of the ravages of warfare, the depopulation of lands, plundering of towns and torture of prisoners.[35]

Philip Augustus's Flemish alliances proved to be short-lived, for both the counts of Flanders and Boulogne went over to Richard in the summer of 1197 in another 'diplomatic revolution' that the Angevin monarch engineered. Baldwin, count of Flanders and Hainault, promised that he would not make peace with the French king without Richard's consent. Afterwards, a number of other northern magnates, including the duke of Louvain and the counts of Guines and Namur, all renounced their fealty to Philip and allied with Richard, and costly subsidies ensured their continued loyalty. Joining these Low Country lords in allying with the English king were the counts of Perche and of Blois.[36] Richard won added influence in the Low Countries and in Germany through his nephew, Otto of Brunswick, the anti-Hohenstaufen candidate for the imperial throne. He had named the youth count of Poitou in 1196, but on the death of Emperor Henry VI the next year, young Otto returned to Germany to pursue his candidacy for the imperial title. Otto was elected king of the Romans, a step toward becoming

---

34 Baldwin, 90; J. Gillingham, 'Richard I and the Science of War in the Middle Ages', 90; Gillingham, *Richard*, 263–4.
35 Newburgh, 1: 483–4; also his description of Richard's raid on Saint-Valéry, 1: 492, complaints of famine; Howden, 4: 54, also 59–60, Philip's burning of Evreux and John's burning of Neufbourg; Diceto, 2: 152, on Richard's capture of Saint-Valéry.
36 Landon, 118–19, 121; Baldwin, 92; *PRIORI*, 172, 198; Stapleton, 2: 301, 302, 303, 307.

emperor, in March 1198. Another reason for the shift in alliances toward Richard may have been his effective economic blockade that threatened Flanders' economy by denying 'the king's enemies' there the supplies of grain that they imported from eastern England.[37] Direct military action also may have frightened these northern princes into allying with Richard. Whatever the reason, the count of Flanders had made a treaty with the English king by July; and in retaliation, Philip went to war against Baldwin.

Philip was active in the south seeking to counteract Richard's northern alliances, and he lined up the allegiances of the dissatisfied nobles of Angoulême and the Limousin, a task that must have proven easier than Richard's enlistment of allies in the Low Countries. Berry presented another source of conflict, for in 1196, Richard sought to bring the lordship of Vierzon on the Cher River near Bourges under his lordship, although it had traditionally been under the counts of Blois. Richard began proceedings in his own court as lord of Issoudun, summoning William I, lord of Vierzon. William then appealed to Philip Augustus's court at Paris, prompting Richard to attack Vierzon and burn the town in summer 1197.[38]

Fighting that had revived in the north in the spring of 1197 with Richard's ferocious raid on the county of Ponthieu continued in the summer with Baldwin of Flanders' invasion of Artois, a part of Flanders belonging to the French crown, and with a raid by Count John and Mercadier against an episcopal territory, Beauvais, held by Philip Augustus's cousin, Philip of Dreux. The two succeeded in capturing the warrior bishop of Beauvais, Richard's longstanding foe, who had spread malicious rumours about him while on crusade, and who had negotiated with the emperor in an attempt to extend the English king's imprisonment in Germany. Now the Lionheart had his revenge, and he refused to release the bishop. Shortly after this, Richard took the castle of Dangu in the Vexin only four miles from Gisors. Baldwin's advance in Artois continued; he took Douai and besieged Arras. The attack on Arras prompted a response from Philip Augustus, but the French king's vulnerable supply lines caused him to seek a respite from the fighting. In September 1197, the two kings and the count of Flanders met and agreed upon a sixteen-month truce.

This truce found Richard Lionheart in a potent diplomatic position. His alliance with the count of Flanders maintained his influence in the Low Countries; in Germany, his nephew, Otto of Brunswick, was a leading candidate for election as emperor; and his alliance with the count of Toulouse protected his domains in southwestern France. Yet the strength of the

---

37 Gillingham, *Richard*, 267; *PR10RI*, xv.
38 Devailly, *Berry*, 424; Landon, 119.

English king's alliances would not deter Philip Augustus from continuing to apply pressure on Normandy. The 1197 truce was no more effective than earlier ones, and the next year saw still more warfare in Flanders and Normandy. Indeed, Richard's need for warriors led him to propose modifications in his English barons' military obligations; he sought from them the long-term service of small bands of knights in Normandy in lieu of the larger numbers of knights that they owed for the traditional forty days.[39]

The count of Flanders resumed the fighting against Philip Augustus in September 1198 with another invasion of Artois, attacking Saint-Omer. Philip answered an appeal from the citizens of Saint-Omer for aid by relieving the pressure on them with an invasion of Normandy, where he raided the Vexin frontier and burned several places. Richard responded by intruding into the Capetian-controlled Vexin. His army met a French force between his castle of Gamaches and the Capetian's castle at Vernon to the south, and Philip was forced to withdraw. Shortly afterwards, the two forces met at Courcelles on the River Epte near Gisors, 28 September 1198. The battle proved to be a second defeat for Philip Augustus with Richard's mercenary, Mercadier, taking thirty French knights, and it led to still another truce. Once Richard took Courcelles, he pursued Philip and his force to the gates of Gisors, where a bridge collapsed under the weight of the French knights' armour; about twenty drowned, and the Capetian ruler himself barely avoided a watery death. The encounter of the two kings before Gisors reveals Richard's daring; in a newsletter reporting on his victory, he boasted that he had 'staked his own head and his kingdom to boot, overriding the advice of all his counsellors'.[40]

Apparently Philip Augustus was finding it burdensome to fight both Baldwin of Flanders in Artois and Richard Lionheart in the Vexin, and futile attempts were made to negotiate a treaty between the two monarchs in October 1198. The French king offered to return all territory that he had taken except Gisors, but Richard refused to violate the terms of his alliance with Baldwin by making a separate peace with Philip. In January 1199, the two rulers met on the Norman frontier, with a papal legate as mediator; and despite harsh recriminations on both sides, they agreed to another truce, to last five years. Under its terms, Philip Augustus could keep the Norman castles that he occupied, but harrying by Richard's men made it nearly impossible for him to supply them. Within a month, Richard renounced the truce when he learned that his Capetian rival had begun building a new castle near Gaillon on the Seine just above Château-Gaillard. Philip Augustus

---

39 *PR1ORI*, xix–xxi.
40 Norgate, *Richard the Lion Heart*, 320, citing Howden, 4: 58–9.

agreed to demolish his new fortress, and talks in February 1199 proceeded toward a peace settlement, again with the papal legate as peacemaker. Richard was to surrender his claim to Gisors in exchange for Philip's grant to him of his royal rights over the archbishopric of Tours; and a marriage between Philip's son, Louis, and Richard's niece, Blanche of Castile, would seal the agreement. Due to Richard's departure for the South in March, however, he did not live to ratify its terms.

Philip succeeded in stirring up troubles for Richard in his southern domains. The Lionheart was almost constantly embroiled with the count of Angoulême, the viscount of Limoges and their allies on the southern frontier of Poitou, just as he had been during his father's lifetime. As early as April 1198, the viscount of Limoges, Aimar, had agreed to an alliance with Philip Augustus. Richard moved south to discipline him and his son, Guy, for their disloyalty in the spring of the following year, intending to ravage the viscount's lands and to destroy three of his castles, Châlus-Chabrol, Nontron and Montagut. His 'characteristically violent' actions impelled Adémar, count of Angoulême, to take up arms on the rebels' side.[41] This is the explanation for Richard's siege in April 1199 of Châlus-Chabrol, a fortress situated between Limoges and Angoulême, the chief towns of his two enemies. He was not merely asserting his right of treasure-trove to claim some Roman coin hoard that had been unearthed in a nearby field, as the legend long accepted by historians would have it; he was confronting a major crisis for his 'empire', a rebellion by magnates of a crucial region in league with his chief enemy.[42] Richard Lionheart died on 6 April 1199 at Châlus, aged 41, wounded by an arrow fired by a crossbowman on the castle's ramparts.

Richard's death left the Plantagenet–Capetian rivalry unresolved, to be concluded in 1204 with John Lackland's loss of Normandy and confirmed in 1214 with Philip Augustus's victory over John's grand coalition at Bouvines. Richard Lionheart's unexpected demise in the prime of life and the drastic defeat of the Plantagenets during his brother's reign have led to much speculation, with historians questioning the inevitability of the loss of the Angevin 'empire' north of the Loire River. Disputes still divide historians on the situation in 1199 at the time of the Lionheart's death: could Richard have achieved a decisive military victory over Philip Augustus, ending the Capetian threat to the Plantagenet legacy? Or would Philip's dogged determination have worn down his opponent in a war of attrition in which the French prince lost most battles but won the war?

---

41   J. Gillingham, 'The Unromantic Death of Richard I', *Speculum* 54 (1979), 28–31, 37–8.
42   F. Arbellot, *La Vérité sur la mort de Richard Coeur-de-lion* (Paris, 1878), 103–4; Gillingham, 'Unromantic Death', acknowledges his debt to Arbellot's work, 20, 41.

Most historians conclude that Richard Lionheart was winning at the time of his death, but the outcome was in fact far from certain. A recent biographer of Philip Augustus characterises the conflict as 'a war of ups and downs, by no means always going Richard's way'.[43] Richard never succeeded in regaining all that Philip had won during his German captivity; his losses in the Norman Vexin, the southeastern marches, and the county of Aumâle had contracted the frontiers of Upper Normandy with Capetian France, edging the French closer to Rouen. The Lionheart's position within these narrower limits was far from impregnable, even with the protection afforded by Château-Gaillard to Rouen and the lower Seine valley. His death during a rebellion in Aquitaine accentuates the instability of his authority in south-western France, despite his alliance with the count of Toulouse. Yet many scholars today would agree that questions about the survival of the Angevin 'empire' cannot be addressed solely in terms of one side or the other's military advantage. Much larger structural questions about the resources of the Plantagenet and Capetian antagonists, the nature of their two governments, and the attitudes of their subjects would determine the fate of Richard's territories.

---

43 Bradbury, *Philip Augustus*, 116–17, also 127–9.

CHAPTER THIRTEEN

Richard in retrospect

Having reviewed some of the accomplishments and problems associated with Richard Lionheart, we are presented with a tangled skein. It is readily apparent that Richard's reputation is tied directly to the value structures of the historians writing about him, a reality that we cannot ourselves escape. The Victorians operated from principles that considered essential a notion of unchanging truth and certainty, whether founded on religious or Enlightenment principles, but which failed to appreciate the context in which events happened. Today's scholars, embracing to differing degrees the notion of the relativity of right and wrong, good and bad, are reluctant to project onto the twelfth century anachronistic values of a later period, but in so doing tacitly ratify behaviour and policies that are clearly obnoxious to late twentieth-century sensibilities. So the dilemma remains: if Richard Lionheart conforms to medieval standards of kingship, then he fails to meet the test set by twentieth-century scholars.

Richard Lionheart's historical reputation is based primarily on his invincibility in warfare, and he spent most of his life on military campaigns. During his years as count of Poitou, acting as his father's viceroy in Aquitaine after the great rebellion of 1173–74, he had to suppress frequent uprisings by regional lords in Aquitaine. Once Richard succeeded Henry II, his reign was spent in wars, first crusading warfare in the Holy Land, 1190–93, then on his return from captivity in 1194, resisting Philip Augustus in Normandy and in Berry and crushing continued rebellions in Aquitaine until his death on 6 April 1199.

The key to the Lionheart's fame as a warrior is his leadership in the Third Crusade, which his contemporaries saw as the central event of his life, and his role as a crusading general must be a major factor in any evaluation of him that is not totally anachronistic. Indeed, modern historians continue to find in the crusade evidence for his greatness. They present Richard taking a larger view of the problem of Christian control over the Holy Land than many of his contemporaries. For him, strengthening the crusader kingdom ranked higher than simply recovering the holy city of Jerusalem. This earned him criticism, for the crusade's primary goal in the eyes of the pope, his propagandists and the men in the crusading army was liberating Jerusalem from Muslim rule.[1] Richard shared with resident Western nobles and leaders of the crusading orders a concern for the future of a Latin Christian kingdom in the East.

Not only does the crusade demonstrate Richard's prowess as a military commander on land, but also his grasp of the significance of sea power and his broad strategic vision. First proof of his command of strategy came with his conquest of the island of Cyprus, a site of great significance, that gave him a valuable source of revenues and supplies off the Palestinian coast.[2] It seems unlikely that Richard's diversion to Cyprus was an accident, as he and subsequent historians have represented it. Indeed, his conquest of Cyprus turned out to be the 'most enduring practical legacy' of the Third Crusade, for it remained the only surviving portion of the Kingdom of Jerusalem in the later Middle Ages.[3] Also the Cyprus campaign and subsequent combat in the East reveal his mastery of galley warfare in the Mediterranean. In his later struggles on the Seine against Capetian forces, he put this knowledge of galleys into practice.[4] Scholars today also find support in Richard's crusading activity for placing him among exemplars of 'administrative kingship', seeing proof of his administrative and organisational skills: amassing treasure for the costs of the conflict in the Holy Land, ensuring discipline for his crusading host both on the voyage and in the Holy Land, seizing Cyprus as a source of supply, and making provision for his soldiers' material well-being.[5]

Not only is condemnation of the Lionheart's crusading adventure anachronistic; condemning him for neglecting England at the expense of his French domains is another anachronism to be avoided. Richard ruled over an empire of which the kingdom of England was only one part, yet he hardly neglected it; his attention to filling appointments in both Church and state attests to his concern for its government. Moreover, war was a medieval monarch's vocation, and Richard could hardly have ignored either Philip

---

1   M. Markowski, 'Richard Lionheart: Bad King, Bad Crusader?', *JMH* 23 (1997), 351–65.
2   J. Gillingham, 'Richard I and Science of War in the Middle Ages', 88.
3   J.O. Prestwich, 'Richard Coeur de Lion: Rex Bellicosus', in *Riccardo Cuor di Leone nella storia et nella leggenda* (Rome, 1981), 7–9, 12–13, 16; S. Painter, 'The Third Crusade: Richard the Lionhearted and Philip Augustus', in K. Setton (ed.), *A History of the Crusades*, 5 vols (Philadelphia, 1962), 2: 64.
4   J. Gillingham, 'Richard I, Galley Warfare and Portsmouth: The Beginnings of a Royal Navy', *Thirteenth Century England* VI (Woodbridge, 1997), 6–8.
5   For example, Prestwich, 'Rex Bellicosus', 13–14.

Augustus's threat to his continental possessions or Saladin's menace to the Holy Land. Indeed, his adversary, Philip, also exemplifies medieval rulers' preoccupation with warfare, spending about the same proportion of his time in wars or planning for war as Richard, first as his companion-in-arms against Henry II, then against Saladin, and finally as his opponent. Philip, unlike Richard, did not need to spend prolonged periods away from Paris, since most of the fighting occurred on the frontiers of the Ile de France.

Historians today must agree with Gillingham that Richard Lionheart through his generalship largely fulfilled much of his contemporaries' criteria for good kingship. Yet, as he has noted, that monarch's very success in attaining a twelfth-century ideal guarantees his failure to meet the standards of kingship applied by modern scholars. Scholars writing today should be more tolerant of Richard's warfare – both his crusade and his battles defending his polyglot dynastic heritage – than were nineteenth-century nationalist writers.

To condemn Richard for slighting administrative matters is to dismiss the evidence, for a careful examination of the sources can expose the workings of his government to a degree not previously attempted. Indeed, he may have been the example of 'administrative kingship' *par excellence*, for he knew how to keep the administrative machine that he found in his English kingdom and Norman duchy well oiled and running properly, despite his failure to gain experience in managing administrative mechanisms during his Poitevin apprenticeship. His servants in England sought to prevent matters within their competence from diverting the king's attention. In the course of an 1198 lawsuit by the men of Thanet against the abbot of Saint Augustine's, Canterbury, two of their leaders crossed the Channel to complain to the king; because they had not first brought their complaint before the justices at Westminster, they were imprisoned and released only on the justiciar's order.[6] Yet Richard stood at the apex of decision-making, and some matters had to await his will. Following the king's return from Germany in 1194, the royal judges adjourned important lawsuits until they could learn the king's will.[7] During his absences, some of his subjects sought to petition him, no matter how far they had to travel.[8]

---

6   C.T. Flower (ed.), *Curia Regis Rolls*, 17 vols, Public Record Office (London, 1923–), 7: 343.

7   Question of whether or not a woman can plead without her leprous husband, F.W. Maitland (ed.), *Rolls of the King's Court Richard I*, PRS 14 (1891), 8–9; conflict over criminal jurisdiction of the courts of the bishop of Norwich and the abbot of Bury Saint Edmunds, 18; dispute between the bishop of Coventry and Coventry Priory, F. Palgrave (ed.), *Rotuli Curiae Regis*, Record Commission (London, 1835), 1: 66–7.

8   Monks of Saint-Trinité de Beaumont, Normandy, securing right to tithes at Palermo, Landon, no. 343: a Norman's right to his stronghold of Illiers confirmed by the king at Jaffa, 1192, Fagnen thesis, no. 79; Walden monks seeking confirmation of their possessions in Poitou, H.G. Richardson and G.O. Sayles, *The Governance of Mediaeval England* (Edinburgh, 1963), 365; Landon, 32.

Richard's most important task in keeping the administrative machinery that he inherited operating smoothly was to select capable servants, and apart from an initial misstep with his naming of his ducal chancellor, William Longchamp, as chief deputy in England, his appointments of officials show that he succeeded splendidly in selecting capable men, not simply elevating longstanding companions. No doubt Richard revelled in the power that he could wield in his English kingdom and his Norman duchy, compared to the limited authority allowed to him in Aquitaine, and he played an active part in governing the Anglo-Norman realm. An example is his personal part in adding increments to newly appointed sheriffs' farms in 1194. He was pleased to find a corps of capable civil servants dedicated to implementing their king/duke's will; their royalist feeling is illustrated by the justices' labelling a sheriff's excommunication by the archbishop of York in 1194 as 'against the royal dignity and excellence'.[9] There can be little astonishment at Richard's staffing his household primarily with Anglo-Normans, who were learned in the arts of government, along with a few Poitevin knights, skilled in military science and markedly loyal, in contrast to most of his Aquitanian subjects.

Few academic historians find speculation on counter-factual questions to be fruitful, usually leaving such surmises to armchair historians. Yet no one seeking to evaluate Richard Lionheart's rule can fail to ask what might have happened, had he not died at age 41, but lived for another decade or more. Would harsh revenue-raising expedients have led to rebellion by the English baronage? Would Richard have found Philip Augustus as formidable an opponent as did his brother? Would the Lionheart's superior generalship have given him success on the battlefield over Philip Augustus instead of his brother's military failures, enabling Richard to hold on to Normandy? Would his reputation have bound his diverse subjects more firmly in loyalty to the Plantagenet line?

It cannot be overlooked that Richard Lionheart viewed England mainly as an inexhaustible treasure house. He was brutal and unrelenting in his financial exactions on the English as well as on the Normans, the two territories where he enjoyed adequate tax-collecting machinery. Despite doctrines of royal responsibility for the realm's general welfare, the true nature of medieval government as predatory is revealed in the reign of Richard little less than in his brother's. In the years 1194–99 as the fighting in Normandy became more ferocious, the rapacious character of Richard's government became clearer. Neither chroniclers' comments about wholesale merchandising of offices nor promises of payments recorded on the pipe

---

9 *Rolls of the King's Court*, 50; also a disseizin labelled *in lesionem coronae domini Regis Ricardi*, Palgrave, *Rotuli Curiae Regis*, 1: 31.

rolls can be denied; and the sources show that Richard, through his sur-rogates, was levying such weighty financial burdens on his Anglo-Norman subjects that King John would not exceed them until his middle years.[10] An entry from the 1198 pipe roll even calls to mind John's wicked sense of humour; the heir to a Somerset barony offered a fine of 100 marks that the king should take 'a reasonable relief, namely £100'.[11]

Indeed, some chroniclers specify Richard's shortcomings in promoting his subjects' well-being, and they hint at mounting dissatisfaction over his exactions. William of Newburgh, surveying late in Richard's reign his early actions before his departure on crusade, judged them irresponsible and compared him unfavourably with his predecessor, Henry II. He noted that 'the experience of present evils has revived the memory of [Henry's] good deeds', and he reminded his readers of the statement by King Solomon's son to the Israelites, 'My father chastised you with whips, but I will chastise you with scorpions.'[12] Other chroniclers made similar, though less pointed criticisms of Richard's reckless expedients at the outset of his reign.[13] Ralph of Coggeshall, writing early in John's reign with high hopes for the new king, complained of the extortions of Richard's last years. He wrote, 'No age can remember, no history can record any preceding king . . . who exacted and received so much money from his kingdom as that king exacted and amassed in the five years after he returned from captivity.'[14]

It is possible that because Richard had the respect of the English barons he might have continued to extract unlimited funds from England without driving them into rebellion. Closer contact with their king, however, could have made them aware that beneath his façade of courtesy lay a prickly personality, readily roused to outbursts of anger.[15] His subjects in Aquitaine had experienced his oppression; even the sparse records from that region preserve evidence of his arbitrary seizures of their property.[16] His capacity

---

10 N. Barratt, 'The English Revenue of Richard I', unpublished paper presented at the Colloque aux Archives du Calvados (Caen, April 1999), 5.

11 *PRIORI*, 222, William of Newmarket.

12 D.C. Douglas and G.W. Greenaway (eds), *English Historical Documents 1042–1189* (London, 1968), 2: 373.

13 D. Carpenter, 'Richard by his Contemporaries. Was he a "Model King"? England in 1189', unpublished paper, Colloque aux Archives du Calvados (April 1999).

14 Coggeshall, cited by D. Carpenter, 'Abbot Ralph of Coggeshall's Account of the Last Years of Richard and the first years of John', *EHR* 113 (1998), 1217.

15 For example, his aggressive behaviour at Messina or his insult to Leopold of Austria at Acre; J. Bradbury, *Philip Augustus: King of France 1180–1223* (London, 1998), 82–3, 91–2.

16 *Cal. Docs. Fr.*, 389, no. 1097, Eleanor's restoration of the vill of Marans to William de Mauzé, a lord of Aunis, that Richard had seized; *Rot. Chart.*, 64b, John's restoration of a house at Bayonne taken by Richard to descendants of Ernald Bertram; P. de Monsabert, 'Documents de l'abbaye de Sainte-Croix de Poitiers', *Revue Mabillon* 9 (1913), 74, no. 33, Eleanor's restoration to the nuns of Sainte-Croix of a wood taken from them by Richard.

for aggressive actions and contemptuous attitudes had become clear to Philip Augustus as well as to lesser-ranking crusading companions first in Sicily and later in the Holy Land. Most likely, the increasing desperation of the warfare and the inflationary spiral in England eventually would have pushed Richard to enforce more sternly the royal *Voluntas*, and his tyrannical acts would have inspired revolt against him, just as happened in the reign of his successor, John Lackland. Royal demands for money were growing steadily more insistent, as a doubling of English royal income after 1194 shows. Indeed, a recent study of Richard's revenues concludes that John's practices before his loss of Normandy in 1204 represent 'nothing more than a continuation of Richard's policies'.[17] This endless and thorough shakedown forms a backdrop for the resistance by English abbots, bishops and barons to royal requests for overseas service from their knights that peaked in John's reign. As their purses emptied, their interest flagged in the fate of their monarch's French lands.

All the Angevin monarchs inspired their subjects' fear, and resistance by a recalcitrant English baronage could easily have inflamed Richard's cruel streak, for he had hardly been hesitant to wage punishing warfare against rebellious Aquitanian nobles. Even in the brutality of crusading warfare, Richard's massacre of 3,000 Muslim prisoners at Acre in 1191 stands out, and in 1194 he foreshadowed one of the harsh punishments that reinforced his brother's reputation for cruelty, when he commanded that one of Count John's imprisoned supporters be starved to death. Luckier partisans of Count John purchased the king's good will by making massive offerings, 2,000 marks each from Gerard de Camville and Hugh de Nonant.[18] Richard continued to extort crippling fines from those who lost his good will. After a prominent French prisoner, committed to the custody of Robert de Ros, escaped in 1196, Robert had to offer a 1,200-mark fine for release from imprisonment and for recovery of his lands seized at the king's command, and his serjeant given guard over the prisoner was hanged.[19]

Regardless of royal revenue-raising measures in England, Richard's final victory over Philip Augustus appears dubious. He never fully recovered bits of Normandy lost to Philip in 1193, and the conflict in Normandy was by no means going entirely the Lionheart's way at the time of his death in the

---

17 Barratt, 'English Revenue of Richard I', 6, 12.
18 Robert Brito, Coggeshall, 63 and n. 2, cited by Carpenter, 'Abbot Ralph of Coggeshall's account', 1218. Hugh de Nonant's fine, *PR7RI*, 191; Gerard de Camville's fine, *PR9RI*, 100; also 300 marks from Roger de Montbegon and 500 from Geoffrey Esturmi, *PR9RI*, 114, 216.
19 *PR9RI*, xviii, 61. Also a 1,000-mark fine in 1196 from the sheriff of Lincolnshire for failure to enforce a royal embargo on overseas shipping, *Memoranda Roll 1 John*, PRS, new ser. 21 (1942): 88, fragment of Originalia Roll of 7 Richard I; and 500 marks offered by the collector of customs for Norfolk and Lincolnshire for financial misdeeds, *PR9RI*, xviii, 233–4.

spring of 1199. Philip had successfully expanded the war on several fronts with both external invasions and internal revolts, raising doubts about Richard's continued ability to beat off attacks by the Capetian king and his allies. How long could he defend such vast holdings along such a long frontier without dispersing his limited assets? Furthermore, as the struggle became more brutal and barbarous, his Norman subjects were bearing the brunt of such heavy violence and destruction that their loyalty was undermined. Yet a decisive victory in a pitched battle putting a permanent stop to Capetian threats against the Angevin territories was unlikely, given the nature of medieval warfare.

When Normandy finally fell to the French in 1203–04, contemporaries lacked the perspective to see it as the culmination of a long process. They laid full blame on King John, and most historians continue to contrast John's supposed 'military incapacity and incredible lethargy' with his brother Richard's tactical genius and prowess on the battlefield.[20] Yet evidence can be compiled that points toward large shifts in politics, economics and society in France that had more to do with the disintegration of the Angevin 'empire' than John Lackland's personal failings, numerous as they were. These structural changes were shifting the balance of power toward the Capetians during the 1190s, even though their consequences did not become clear until the thirteenth century.

Either prompting or exploiting these changes was Philip Augustus, a formidable though unpretentious opponent, who was the first Capetian to bring together wisdom, determination and ample resources in the task of crushing his Angevin rival. Philip's dual advantages of steadily increasing financial resources and his suzerainty over the Plantagenet continental lands could well have proven insurmountable to Richard, had he lived longer, just as they later proved for John. Ever since Philip Augustus had made plans for the government of his kingdom during his absence on crusade, his position as monarch within France had been strengthening. He was setting in motion in France the shift in the balance of power between monarchy and nobility that Henry II had effectuated in England, and modern histories salute him as 'the first great architect of the medieval French monarchy'.[21]

Philip Augustus achieved acknowledgement of the feudal principle that the great lordships of France were fiefs held of the French crown, converting earlier vague suzerainty into something approaching sovereign power.

---

20 B. Lyon, 'John, King of England' in J. Strayer (ed.), *Dictionary of the Middle Ages*, 13 vols (New York, 1982–89), 7: 130.

21 J.W. Alexander, 'Philip II Augustus', *Medieval France: an Encyclopedia*, ed. W. Kibler (New York, 1995), 726; 'responsible for laying the foundations for the ascendancy of the French monarchy in the thirteenth century', J.W. Baldwin, *Dictionary of the Middle Ages*, 9: 552.

Philip succeeded in requiring his nobles to pay ruinous sums as reliefs, demanding custody of deceased French nobles' minor heirs, and controlling the marriages of their daughters; in short, he was exploiting his position as feudal lord in the same manner that Henry II had coerced funds from the English baronage. Eventually, he would succeed in subjecting his vassals to royal jurisdiction, summoning the greatest of them, King John, to his *curia regis* as a contumacious vassal, declaring his fiefs forfeit to the crown, and waging war to enforce his court's judgment.

Even without the problems caused by Philip Augustus's lordship over Richard's French possessions, Richard would have had a difficult time moulding his disparate domains into a long-lasting political entity. The Plantagenets with their hegemonic view of their 'empire' showed little commitment to imposing Anglo-Norman administrative devices on Eleanor's southern lands. Perhaps Richard recognised the risks in trying to impose the strong structures needed to convert the vague vassalage of Poitevin nobles into definite payments and services. Yet he was fighting a rearguard action to retain control in the face of the growing power of regional lords in southern Poitou, relying on military force and violence as the means for asserting his authority. A long period of peace – longer than a single reign – was essential for cementing commercial ties, recruiting a cosmopolitan civil service, weaving networks of patronage and kinship binding the nobilities to the Plantagenet line, and spinning a powerful dynastic myth to inspire his diverse subjects. The French king, however, had no intention of allowing any Plantagenet ruler such a lengthy stretch of tranquillity.

Finally, Richard Lionheart failed at one of a medieval monarch's fundamental tasks; he died without leaving a son as his undoubted heir. Although he apparently had named his brother John as his heir by 1197, repudiating his earlier designation of his nephew, Arthur of Brittany, uncertainty about the succession led to warfare following his death in April 1199, when Loire Valley lords opted for young Arthur. Richard left not only a disputed succession, but a legacy to his brother John in 1199 that was otherwise flimsy. It may be compared to Edward I's legacy in 1307 to his son Edward II of unresolved war, uncontrolled government expenditures and a discontented English baronage. In both cases, military disaster and noble rebellion followed.

Map I   The Angevin Empire

Map II   England, Scotland and Wales

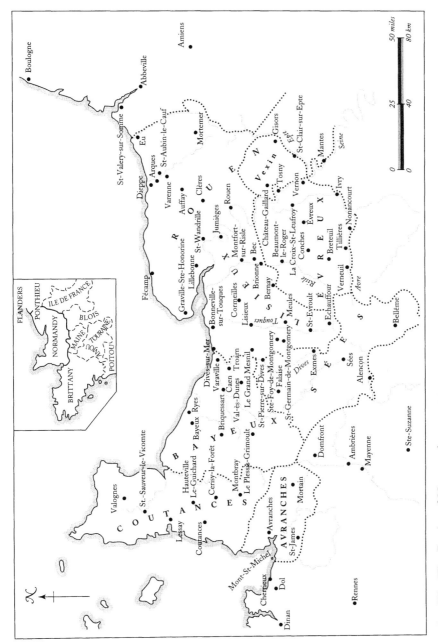

Map III The Duchy of Normandy

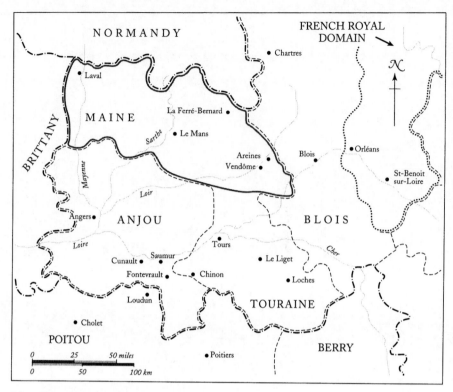

Map IV   Greater Anjou

Map V   The Duchy of Aquitaine

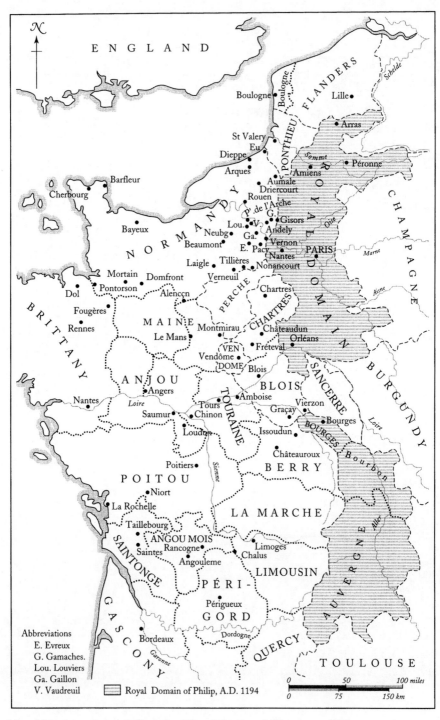

Map VI   Angevin and Capetian Dominions and Theatres of War

254

GENEALOGICAL TABLE

The Angevin Dynasty

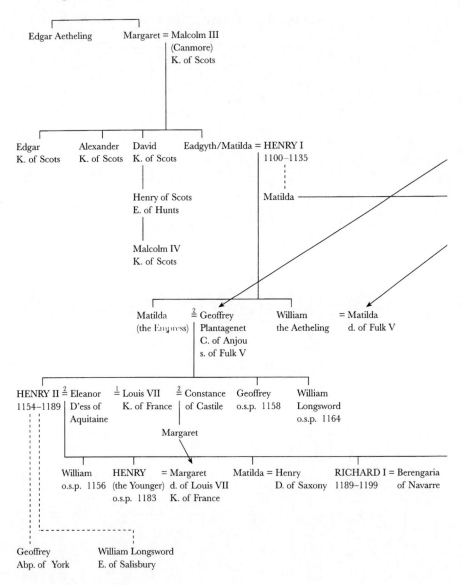

The Angevin Kings
From: King John, Turner, pub 94 © Longman UK

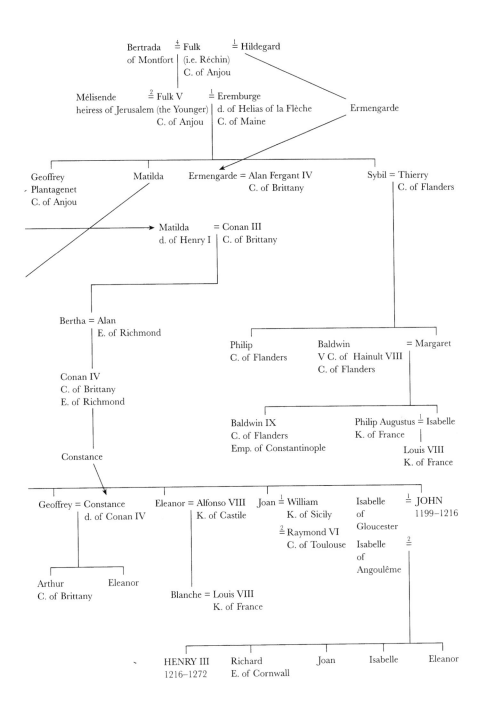

Manuscript sources

Bibliothèque nationale, Paris, nouvelle acquisition Latin 1224.

Primary sources for England and the crusade

Appleby, J.T. (ed. and trans.) *The Chronicle of Richard of Devizes* (London, 1963).

Brewer, J.S., Dimock, J.F. and Warner, G.F. (eds) *Giraldi Cambrensis Opera* (Gerald of Wales), RS, 8 vols (London, 1861–91).

Cheney, C.R. and Semple, W.H. (eds and trans.) *Selected Letters of Pope Innocent III concerning England (1198–1216)* (Edinburgh, 1953).

Clarke, A., Caley, J., Bayley, F., Holbrooke, F. and Clarke, F.W. (eds) *Foedera, Conventiones, Litterae, etc.; or Rymer's Foedera, 1066–1383*, Record Commission, 4 vols in 7 (London, 1816–30, 1869).

Crook, D. *Records of the General Eyre*, Public Record Office Handbook 20 (London, 1982).

Davies, J.C. (ed.) *Cartae Antiquae Rolls 11–20*, PRS, ns. 33 (London, 1957).

Douglas, D. and Greenaway, G.W. (eds) *English Historical Documents, 1042–1189*, vol. 2 (London, 1968).

Douie, D.L. and Farmer, H. (eds and trans.) *The Life of St. Hugh of Lincoln*, 2 vols (Edinburgh, 1961–62).

Feet of Fines of the Reign of Henry II and . . . of Richard I, A.D. 1182 to A.D. 1199, PRS, vols 17, 20, 23, 24 (London, 1894–1900).

Flower, C.T. (ed.) *Curia Regis Rolls*, 17 vols (London, 1923–).

Great Roll of the Pipe for the Reign of King Henry the Second, PRS, vols 1–2, 4–9, 11–13, 15–16, 18–19, 21–2, 25–34, 36–8 (London, 1884–1925) *Richard I*, ns. 1–3, 5–9 (1925–32); *John*, ns. 12, 14–16, 18–22, 24, 30, 35, 37 (1934–64).

Hall, G.D.G. (ed. and trans.) *Tractatus de Legibus et Consuetudinibus Regni Anglie qui Glanvilla vocatur* (London, 1965).

Hall, H. (ed.) *Red Book of the Exchequer*, RS, 3 vols (London, 1896).

Hardy, T.D. (ed.) *Rotuli Chartarum, 1199–1216*, Record Commission (London, 1837).

Hewlett, H.G. (ed.) *Chronica Rogeri de Wendover . . . Flores Historiarum*, RS, 3 vols (London, 1886–89).

Holt, J.C. and Mortimer, R. (eds) *Acta of Henry II and Richard I: Hand-list of documents surviving in . . . the United Kingdom*, List and Index Society, 21 (Gateshead, 1986).

Howlett, R. (ed.) *Historia Rerum Anglicarum of William of Newburgh*, in *Chronicles, Stephen, Henry II and Richard I*, RS, 4 vols (London, 1885–90).

Hunter, J. (ed.) *The Great Roll of the Pipe for the First Year of the Reign of King Richard the First*, Record Commission (London, 1844).

Johnson, C. (ed. and trans.) *Dialogus de Scaccario* (London, 1950).

Landon, L. (ed.) *Cartae Antiquae Rolls 1–10*, PRS, ns. 17 (London, 1939).

Luard, H.R. (ed.) *Annales Monastici*, RS, 5 vols (London, 1864–69).

Luard, H.R. (ed.) *Matthaei Parisiensis Chronica Majora*, RS, 7 vols (London, 1872–84).

Maitland, F.W. (ed.) *Rolls of the King's Court Richard I*, PRS 14 (1891).

Meyer, P. (ed.) *L'Histoire de Guillaume le Maréchal*, Société de l'histoire de France, vols 255, 268, 304 (Paris, 1891–1901).

Migne, J.P. (ed.) *Patrologiae latinae*, 217 vols (Paris, 1844–55).

Millor, W.J., Butler, H.E. and Brooke, C.N.L. (eds) *The Letters of John of Salisbury*, 2 vols (Oxford, 1955, 1986).

Palgrave, F. (ed.) *Rotuli Curiae Regis*, 2 vols, Record Commission (London, 1835).

Richardson, H.G. (ed.) *Memoranda Roll 1 John*, PRS, ns. 21 (London, 1943).

Round, J.H. (ed.) *Ancient Charters, Royal and Private, prior to 1200*, PRS, 10 (London, 1888).

Round, J.H. (ed.) *Calendar of Documents Preserved in France* (London, 1899).

Shirley, W.W. (ed.) *Royal Letters, Henry III*, 2 vols, RS (London, 1862–66).

Stenton, D.M. (ed.) *The Chancellor's Roll, 8 Richard I*, PRS, ns. 7 (London, 1930).

Stenton, D.M. (ed.) *Rolls or Fragments of Rolls From the Years 1199, 1202, 1203–06*, vol. 3, *Pleas Before the King or His Justices, 1198–1212*, Selden Society, vol. 83 (London, 1967).

Stevenson, J. (ed.) *Radulphi de Coggeshall Chronicon Anglicanum*, RS (London, 1875).

Stubbs, W. (ed.) *Chronica Rogeri de Hovedene*, RS, 4 vols (London, 1868–71).

Stubbs, W. (ed.) *Epistolae Cantuarienses*, RS (London, 1865).

Stubbs, W. (ed.) *Gervase of Canterbury, Historical Works*, RS, 2 vols (London, 1879–80).

Stubbs, W. (ed.) *Gesta Regis Henrici Secundi Benedicti Abbatis*, RS, 2 vols (London, 1867).

Stubbs, W. (ed.) '*Itinerarium Peregrinorum et Gesta Regis Ricardi*', in *Chronicles and Memorials of the Reign of Richard I*, RS, 2 vols (London, 1864–65).

Stubbs, W. (ed.) *Memoriale Walteri de Coventria*, RS (London, 1872–73).

Stubbs, W. (ed.) *Radulphi de Diceto, Opera Historica*, RS, 2 vols (London, 1876).

Thorpe, L. (trans.) *Geoffrey of Monmouth: The History of the Kings of Britain* (Harmondsworth, 1966).

Primary sources for continental holdings

Audouin, E. (ed.) *Recueil des documents concernant la commune et la ville de Poitiers*, 1, Archives historiques du Poitou, 44 (1923).

Baldwin, J.W. (ed.) *Les Registres de Philippe Auguste. Receuil des historiens de la France, Documents financières et administratives*, vol. 7 (Paris, 1992).

Baldwin, J.W. and Nortier, M. 'Contributions à l'étude des finances de Philippe Auguste', *BEC* 138 (1980).

Bardonnet, A. (ed.) 'Comptes et enquêtes d'Alphonse, comte de Poitou 1253–1269', *Archives historiques du Poitou*, 8 (1879), 1–160.

Bémont, C. (ed.) *Recueil d'actes relatifs à l'administration des rois d'Angleterre en Gascogne au xiii⁰ siècle* (Paris, 1914).

Borderie, A. de la (ed.) *Recueil d'actes des ducs et princes de Bretagne* (Rennes, 1888).

Boussard, J. (ed.) *Historia Pontifum et comitum Engolismensium* (Paris, 1957).

Boutière, L. de la (ed.) *Cartulaire de l'Abbaye d'Orbestier*, Archives historiques du Poitou, 6 (1879).

Brousillon, Bertrand de (ed.) *Cartulaire de Saint-Aubin d'Angers* (Paris, 1903).

Brutails, J.-A. (ed.) *Cartulaire de l'église collégiale de Saint Seurin de Bordeaux* (Bordeaux, 1897).

Chaplais, P. (ed.) *Diplomatic Documents preserved in the Public Record Office*, 1, 1101–1272 (London, 1964), for treaties: 5, March 1191 Treaty of Messina; 6, 5 January 1196 Treaty of Gaillon or Louviers; 7 July 1197, Treaty with Baldwin of Flanders at La Roche d'Andely; 9, 22 May 1200 Treaty of Le Goulet.

Debord, A. (ed.) *Cartulaire de l'abbaye de Saint-Amand-de-Boixe*, Société archéologique et historique de la Charente (Poitiers, 1982).

Delaborde, H.-F. (ed.) *Oeuvres de Rigord et de Guillaume le Breton*, Société de l'histoire de France, 2 vols (Paris, 1882–85).

Delaborde, H.-F., Petit-Dutaillis, C., Monicat, J., Boussard, J. and Nortier, M. (eds) *Recueil des actes de Philippe Auguste*, 4 vols (Paris, 1916–79).

D'Elbene, M. and Denis, L.J. (eds) *Cartulaire du chapitre-royal de Saint-Pierre de la Cour du Mans*, Archives historiques du Maine, 4 (1903–07).

Delisle, L. (ed.) *Enquête de 1172, Recueil des historiens des Gaules et de la France*, 24 vols (Paris, 1737–1904), 23 (Paris, 1876).

Delisle, L. (ed.) 'Histoire des ducs de Normandie et des rois d'Angleterre', *Recueil des Historiens des Gaules et de la France* 24, pt 2 (Paris, 1906).

Denis, L.-J. *Chartes de St.-Julien de Tours (1002–1300)*, Archives historiques du Maine, 12 (1912–13).

Duplès-Agier, H. (ed.) *Chroniques de Saint-Martial de Limoges* (Paris, 1874).

Font-Reaulx, J. de (ed.) *Cartulaire de Saint-Etienne, Limoges*, Bulletin de la Société archéologique et historique du Limousin, 69 (1921).

Gouiran, G. *L'Amour et la guerre: l'oeuvre de Bertrand de Born* (Paris, 1985).

Grasilier, T. (ed.) *Cartulaires inédits de la Saintonge*, 1, *Cart. de Ste-Etienne de Vaux*; 2, *Cart. de l'abbaye royale de Notre-Dame de Saintes* (Niort, 1871).

Haigueré, D. *Les Chartes de Saint-Bertin*, 5 vols (Saint-Omer, 1886–99).

Halphen, L. (ed.) *Recueil d'annales angevines et vendômoises* (Paris, 1903).

Halphen, L. and Poupardin, R. (eds) *Chroniques des comtes d'Anjou* (Paris, 1913).

Hardy, T.D. (ed.) *Rotuli Litterarum Clausarum*, 2 vols, Record Commission (London, 1833–44).

Hardy, T.D. (ed.) *Rotuli Litterarum Patentium*, Record Commission (London, 1835).

Hardy, T.D. (ed.) *Rotuli Normanniae in Turri Londinensi asservati*, Record Commission (London, 1835).

Hartigan, F. (ed.) *Accounts of Alphonse of Poitiers 1243–1248* (Lanham, MD, 1984).

Higounet, C. and Higounet-Nadal, A. (eds) *Grande Cartulaire de la Sauve Majeure*, Etudes et documents d'Aquitaine, 8, 2 vols (Bordeaux, 1996).

Howlett, R. (ed.) *Chronicle of Robert of Torigny* in *Chronicles, Stephen, Henry II and Richard I*, RS, 4 vols (London, 1885–90).

Hubert, E. (ed.) *Cartulaire des seigneurs de Chateauroux (967–1789)* (Chateauroux, 1931).

Labbe, P. (ed.) *Geoffroi de Vigeois, Chronica*, in *Novae Bibliotheca Manuscriptorum*, 11 (Paris, 1657).

Leroux, A. and Boisvieux, A. (eds) *Chartes de chroniques et mémoriaux pour servir à l'histoire de la Marche et du Limousin* (Tulle and Limoges, 1886).

Lewis, A. 'Six Charters of Henry II and his Family for the Monastery of Dalon', *EHR* 110 (1995), 652–5.

Lot, F. and Fawtier, R. (eds) *Le Premier Budget de la monarchie française, le compte générale de 1202–1203* (Paris, 1932).

Marchegay, P. (ed.) *Cartulaires du Bas-Poitou* (Les Roches-Baritaud, 1877).

Marchegay, P. (ed.) 'Chartes angevines des onzième et douzième siècles', *BEC* 36 (1875), 380–441.

Marchegay, P. (ed.) 'Chartes de Fontevraud concernant l'Aunis et La Rochelle', *BEC*, 4th ser., 19 (1858), 321–47.

Marchegay, P. (ed.) *Documents inédits sur la Saintonge et l'Aunis*, Archives historiques de la Saintonge et l'Aunis, 5 (1878).

Marchegay, P. and Mabille, E. (eds) *Chroniques des églises d'Anjou*, Société de l'histoire de France (Paris, 1869).

Martene, E. and Durand, U. *Thesaurus novus Anecdotorum*, 5 vols (Paris, 1717).

Martene, E. and Durand, U. *Veterum Scriptorum et Monumentorum Amplissima Collectio*, 9 vols (Paris, 1724–39).

Metais, C. (ed.) *Cartulaire de l'abbaye cardinalice de la Trinite de Vendome* (Paris, 1893).

Monsabert, D.P. de (ed.) *Chartes et documents pour servir à l'histoire de l'abbaye de Charroux*, Archives historiques du Poitou, 39 (Poitiers, 1910).

Musset, G. (ed.) *Cartulaire de Saint-Jean d'Angely*, Archives historiques de la Saintonge et de l'Aunis, 30, 33 (1901, 1903).

Packard, S.R. (ed.) *Miscellaneous Records of the Norman Exchequer*, Smith College Studies in History, 12 (1926–27).

Paden, W.D., Sankovitch, T. and Stäblein, P.H. *Poems of the Troubadour Bertran de Born* (Berkeley and Los Angeles, CA, 1986).

Pon, G. (ed.) *Recueil des documents de l'Abbaye de Fontaine-le-Comte (xii*–xiii* siècles)*, Archives historiques du Poitou, 61 (1982).

Poupardin, R. (ed.) *Recueil des chartes de l'Abbaye de Saint-Germain-des-Prés*, 2, *1183–1216*, Société de l'histoire de Paris et de l'Ile de France (Paris, 1930).

Redet, L. 'Documents pour l'histoire de l'Eglise de Saint-Hilaire de Poitiers', *MSAO* lst ser. 1, 14, 18 (1847, 1852).

Richard, A. (ed.) *Chartes et documents pour servir à l'histoire de l'Abbaye de Saint-Maixent*, Archives historiques du Poitou, 16 (1886).

Sainte-Marthe, D. (ed.) *Gallia Christiana in Provincias Ecclesiasticas Distributa*, 16 vols (Paris, 1739–1877).

Salmon, A. *Recueil de chroniques de Touraine*, Société archéologique de Touraine (Tours, 1854).

Stapleton, T. (ed.) *Magni Rotuli Scaccarii Normanniae Sub Regibus Angliae*, 2 vols (London, 1840–44).

Tardiff, E.J. (ed.) *Le Très Ancien Coutumier*, in *Coutumiers de Normandie*, 1 (Rouen, 1881).

Teulet, A. (ed.) *Layettes du trésor des chartes*, 5 vols (Paris, 1863–1909).

F. Villard (ed.) *Recueil des documents relatifs à l'Abbaye de Montierneuf de Poitiers (1076–1319)*, Archives historiques du Poitou, 59 (1973).

Secondary sources for England, the Celtic fringe and crusade

Accademia dei Lincei. *Riccards Chor di Leone nella Storia e nella Leggenda*, Problemi altuali di scienza e di cultura, 253 (Rome, 1981).

Alexander, J.W. *Ranulf of Chester, a Relic of the Conquest* (Athens, GA, 1983).

Amt, E. *The Accession of Henry II in England: Royal Government Restored 1149–1159* (Woodbridge, 1993).

Appleby, J.T. *England Without Richard, 1189–1199* (Ithaca, NY, 1965).

Balfour, D. 'William Longchamp: Upward Mobility and Character Assassination in Twelfth-century England', PhD dissertation (University of Connecticut, 1996).

Barlow, F. *The Feudal Kingdom of England 1042–1216*, 4th edn (London, 1988).

Barratt, N. 'The English Revenue of Richard I', unpublished paper presented at the Colloque aux Archives du Calvados, (Caen, April 1999).

Barratt, N. 'The Revenues of John and Philip Augustus Revisited', in S.D. Church (ed.) *King John: New Interpretations* (Woodbridge, 1999), 75–99.

Barratt, N. 'The Revenue of King John', *EHR* 111 (1996), 835–55.

Barrow, G.W.S. *The Kingdom of the Scots: Government, Church and Society from the Eleventh to the Fourteenth Century* (London, 1973).

Bartlett, R. *Gerald of Wales* (Oxford, 1982).

Bates, D.B. 'Normandy and England after 1066', *EHR* 104 (1989), 851–76.

Bates, D.B. 'The Prosopographical Study of Anglo-Norman Royal Charters', in K.S.B. Keats-Rohan (ed.) *Family Trees and the Roots of Family Politics: The Prosopography of Britain and France from the Tenth to the Twelfth Century* (Woodbridge, 1997), 89–102.

Bates, D. and Curry, A. (eds) *England and Normandy in the Middle Ages* (London, 1994).

Bolton, J.L. *The Medieval English Economy 1150–1500* (London, 1980).

Bond, S. 'The Medieval Constables of Windsor Castle', *EHR* 82 (1967), 225–49.

Bridge, A. *Richard the Lionheart* (New York, 1989).

Brooke, C.N.L. *From Alfred to Henry III 871–1272* (London, 1961).

Brooke, Z.N. *The English Church and the Papacy from the Conquest to the Reign of John* (Cambridge, 1931).

Brooks, F.W. 'William of Wrotham and the Office of the Keeper of the King's Ports and Galleys', *EHR* 49 (1925), 570–9.

Brown, R.A. 'Framlingham Castle and Bigod, 1154–1216', in *Castles, Conquest and Charters: Collected Papers of R. Allen Brown* (Woodbridge, 1989).

Brown, R.A. 'A List of Castles, 1154–1216', in *Castles, Conquest and Charters: Collected Papers of R. Allen Brown* (Woodbridge, 1989).

Brown, R.A. 'Royal Castle-building in England, 1154–1216', in *Castles, Conquest and Charters: Collected Papers of R. Allen Brown* (Woodbridge, 1989).

Brundage, J.A. *Richard Lion Heart* (New York, 1974).

Carpenter, D. 'Abbot Ralph of Coggeshall's Account of the Last Years of Richard and the First Years of John', *EHR* 3 (1998), 1210–30.

Carpenter, D. 'The Decline of the Curial Sheriff 1194–1285', *EHR* 91 (1976), 1–32.

Carpenter, D. 'Richard by his Contemporaries. Was he a "Model King"? England in 1189', unpublished paper, Colloque de Caen (April 1999).

Cawley, A. 'The King and his Vassals: A Study of the Chancery of Richard I', BA thesis (University of Cambridge, 1962).

Cazel, F. (ed.) *Feudalism and Liberty, Articles and Addresses of Sidney Painter* (Baltimore, 1961).

Cheney, C.R. *From Becket to Langton: English Church Government 1170–1213* (Manchester, 1956).

Cheney, C.R. *Hubert Walter* (London, 1967).

Cheney, C.R. *Innocent III and England* (Stuttgart, 1979).

Cheney, C.R. *The Papacy and England 12th–14th Centuries* (London, 1982).

Chibnall, M. *Anglo-Norman England 1066–1166* (Oxford, 1986).

Church, S.D. (ed.) *King John: New Interpretations* (Woodbridge, 1999).

Clanchy, M.T. *England and its Rulers 1066–1272* (London, 1983).

Clanchy, M.T. *From Memory to Written Record: England 1066–1307*, 2nd edn (Oxford, 1993).

Colvin, H.M. (ed.) *The History of King's Works*, 2 vols (London, 1963).

Crouch, D. 'Normans and Anglo-Normans: A Divided Aristocracy?', in D. Bates and A. Curry (eds) *England and Normandy in the Middle Ages* (London, 1994).

Crouch, D. 'Strategies of Lordship in Angevin England and the Career of William Marshal', in *The Ideals and Practice of Medieval Knighthood*, vol. 2 (Woodbridge, 1988).

Crouch, D. *William Marshal: Court, Career, and Chivalry in the Angevin Empire, 1147–1219* (London, 1990).

Davies, R.R. *The Age of Conquest: Wales 1063–1415*, vol. 2 of *The Oxford History of Wales* (Oxford, 1987).

Davies, R.R. *Domination and Conquest: The Experience of Ireland, Scotland and Wales, 1100–1300* (Cambridge, 1990).

Davies, R.R. 'Kings, Lords and Liberties in the March of Wales, 1066–1272', *TRHS*, 5th ser. 29 (1979), 41–61.

Davies, R.R. 'Presidential Address: The Peoples of Britain and Ireland, 1100–1400, Identities', *TRHS*, 4, 6th ser. (1994), 1–20.

Desborough, D.E. 'Politics and Prelacy in the Late Twelfth Century: The Career of Hugh de Nonant, Bishop of Coventry, 1188–98', *Historical Research* 64 (1991), 1–14.

Douie, D.L. *Archbishop Geoffrey Plantagenet and the Chapter at York* (York, 1960).

Duncan, A.A.M. *Scotland: The Making of the Kingdom*, vol. 2, *The Edinburgh History of Scotland* (New York, 1975).

Edwards, J.G. 'The "Itinerarum Regis Ricardi" and the "Estoire"', in *Historical Essays in Honour of James Tait* (Manchester, 1933).

Flanagan, M.T. *Irish Society, Anglo-Norman Settlers, Angevin Kingship: Interactions in Ireland in the Late Twelfth Century* (Oxford, 1989).

Flower, C.T. *Introduction to the Curia Regis Rolls*, Selden Society, vol. 62 (London, 1943).

Freedman, P. and Spiegel, G. 'Medievalisms Old and New: The Rediscovery of Alterity in North American Medieval Studies', *AHR* 103 (1998), 689–90.

Galbraith, V.H. 'Good kings and Bad kings in English History', *History*, 30 (1945); rpt. in *Kings and Chronicles* (London, 1982).

Gillingham, J. 'The Art of kingship: Richard I, 1189–99', *History Today* (April 1985); rpt. in *Coeur de Lion*.

Gillingham, J. 'The Beginnings of English Imperialism', *Journal of Historical Sociology* 5 (1992).

Gillingham, J. 'Conquering Kings: Some Twelfth-century Reflections on Henry II and Richard I', in *Warriors and Churchmen in the High Middle Ages: Essays Presented to Karl Leyser* (London, 1992).

Gillingham, J. 'The Fall of the Angevin Empire', in N. Saul (ed.) *England in Europe 1066–1453* (New York, 1994).

Gillingham, J. 'Henry II, Richard I and the Lord Rhys', *Peritia* 10 (1996), 225–36.

Gillingham, J. *Richard Coeur de Lion: Kingship, Chivalry, and War in the Twelfth Century* (London, 1994).

Gillingham, J. 'Richard I, Galley Warfare and Portsmouth: The Beginnings of a Royal Navy', *Thirteenth Century England* VI (Woodbridge, 1997).

Gillingham, J. 'Richard I and Berengaria of Navarre', *BIHR* 53 (1980), 157–73.

Gillingham, J. 'Richard I and the Science of War in the Middle Ages', in *War and Government in the Middle Ages* (Woodbridge, 1984).

Gillingham, J. *Richard the Lionheart* (London, 1978).

Gillingham, J. 'Roger of Howden on Crusade', in *Richard Coeur de Lion: Kingship, Chivalry, and War in the Twelfth Century* (London, 1994).

Gillingham, J. 'The Unromantic Death of Richard I', *Speculum* 54 (1979), 18–41.

Gillingham, J. 'War and Chivalry in the History of William the Marshal', in *Thirteenth Century England* II (Woodbridge, 1987).

Gillingham, J. and Holt, J.C. (eds) *War and Government in the Middle Ages* (Woodbridge, 1988).

Golding, B. 'Simon of Kyme, the Making of a Rebel', *Nottingham Medieval Studies* 27 (1983), 24–36.

Gransden, A. *Historical Writing in England c. 550–1307* (Ithaca, NY, 1974).

Grant, L. 'Gothic Architecture in Southern England and the French Connection in the Early Thirteenth Century', in P. Coss and S. Lloyd (eds) *Thirteenth Century England*, 4 (1991).

Green, J.A. *The Government of England under Henry I* (Cambridge, 1986).

Green, J.A. 'Unity and Disunity in the Anglo-Norman State', *Historical Research* 63 (1989), 115–34.

Harris, B.E. 'King John and Sheriffs' Farms', *EHR* 79 (1964), 532–42.

Harvey, P.D.A. 'The English Inflation of 1180–1220', *Past and Present* 61 (1973), 3–30.

Heiser, R.R. 'The Extent of the Lionheart's Folly: Richard I's Arrangements for Count John and Archbishop Geoffrey prior to the Third Crusade', *Nottingham Medieval Studies* 43 (1999), 79–89.

Heiser, R.R. 'The *Familiares* of the Court of King Richard I', Florida State University M.A. Thesis (Tallahassee, 1988).

Heiser, R.R. 'The Households of the Justiciars of Richard I: An Inquiry into the Second Level of Medieval English Government', *HSJ* 2 (1990), 223–36.

Heiser, R.R. 'Richard I and His Appointments to English Shrievalties', *EHR* 112 (1997), 1–19.

Heiser, R.R. 'The Royal *Familiares* of Richard I', *Medieval Prosopography* 10 (1989), 25–50.

Heiser, R.R. 'The Sheriffs of Richard I: Trends of Management as Seen in the Shrieval Appointments from 1189 to 1194', *HSJ* 4 (1992), 109–22.

Heiser, R.R. 'The Sheriffs of Richard the Lionheart: A Prosopographical Survey of Appointments, Politics, and Patronage, 1189–1199', PhD dissertation (Florida State University, 1993).

Holden, B. 'The Rise of a Royal Bastard: William Longespée, Earl of Salisbury, 1198–1226', MA thesis (Florida State University, 1996).

Hollister, C.W. *Monarchy, Magnates and Institutions in the Anglo-Norman World* (London, 1986).

Hollister, C.W. and Baldwin, J.W. 'The Rise of Administrative Kingship: Henry I and Philip Augustus', *AHR* 83 (1978), 867–905.

Holt, J.C. 'The Acta of Henry II and Richard I of England 1154–1199: The Archive and its Historical Implications', in Peter Rück (ed.) *Sammlungen mittelalterlicher Urkunden in Europa* (Sigmaringen, 1989).

Holt, J.C. 'Feudal Society and the Family in Early Medieval England: II. Notions of Patrimony', *TRHS* 5th ser. 33 (1983), 192–220.

Holt, J.C. *Magna Carta*, 2nd edn (Cambridge, 1991).

Holt, J.C. (ed.) *Magna Carta and the Idea of Liberty* (New York, 1972).

Holt, J.C. *Magna Carta and Medieval Government* (London, 1985).

Holt, J.C. *The Northerners: A Study in the Reign of King John* (Oxford, 1961).

Holt, J.C. 'Politics and Property in Early Medieval England', *Past and Present* 57 (1972), 31–52.

Holt, J.C. 'Ricardus Rex Anglorum et Dux Normannorum', in *Magna Carta and Medieval Government* (London, 1985).

Holt, J.C. 'The Writs of Henry II', in J. Hudson (ed.) *The History of English Law: Centenary Essays on 'Pollock and Maitland'* (Oxford, 1996), 47–64.

Jamison, E. 'The Alliance of England and Sicily in the Second Half of the Twelfth Century', *Journal of Warburg and Courtauld Institutes* 6 (1943).

Jolliffe, J.E.A. *Angevin Kingship*, 2nd edn (London, 1963).

Jolliffe, J.E.A. 'The Chamber and Castle Treasuries under King John', in R.W. Hunt, W.A. Pantin and R.W. Southern (eds) *Studies in Medieval History Presented to F.M. Powicke* (Oxford, 1948).

Keefe, T.K. 'Counting Those Who Count: A Computer-assisted Analysis of Charter Witness-lists and the Itinerant Court in the First Year of the Reign of King Richard I', *HSJ* 1 (1989), 135–45.

Keefe, T.K. *Feudal Assessments and the Political Community under Henry II and His Sons* (Berkeley and Los Angeles, CA, 1983).

Keefe, T.K. 'Henry II and the Earls: The Pipe Roll Evidence', *Albion*, 13 (1981), 191–222.

Keefe, T.K. 'Place–date Distribution of Royal Charters and the Historical Geography of Patronage Strategies at the Court of Henry II Plantagenet', *HSJ* 2 (1990), 179–88.

Keefe, T.K. 'Proffers for Heirs and Heiresses in the Pipe Rolls: Some Observations on Indebtedness in the Years before the Magna Carta (1180–1212)', *HSJ* 5 (1993), 99–109.

Keen, M. 'War, Peace and Chivalry', in *Nobles, Knights and Men-at-Arms in the Middle Ages* (London, 1996).

Kemp, B. 'Exchequer and Bench in the Later Twelfth Century – Separate or Identical Tribunals?', *EHR* 88 (1973), 559–73.

Knowles, D. *The Monastic Order in England 940–1216*, 2nd edn (Cambridge, 1963).

Lally, J.E. 'Secular Patronage at the Court of Henry II', *BIHR* 49 (1976), 159–84.

Landon, L. *The Itinerary of King Richard I*, PRS, ns. 13 (London, 1935).

Latham, R.E., *Revised Medieval Latin Word-list* (Oxford, 1965).

Lewis, A.W. 'Six Charters of Henry II and his Family for the Monastery of Dalon', *EHR* 110 (1995), 652–65.

Lewis, P.N. 'The Wars of Richard I in the West', M.Phil. thesis (University of London, 1997).

Loengard, J.S. ' "Of the Gift of her Husband": English Dower and its Consequences in the Year 1200', in J. Kirshner and S.F. Wemple (eds) *Women of the Medieval World* (Oxford, 1985).

Lovatt, M.B. 'The Career and Administration of Geoffrey Plantagenet, Archbishop of York? 1151–1212', PhD thesis (Cambridge University, 1975).

Loyd, L. *The Origins of Some Anglo-Norman Families*, ed. C.T. Clay and David C. Douglas, Harleian Society, 103 (1951) (Baltimore, 1975).

Lyon, B. *A Constitutional and Legal History of Medieval England* (New York, 1960).

Lyon, B. 'Henry II: A Non-Victorian Interpretation', in J.S. Hamilton and P.J. Bradley (eds) *Documenting the Past: Essays in Medieval History Presented to George Peddy Cuttino* (Woodbridge, 1989).

Lyon, B. 'John, King of England', in J. Strayer (ed.) *Dictionary of the Middle Ages*, 13 vols (New York, 1982–89), 7: 129–30.

Lyon, B. 'Richard I the Lionhearted', in J.R. Strayer (ed.) *Dictionary of the Middle Ages*, 13 vols (New York, 1982–89), 10: 383–84.

Markowski, M. 'Richard Lionheart: Bad King, Bad Crusader?', *JMH* 23 (1997), 351–65.

Mason, E. 'The Hero's Invincible Weapon: An Aspect of Angevin Propaganda', in *The Ideals and Practices of Medieval Knighthood*, vol. 3, *Papers from the Fourth Strawberry Hill Conference, 1988*, ed. C. Harper-Bill and R. Harvey (Woodbridge, 1989).

Mayhew, N.J. 'Frappes de monnaies et hausse des prix en Angleterre de 1180 à 1220', in *Etudes d'histoire monétaire* (Lille, 1984).

Miller, E. and Hatcher, J. *Medieval England: Society and Economic Change 1086–1348* (London, 1978).

Milsom, S.F.C. *The Legal Framework of English Feudalism* (Cambridge, 1976).

Mitchell, M. *Berengaria: Enigmatic Queen of England* (Burwash, 1986).

Mitchell, S.K. *Studies in Taxation under John and Henry III* (New Haven, CT, 1914).

Morillo, S. *Warfare under the Anglo-Norman Kings 1066–1135* (Woodbridge, 1994).

Morris, W.A. *The Medieval English Sheriff to 1300* (Manchester, 1927).

Mortimer, R. 'The Family of Rannulf de Glanville', *BIHR* 54 (1981).

Nelson, J. (ed.) *Richard Coeur de Lion in History and Myth*, King's College London Medieval Studies, 7 (London, 1992).

Norgate, K., *England under the Angevin Kings*, 2 vols (London, 1887; rprt New York, 1969).

Norgate, K. *Richard the Lion Heart* (London, 1924).

Painter, S. 'The Earl of Clare: Richard de Clare, Earl of Hertford', in F. Cazel (ed.) *Feudalism and Liberty, Articles and Addresses of Sidney Painter* (Baltimore, 1961).

Painter, S. *The Reign of King John* (Baltimore, 1949).

Painter, S. *Studies in the History of the English Feudal Barony* (Baltimore, 1943).

Painter, S. 'The Third Crusade: Richard the Lionhearted and Philip Augustus', in K. Setton (ed.) *A History of the Crusades*, 5 vols (Philadelphia, 1962).

Painter, S. *William Marshal: Knight-Errant, Baron, and Regent of England* (Baltimore, 1933).

Painter, S. and Tierney, B. *Western Europe in the Middle Ages 300–1475*, 3rd edn (New York, 1978).

Partner, N. *Serious Entertainments: The Writing of History in Twelfth-Century England* (Chicago, 1977).

Poggioli, P. 'From Politician to Prelate: The Career of Walter of Coutances, Archbishop of Rouen, 1184–1207', PhD dissertation (Johns Hopkins University, 1984).

Poole, A.L. *From Domesday Book to Magna Carta 1087–1216*, 2nd edn, Oxford History of England, 2 (Oxford, 1954).

Poole, A.L. *Obligations of Society in the 12th and 13th Centuries* (Oxford, 1946).

Postan, M.M. *The Medieval Economy and Society: An Economic History of Britain in the Middle Ages* (Berkeley, CA, 1972).

Pounds, N.J.G. *The Medieval Castle in England and Wales: A Social and Political History* (Cambridge, 1990).

Powell, W.R. 'The Administration of the Navy and the Stannaries, 1189–1216', *EHR* 71 (1956), 177–88.

Powicke, F.M. 'England: Richard I and John', in *Cambridge Medieval History*, 6 (Cambridge, 1929).

Prestwich, J.O. 'Richard Coeur de Lion: Rex Bellicosus', in *Riccardo Cuor di Leone nella storia et nella leggenda* (Rome, 1981).

Prestwich, J.O. 'War and Finance in the Anglo-Norman Realm', *TRHS*, 5 ser. 4 (1954), 19–43.

Public Record Office *Lists of Sheriffs for England and Wales: From earliest times to AD 1831*, Lists and Indexes 9 (London, 1963).

Ramsey, J. *A History of the Revenues of the Kings of England, 1066–1399*, 2 vols (Oxford, 1925).

Reynolds, S. *Kingdoms and Communities in Western Europe, 900–1300* (Oxford, 1984).

Reynolds, S. 'Medieval *Origines gentium* and the Community of the Realm', *History* 68 (1983), 375–90.

Richardson, H.G. 'William of Ely, the King's Treasurer, 1195–1215', *TRHS* 4th ser. 15 (1932), 45–90.

Richardson, H.G. and Sayles, G.O. *The Governance of Mediaeval England* (Edinburgh, 1963).

Round, J.H. 'Some English Crusaders of Richard I', *EHR* 18 (1903), 475–81.

Sanders, I.J. *English Baronies: A Study of their Origin and Descent 1086–1327* (Oxford, 1960).

Saul, N. (ed.) *England and Europe 1066–1453* (New York, 1994).

Scammell, G. *Hugh du Puiset, Bishop of Durham* (Cambridge, 1956).

Smail, R.C. *Crusading Warfare 1097–1193* (Cambridge, 1956).

Smalley, B. *Historians in the Middle Ages* (New York, 1974).

Southern, R.W. *The Making of the Middle Ages* (London, 1953).

Southern, R.W. *Medieval Humanism and Other Studies* (New York, 1970).

Southern, R.W. 'Peter of Blois and the Third Crusade', in H. Mayr-Harting and R.I. Moore (eds) *Studies in Medieval History presented to R.H.C. Davis* (London, 1985).

Southern, R.W. 'The Place of Henry I in English History', in *Medieval Humanism and Other Studies* (New York, 1971).

Sprey, I. 'William Longchamp: Papal *legatus a latere* and Faithful Royal Servant', unpublished paper presented at the American Historical Association annual meeting (Seattle, January 1998).

Stacey, R. *Politics, Policy and Finance under Henry III 1216–1245* (Oxford, 1987).

Stenton, D.M. *English Justice between the Norman Conquest and the Great Charter* (Philadelphia, 1964).

Stenton, D.M. 'Roger of Howden and Benedict', *EHR* 58 (1953), 574–82.

Stones, E.L.G. (ed. and trans.) *Anglo-Scottish Relations 1174–1328: Some Selected Documents* (Oxford, 1965).

Strickland, M. *War and Chivalry: The Conduct and Perception of War in England and Normandy 1066–1217* (Cambridge, 1996).

Stubbs, W. *Historical Introductions to the Rolls Series*, ed. A. Hassall (London, 1902).

Summerson, H. 'Problems of Biography: Revising the DNB', *Medieval Prosopography*, 17 (1996), 210–11.

Thomas, H. 'The Knights of the York County Court in 1212', in E. King and S. Ridyard (eds) *Law in Mediaeval Life and Thought* (Sewanee, TN, 1990).

Thomas, H. 'Portrait of a Medieval Anti-Semitic: Richard Malebisse *Ver Agnomine Mala Bestia*', *HSJ* 5 (1993), 1–15.

Turner, R.V. 'Changing Perceptions of the New Administrative Class in Anglo-Norman and Angevin England: The Curiales and their Conservative Critics', *JBS* 29 (1990), 93–117; reprinted in *Judges, Administrators and the Common Law in Angevin England* (London, 1994).

Turner, R.V. *The English Judiciary from Glanvill to Bracton c. 1176–1239* (Cambridge, 1985).

Turner, R.V. 'Henry II's Legal Reforms: Feudal or Royalist?', *Sewanee Mediaeval Studies* 3 (1990), 121–35.

Turner, R.V. *Judges, Administrators and the Common Law in Angevin England* (London, 1994).

Turner, R.V. *King John* (London, 1994).

Turner, R.V. 'King John's Concept of Royal Authority', *History of Political Thought* 17 (1996), 157–78.

Turner, R.V. 'The Mandeville Inheritance, 1189–1236: Its Legal, Political and Social Context', *HSJ* 1 (1989).

Turner, R.V. *Men Raised from the Dust: Administrative Service and Upward Mobility in Angevin England* (Philadelphia, 1988).

Turner, R.V. 'The Origins of Common Pleas and King's Bench', *American Journal of Legal History* 21 (1977), 238–54; reprinted in *Judges, Administrators and the Common Law in Angevin England* (London, 1994).

Turner, R.V. 'Richard Lionheart and English Episcopal Elections', *Albion* 29 (1997), 1–13.

Turner, R.V. 'Simon of Pattishall, Northamptonshire Man, Early Common Law Judge', *Northamptonshire Past and Present*, 6 (1978), 5–14; reprinted in *Judges, Administrators and the Common Law in Angevin England* (London, 1994).

Turner, R.V. 'William de Forz, Count of Aumale', *Proceedings of the American Philosophical Society* 115 (1973), 221–49.

Vincent, N. *Peter des Roches: An Alien in English Politics 1205–1238* (Cambridge, 1996).

Walker, D. *Medieval Wales* (Cambridge, 1990).

Walker, S.S. 'Feudal Constraint and Free Consent in the Making of Marriages in Medieval England: Widows in the King's Gift', in T. Cook and C. Lacel (eds) *Historical Papers, Saskatoon, 1979*, Canadian Historical Association (Ottawa, 1979).

Walker, S.S. (ed.) *Wife and Widow in Medieval England* (Ann Arbor, MI, 1994).

Warren, W.L. *The Governance of Norman and Angevin England, 1086–1272* (Palo Alto, CA, 1987).

Warren, W.L. *Henry II* (Berkeley and Los Angeles, CA, 1987).

Warren, W.L. 'King John and Ireland', in J. Lydon (ed.) *England and Ireland in the Later Middle Ages* (Dublin, 1981).

Waugh, S.L. *The Lordship of England: Royal Wardships and Marriages in English Society and Politics, 1217–1327* (Princeton, NJ, 1988).

West, F.J. *The Justiciarship in England, 1066–1232* (Cambridge, 1966).

White, G. 'The End of Stephen's Reign', *History* 75 (1990), 3–22.

Wightman, W.E. *The Lacy Family in England and Normandy 1066–1194* (Oxford, 1966).

Wilkinson, B. 'The Government of England during the Absence of Richard I on the Third Crusade', *Bulletin of the John Rylands Library* 28 (1944), 485–509.

Young, C.R. *Hubert Walter, Lord of Canterbury and Lord of England* (Durham, NC, 1968).

Young, C.R. *The Royal Forests of Medieval England* (Philadelphia, 1976).

Secondary sources for continental holdings

Alexander, J.W. 'Philip II Augustus', *Medieval France: An Encyclopedia*, ed. W. Kibler (New York, 1995).

Arbellot, F. *La vérité sur la mort de Richard Coeur-de-lion* (Paris, 1878).

Arnoux, M. 'Classe agricole, pouvoir seigneurial et authorité ducale. L'évolution de la Normandie féodale d'après le témoignage des chroniquers (x^e–xiie siècles)', *Moyen Age* 98 (1992), 35–60.

Avril, J. *Le Gouvernement des évêques et la vie religieuse dans le diocèse d'Angers (1148–1240)*, 2 vols (Paris, 1984).

Bachrach, B. 'The Angevin Economy 360–1060: Ancient or Feudal', *Studies in Medieval and Renaissance History*, new ser. 10 (New York, 1988).

Bachrach, B. *Fulk Nerra, a Neo-Roman Consul 987–1040* (Berkeley and Los Angeles, CA, 1993).

Bachrach, B. 'Henry II and the Angevin Tradition of Family Hostility', *Albion* 16 (1984), 112–30.

Bachrach, B. 'The Idea of Angevin Empire', *Albion* 10 (1978), 293–9.

Baldet, I. 'Essai d'itinéraire et registre d'Aliénor, reine d'Angleterre, duchesse d'Aquitaine (1189–1204)', Mémoire principal pour le D.E.S. (Bibliothèque du CESCM, D.E.S., no. 37), Poitiers.

Baldwin, J.W. 'The Capetian Court at Work under Philip Augustus', in E. Haymes (ed.) *The Medieval Court in Europe* (Munich, 1986).

Baldwin, J.W. *The Government of Philip Augustus: Foundations of French Royal Power in the Middle Ages* (Berkeley, 1986).

Baldwin, J.W. 'Philip Augustus', in J.R. Strayer (ed.) *Dictionary of the Middle Ages*, 13 vols (New York, 1982–89), 9: 552–3.

Baldwin, J.W. 'Philip Augustus and the Norman Church', *French Historical Studies* 6 (1969), 1–30.

Baldwin, J.W. and Nortier, M. 'Contributions à l'étude des finances de Philippe Auguste', *BEC* 138 (1980), 5–53.

Barthélemy, D. *La Mutation de l'an mil, a-t-elle eu lieu?* (Paris, 1997).

Barthélemy, D. *Nouvelle Histoire de la France médiévale*, vol. 3 of *L'Ordre seigneurial XIᵉ–XIIᵉ siècles* (Paris, 1990).

Bates, D. *Normandy before 1066* (London and New York, 1982).

Bates, D. 'Normandy and England after 1066', *EHR* 104 (1989), 851–76.

Bates, D. 'The Rise and Fall of Normandy c.911–1204', in D. Bates and A. Curry (eds) *England and Normandy in the Middle Ages* (London, 1994).

Bates, D. 'Rouen from 900 to 1204: From Scandinavian Settlement to Angevin "Capital",' *Medieval Art, Architecture, and Archaeology at Rouen*, ed. J. Stratford, *British Archaeological Association, Transactions*, 12 (1993).

Bautier, R.-H. 'Conclusion. "Empire Plantagenêt" ou "Espace Plantagenêt". Y eut-il une civilisation du monde Plantagenêt?', *CCM* 29 (1986), 139–47.

Bautier, R.-H. (ed.) *La France de Philippe Auguste: le temps de mutations* (Paris, 1982).

Bautier, R.-H. 'La place du regne de Philippe Auguste dans l'histoire de la France médiévale', reprinted in *Etudes sur la France capétienne* (London, 1992).

Bautier, R.-H. 'Le traité d'Azay et la mort de Henri II Plantagenêt: un tournant dans la première guerre de Cent ans entre Capétiens et Plantagenêts (juillet 1189)'; reprinted in *Etudes sur la France capétienne* (London, 1992).

Beauchet-Filleau, H. 'Recherches sur Airvaux, son château et son abbaye', *MSAO* 24 (1857).

Beautemps-Beaupré, C.-J. *Coutumes et institutions de l'Anjou et de Maine antérieures au xviᵉ siècle*, 8 vols (Paris, 1877–97).

Beech, G.T. 'The Lord/Dependent (Vassal) Relationship: A Case Study from Aquitaine c. 1030', *JMH* 24 (1998), 1–30.

Beech, G.T. *A Rural Society in Medieval France: The Gâtine of Poitou in the Eleventh and Twelfth Centuries* (Baltimore, 1964).

Benjamin, R. 'A Forty Years War: Toulouse and the Plantagenets, 1156–1196', *Historical Research* 61 (1988), 270–85.

Bisson, T. 'Les Comptes des domaines au temps de Philippe Auguste: essai comparatif', in R.-H. Bautier (ed.) *La France de Philippe Auguste: le temps des mutations* (Paris, 1982); reprinted in *Medieval France and her Pyrenean Neighbours: Studies in Early Institutional History* (London, 1989).

Bisson, T.N. 'The "Feudal Revolution"', *Past and Present* 142 (February 1994), 6–42.

Bisson, T. *Medieval France and her Pyrenean Neighbours: Studies in Early Institutional History* (London, 1989).

Bisson, T.N. 'The Organized Peace in Southern France and Catalonia', in *Medieval France and her Pyrenean Neighbours: Studies in Early Institutional History* (London, 1989).

Boase, T.S.R. 'Fontevrault and the Plantagenets', *Journal of the British Archaeology Association* 3rd ser. 34 (1971), 1–10.

Boissonade, P. 'Administrateurs laïques et ecclésiastiques Anglo-Normands en Poitou à l'époque d'Henri II Plantagenêt (1152–1189)', *BSAO* 3rd ser. 5 (1919), 156–90.

Boüard, M. de, 'Le Duché de Normandie', in F. Lot and R. Fawtier (eds) *Histoire des institutions françaises au moyen âge*, 3 vols (Paris, 1951).

Boüard, M. 'La Salle de l'Echiquier au château de Caen', *Medieval Archaeology* 9 (1965), 64–81.

Boussard, J. 'Aspects particuliers de la féodalité dans l'empire Plantagenêt', *BSAO*, 4th ser. 7 (1963), 29–47.

Boussard, J. *Le comté d'Anjou sous Henri Plantagenêt et ses fils 1151–1204* (Paris, 1938).

Boussard, J. 'La diversité et les traits particuliers du régime féodal dans l'Empire Plantagenêt', *Annali della Fondazione italiana per la storia amministrativa* 1 (1964), 157–82.

Boussard, J. *Le Gouvernement d'Henri II Plantagenêt* (Paris, 1956).

Boussard, J. 'Les influences anglaises dans le développement des grandes charges de l'empire plantagenêt', *Annales de Normandie* 5 (1955), 215–31.

Boussard, J. 'Les institutions de l'Empire plantagenêt', in F. Lot and R. Fawtier (eds) *Histoire des institutions françaises au moyen âge*, 3 vols (Paris, 1951).

Boussard, J. 'Les mercenaires au XIIe siècle: Henri II Plantagenêt et les origines de l'armée de métier', *BEC* 106 (1945–46), 189–224.

Boussard, J. 'Philippe Auguste et les Plantagenêts', in R.-H. Bautier (ed.) *La France de Philippe-Auguste* (Paris, 1982).

Boutruche, R. *Une Société provinciale en lutte contre le régime féodal* (Paris, 1947).

Bradbury, J. 'Geoffrey V of Anjou, Count and Knight', in C. Harper-Bill and R. Harvey (eds) *The Ideals and Practices of Medieval Knighthood*, vol. 3, *Papers from the Fourth Strawberry Hill Conference, 1988* (Woodbridge, 1989).

Bradbury, J. *Philip Augustus: King of France 1180–1223* (London, 1998).

Broussillon, B. *La Maison de Craon 1050–1480*, 2 vols (Paris, 1893).

Brown, E.A.R. 'Eleanor of Aquitaine: Parent, Queen, Duchess', in W.W. Kibler (ed.) *Eleanor of Aquitaine, Patron and Politician* (Austin, TX, 1976).

Brutails, J.A. 'Les fiefs du roi et les alleux en Guyenne', *Annales du Midi* 29 (1917).

Burns, J.H. (ed.) *The Cambridge History of Medieval Political Thought* (Cambridge, 1988).

Carter, K. 'Arthur I, Duke of Brittany, in History and Literature', PhD dissertation (Florida State University, 1996).

Chaline, N.-J. (ed.) *Le Diocèse de Rouen-Le-Havre* (Paris, 1976).

Chamard, F. 'Chronique historique de Châtellerault avant la fin du xiiie siècle d'après les documents inédits', *MSAO* 35 (1970–71), 103–8.

Chaplais, P. 'Le Traité de Paris de 1259 et l'inféodation de la Gascogne allodiale', *Le Moyen Age* 61 (1955); rpt in *Essays in Medieval Diplomacy and Administration* (London, 1981).

Chartrou, J. *L'Anjou de 1109 à 1151: Foulque de Jerusalem et Geoffroi Plantagenêt* (Paris, 1928).

Chaytor, H.J. *Savaric de Mauléon; Baron and Troubabour* (Cambridge, 1939).

Chedeville, A. and Tonnèrre, N.-Y. *La Bretagne féodale xie–xiiie siècles* (Rennes, 1987).

Cirot de la Ville *Histoire de l'abbaye et la congrégation de Notre Dame de la Grande-Sauve*, 2 vols (Paris/Bordeaux, 1844–45).

Clédat, L. *Du Rôle historique de Bertrand de Born (1175–1200)* (Paris, 1879).

Conklin, G. 'Les Capétiens et l'affaire de Dol de Bretagne 1179–1199', *Revue d'histoire de l'Eglise de France* 78 (1992), 241–63.

Coulson, C. 'Fortress-policy in Capetian Tradition and Angevin Practice: Aspects of the Conquest of Normandy by Philip II', *ANS* 6 (1984), 13–38.

Coulson, C. 'Rendability and Castellation in Medieval France', *Château Gaillard, Etudes de castellogie médiévale* 6 (1972), 59–67.

Courteault, P. *Histoire de la Gascogne et de Béarn* (Paris, 1938).

Crouch, D. 'Normans and Anglo-Normans: A Divided Aristocracy?', in D. Bates and A. Curry (eds) *England and Normandy in the Middle Ages* (London, 1994).

Crozet, R. 'Recherches sur les sites de châteaux et de lieux fortifiés en Haut-Poitou au moyen âge', *BSAO*, 4th ser. 11 (1971), 187–217.

Debord, A. *La Société laïque dans les pays de la Charente X^e–XIIe siècles* (Paris, 1984).

Debord, A. 'The Castellan Revolution and the Peace of God in Aquitaine', in Thomas Head and Richard Landes (eds) *The Peace of God: Social Violence and Religious Response in France around the Year 1000* (Ithaca, NY, 1992), 156–9.

de Chergé, M. 'Mémoire historique sur l'abbaye de Montierneuf de Poitiers', *MSAO*, ser. 1, 11 (1844), 147–276.

Delisle, L. 'Des revenues publiques en Normandie au 12e siècle', *BEC*, 2nd ser. 5 (1848–49), 257–89.

de Longuemar, M. (ed.) 'Documents pour l'histoire de Saint-Hilaire de Poitiers', *MSAO* 14 (1847).

de Longuemar, M. 'Essai historique sur l'église collégiale de Saint-Hilaire le Grand de Poitiers', *MSAO*, ser. 1, 23 (1856), 1–381.

Delumeau, J. (ed.) *Le Diocèse de Rennes* (Paris, 1979).

Devailly, G. *Le Berry du Xe au milieu du XIIIe siècle* (Paris, 1973).

Dez, G. 'Histoire de Poitiers', *MSAO*, ser. 4, 10 (1966), 39–58.

Dillay, M. 'Le régime de l'église privée du XIe au XIIIe siècle, dans l'Anjou, le Maine, le Touraine', *Revue historique de droit français et étranger* (1925), 253–94.

Dubois, G. 'Recherches sur la vie de Guillaume des Roches, seneschal d'Anjou, du Maine et de la Touraine', *BEC* 6th ser. 5 (1869), 377–424; (1871), 88–145.

Dubourg-Noves, P. (ed.) *Histoire d'Angoulême et de ses alentours* (Toulouse, 1989).

Duby, G. *La Dimanche de Bouvines* (Paris, 1973), *The Legend of Bouvines: War, Religion and Culture in the Middle Ages*, trans. C. Tihanyi (Cambridge, 1990).

Duby, G. *France in the Middle Ages*, trans. J. Vale (Oxford, 1991).

Duby, G. 'Les "jeunes" dans la société aristocratique dans la France du Nord-Ouest au XIIe siècle', *Annales* 27 (1964), 835–46; rpt C. Postan (trans.) 'Youth in Aristocratic Society: Northwestern France in the Twelfth Century', *The Chivalrous Society* (Chicago, 1974).

Duby, G. *La Société aux XIe et XIIe siècles dans la région mâconnaise* (Paris, 1971).

Duby, G. *The Three Orders: Feudal Society Imagined*, trans. A. Goldhammer (Chicago, 1980).

Duguet, J. 'Notes sur quelques vicomtes de Châtellerault', *BSAO* 4th ser. 16 (1981–82), 261–70.

Dumas, F. 'La monnaie dans les domaines Plantagenêt', *CCM* 29 (1986), 53–9.

Dunbabin, J. *France in the Making 842–1180* (Oxford, 1985).

Durand, Y. *Le Diocèse de Nantes*, ser. *Histoire des diocèses de France* (Paris, 1985).

Everard, J. 'The "Justiciarship" in Brittany and Ireland under Henry II', *ANS* 20 (1998), 81–105.

Evergates, T. *Feudal Society in the Bailliage of Troyes under the Counts of Champagne, 1152–1284* (Baltimore, 1975).

Evergates, T. 'Nobles and Knights in Twelfth-century France', in T.N. Bisson (ed.) *Cultures of Power: Lordship, Status, and Process in Twelfth-century Europe*, (Philadelphia, 1995).

Fagnen, C. 'Essai sur quelques actes normands de Richard Coeur-de-Lion', *Ecole nationale des Chartes, Positions des thèses* (Paris, 1971), 72.

Fagnen, C. 'Le Vocabulaire du pouvoir dans les actes de Richard Coeur de Lion, duc de Normandie (1189–1199)', *Actes du 105e Congrès Nationale des Sociétés savantes, Caen 1980*, 1 (Paris, 1984).

Favreau, R. 'Les débuts de la ville de La Rochelle', *CCM* 30 (1987), 3–32.

Favreau, R. (ed.) *Le Diocèse de Poitiers* (Paris, 1988).

Favreau, R. *Histoire de Poitiers* (Toulouse, 1985).

Favreau, R. 'Les juifs en Poitou et dans les pays de la Charente au moyen âge', *Revue des études juives* 147 (1988), 5–29.

Fawtier, R. *The Capetian Kings of France*, trans. L. Butler and R.J. Adam (London, 1960).

Folz, R. *The Concept of Empire in Western Europe from the Fifth to the Fourteenth Century*, trans. S. Ogilvie (London, 1985).

Foreville, R. 'Innocent III et les élections épiscopales dans l'espace Plantagenêt', *Cahiers des annales de Normandie* 23 (1990), 293–9.

Galliou, P. and Jones, M. *The Bretons* (Oxford, 1991).

Garaud, M. 'Les Châtelains de Poitou et l'avènement du régime féodal, xie et xiie siècles', *MSAO*, 4th ser. 8 (1964).

Garaud, M. 'Les vicomtes du Poitou (xie–xiie siècles)', *Tijdschrift voor Rechtsgischeidnis* 4th ser. 16 (1937), 426–49.

Geary, P. 'Vivre en conflit dans une France sans Etat: typologie des mécanismes de règlement de conflits (1050–1200)', *Annales, économies, sociétés, civilisations* (1986), 1107–33; trans. 'Living with Conflicts in Stateless France: A Typology of Conflict Management Mechanisms, 1050–1200', in P. Geary, *Living with the Dead in the Middle Age* (Ithaca, NY, 1994).

Genicot, L. 'Provinces de France au coeur du moyen âge', *Revue d'histoire ecclésiastique* 72 (1977), 614–15; rpt in L. Genicot, *La Noblesse dans l'Occident médiéval* (London, 1982).

Géraud, H. 'Mercadier: les routiers au treizième siècle', *BEC* 3 (1841–42), 417–43.

Gillingham, J. *The Angevin Empire* (New York, 1984); rpt in J. Gillingham, *Richard Coeur de Lion: Kingship, Chivalry and War in the Twelfth Century* (London, 1994).

Gillingham, J. 'The Fall of the Angevin Empire', *History Today* 36 (1986), 30–5; rpt in *Coeur de Lion*.

Gillingham, J. 'Richard I and Berengaria of Navarre', *BIHR* 53 (1980), 157–73.

Gleason, S.E. *An Ecclesiastical Barony of the Middle Ages: The Bishopric of Bayeux, 1066–1204* (Cambridge, MA, 1936).

Green, J. 'Lords of the Vexin', in *War and Government in the Middle Ages*.

Grenier, P. *La Cité de Limoges, ses évêques, sa chapitre, son consulat, xiie–xiiie siècles* (Limoges, 1908).

Griffiths, Q. 'The Capetian Kings and St. Martin of Tours', *Studies in Medieval and Renaissance History*, new ser. 9 (New York, 1987), 83–133.

Guillemain, B. *Le Diocèse de Bordeaux* (Paris, 1974).

Guillemain, B. 'Les moines sur les sièges épiscopaux du sud-ouest de la France au xie et xiie siècles', *Mélanges E.-R. Labande* (Poitiers, 1976).

Guillot, O. 'Administration et gouvernement dans les états du comte d'Anjou au milieu du XIe siècle', *Beihefte der Francia* 9, *Histoire comparée de l'administration (IVe–XVIIIe siècles)*, ed. W. Paravicini and K.F. Werner (Munich, 1980), 311–26.

Guillot, O. *Le Comte d'Anjou et son entourage*, 2 vols (Paris, 1973).

Hajdu, R. 'Castles, Castellans and the Structure of Politics in Poitou, 1152–1271', *JMH* 4 (1978), 27–53.

Hajdu, R. 'Family and Feudal Ties in Poitou 1100–1300', *Journal of Interdisciplinary History* 8 (1977), 117–39.

Hallam, E.M. *Capetian France, 987–1328* (London, 1980).

Hallam, E.M. 'Henry II, Richard I and the Order of Grandmont', *JMH* 1 (1975), 165–86.

Hallam, E.M. *The Plantagenet Chronicles* (New York, 1986).

Hallam, E.M. 'Royal Burial and the Cult of Kingship in England and France, 1060–1330', *JMH* 8 (1982), 359–80.

Hartigan, F. *The Accounts of Alphonse of Poitiers 1243–48* (Lanham, MD, 1984).

Haskins, C.H. *Norman Institutions* (Cambridge, MA, 1918).

Hassig, R. *Aztec Warfare: Imperialism, Expansion and Political Control* (Norman, OK, 1988).

Higounet, C. *Histoire de l'Aquitaine* (Toulouse, 1971).

Higounet, C. 'En Bordelaise: "Principes castelli tenentes"', in P. Contamines (ed.) *La Noblesse au moyen âge, xie–xve siècles: essais à la mémoire de Robert Boutruche* (Paris, 1976).

Higounet, C. 'La société nobiliaire en Bordelaise à la fin du xiiie siècle', in *Sociétés et groupes sociaux en Aquitaine et Angleterre* (Bordeaux, 1976).

Hillion, Y. 'La Bretagne et la rivalité Capétiens–Plantagenêts. Un exemple: la duchesse Constance (1186–1202)', *Annales de Bretagne* 92 (1985), 111–44.

Hivergneaux, M. 'Aliénor d'Aquitaine: le pouvoir d'une femme à la lumière de ses chartes', Colloque de Thouars (29 April–1 May 1999).

Hollister, C.W. 'Normandy, France and the Anglo-Norman *Regnum*', *Speculum* 51 (1976); rpt in *Monarchy, Magnates and Institutions*.

Hollister, C.W. and Keefe, T.K. 'The Making of the Angevin Empire', *JBS* 12 (1973), 1–25.

Holt, J.C. 'Aliénor d'Aquitaine, Jean sans Terre et la succession de 1199', *CCM* 29 (1986), 95–100.

Holt, J.C. 'The End of the Anglo-Norman Realm', in *Magna Carta and Medieval Government* (London, 1985).

Holt, J.C. 'The Loss of Normandy and Royal Finances', in *War and Government in the Middle Ages* (Woodbridge, 1984).

Imbart de la Tour, P. *Les Elections épiscopales dans l'Eglise de France du IXe au XIIe siècle* (Paris, 1891).

Imbert, H. 'Notice sur les vicomtes de Thouars', *MSAO* 29 (1864), 365–8.

Jeanne-Rose, O. 'Ports, marchands et marchandises: aspects économiques du littoral poitevin (IXe–XIIe siècles)', *MSAO*, 5th ser. 4 (1996), 115–42.

Jessee, W.S. 'Count Fulk Rechin of Anjou and the Acquisition of Maine: A Reassessment', unpublished paper presented at the International Congress of Medievalists (Kalamazoo, MI, May 1996).

Johnson, P. *Prayer, Patronage, and Power: The Abbey of La Trinité, Vendôme, 1032–1187* (New York, 1981).

Jouet, R. *Et la Normandie devint française* (Paris, 1983).

Keefe, T.K. 'Geoffrey Plantagenet's Will and the Angevin Succession', *Albion* 6 (1974),

Koziol, G. 'England, France, and the Problem of Sacrality in Twelfth-century Ritual', in T. Bisson (ed.) *Cultures of Power: Lordship, Status, and Process in Twelfth-century Europe* (Philadelphia, 1995).

Labande, E.-R. 'La civilisation de l'Aquitaine à la fin de la période ducale', *Bulletin du Centre International d'Etudes Romanes* 1–2 (1964), 15–30.

Labande, E.-R. 'Pour une image véridique d'Aliénor d'Aquitaine', *BSAO*, 4th ser. 2 (1952), rpt in *Histoire de l'Europe occidentale XIe–XIVe siècles* (London, 1973).

Latouche, R. 'La commune du Mans (1070)', *Mélanges d'histoire du moyen âge dédiés à la mémoire de Louis Halphen* (Paris, 1950).

Lebrun, F. *Le Diocèse d'Angers* (Paris, 1981).

Legohérel, H. 'Le parage en Touraine–Anjou au moyen âge', *Revue historique de droit français et étranger*, 4th ser. 43 (1965), 222–46.

Le Patourel, J. 'Angevin Successions and the Angevin Empire', in *Feudal Empires, Norman and Plantagenet* (London, 1984).

Le Patourel, J. *Feudal Empires, Norman and Plantagenet* (London, 1984).

Le Patourel, J. 'Henri II Plantagenêt et la Bretagne', app. 2, in *Feudal Empires, Norman and Plantagenet* (London, 1984); rpt from *Mémoires de la Société de l'histoire et d'archéologie de Bretagne* 58 (1981).

Le Patourel, J. *The Norman Empire* (Oxford, 1976).

Le Patourel, J. 'The Plantagenet Dominions', in *Feudal Empires, Norman and Plantagenet* (London, 1984).

Lewis, A.W. *Royal Succession in Capetian France: Studies on Familial Order and the State* (Cambridge, MA, 1981).

Limouzin-Lamothe, R. *Le Diocèse de Limoges des origines à la fin du moyen âge* (Paris, 1951).

Lot, F. and Fawtier, R. (eds) *Histoire des institutions françaises au moyen âge*, 3 vols (Paris, 1957–62).

Lot, F. and Fawtier, R. *Le Premier Budget de la monarchie française, le compte générale de 1202–1203* (Paris, 1932).

Luttwak, E. *The Grand Strategy of the Roman Empire from the First Century A.D. to the Third* (Baltimore, 1976).

Maitre, L. 'Situation du diocèse de Nantes au XIe et au XIIe siècles', *Annales de Bretagne* 27 (1911–12), 109–20, 342–61.

Mallet, J. 'Une capitale militaire aux origines incertaines (jusqu'en 1475)', in F. Lebrun (ed.) *Histoire d'Angers* (Toulouse, 1975).

Marsh, F.B. *English Rule in Gascony (1199–1259) with Special Reference to the Towns* (Ann Arbor, MI, 1912).

Martindale, J. 'Aimeri of Thouars and the Poitevin Connection', *ANS* 7 (1985), 224–45; rpt in J. Martindale, *Status, Authority and Regional Power* (Aldershot, 1997).

Martindale, J. ' "Cavalaria et orgueill": Duke William IX of Aquitaine and the Historian', in C. Harper-Bill and R. Harvey (eds) *The Ideals and Practice of Knighthood*, vol. 2, (Woodbridge, 1988), 87–116; rpt in J. Martindale, *Status, Authority and Regional Power* (Aldershot, 1997).

Martindale, J. 'Conventum inter Guillelmum Aquitanorum Comes et Hugonem', *EHR* 84 (1969), 528–48.

Martindale, J. 'Eleanor of Aquitaine', in J. Nelson (ed.) *Richard Coeur de Lion in History and Myth* (London, 1992); rpt in *Status, Authority and Regional Power* (Aldershot, 1997).

Martindale, J. ' "His Special Friend?" The Settlement of Disputes and Political Power in the Kingdom of the French (Tenth to Mid-twelfth Century)', *TRHS* 6th ser. 5 (1995), 21–57.

Meade, M. *Eleanor of Aquitaine* (New York, 1977).

Mesmin, S. 'Du Comté à la commune: le léproserie de Saint-Gilles de Pont-Audemer', *Annales de Normandie* 37 (1987), 30–40.

Miyamtsu, H. 'A-t-il existé une commune à Angers au xiie siècle?', *JMH* 21 (1995), 117–52.

Moss, V. 'Normandy and the Angevin Empire: A Study of the Norman Exchequer Rolls 1180–1204', PhD thesis (University of Wales College, Cardiff, 1996).

Moss, V. 'Normandy and England in 1180: Pipe Roll Evidence', in D. Bates and A. Curry (eds) *England and Normandy in the Middle Ages* (London, 1994).

Musset, L. 'Aux origines d'une classe dirigeante, les Tosny, grands barons normands du xᵉ au xiiiᵉ siècle, *Francia* 5 (1977), 45–80.

Musset, L. 'Quelques problèmes posés par l'annexion de la Normandie au domaine royal français', in *La France de Philippe Auguste* (Paris, 1982).

Nelson, J. *Charles the Bald* (London, 1992).

Neveux, F. 'Trois villes épiscopals de Normandie du xiiᵉ au xvᵉ siècle', *Receuil d'études en hommage à Lucien Musset*, Cahiers des Annales de Normandie, 23 (Caen, 1990).

Nouaillac, J. *Histoire du Limousin et de la Marche*, 4th edn (Paris, 1931).

Ogé, N. 'Hamelin, évêque du Mans, 1199–1214', *La Province du Maine*, 96, 5th ser., 8 (July–September 1994), 233–49; (October–December 1994), 347–60.

Orliac, P. 'Législation, coutumes et coutumiers au temps de Philippe Auguste', in R.-H. Bautier (ed.) *La France de Philippe Auguste: le temps de mutations* (Paris, 1982).

Owen, D.D.R. *Eleanor of Aquitaine: Queen and Legend* (Oxford, 1993).

Packard, S.R. 'The Judicial Organization of Normandy, 1189–1204', *Law Quarterly Review*, 40 (1909), 442–64.

Packard, S.R. 'The Norman Communes under Richard and John', in C. Taylor (ed.) *Anniversary Essays in Medieval History by Students of Charles H. Haskins* (Boston, 1929).

Painter, S. 'Castellans of the Plain of Poitou in the Eleventh and Twelfth Centuries', reprinted from *Speculum* 31 (1956) in Fred A. Cazel Jr. (ed.) *Feudalism and Liberty* (Baltimore, 1961).

Painter, S. 'The Houses of Lusignan and Châtellerault, 1150–1250', rpt in F. Cazel Jr. (ed.) *Feudalism and Liberty* (Baltimore, 1961).

Painter, S. 'The Lords of Lusignan in the Eleventh and Twelfth Centuries', rpt in F.A. Cazel Jr. (ed.) *Feudalism and Liberty* (Baltimore, 1961).

Paterson, L. *The World of the Troubadours: Medieval Occitan Society* c. *1100–1300* (Cambridge, 1993).

Pernoud, R. *Aliénor d'Aquitaine* (Paris, 1965).

Petit-Dutaillis, C. *La Monarchie féodale en France et en Angleterre* (Paris, 1933; rpt 1971).

Pocquet du Haut-Jussée, B.-A. 'Le grand fief breton', in F. Lot and R. Fawtier (eds) *Histoire des institutions françaises au moyen âge* (Paris, 1957–62), 1.

Pocquet du Haut-Jussée, B.-A. 'Les Plantagenêts et la Bretagne', *Annales de Bretagne* 53 (1946), 1–27.

Poly, J.-P. and Bournazel, E. *The Feudal Transformation 900–1200* (New York and London, 1991).

Pontal, O. 'Les évêques dans le monde Plantagenêt', *CCM* 29 (1986), 1229–37.

Power, D. 'Between the Angevin and Capetian Courts: John de Rouvray and the Knights of the Pays de Bray, 1185–1214', in *Family Trees and the Roots of*

Family Politics: The Prosopography of Britain and France from the Tenth to the Twelfth Century (Woodbridge, 1996).

Power, D. 'The Norman Frontier in the Twelfth and Early Thirteenth Centuries', PhD thesis (Cambridge, 1994).

Power, D. 'What did the Frontier of Angevin Normandy Comprise?', *ANS* 17 (1995), 181–201.

Powicke, F.M. 'The Angevin Administration of Normandy I', *EHR* 21 (1906), 625–49; 'The Angevin Administration of Normandy II', *EHR* 22 (1907), 15–42.

Powicke, F.M. 'England: Richard I and John', in *Cambridge Medieval History*, 8 vols (Cambridge, 1929).

Powicke, F.M. *The Loss of Normandy, 1189–1204*, 2nd edn (Manchester, 1960).

Redet, L. 'Essai historique sur l'église collégiale de St.-Hilaire le Grand de Poitiers', *MSAO*, ser. 1, 23 (1856), 1–381.

Renouard, Y. 'Essai sur le rôle de l'empire angevin dans la formation de la France et de la civilisation française aux XIIe et XIIIe siècles', in *Etudes d'histoire médiévale*, 2 vols (Paris, 1968).

Renouard, Y. 'Les institutions du duché d'Aquitaine (des origines à 1453)', in F. Lot and R. Fawtier (eds) *Histoire des Institutions francaises au moyen âge* (Paris, 1957–62), 1.

Reynolds, S. *Fiefs and Vassals* (Oxford, 1995).

Richard, A. *Histoire des comtes de Poitou*, 2 vols (Paris, 1903).

Rosenthal, J.T. 'The King's "Wicked Advisers" and Medieval Baronial Rebellions', *Political Science Quarterly* 82 (1967), 595–618.

Salch, C.-L. *Dictionnaire des châteaux et des fortifications du moyen âge en France* (Strasbourg, 1979).

Schaffer, M. 'Rhetorics of Authority: Feudal Ideologies in Twelfth-century Anjou', unpublished paper presented at the International Congress on Medieval Studies (Kalamazoo MI, May 1992).

Searle, E. *Predatory Kinship and the Creation of Norman Power, 840–1066* (Berkeley, CA, 1988).

Shaw, I.P. 'The Ecclesiastical Policy of Henry II on the Continent', *Church Quarterly Review* 151 (1951), 137–55.

Spear, D. 'Les chanoines de la Cathédral de Rouen pendant la période ducale', *Annales de Normandie* 41 (1991), 135–76.

Spear, D. 'The Norman Empire and the Secular Clergy, 1066–1204', *JBS* 21 (1981–82), 1–10.

Spiegel, G.M. *The Chronicle Tradition of Saint Denis: A Survey* (Leyden, 1978).

Spiegel, G.M. '"Defense of Realm" Evolution of a Capetian Propaganda Slogan', *JMH* 3 (1977), 115–33.

Stephenson, C. 'The Aids of the French Towns in the Twelfth and Thirteenth Centuries'; 'Origins and Nature of the *Taille*', in B. Lyon (ed.) *Medieval Institutions: Selected Essays* (Ithaca, NY, 1954).

Stephenson, C. *Medieval Feudalism* (Ithaca, NY, 1942).

Strayer, J.R. 'Fief', in *Dictionary of the Middle Ages*, vol. 5 (New York, 1982–89).

Tabuteau, E.Z. 'The Role of Law in the Succession to Normandy and England 1087', *HSJ* 3 (1991), 144–69.

Thompson, K. 'The Lords of the Laigle: Ambition and Insecurity on the Borders of Normandy', *ANS* 18 (1995), 177–99.

Thompson, K. 'William Talvas', in D. Bates and A. Curry (eds) *England and Normandy in the Middle Ages* (London, 1994).

Trabut-Cussac, J.-P. *Bordeaux sous les rois d'Angleterre, Histoire de Bordeaux*, ed. Y. Renouard, 3 (Bordeaux, 1965).

Trabut-Cussac, J.-P. 'Les coutumes ou droits de douane perçues à Bordeaux', *Annales du Midi* 42 (1950), 135–50.

Tricoire, P.G. *Les Évêques d'Angoulême. Recherches historiques depuis les origines jusqu'à nos jours* (Angoulême, 1912).

Turner, R.V. 'Eleanor of Aquitaine and her Children: An Inquiry into Medieval Family Attachment', *JMH* 14 (1988), 21–35.

Turner, R.V. 'The Households of the Sons of Henry II', Colloque de Thouars, France (May 1999).

Turner, R.V. 'The Problem of Survival for the Angevin "Empire": Henry II's and His Sons' Vision versus Late Twelfth-century Realities', *AHR* 100 (1995), 78–96.

Turner, R.V. 'Richard Lionheart and the Episcopate in his French Domains', *French Historical Studies* 21 (1998), 518–42.

Vale, M. *The Angevin Legacy and the 100 Years War 1250–1340* (Oxford, 1990).

Valin, L. *Le Duc de Normandie et sa cour 912–1204* (Paris, 1910).

Verynaud, G. *Histoire de Limoges* (Limoges, 1973).

Walker, D. 'Crown and Episcopacy under the Normans and Angevins', *ANS* 5 (1982), 220–33.

Warren, W.L. *Henry II* (Berkeley, CA, 1973).

Watson, R. 'The Counts of Angoulême from the 9th to the Mid-13th Century', PhD thesis (University of East Anglia, 1979).

Watson, R. 'Scribes and Writing Offices: The Charters of the Counts of Angoulême before the Late Thirteenth Century', *Münchener Beiträge zur Mediävistik und Renaissance Forschung, 35 Landesherrliche Kanzleien im Spätmittelalter*, 2 (1984), 659–80.

Werner, K.F. 'Kingdom and Principality in Twelfth-century France', in T. Reuter (ed.) *The Medieval Nobility* (Amsterdam, 1978).

Werner, K.F. 'Les nations et le sentiment national dans l'Europe médiévale', *Revue Historique* 244 (1970), 285–304.

White, S. '*Pactum . . . Legem Vincit et Amor Judicium*: The Settlement of Disputes by Compromise in Eleventh-century Western France', *American Journal of Legal History* 22 (1978), 281–308.

Wood, C.T. *The French Apanages and the Capetian Monarchy, 1224–1328* (Cambridge, MA, 1966).

Yver, J. 'Contribution à l'étude du développement de la compétence ducale en Normandie', *Annales de Normandie* 8 (1958), 139–83.

INDEX

281

Vau de Vire, 176
Vendée, 216
Vendôme, 181, 187, 191, 193, 197, 231, 234
Ventadour, 62, 206
Vermandois, 42
Verneuil, 46n20, 230
Vernon, 232, 238
Vexin, 36, 42, 68, 71, 83, 84, 175, 226, 228, 231–3, 235, 237, 238, 240
Vézelay, 82
Vézian, viscount of Lomagne, 65
Vienne river, 61, 205
Vierzon, 203n9, 237
Vouvent, 212
Vulgrin III Taillefer, count of Angoulême, 61, 63, 64, 65, 206, 210

Walden abbey, 243n8
Wales, 31, 74, 79, 107, 118, 133, 137, 143, 159, 162
Walkelin de Ferrers, 80
Walkern barony, 162
Wallingford, 75, 88, 104, 116, 133, 136, 137, 138, 146
Walter de Clifford, 117n22
Walter de Mayenne, 189n37
Walter of Coutances, archbishop of Rouen, 10, 34, 53, 73, 88, 110, 116, 121, 123–40, 141, 143, 149, 151, 169, 178, 179, 228, 236
Warenne, 81, 143
Warin fitz Gerold, 93
Warwick, 81
Welshpool, 159
Westminster, 11, 73, 80, 94, 112, 113, 114, 115, 119, 120, 121, 132, 137, 151, 162, 189, 243
William, abbot of Saint-Aubin, 193
William, archbishop of Montreale, 120
William, bishop of Hereford, 132
William, count of Ponthieu, 232, 234
William IX, duke of Aquitaine, 33, 59, 203
William II, duke of Normandy, 177
William Blanchard, 146n11
William Briwerre, 96, 98, 99, 100, 103, 116, 129, 133
William Cook, 208
William d'Aubigny, earl of Sussex, 93, 94
William de Beauchamp, 102, 103, 104, 107
William de Braose, 93, 103, 104, 133, 145, 159, 161, 176
William de Chimellé, bishop of Avranches, 95, 178–9, 190

William de Chisi, 84
William de Forz, count of Aumale, 35, 79, 80, 82, 172, 235
William de Lanvaley, 162
William de l'Etang, 34, 35
William de Mandeville, earl of Essex, co-justiciar, 82, 96–7, 98
William de Mauléon, 60n9
William de Mauzé, 245n16
William de Montsoreau, 190
William de Rupière, bishop of Lisieux, 179
William de Saint John, 80
William de Sainte-Mère-Église, 95, 143, 146, 151, 152
William de Stuteville, 116, 132, 157
William de Tancarville, 176
William de Wenneval, 125, 146
William de Wrotham, 153
William des Roches, 186, 199
William du Hommet, constable of Normandy, 80, 81, 169
William fitz Alan, 93, 107, 159
William fitz Aldelin, 104, 150
William fitz Osbert, 150, 158
William fitz Patrick, earl of Salisbury, 78, 132
William fitz Ralph, seneschal of Normandy, 34, 35, 81, 85, 169, 226
William le Templier, archbishop of Bordeaux, 223n94
William Longchamp, bishop of Ely, chief justiciar, 10, 11, 34, 50, 74, 79, 80, 88, 89, 92, 95, 98, 99, 100, 102, 103, 107, 109, 110–29, 130, 131, 132, 133, 135–6, 138, 139, 142, 144, 145, 146, 149, 151, 155, 160, 175, 228, 244
William Longsword, bastard son of Henry II, earl of Salisbury, 78, 90, 123
William III Maingot, 205
William Marshal, earl of Pembroke, 35, 76, 78, 79, 80, 86, 88, 93, 94, 96, 98, 100, 103, 104, 107, 122, 123–4, 125, 129, 132, 133, 138, 176, 201
William Mauduit, 100, 103
William Puintel, 116
William Rufus, king of England, 24
William Taillefer, 61, 65
William Toleran, bishop of Avranches, 179
William I Vierzon, 237
William of Newburgh, 3, 6n22, 91, 101, 105, 111, 236, 245
William of Newmarket, 245n11
William of Poitiers, 38
William the Conqueror, king of England, 19, 21, 24, 38, 143, 183, 201

William the Lion, king of Scotland, 107–8, 147–8
Winchester, 34n44, 74, 78, 95, 101, 102, 106, 116, 122, 125–7, 129, 132, 148, 162, 230
Windsor castle, 104, 113, 116, 136, 137, 138, 146
Wissant, 228

Worcester, 80, 95, 102, 104, 107, 119, 134, 160, 176

York, 78, 89, 90, 92, 95, 96, 99, 102, 107, 112, 116, 118, 119, 122, 123, 126, 127, 133, 134, 147, 244
York minster, 79, 89, 112, 160